UPGRADER'S GUIDE

murach's
ASP.NET 2.0
upgrader's guide

VB EDITION

Anne Boehm
Joel Murach

 MIKE MURACH & ASSOCIATES, INC.
1-800-221-5528 • (559) 440-9071 • Fax: (559) 440-0963
murachbooks@murach.com • www.murach.com

Authors:	Anne Boehm
	Joel Murach
Cover Design:	Zylka Design
Production:	Tom Murach
	Judy Taylor

Books for .NET programmers

Murach's ASP.NET 2.0 Upgrader's Guide: C# Edition
Murach's ASP.NET 2.0 Upgrader's Guide: VB Edition
Murach's ASP.NET Web Programming with VB.NET
Murach's C#
Murach's Beginning Visual Basic .NET
Murach's VB.NET Database Programming with ADO.NET
Murach's SQL for SQL Server

Two books for every Java programmer

Murach's Beginning Java 2, JDK 5
Murach's Java Servlets and JSP

Four books for every IBM mainframe programmer

Murach's OS/390 and z/OS JCL
Murach's Mainframe COBOL
Murach's CICS for the COBOL Programmer
DB2 for the COBOL Programmer, Part 1

Please check www.murach.com for other books on .NET 2.0 subjects

Contents

Expanded contents

Section 1   Introduction to ASP.NET 2.0

Chapter 5   How to use the GridView control

Chapter 6   How to use the DetailsView and FormView controls

Chapter 7   How to use object data sources

Section 3   New ASP.NET 2.0 features

Chapter 8   How to use site navigation

Introduction

If you're a Visual Basic developer who's going to be upgrading to ASP.NET 2.0 from ASP.NET 1.0 or 1.1, this book can save you many of hours of research. It can do that because we've already done that research for you. Then, we put that information into this single book that will help you upgrade to ASP.NET 2.0 as quickly and easily as possible.

Unlike most competing books, this one doesn't just tell you what the new features are and how great they are and then let you figure out how to use them on your own. Instead, our book also shows you exactly how to use all of the new features so you get the most from them. That's why we say that the purpose of this book is to show you: *"What's new and how to use it."*

What this book does

To be more specific about what this book presents, here is a brief description of each of the four sections of the book:

- The goal of section 1 is to get you started right. So chapter 1 gives you a quick introduction to the new features of ASP.NET 2.0, and chapter 2 shows you how to develop a complete ASP.NET 2.0 application using the new code-behind model and the new data source controls. Then, chapter 3 shows you how to use the new *master pages* feature, because you'll probably want to use that feature with every ASP.NET 2.0 application you develop.

- In section 2, you'll learn how to use the new data access features of ASP.NET 2.0. That includes a new feature called *data sources*, which can dramatically reduce the amount of data access code that you need for an application. It includes some new bound controls that are designed to work with data sources. And it includes *object data sources*, which make it easier for you to separate presentation code from data access code. This is powerful stuff, so you're going to want to read this section from start to finish.

- In section 3, you'll learn how to use the other new ASP.NET 2.0 features. These include the new *navigation* features; the new *login controls* that make user authentication easier than ever; the new *profile* feature that makes it easy to capture user preferences in a persistent data store; *themes* that help you separate graphic details from the rest of the application; and *web parts* that make it easy for you to develop portals. Most of these features let you develop better applications with less code. And no other book will get you up and running with these features faster and better than this one.

- In section 4, you'll learn the other skills that you need for upgrading to ASP.NET 2.0. To start, you'll learn the several ways that your old 1.x applications can co-exist with your new 2.0 applications because you usually won't need to convert your old applications to ASP.NET 2.0. In some cases, though, it does make sense, so you'll also learn how to convert your old applications to 2.0. Last, you'll learn the several ways that you can configure and deploy your ASP.NET 2.0 applications, including the use of the new Web Site Administration Tool, the Copy Web Site command, and the Publish Web Site command for precompiled deployment.

To get the most from this book, we recommend that you start by reading the first section from start to finish. But after that, you can skip to any of the other three sections to get the information that you need whenever you need it. Since this book has been carefully designed to work that way, you won't miss anything by skipping around.

Why you'll learn faster and better with this book

Like all our books, this one has features that you won't find in competing books. That's why we believe you'll learn faster and better with our book than with any other. Here are just three of those features.

- To make sure that you learn the new ASP.NET 2.0 features as quickly and easily as possible, all of the features are presented in the context of complete applications. These applications include the web forms, the aspx code, and the Visual Basic code. As we see it, the best way to learn is to study applications like these, even though you won't find them in most competing books.

- Unlike many ASP.NET books, this one shows you how to get the most from Visual Studio 2005 as you develop your applications. Because we've found that this IDE is one of the keys to development productivity, we're still surprised that most books ignore or neglect it.

- If you page through this book, you'll see that all of the information is presented in "paired pages," with the essential syntax, guidelines, and examples on the right page and the perspective and extra explanation on the left page. This not only helps you learn faster by reading less, but it is also the best reference format that you'll find anywhere. That's why this book works so well for both training and reference.

What software you need

To develop ASP.NET 2.0 applications that take advantage of the new features presented in this book, you can use any of the full versions of Visual Studio 2005, including Visual Studio 2005 Standard Edition, Professional Edition, or Team System. You can also use the inexpensive Visual Web Developer 2005 Express Edition.

All of these Visual Studio editions come with everything you need to develop ASP.NET 2.0 applications, including the Visual Studio development environment, version 2.0 of the Microsoft .NET Platform and ASP.NET, the C# 2005 and Visual Basic 2005 language compilers, a built-in web server that's ideal for testing ASP.NET applications, and a scaled-back version of SQL Server called SQL Server Express.

For professional development work, you'll probably want to use IIS rather than the built-in web server and the full version of SQL Server rather than SQL Server Express. But the tools that come with Visual Studio 2005 are more than adequate for simple application development and for learning the new features of ASP.NET 2.0.

What you can get from our website

Because this book is based on the "Go Live" Beta 2 release of ASP.NET 2.0, it's possible that there will be some minor changes when the final product is released in late 2005. But if there are, we'll be summarizing the changes on our web site shortly after the product is released. Just go to www.murach.com, find the page for this Upgrader's Guide, and look for an appropriate link. (You'll also find a few references in this book to changes that will probably be made in the final release.)

You can also download the source code and databases for all of the applications presented in this book, as summarized in appendix A. Then, you can test and review these applications on your own to see exactly how they work. And you can copy and paste the code that you want to use in your own applications.

Related books

If you or your colleagues haven't yet mastered all of the ASP.NET 1.x features and skills, you may be interested in *Murach's ASP.NET Web Programming with VB.NET*. This book presents all of the 1.x classes, methods, and skills that you need for using validation controls, security, email, custom error pages, back-button control, Crystal Reports, web services, user controls, custom server controls, and the Repeater and DataList controls. It also has a great section on database programming with ADO.NET. In fact, this book plus our Upgrader's Guide will tell you everything you need to know for maintaining ASP.NET 1.x applications and for developing new ASP.NET 2.0 applications.

Similarly, if you realize that your Visual Basic skills aren't as strong as they ought to be, *Murach's Beginning Visual Basic .NET* is a book that you may be interested in. It will get you up-to-speed with the language. It will show you how to work with the most useful .NET classes. And it will show you how to develop Windows Forms applications.

A third book that we recommend for all ASP.NET programmers is *Murach's SQL for SQL Server*. To start, it shows you how to write SQL statements in all their variations so you can code the right statements for your data sources. This often gives you the option of having Microsoft SQL Server do more so your applications do less. Beyond that, this book shows you how to design and implement databases and how to use advanced features like stored procedures.

Last, please check our web site periodically for new books. In particular, we intend to publish comprehensive books on ASP.NET 2.0 that will integrate the old and new features and skills. We'll also be publishing new books on C# 2005 and Visual Basic 2005.

Please let us know how this book works for you

When we started working with ASP.NET 2.0, we realized that developers who were upgrading from ASP.NET 1.x needed one type of book and people who were new to ASP.NET web programming needed another. With that in mind, we decided to start with a book that provides just the information that upgraders need.

Now that we're done, we hope that the many hours that we put into the research and development for this book will save you both time and effort as you upgrade to ASP.NET 2.0. So, if you have any comments about our book, we would appreciate hearing from you. And thanks very much for buying our book.

Anne Boehm, Author
anne@murach.com

Joel Murach, Author
joelmurach@yahoo.com

Section 1

Introduction to ASP.NET 2.0

The three chapters in this section present an introduction to the new features of ASP.NET 2.0. Chapter 1 presents an overview of the most important new features for not only ASP.NET 2.0, but also for Visual Studio 2005 and Visual Basic 2005. This chapter gives you the big picture, but doesn't go into detail or specifics on the new features.

Next, chapter 2 shows you how to use Visual Studio 2005 to create an ASP.NET 2.0 application. In this chapter, you'll learn how the new code-behind model for ASP.NET 2.0 works. You'll also learn how to work with several new programming techniques for ASP.NET 2.0, such as cross-page posting and data sources.

Finally, chapter 3 presents master pages, one of the most important new features of ASP.NET 2.0. Once you see the benefits of master pages, you'll probably want to use them in all your ASP.NET 2.0 applications.

When you finish all three of these chapters, you'll have a solid understanding of the new ASP.NET 2.0 features that affect almost every web application you'll write. And you'll be ready to learn all of the other new features of ASP.NET 2.0 that are presented in the rest of this book.

1

What's new in ASP.NET 2.0

This chapter introduces you to the new features that are available in ASP.NET 2.0, as well as the new features of Visual Studio 2005 and the new version of the Visual Basic programming language. Once you get the big picture from this chapter, you can learn how to use each of the new features in the other chapters of this book.

An introduction to Visual Studio 2005 and ASP.NET 2.0

In the fall of 2005, Microsoft released the final versions of its long-awaited update to Visual Studio and the .NET Framework for developers. While these new products were being developed, they were known by the code name "Whidbey." But the final release of Visual Studio is called Visual Studio 2005, and the final release of the .NET Framework is called .NET Framework 2.0. Visual Studio 2005 includes Visual Basic 2005 and C# 2005, and the .NET Framework 2.0 includes ADO.NET 2.0 and ASP.NET 2.0.

Visual Studio 2005 editions

As the first table in figure 1-1 shows, Visual Studio 2005 is available in several editions. Most professional developers will work with either the Standard Edition or the Professional Edition. But large development teams may use the Team System edition, which includes features designed for specialized development roles such as architects, developers, and testers.

Visual Studio 2005 also comes in several inexpensive Express Editions. These editions sell for about $100. For web development, you can use Visual Web Developer 2005 Express Edition, which is sometimes referred to as VWD. It's designed for individual developers, students, and hobbyists who want to get started with ASP.NET development. With VWD, you can do web development in Visual Basic, C#, or J#.

All of the features described in this book will work with Visual Studio 2005 Standard, Professional, or Team System. They will also work with Visual Web Developer 2005 Express Edition. Although you can also get language-specific Express versions, these editions support only Windows forms development so you can't use them to develop ASP.NET applications.

New programming features for ASP.NET 2.0

The second table in this figure lists some of the most important new features of ASP.NET 2.0. Each of these features is described in detail later in this chapter, so I won't describe them here. But this table should show you that ASP.NET 2.0 is a significant upgrade with several major new features that you'll probably want to use in your ASP.NET 2.0 applications.

Visual Studio 2005 Editions

Edition	Description
Visual Studio 2005 Standard Edition	Supports Windows and Web development using Visual Basic, C#, C++, and J#.
Visual Studio 2005 Professional Edition	Same as Standard Edition with several additional features such as additional deployment options and integration with SQL Server 2005.
Visual Studio 2005 Team System	The top-of-the-line version of Visual Studio, with special features added to support large development teams with distinct team roles such as software architects, developers, and testers.
Visual Web Developer 2005 Express Edition	Inexpensive web development in Visual Basic, C#, or J# for hobbyists and novices.
Express Editions (Visual Basic, C#, C++, J#)	Inexpensive language-specific versions that support Windows forms development for hobbyists and novices. These editions don't support web development.

New programming features for ASP.NET 2.0

Feature	Chapters	Description
New code-behind model	2	Improves the relationship between aspx files and code-behind files.
Master pages	3	Lets you easily create pages with consistent elements such as banners and navigation menus.
New data-access features	4-7	New data source controls and bound-data controls drastically reduce the amount of code required for most database applications.
Site navigation	8	Provides controls that make it easy to create site navigation menus.
Login and user registration	9	Provides controls to automatically register users and allow them to log in to a web site.
Profiles	10	Stores data about users between sessions.
Themes	12	Lets you easily customize formatting elements.
Web parts	13	Lets the user choose which elements to include in a web page.

Description

- Visual Studio 2005 is a development environment that supports version 2.0 of the .NET Framework.
- Version 2.0 of the .NET Framework includes ASP.NET 2.0, which has several major improvements over previous versions of ASP.NET.

Figure 1-1   An introduction to Visual Studio 2005 and ASP.NET 2.0

ASP.NET 2.0's new code-behind model

One of the basic changes in ASP.NET 2.0 is its new code-behind model. This model is a major improvement over ASP.NET 1.x that affects the way the code-behind file is created in Visual Studio and the way ASP.NET 2.0 applications are compiled. Although the new model doesn't radically change the way you code ASP.NET applications, you should understand how the new model works and what its advantages are.

The ASP.NET 2.0 code-behind model

Figure 1-2 presents an overview of the new *code-behind model* and how it differs from previous versions. In ASP.NET 1.x, the code behind file was a class file that inherited the System.Web.UI.Page class, and the web page inherited the code-behind file. As a result, all of the controls that appeared on the page were declared in the code-behind file so they would be available to both the code-behind file and the page file.

To make that work, Visual Studio added a declaration to the code-behind file for each control that you created in the page file. This declaration was placed in a hidden code region of the code-behind file that you weren't supposed to modify. Unfortunately, it was all too easy for the code-behind file to become out of sync with the page file. If, for example, you deleted a control in the page file, the declaration in the code-behind file might not be deleted. Worse, if you changed the name of a control in the page file, the name of the control in the code-behind file might not get changed.

The new code-behind model completely avoids the need for a hidden code region and generated code in the code-behind file. Instead, the new model uses a new feature of Visual Basic 2005 called *partial classes*, which lets you create a class that's defined by two or more source files. So now, the control declarations are placed in a separate file that's compiled together with the code-behind file to create the final code-behind class. Furthermore, these declarations aren't created by Visual Studio while you're developing the application. Instead, they're generated by the ASP.NET runtime when it compiles the application.

The two main benefits of the new code-behind model are also listed in this figure. First, since there's no generated code in the code-behind file, there's no hidden code region that contains code you shouldn't edit. That means it's impossible to inadvertently mess up the generated code, and there's never a need to manually edit the generated code. Second, eliminating the generated code in the code-behind file makes it easier to keep the page file and the code-behind file in sync.

The ASP.NET 1.x code-behind model

- The code-behind file (.aspx.vb) is a class that inherits System.Web.UI.Page.
- The ASP.NET runtime generates a Visual Basic class for the web page (.aspx). This class inherits the class defined by the code-behind file.
- The code-behind class must contain a declaration for each control used by the web page. Visual Studio adds these declarations automatically when you add a control using the Web Forms Designer.

The ASP.NET 2.0 code-behind model

- The code-behind file (.aspx.vb) is a *partial class* that inherits System.Web.UI.Page.
- The ASP.NET runtime generates a partial class that contains the declarations required for the web page (.aspx). This partial class is compiled with the partial class of the code-behind file into one class that includes the declarations for the web controls and the Visual Basic event handlers.
- The ASP.NET runtime also generates another Visual Basic class for the web page. Then, when this Visual Basic file is compiled, it inherits the class that includes the declarations and the Visual Basic event handlers.

Benefits of the new code-behind model

- No generated code in the code-behind file.
- Easier to keep the web page file (.aspx) in sync with the code-behind file (.aspx.vb).

Description

- One of the most important differences between ASP.NET 1.x and ASP.NET 2.0 is the new way of handling a web page's code-behind file.
- ASP.NET 1.x relied on Visual Studio .NET to generate code in both the .aspx file and the code-behind file. Unfortunately, this cluttered the code-behind file with generated code and often led to inconsistencies between the page file and the code-behind file.
- The ASP.NET 2.0 *code-behind model* requires less synchronization between the page file and the code-behind file because the declarations are in one partial class and the event handlers are in another partial class.

Figure 1-2   The ASP.NET 2.0 code-behind model

How ASP.NET 2.0 applications are compiled

The diagram in figure 1-3 shows what actually happens behind the scenes when a user requests a page of an ASP.NET 2.0 application. First, the ASP.NET runtime reads the aspx file for the requested web page and generates a Visual Basic source file that contains two classes. The first generated class is a partial class that contains the declarations for each of the controls contained on the page. This class has the same name as the web page. That same name is also used for the partial class for the code-behind file. Later, these partial classes are compiled to create a single class that provides all of the event-handling code for the page.

The other class that's generated by the ASP.NET runtime contains the code that actually creates the ASP.NET page. This class gets its name from the aspx file plus _aspx, so its name is Order_aspx in this example. Because this class inherits the Order class, an object that is instantiated from the Order_aspx class will contain the code that creates the page, as well as the event-handling code provided by the Order class.

After the page classes are compiled, the ASP.NET runtime calls the Visual Basic compiler to compile any class files that are in the application's App_Code folder. If, for example, this Order application requires a business class named Order.vb and a database class named OrderIO.vb, both of these files will be compiled and the result will be saved in a single assembly (dll file).

Please note that this entire process happens only the first time an aspx page is accessed. Then, when the page is accessed again, the saved assemblies are reused, so the application doesn't have to be recompiled. However, ASP.NET does compare the time stamps on the source files with the time stamps on the dll files. If any of the source files have been modified since they were last compiled, ASP.NET automatically recompiles them.

Before I go on, you should realize that it isn't necessary to use code-behind files at all. If you prefer, you can put Visual Basic code right in the aspx file. In that case, the compiler doesn't combine the partial classes when it compiles the page. Instead, the runtime generates a single source file that contains all of the code for the page, and then calls the compiler to compile the generated code.

Note, however, that storing the aspx code and Visual Basic code in separate files can simplify application development because it lets you separate the presentation elements for a page from its logic elements. In fact, it's not uncommon to have HTML designers work on the aspx files while Visual Basic programmers work on the corresponding code-behind files.

How an ASP.NET application is compiled

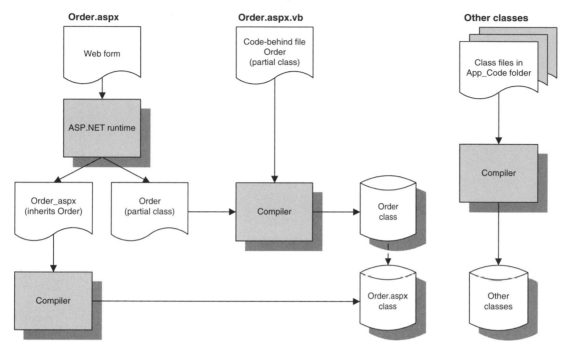

Description

- When a user requests an .aspx page, the ASP.NET runtime processes the .aspx file and generates a Visual Basic file that contains two classes. The first is a partial class that has the same name as the web page (Order). It contains the declarations for each of the controls. The second class has the same name as the web page plus _aspx, and it has the code that will create and render the web page.

- Next, the Visual Basic compiler compiles the two partial classes into a class (Order) that provides the event-handling code for the requested page. This class is saved as an assembly (.dll).

- Then, the Visual Basic compiler compiles the second generated class (Order_aspx), which inherits the first compiled class (Order). The resulting class is saved as an assembly (.dll) that's executed when the page is requested.

- If necessary, the Visual Basic compiler compiles any other class files that are stored in the application's App_Code folder. These classes are saved in a single assembly (.dll).

- This process is done only the first time the .aspx page is requested. After that, the page is processed directly from the compiled assemblies.

Note

- For the Default page, the name of the code-behind class is _Default.

Figure 1-3   How ASP.NET 2.0 applications are compiled

New features of ASP.NET 2.0

Besides the new code-behind model, ASP.NET 2.0 includes many new features. You'll use some of these new features, such as master pages and the new data access features, in almost every ASP.NET page you develop. Other features have more limited application. The following topics provide a brief introduction to the most important of these new features.

An introduction to master pages

Master pages make it easy for you to create pages that have common elements such as banners and navigation menus. That's why it is one of the most important new features of ASP.NET 2.0.

As figure 1-4 shows, a *master page* is a page that provides a framework within which the content from other pages can be displayed. The page that's actually sent to the browser is created by combining elements from a master page and a *content page*. The content page provides the content that's unique to each page in the application, while the master page provides the elements that are common to all pages.

In the example in this figure, the master page (MasterPage.master) provides a banner at the top of each page, a simple navigation menu at the side of each page, and a message that indicates how many days remain until Halloween at the bottom of each page. In addition, the master page contains a *content place-holder* that indicates where the content from each content page should be displayed. In this case, the content page is the Order.aspx page, and its content is displayed in the content placeholder in the master page.

In chapter 3, you'll learn just how powerful the master pages feature can be. In fact, you may decide that you're going to use one master page for every group of web pages that you develop.

An application that uses a master page

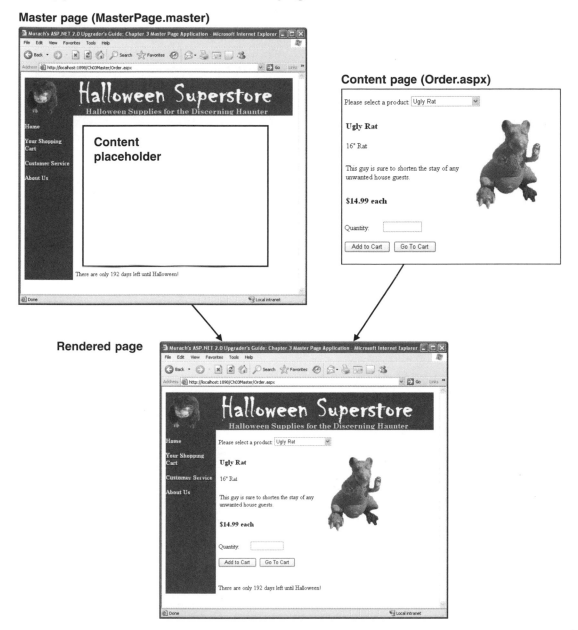

Description

- A *master page* provides a framework in which the content of each page on a web site is presented. Master pages make it easy to create pages that have a consistent look.
- The pages that provide the content displayed in a master page are called *content pages*.
- The content of each content page is displayed in the master page's *content placeholder*.
- The master pages feature is presented in chapter 3.

Figure 1-4   An introduction to master pages

An introduction to the ASP.NET 2.0 data access features

As figure 1-5 shows, Microsoft has thoroughly revamped data access and *data binding* for ASP.NET 2.0. For starters, ASP.NET 2.0 introduces a new type of data access object called a *data source* that is designed to eliminate the need to write code that directly accesses ADO.NET databases. In fact, with ASP.NET 2.0, you can create surprisingly advanced database applications without writing a single line of code.

As in previous versions, ASP.NET 2.0's *data access controls* are found in the Data tab of the Toolbox. This tab includes the five controls that are listed in the first table in this figure. The GridView control is a replacement for the DataGrid control. The DetailsView and FormView controls are entirely new. And the DataList and Repeater controls were available in ASP.NET 1.x, but they've been updated to work with the new data source controls.

The second table in this figure lists the five *data source controls* that come with ASP.NET 2.0. Of these controls, the one you'll use the most for database access is SqlDataSource. This control is designed primarily to work with Microsoft SQL Server databases, but you can also use it with other SQL databases, including Oracle, Access, and any database that supports ODBC.

In contrast, the AccessDataSource control is a special version of the SqlDataSource control that's designed to make it easy to use Microsoft Access databases. Instead of a connection string, the AccessDataSource control lets you specify the path for an Access database.

Finally, the ObjectDataSource control lets you create your own custom data access classes and use them with the data binding features of the GridView and other bound data controls. The XmlDataSource control lets you bind data controls to XML data. And the SiteMapDataSource control is used with ASP.NET 2.0's site navigation features.

The last control shown in the Data tab of the Toolbox is ReportViewer, which isn't really a data access control. Instead, it lets you view a report created with Crystal Reports. This control is similar to the CrystalReportViewer control of ASP.NET 1.x, so you shouldn't have any difficulty using it if you know how to use that control.

In this book, you'll learn how to use all of the data source controls except for the ReportViewer control. And you'll learn how to use the three new data access controls. This figure directs you to the chapter or chapters that present each type of control.

The Data tab of the Visual Studio Toolbox

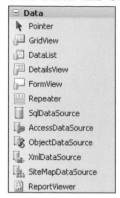

ASP.NET data access controls

Control	Chapter	Description
GridView	5	Displays data in a grid that's rendered as an HTML table.
DataList		Displays a list of data items (available with ASP.NET 1.x).
DetailsView	6	Displays the details of a single record in an HTML table.
FormView	6	Displays the details of a single record in a form.
Repeater		Displays a list of data items (available with ASP.NET 1.x).

ASP.NET data source controls

Control	Chapter	Description
SqlDataSource	4-6	Binds to SQL database.
AccessDataSource	2	Binds directly to Microsoft Access database files.
ObjectDataSource	7	Binds to an object created from a custom data access class.
XmlDataSource	4	Binds to XML data.
SiteMapDataSource	8	A data source used to provide site navigation features.

Description

- The use of *data sources* helps make *binding* a *data access control* in ASP.NET 2.0 significantly easier and more flexible than it was in ASP.NET 1.x.

- With ASP.NET 2.0, *data source controls* handle the details of accessing data in a database. In most ASP.NET 2.0 applications, you'll use data source controls instead of datasets, data adapters, data readers, and other ADO.NET classes.

- The GridView control is a replacement for the ASP.NET 1.x DataGrid control. The DataGrid control is still available, but it's no longer in the Toolbox.

- The ReportViewer control lets you add a Crystal Reports report to a web page.

- All editions of Visual Studio 2005 come with a scaled-back version of SQL Server 2005 called SQL Server Express. You can use SQL Server Express to test applications that use SQL Server databases without installing SQL Server on your development system.

Figure 1-5   An introduction to the ASP.NET 2.0 data access features

An introduction to site navigation

Another important new feature of ASP.NET 2.0 is *site navigation*, which makes it easy to add menus and other navigation features to a web application. In fact, providing site navigation is as simple as (1) creating an XML file that documents the structure of your application, (2) dragging a navigation control to the master page, and (3) binding the navigation control to a site navigation data source. In contrast, you had to develop your own navigation features with previous versions of ASP.NET.

Figure 1-6 shows a page from an ASP.NET 2.0 application that uses the new site navigation features. This page includes a SiteMapDataSource control and the three navigation controls: TreeView, Menu, and SiteMapPath.

The SiteMapDataSource control is a special type of data source control that provides information about the organization of a web site's pages to a TreeView or Menu navigation control. By default, this data source obtains its information from an XML file called web.sitemap, which resides in the application's root folder. You must manually create this file before you can use a site map data source.

The TreeView control displays all of the pages in the web.sitemap file in a tree structure that's similar to a directory tree displayed by the Windows Explorer. The user can expand or collapse each node by clicking the + or – button that appears next to each node that has children. This control is most useful when you want to give users a view of all the pages in a web site.

The Menu control creates dynamic menus that expand when you hover the mouse over a menu item that contains subitems. If, for example, you were to hover the mouse over the Projects item in the menu in this figure, a submenu listing Costumes, Static Props, and Animated Props would appear. Although the menu shown in this figure is a *vertical menu*, which means that the items are stacked vertically, you can also use the Menu control to create a *horizontal menu*.

The SiteMapPath control displays a list of links that lead from the current page back to the web site's home page. This makes it easy for the user to quickly return to the home page or to a parent of the current page.

A page with three site navigation controls

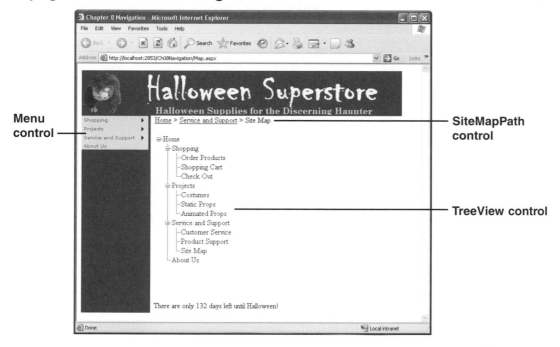

Menu control

SiteMapPath control

TreeView control

ASP.NET navigation controls

Control	Description
TreeView	Provides a hierarchical view of the site's structure. The user can click + or – icons next to each node to expand or collapse the node. Must be bound to a SiteMapDataSource control. Located in the Navigation tab of the Toolbox.
Menu	Creates a horizontal or vertical menu. Must be bound to a SiteMapDataSource control. Located in the Navigation tab of the Toolbox.
SiteMapPath	Displays a list of links from the application's root page (the home page) to the current page. Doesn't need to be bound to a SiteMapDataSource control. Located in the Navigation tab of the Toolbox.
SiteMapDataSource	Connects a navigation control to the site hierarchy specified by the web.sitemap file. Located in the Data tab of the Toolbox.

Description

- ASP.NET provides three user-interface controls and a data source control designed to let the user navigate the pages in a web site.
- The navigation structure of a web site is defined by an XML file named web.sitemap located in the application's root folder. You must create this file before you can work with the Menu and TreeView controls.
- These features are presented in chapter 8.

Figure 1-6   An introduction to site navigation

An introduction to the login controls

ASP.NET 2.0 supports forms-based authentication just as in previous versions of ASP.NET. However, as figure 1-7 shows, ASP.NET 2.0 has added several *login controls* that are designed to simplify the job of creating login pages and other pages related to user authentication. For example, the Login control lets the user enter a username and password to log in. The other controls listed in this figure include such common functions as creating a new user account, changing a password, or recovering a lost password.

The result is that you can do all of the essential login and authentication functions without writing any code. In contrast, with previous versions of ASP.NET, you had to provide all of this functionality. That's why the login controls are another important new feature.

The Login tab of the Visual Studio Toolbox

ASP.NET 2.0 login controls

Control	Description
Login	Lets the user log in to an application.
LoginView	Lets you change what's displayed on the web page depending on whether the user is anonymous (unauthenticated) or logged in (authenticated).
PasswordRecovery	Provides a standard way for the user to recover a forgotten password.
LoginStatus	If the user isn't logged in, offers the user a chance to log in. If the user is logged in, provides a link the user can click to log out.
LoginName	Displays the user name for the current user.
CreateUserWizard	Provides an easy and consistent way for a user to register.
ChangePassword	Lets the user change his or her password.

Description

- The controls on the Login tab of the Toolbox let you easily add user login management to ASP.NET applications that use forms-based authentication.
- ASP.NET 2.0 also includes a web-based site administration tool that lets you configure forms-based authentication.
- By default, a SQL Server database in the application's App_Data folder is used to store the membership and role data that these controls require.
- The login controls and other new authentication features are presented in chapter 9.

Figure 1-7   An introduction to the login controls

An introduction to profiles

As figure 1-8 shows, *profile* is a new type of state that stores data for an individual user. Although profile state is similar to session state, it has two key differences. First, profile data is maintained between user sessions. For example, if you store a user's shopping cart in profile instead of session state, the user can leave your web site, come back at a later date, and find the same items still in the cart.

Second, profile data is strongly typed because the data is stored using custom properties that are defined in the application's web.config file. There, each definition specifies the name of a property and its data type. In contrast, data stored in session state is saved as simple key-value pairs, where the data type of the value for each pair is always Object and the key value can be any value you want.

The first example in this figure shows how you can define profile properties. Here, the first two properties store a user's first and last name as strings named FirstName and LastName. Then, the third property stores a DateTime object named LastActivityDate.

This first example also enables the *anonymous identification* feature, another new feature of ASP.NET 2.0. This feature automatically creates a unique ID that can be used to identify each user, even if the user hasn't logged in. Since all three properties in the first example allow anonymous identification, these profile properties can be used with authenticated users who have logged in to the application or with anonymous users who haven't logged in.

The second example shows how you can get profile properties from the data store. Here, the Profile class is used to retrieve the first and last name of the user. Then, it is used to retrieve the last activity date for the user.

The third example shows how you can store profile properties in a data store. Here, the FirstName and LastName properties of the Profile class are used to store the text that's in the text boxes named txtFirstName and txtLastName. Then, the Profile class is used to store the current date as the last activity date.

By default, profile data is stored in a predefined SQL Server database in the application's App_Data folder. This lets you use the profile feature without having to create a database to store profile data. However, if you need to work with an existing SQL Server database, or if you need to use another type of database such as an Oracle or MySQL database, you can write a custom profile provider as described in chapter 10. Although this requires some serious coding, it allows you to use the profile feature to work with existing data in just about any type of data store.

A section of a web.config file that defines profile properties

```
<anonymousIdentification enabled="true" />

<profile>
    <properties>
        <add name="FirstName" type="System.String"
            allowAnonymous="true" />
        <add name="LastName" type="System.String"
            allowAnonymous="true" />
        <add name="LastActivityDate" type="System.DateTime"
            allowAnonymous="true" />
    </properties>
</profile>
```

Visual Basic code that gets a profile property

```
Protected Sub Page_Load(ByVal sender As Object, _
        ByVal e As System.EventArgs) Handles Me.Load
    If Not IsPostBack Then
        txtName.Text = Profile.FirstName & " " & Profile.LastName
        lblLastActivityDate.Text = _
            FormatDateTime(Profile.LastActivityDate, DateFormat.ShortDate)
    End If
End Sub
```

Visual Basic code that sets a profile property

```
Protected Sub btnSave_Click(ByVal sender As Object, _
        ByVal e As System.EventArgs) Handles btnSave.Click
    Profile.FirstName = txtFirstName.Text
    Profile.LastName = txtLastName.Text
    Profile.LastActivityDate = DateTime.Now
End Sub
```

Description

- *Profile* state is similar to session state but persists between user sessions.
- Unlike session state, the data stored in a profile is strongly typed. When you create an application, you specify the profile properties in the web.config file.
- By default, profiles only allow you to work with authenticated users (users who have identified themselves by logging in). However, it's also possible to store data about anonymous users (users who haven't logged in). To do that, you need to enable ASP.NET 2.0's new *anonymous identification* feature. This feature creates a unique ID that can be used to identify each user.
- By default, profile data is stored in a predefined SQL Server database in the application's App_Data folder. However, you can also write a custom profile provider to work with data in an existing SQL Server database or in another type of database such as Oracle or MySQL.
- The profile feature is presented in chapter 10.

Figure 1-8   An introduction to profiles

An introduction to themes

Figure 1-9 describes another new feature called *themes*. Themes provide three types of elements that let you quickly change the overall appearance of an application. *Style sheets* control the formatting used for the HTML elements in a page. *Skins* control the appearance of ASP.NET web server controls. And *images* can be used by the style sheets and skins of a theme to supply backgrounds and other design elements.

An introduction to web parts

Figure 1-9 also describes a new feature called *web parts*. This feature lets you create *portals*, which are web pages that the users can easily customize by choosing and arranging the web parts that should appear on the pages. In this figure, for example, you can see a portal page that displays four web parts that might be used by a salesperson for a store that sells Halloween products. However, the web parts on a portal can provide just about any type of information. For example, you might let the user choose to include a news feed, a weather report, or a stock market ticker on a portal page of your web site.

Although creating a web site that uses web parts is relatively easy, the hard part is creating the web parts themselves. That is done in a way that's similar to creating custom controls. Fortunately, the web parts feature automatically treats ASP.NET user controls as web parts. This allows you to use existing user controls as web parts, and it allows you to quickly develop new user controls that can be used as web parts. In addition, in the future, web parts that have been created by other developers may become available on the Internet. As a result, before you go to the trouble of creating your own web parts, you should check to see if someone has already done the work for you.

An ASP.NET page that uses themes and web parts

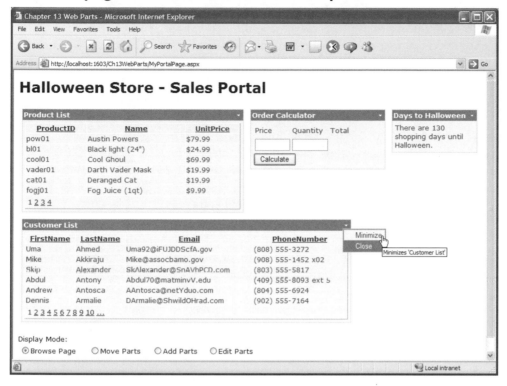

What the themes feature does

- Uses *style sheets* to define the formatting used for HTML elements, uses *skins* to determine the appearance of ASP.NET controls, and stores *images* that can be used by the style sheets and skins of a theme.
- Lets you consistently apply formatting to all of the pages of an application.
- Lets you separate the formatting from the function of an application.
- Lets you easily switch the formatting of a page at design time or runtime.
- Themes are presented in chapter 12.

What the web parts feature does

- Lets you develop *portals*, which are web pages that can be customized by the user. A portal typically defines several zones that can contain *web parts*, which are special controls that can be displayed within certain zones of a portal. These controls can be minimized, restored, closed, and moved by the user.
- Lets you use ASP.NET user controls as web parts.
- Lets you develop custom web parts.
- Web parts are presented in chapter 13.

Figure 1-9   An introduction to themes and web parts

Other new features of ASP.NET 2.0

The previous figures have introduced you to six major new features of ASP.NET 2.0, each of which merits its own chapter in this book. However, ASP.NET 2.0 also includes many minor new features and improvements. Some of the most useful of these features are summarized in figure 1-10.

The Wizard and MultiView controls are new ASP.NET controls that let you create two or more pages of input controls on a single ASP.NET page. The Wizard control includes built-in navigation controls (such as Next and Prev buttons), while the MultiView control requires that you create your own navigation controls. These controls are presented in chapter 11, and the other controls listed in this figure are presented in chapter 14.

Cross-page posting is a new feature that lets you create a button control that posts to a different web page. In previous versions, the most common way to accomplish this was to write a Click event handler for the button, and then use Response.Redirect or Server.Transfer to go to another page. But now, you can specify a postback URL on a button. Then, when the user clicks the button, the page posts to the specified URL rather than to the page that's currently displayed. Because this feature is so useful, it is described in chapter 2.

Another new feature for ASP.NET 2.0 is the special folders that are used to store the code and data used by an application. For instance, class files (other than code-behind files) are stored in a special folder named App_Code. And database files can be stored in a folder named App_Data. In chapter 2, you'll learn more about these and the other special folders that you're going to be using.

Other new ASP.NET 2.0 server controls

- Wizard, which lets you create a multi-step wizard with built-in navigation controls.
- MultiView, which is similar to a Wizard but doesn't include navigation controls.
- ImageMap, which lets you create images with different links for separate regions of the image.
- BulletedList, which can create an HTML bullet list from bound data.
- FileUpload, which lets the user upload a file to your application.
- Hidden field, which lets you save data in a hidden field on a page.
- Substitution, which lets you include small amounts of dynamic data on otherwise static pages and still take advantage of page caching.

Other ASP.NET 2.0 features

- *Cross-page posting*, which lets you create a button control that posts back to a different page.
- Special folders such as App_Code and App_Data that contain the class and database files used by an application.

Description

- In addition to the major features described in the previous figures, ASP.NET 2.0 includes several new controls that are presented in chapter 14.
- ASP.NET 2.0 also includes some other improvements like cross-page posting and the App_Code folder that are presented in chapter 2.

Figure 1-10   Other new features of ASP.NET 2.0

New features of Visual Studio 2005 and Visual Basic 2005

ASP.NET isn't the only thing that has been improved with the release of Visual Studio 2005 and version 2.0 of the .NET Framework. Visual Studio itself has received some nice improvements, and a few new features have been added to the Visual Basic programming language. The topics that follow describe these new features.

New features of Visual Studio 2005

Microsoft has made many improvements to the integrated development environment for Visual Studio 2005. Figure 1-11 describes just a few of the more significant ones.

One that you'll notice right away is that grid layout mode is no longer supported. In Visual Studio 2005, you must use flow layout when you design web pages. In most cases, though, flow layout was the preferred way to develop web applications, so you probably won't miss grid layout.

Another change is that Visual Studio 2005 has done away with project files. Most of the configuration information that was stored in these files is now stored in the web.config file. Also, ASP.NET 2.0 applications are now known as *web sites* rather than web projects.

Visual Studio 2005 also includes a built-in web server called the *development server* that lets you test web applications on your computer without installing IIS or using a remote server. Although this development server has a few important limitations, it makes the initial stages of application development and testing much easier.

Finally–and perhaps most important to some of us–Visual Studio's Web Forms Designer no longer makes arbitrary changes to the HTML in your aspx files. In contrast, previous versions of the Web Forms Designer would frequently adjust the indentation of your HTML or make other arbitrary changes. In fact, just switching to Design view could cause changes in your aspx files. But not any more!

You'll learn more about these and other changes to Visual Studio 2005 in chapter 2.

An ASP.NET 2.0 application displayed in Visual Studio 2005

Major changes for Visual Studio 2005

- Grid layout mode is no longer supported. The Web Forms Designer now works in flow layout mode.
- The Solution/Project model has been simplified. You now work with *web sites* instead of projects.
- Visual Studio 2005 includes a built-in web server called the *development server* that lets you test web applications without installing IIS.
- In previous versions, the web designer frequently changed the HTML in the application's aspx files. In Visual Studio 2005, the web designer doesn't make unwanted changes to your HTML.

Description

- Although Visual Studio 2005 includes many changes that make it easier to develop ASP.NET web applications, most of the basic techniques for working with aspx pages and code are the same as in previous versions.

Figure 1-11   New features of Visual Studio 2005

New Visual Basic language features

Figure 1-12 introduces six new features that have been added to the Visual language with version 2.0 of .NET. Other than partial classes, none of these features are essential for ASP.NET applications. Still, you may want to research some of these new features on your own so you'll be able to use them where appropriate.

I've already mentioned *partial classes*, which are used by the ASP.NET 2.0 code-behind model. These classes let you spread the code for a class over two or more source files. Then, when the application is compiled, the partial classes are combined to create the complete class.

The *generics* feature lets you create classes that include type information as a parameter. The main use of this feature is to create strongly-typed collection classes. The code example shown for this feature creates an instance of a new collection class called List, which can contain only objects of type Customer.

Continue is a new statement that lets you control the execution of a Do, For, or While loop. In most cases, you'll want each statement in a loop to execute for each iteration of the loop. If you want to end the current iteration of a loop before the last statement, however, you can use the Continue statement as shown in the example in this figure. This statement skips immediately to the next iteration of the loop.

The IsNot keyword has been added to make it easier to compare two objects. For example, the If statement in this figure that uses the IsNot keyword checks if an object named Customer is not equal to Nothing. Prior to Visual Basic 2005, you would have had to code this statement like this:

```
If Not Customer Is Nothing Then...
```

I think you'll agree that the statement that uses the IsNot keyword is less awkward than the statement that doesn't.

The last example in this figure shows how to work with unsigned integer types. Although version 1.x of the .NET Framework provided for these types, Visual Basic 2002 and 2003 didn't support them. As you can see in this figure, the Visual Basic keywords for using these data types are UShort, UInteger, and ULong. This figure also shows the Visual Basic functions you can use to convert values with other types to these new types.

New Visual Basic features

- *Partial classes* let you spread the definition of a class over two or more source files:

```
Partial Class Order
    Inherits System.Web.UI.Page
    ...
End Class
```

- *Generics* are used primarily to create strongly-typed collection classes:

```
Dim customerList As New List(Of Customer)
```

- The *Continue statement* lets you skip immediately to the next iteration of a Do, For, or While loop:

```
Protected Sub btnRandom_Click(ByVal sender As Object, _
        ByVal e As System.EventArgs) Handles btnRandom.Click
    Dim i As Integer
    For i = 1 To 10
        Dim iNumber As Integer = CInt(Rnd() * 10)
        If iNumber <= 5 Then
            Continue For
        End If
        lstNumbers.Items.Add(iNumber.ToString)
    Next
End Sub
```

- The *IsNot keyword* can be used to avoid awkward constructs that compare two objects using the Not and Is keywords:

```
If Customer IsNot Nothing Then...
```

- The *unsigned integer types* let you store and convert unsigned integer values:

```
Dim usNumber As UShort
Dim uiNumber As UInteger
Dim ulNumber As ULong
usNumber = CUShort(txtShort.Text)
uiNumber = CUInt(txtInteger.Text)
ulNumber = CULng(txtLong.Text)
```

Description

- Visual Studio 2005 includes Visual Basic 2005, which includes several new programming features. Although this isn't a complete list, these are the most significant changes to the Visual Basic language.

Figure 1-12   New Visual Basic language features

Perspective

Now that you've been introduced to the new features of ASP.NET 2.0, Visual Studio 2005, and Visual Basic 2005, you're ready to learn how to use them. To start, I recommend that you read the next two chapters to get better acquainted with the new features that you're going to use all the time. After that, you can skip to the chapters that present the features you're most interested in.

Terms

code-behind model
partial class
master page
content page
content placeholder
data source
data binding
data access control
data source control
site navigation
vertical menu
horizontal menu
login control
profile
theme
style sheet
skin
image
web part
cross-page posting
web site
development server
generics

2

How to create an ASP.NET 2.0 application in Visual Studio 2005

In the last chapter, you were introduced to the new features of ASP.NET 2.0. Now, in this chapter, you'll learn how to build a simple web site using Visual Studio 2005. Along the way, you'll learn first-hand how to work with ASP.NET 2.0's new code-behind model as well as several other new features.

The Shopping Cart application

To illustrate the skills that you'll learn in this chapter, I'll use a simple Shopping Cart application. It uses two pages, requires access to a database, stores data in session state, uses several different types of input controls and validators, and requires code-behind files for both of its pages. In short, although this is a simple application, it isn't trivial.

This application lets the user select a product from a drop-down list and displays those products in a shopping cart that the user can modify. The application is used by a company that sells Halloween products such as costumes and decorations. I'll describe the two pages of this application in the topics that follow.

The Order page

Figure 2-1 presents the first page of the Shopping Cart application. This page, named Order.aspx, includes a drop-down list from which the user can select a product. The products are retrieved from an Access database via an AccessDataSource control, one of the new data source controls provided by ASP.NET 2.0. Since the drop-down list is bound to the data source, the products are displayed automatically.

Although it isn't apparent in this figure, the product data is retrieved from an Access database named Halloween.mdb. This database includes a table named Products. The Products table has these columns: ProductID, Name, ShortDescription, LongDescription, CategoryID, ImageFile, UnitPrice, and OnHand. All of these columns except CategoryID and OnHand are used by the Shopping Cart application.

The AutoPostBack property of the drop-down list is set to True. That way, when the user selects a product, the page is posted back to the server. Then, the code for the page retrieves the data for the selected product from the data source. Because this data is already available in the AccessDataSource object, though, the program doesn't have to access the database again to get this information. Instead, it extracts the data from the data source, and this data is displayed in several labels. In addition, the ImageUrl property of an Image control is set to the value of the ImageFile column so the product image is displayed.

Once a product is selected, the user can enter a quantity and click the Add to Cart button. However, if the user clicks the Add to Cart button without entering a valid quantity, an error message is displayed. To accomplish that, two validation controls are included on the page. A required field validator makes sure that the user enters a quantity, and a compare validator makes sure that the user enters an integer greater than zero. Because validation controls haven't changed from ASP.NET 1.x, you shouldn't have any trouble using them in your ASP.NET 2.0 applications.

The design of the Order page

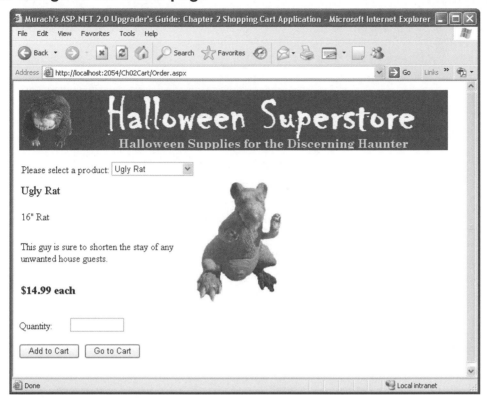

Description

- The Order page of this application accepts an order for any items in the online store.
- To order an item, the user selects the product from the drop-down list, enters a quantity in the text box, and clicks the Add to Cart button.
- When the user clicks the Add to Cart button, the selected product is added to the shopping cart. If the product is already in the shopping cart, the quantity is added to the quantity in the existing shopping cart item. Then, the Shopping Cart page is displayed.
- The product information is retrieved from an Access database by an AccessDataSource control that's bound to the drop-down list.
- The AutoPostBack property of the drop-down list is set to True so the page is posted when the user selects a product. Then, the information for the selected product is displayed.
- The shopping cart information is stored in a SortedList object. This sorted list is saved in session state so it can be retrieved and updated each time a product is ordered.
- Validation controls ensure that the user enters a positive integer for the quantity.

Figure 2-1   The Order page of the Shopping Cart application

If the user enters a valid quantity, a sorted list that contains the user's shopping cart is updated with the product information. If the product isn't already in the shopping cart, a new item is added to the sorted list. But if the product already exists in the shopping cart, the quantity entered is added to the quantity for the product that's in the shopping cart.

Because the shopping cart must be retrieved and updated each time a product is added or updated, the sorted list that represents the shopping cart is saved in session state. This shopping cart is also retrieved by the Cart page of this application, which I'll describe next.

The Cart page

After the user selects a product from the Order page, enters a quantity, and clicks the Add to Cart button, the Cart page in figure 2-2 is displayed. This page lists all the items currently in the shopping cart in a list box. To do that, it must retrieve the shopping cart from session state.

To work with the items in the shopping cart, the user can use the two buttons to the right of the list box. To remove an item from the shopping cart, the user can select the item and click the Remove Item button. Or, to remove all the items from the shopping cart, the user can click the Empty Cart button.

If the user wants to add items to the shopping cart, he can click the Continue Shopping button to return to the Order page. Then, the user can add additional items to the shopping cart.

Alternatively, the user can click the Check Out button to complete the order. However, the check out function hasn't yet been implemented in this version of the Shopping Cart application. So if the user clicks the Check Out button, a message is displayed to indicate that the check out feature isn't implemented. In a complete application, of course, clicking this button would cause additional pages to be displayed to complete the order. But since those pages aren't required to illustrate the skills presented in this chapter, I omitted them.

Like most applications, there are several different ways to implement a shopping cart in ASP.NET. For instance, one design decision is how to save the shopping cart data. For this application, I decided to save the shopping cart data in session state. As an alternative, though, you could save the shopping cart data in a database table. Or, you could use ASP.NET 2.0's new profile feature. Each approach has its advantages and disadvantages.

A second design decision for a shopping cart application is what type of ASP.NET control to use when you display the shopping cart. To keep this application simple, I used a list box. However, you can create a more advanced shopping cart by using a Repeater or DataList control or the new GridView control. With these controls, you can display the shopping cart data in neatly arranged columns and include buttons or other controls in each row to let the user delete or modify the cart items.

The design of the Cart page

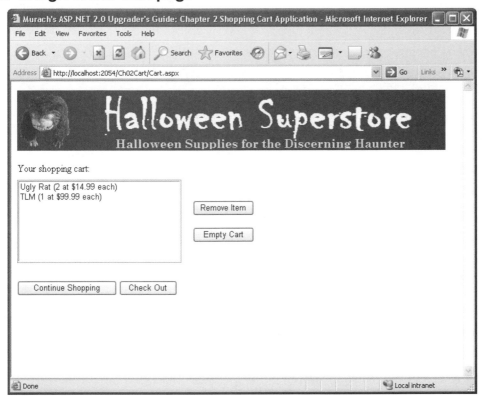

Description

- The Cart page displays the items in the shopping cart in a list box control. To load the list box, it uses the shopping cart information that's saved in session state by the Order page.

- The user can select any item in the shopping cart and then click the Remove Item button to remove the item from the cart. To remove all the items from the cart, the user can click the Empty Cart button.

- After reviewing the cart, the user can click the Continue Shopping button to return to the Order page and order additional products.

- If the user clicks the Check Out button, a message is displayed that indicates that the check out function hasn't been implemented yet.

Figure 2-2   The Cart page of the Shopping Cart application

The files and folders used by the Shopping Cart application

Web applications are organized differently in ASP.NET 2.0 than in previous versions. To illustrate these differences, figure 2-3 describes the files and folders used by the Shopping Cart application.

By default, Visual Studio 2005 places new web page files and their related code-behind files in the application's root folder, but other files used by the application are placed in special folders. The first table in this figure lists the most commonly used special folders. Besides these folders, though, you can also create your own folders. For example, it's common to create an Images folder to store any image files used by the application.

The App_Code, App_Data, App_Themes, and Bin folders are used for certain types of files required by the application. For instance, class files (other than the class files for web pages) are stored in the App_Code folder, and any Access database files used by the application are stored in the App_Data folder. In contrast, the App_Themes folder is used to store any theme data, which you'll learn more about in chapter 12. And the Bin folder is where the application's compiled assemblies are stored.

Note that the special folders aren't available to the application through normal means. For example, you can't store an image file in the App_Data folder, and then refer to it in the ImageUrl attribute of an Image control. The only exception is that you can refer to the App_Data folder in a connection string for an Access database.

The second table in this figure lists the specific files and folders that make up the Shopping Cart application. As you can see, the App_Code folder contains two class files named CartItem.vb and Product.vb that define the CartItem and Product classes required by the application. And the App_Data folder contains an Access database named Halloween.mdb, plus an .ldb file that stores the record locking information for that file.

The Shopping Cart application also includes a folder named Images. This folder includes just one image file, banner.jpg, which provides the banner displayed at the top of each page. However, this folder also includes a subfolder named Products, which includes a separate image file for each product in the Products table of the database. Because the Products table includes a column named ImageFile that provides the file name for each product's image, the application can display the correct image for each product.

Finally, the root folder for the application contains two files for each of the application's web pages: one for the page itself, the other for the code-behind file. For example, the Cart.aspx file contains the aspx code that defines the Cart page, and the Cart.aspx.vb file is the code-behind file that contains the Visual Basic code for the Cart page.

Please note that the root folder also contains a web.config file. This file is added the first time you run an application with debugging. Although the format of this file has changed a bit for ASP.NET 2.0, it still works the same as for ASP.NET 1.x.

The Solution Explorer for the Shopping Cart application

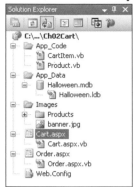

Special folders used in ASP.NET 2.0 applications

Folder	Description
App_Code	Non-page class files that are compiled together to create a single assembly.
App_Data	Database files used by the application.
App_Themes	Themes used by the application.
Bin	Compiled code.

Files in the Shopping Cart application

Folder	File	Description
App_Code	CartItem.vb	A class that represents an item in the shopping cart.
App_Code	Product.vb	A class that represents a product.
App_Data	Halloween.mdb	The Access database file that contains the Halloween database.
App_Data	Halloween.ldb	The locking file associated with the Halloween.mdb database file.
Images	Banner.jpg	An image file that displays the banner used at the top of each page.
Images\Products	(multiple)	Contains an image file for each product in the database.
(root)	Cart.aspx	The aspx file for the Cart page.
(root)	Cart.aspx.vb	The code-behind file for the Cart page.
(root)	Order.aspx	The aspx file for the Order page.
(root)	Order.aspx.vb	The code-behind file for the Order page.
(root)	web.config	The application configuration file.

Description

- The Solution Explorer in Visual Studio 2005 is similar to the Solution Explorer in previous versions of Visual Studio. However, ASP.NET 2.0 web projects use a new folder structure with special folders such as App_Code and App_Data.
- The Images folder is a custom folder that I created to hold the image files used by this application. The Products subfolder contains the image files for the products in the Products table of the Halloween database.

Figure 2-3   The files and folders used by the Shopping Cart application

How to work with ASP.NET 2.0 web sites

The basic file and project management tasks for Visual Studio 2005 work much as they did in previous versions. However, there are a few minor variations that I'll describe next.

How to create a new ASP.NET 2.0 web site

In Visual Studio 2005, a web project is called a *web site*, and figure 2-4 shows the dialog box for creating a new ASP.NET 2.0 web site. This dialog box is displayed when you choose the File→New→Web Site command. From this dialog box, you can select the language used for the web site, the name of the web site, and the location at which the web site will be created.

The Location drop-down list in this dialog box gives you three options for specifying the location of the web site. The simplest method is to create a *file-system web site*. This type of web site can exist in any folder on your local hard disk, or in a folder on a shared network drive. File-system web sites can be run directly by Visual Studio's built-in web server. But you can also run a file-system web site with IIS by creating a Virtual Directory for the folder.

If you choose HTTP in the Location drop-down list, Visual Studio uses HTTP to create a web site in an IIS Virtual Directory. This eliminates the need to manually create a Virtual Directory for the application, but requires that you have access to an IIS server. In addition, if the IIS server isn't on your local computer, it must have FrontPage 2002 Server Extensions installed.

If you want to create a web site on a remote IIS server that doesn't have FrontPage 2002 Server Extensions installed, you can use the FTP option. This uses File Transfer Protocol to upload the application's files to the server.

This figure also points out that, by default, Visual Studio 2005 creates a solution file for your web site in My Documents\Visual Studio 2005\Projects. This solution file is stored in this folder regardless of the location of the web site itself. However, you can change this location as well as other project and solution options by choosing Tools→Options, checking the Show All Settings checkbox, and selecting Projects and Solutions in the settings list. Usually, though, there's no reason to change these settings.

Unlike previous versions, Visual Studio 2005 doesn't use project files. Instead, the settings that were stored in project files are now stored in the web.config file.

The New Web Site dialog box

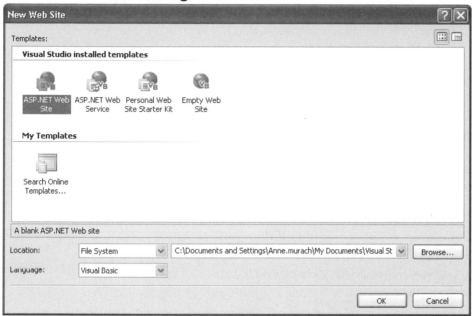

Three location options for ASP.NET web sites

Location option	Description
File System	A web site created in a folder on your local computer or on a shared network. You can run the web site directly from the built-in web server or create an IIS Virtual Directory for the folder and run the application under IIS.
HTTP	A web site created under the control of an IIS web server. If the IIS server isn't on your local computer, the server must have FrontPage 2002 Server Extensions installed.
FTP	A web site created on a remote hosting server that has IIS and ASP.NET 2.0 installed but doesn't have FrontPage 2002 Server Extensions installed.

Description

- An ASP.NET project is called a *web site* under ASP.NET 2.0. So you use the File→New →Web Site command to create a new ASP.NET 2.0 web site.

- The default location for a *file-system web site* is My Documents\Visual Studio 2005\WebSites.

- Visual Studio creates a solution file for the web site in the default location for solution files, which is normally My Documents\Visual Studio 2005\Projects. Unlike previous versions, though, ASP.NET 2.0 web sites don't use project files. Instead, they use web.config files to store project information.

Figure 2-4   How to create a new ASP.NET 2.0 web site

How to add items to a web site

Figure 2-5 presents the skills you need to add items to a web site. Specifically, this figure shows how to add new items such as web pages or class files, how to create new folders such as the Images folder used by the Shopping Cart application, and how to copy existing items such as image files, class files, and web pages from other applications into a web site.

To add a new item to a project, right-click the folder you want to add the item to, and choose the Add New Item command from the shortcut menu that appears. This brings up the Add New Item dialog box shown in this figure. Then, choose one of the templates such as Web Form or Class to indicate the type of item you want to add, type a name for the item, and click Add.

When you add a new web form, be sure that the language setting is Visual Basic and that the Place Code in Separate File box is checked. These settings are easy to overlook, but difficult to change manually if they're set wrong when you create the page.

To add a folder to a web site, right-click the web site itself in the Solution Explorer and choose Add Folder. From the menu that's displayed, you can select the special folder you want to add, or you can select Regular Folder and then enter the name for the folder. You can then add items to the folder you've created.

You can also add an existing item such as an image file or a web page from another web application. To do that, right-click the folder you want to add the existing item to and choose Add Existing Item. This brings up a dialog box that lets you select the item you want to add.

The Add New Item dialog box

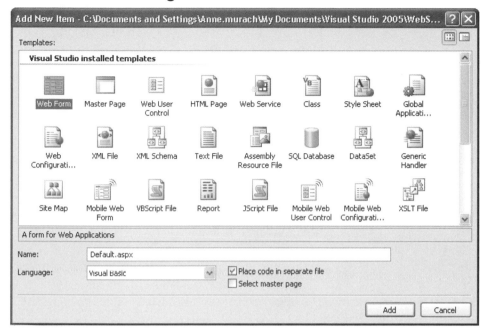

How to add a new item

- One way to open the Add New Item dialog box is to choose the Website→Add New Item command. The other way is to right-click the folder in the Solution Explorer that you want to add the item to, and then choose Add New Item from the shortcut menu.

- From the Add New Item dialog box, select the type of item you want to add from the list of available templates, and enter a name for the item. Next, choose the language you want to use. Then, if you're adding a web form, check the Place Code in Separate File box to create a code-behind file. Last, click the Add button.

How to add a folder to a web site

- In the Solution Explorer, right-click the web site and choose Add Folder. Then, select the special folder you want to add. Or select Regular Folder, and then type a name for the new folder and press Enter.

How to add an existing item to a web site

- In the Solution Explorer, right-click the folder you want to add the item to (or the web site itself if you don't want the item to be placed in a folder) and choose Add Existing Item. Then, locate the item you want to add, select it, and click the Add button.

Figure 2-5   How to add items to a web site

How to design an ASP.NET 2.0 web page

The Web Forms Designer for Visual Studio 2005 has been significantly redesigned to make it easier to work with web pages, both in Design view and Source view (which used to be called HTML view). The topics that follow present these improvements.

The HTML code for a new web page

Figure 2-6 shows the HTML code that's generated for the Default.aspx file when you create a new web site. Similar code is generated when you add a new web form to an existing application. The only difference is that different names are used in the CodeFile and the Inherits attributes of the Page directive.

This code provides a skeleton that you can use to create the web pages for a web application. It begins with a Page directive that controls how the page is compiled. This directive provides the four attributes listed in the table. For the default page for this web site, the Language attribute is set to VB, AutoEventWireup is set to False, CodeFile is set to Default.aspx.vb, which is the code-behind file, and Inherits is set to _Default.

You may remember from chapter 1 that the code-behind model for ASP.NET 2.0 uses partial classes for the aspx file and the code-behind file for each web page. Later, these partial classes are compiled into a single class with a name that's prefixed by an underscore. For this default page, the name of that class is _Default. Then, this class is inherited by the class named Default, which contains the code that is used to instantiate the page. If you want to refresh your memory about this, please refer back to figures 1-2 and 1-3.

In any event, the CodeFile attribute is similar to the CodeBehind attribute that was used in the Page directive for ASP.NET 1.x. However, because the code-behind model works differently in ASP.NET 2.0, Microsoft decided to create a new attribute named CodeFile rather than redefine the meaning of the old CodeBehind attribute.

You may notice a few other differences between the ASP.NET 2.0 template and the template used for previous versions. For example, the Body tag in ASP.NET 1.x used a non-standard attribute named MS-POSITIONING to set the positioning mode for the page. But in ASP.NET 2.0, non-standard HTML attributes aren't used.

Another difference is that the Form element in the ASP.NET 2.0 template includes a Div element. Then, when you use the Web Forms Designer to add elements to the page, those elements are inserted between the start and end tags for this Div element.

The HTML code for a new web page

```
<%@ Page Language="VB" AutoEventWireup="false" CodeFile="Default.aspx.vb"
Inherits="_Default" %>

<!DOCTYPE html PUBLIC "-//W3C//DTD XHTML 1.1//EN"
"http://www.w3.org/TR/xhtml11/DTD/xhtml11.dtd">

<html xmlns="http://www.w3.org/1999/xhtml" >
<head runat="server">
    <title>Untitled Page</title>
</head>
<body>
    <form id="form1" runat="server">
    <div>

    </div>
    </form>
</body>
</html>
```

Attributes of the Page directive for ASP.NET 2.0

Attribute	Description
AutoEventWireup	If false (the default for Visual Basic), you must wire page-level events to procedures in the code-behind file using the Handles clause. If true, page-level events are automatically wired to procedures in the code-behind file with predefined names such as Page_Load and Page_PreRender.
CodeFile	Specifies the name of the code-behind file that contains the event-handling code for the page.
Inherits	Specifies the name of the class that will get inherited. By convention, this is the name of the page prefixed with an underscore. See figures 1-2 and 1-3 for details about how this works.
Language	Specifies the language used to implement the processing for the page. For VB.NET applications, this attribute is set to *VB*.

Description

- The Page directive is processed by ASP.NET when the page is compiled. It uses two new attributes to specify the name of the code-behind file and the class that the page inherits.
- As in previous versions, a Form element defines the form for the ASP.NET page. But in ASP.NET 2.0, the Form element contains a Div element. Then, any elements you add to the page in the Web Forms Designer are inserted within the Div element.

Figure 2-6   The HTML code for a new web page

How to work in Source view

When you open a web page in Visual Studio, the page is initially displayed in Source view, as shown in figure 2-7. In this view, you can work directly with the HTML for the page. In fact, if you're proficient with HTML, you'll often work in Source view to tweak the layout and appearance of the page's controls. You can also drag controls from the Toolbox and drop them into a page while you're working in Source view. And you can use the Properties window to set attribute values while working in Source view. However, some developers prefer to work in Design view as described in the next figure. To switch to Design view, you just click the Design button located at the bottom left corner of the editor window.

A web form displayed in Source view

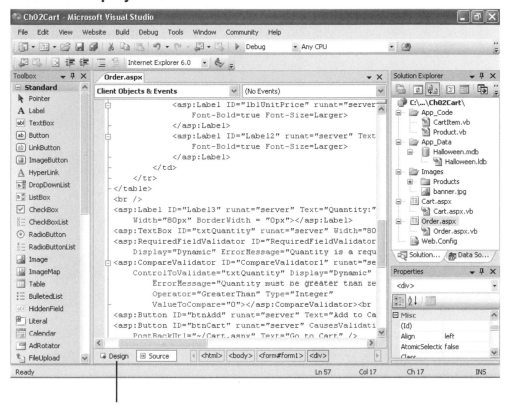

Design button

Description

- By default, Visual Studio 2005 displays aspx pages in Source view so you can work directly with the source code. You can switch to Design view by clicking the Design button located at the bottom left of the window.

- The HTML Editor for Visual Studio 2005 supports IntelliSense, which makes it easier to add HTML and other elements to the page while working in Source view.

- While you're working in Source view with Visual Studio 2005, you can use the Toolbox to create new controls. You can also use the Properties window to create and modify properties.

Figure 2-7   How to work in Source view

How to work in Design view

Figure 2-8 shows an ASP.NET page displayed in Design view with Visual Studio 2005. The change you'll probably notice first when you use this view is that it no longer defaults to grid layout mode. In fact, Microsoft has almost done away with grid layout mode altogether. Although it's still available via the new Layer control, Visual Studio 2005 is designed to work in flow layout mode.

One of the biggest frustrations of previous versions of Visual Studio is that when you switched to Design view, the Web Forms Designer often made arbitrary changes to your HTML. For example, it would sometimes change the indentation or the order in which attributes appeared. But that's not so with Visual Studio 2005.

Another new feature that you'll notice right away is that many ASP.NET 2.0 controls have a *smart tag menu*. To display this menu, click the Smart Tag icon that appears above and to the right of a control. Then, the smart tag menu reveals a list of common tasks for the control. To illustrate, this figure shows a smart tag menu for a drop-down list. As you can see, it lists the tasks that are commonly required for drop-down lists, such as choosing a data source, editing the items in the list, and enabling the AutoPostBack property.

A web form in Design view

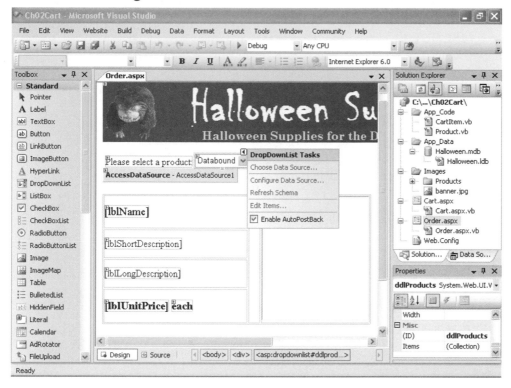

Description

- The Web Forms Designer now works entirely in flow layout mode. Grid layout mode has been dropped.

- Changes that you make while working in Design view will be reflected in the HTML for the page. However, the Web Forms Designer no longer makes arbitrary changes to your HTML.

- Many server controls have a *smart tag menu* that provides options for the commonly performed tasks.

- To activate a smart tag menu, click the Smart Tag icon to the upper right of a control.

Figure 2-8   How to work in Design view

How to create and use data sources

In ASP.NET 1.x, you used data adapters and other ADO.NET data objects to connect to database tables and bind web controls to the data. Although you could often save time by using the Data Adapter Configuration Wizard to automatically create and configure the ADO.NET objects, you still had to write code to retrieve or update data and to handle database errors.

But now, ASP.NET 2.0 offers a new type of control called a *data source* that handles the details of working with ADO.NET objects for you. To illustrate how that works, the following topics show you how to create a data source that connects to a Microsoft Access database and bind it to a drop-down list. Keep in mind, though, that there's much more to working with data sources than these topics let on. That's why the four chapters in section 2 of this book are devoted to working with data sources and data binding.

How to create an Access data source

ASP.NET 2.0 provides several data source controls in the Data tab of the Toolbox. The simplest of these controls is the AccessDataSource, which is designed to retrieve data from a Microsoft Access database file. Figure 2-9 shows how to create this type of data source.

Before you can use an Access data source, though, you must first create an Access database and add it to the App_Data folder of the web site. As I've mentioned before, the Shopping Cart application for this chapter uses a database named Halloween.mdb.

To create an AccessDataSource control, open the Data tab of the Toolbox, drag the AccessDataSource control, and drop it onto the form. Since the data source isn't displayed on the page when the application is run, it doesn't matter where you drop the data source on the page. However, if the data source is going to be bound to a web control, it makes sense to place it near that control.

When you drop the Access data source on the page, a smart tag menu will appear. Then, choose the Configure Data Source command to bring up the first page of the Configure Data Source wizard, which is shown in this figure. From this dialog box, select the Access database file you want to use for the data source.

Once you've selected the database file for the data source, you must configure the data source as described in the next figure. Then, you can bind it to the drop-down list as described in figure 2-11.

The Configure Data Source dialog box

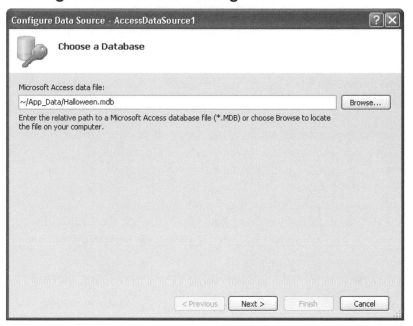

How to create an Access data source

1. In the Web Forms Designer, open the Data tab of the Toolbox and drag the AccessDataSource control to the form.

2. Select Configure Data Source from the smart tag menu of the data source control to display the Configure Data Source dialog box.

3. Identify the Access database that you want to use in the App_Data folder and click Next. Then, complete the Configure Data Source wizard as described in the next figure.

Description

*   Before you can create an Access *data source*, you must add the Access database file to the App_Data folder.

*   The Shopping Cart application uses an AccessDataSource control to provide the list of products that's displayed in the drop-down list. This control reads data from a Microsoft Access database file.

*   Although data source controls are visible in the Web Forms Designer, they don't render any HTML to the browser. As a result, they aren't visible when the application runs.

Figure 2-9   How to create an Access data source

How to configure an Access data source

Figure 2-10 shows how to configure an Access data source using the Configure Data Source wizard. After the first page of this wizard lets you select the Access database file you want to use (as in the previous figure), the second page that's shown in this figure lets you specify the query that retrieves data from the database.

To create a query, you can code a SQL SELECT statement. Or, you can choose columns from a single table or view and let the wizard generate the SELECT statement for you. For now, we'll use the second technique.

To select columns from a table, use the Name drop-down list to select the table you want to select the columns from. Then, check each of the columns you want to retrieve in the Columns list box. In this figure, I chose the Products table and selected six of the columns. As you check the columns, the Configuration wizard creates a SQL SELECT statement that's shown in the text box at the bottom of the dialog box.

The buttons to the right of the Columns list box let you specify additional options for selecting data. If you want to select just rows that meet a certain criteria, click the WHERE button, then specify the criteria you want. Or, if you want to specify a sort order, click the ORDER BY button, then choose the columns you want the data sorted by. In this figure, I used this button to specify that the data should be sorted on the Name column so the SELECT statement includes an ORDER BY [Name] clause.

When you've finished specifying the data you want the data source to retrieve, click Next. This takes you to a page that includes a Test Query button. If you click this button, the Wizard immediately retrieves the data that you have specified. You can then look over this data to make it's what you expected. If it isn't, click the Back button and adjust the query as needed.

The Configure Data Source wizard

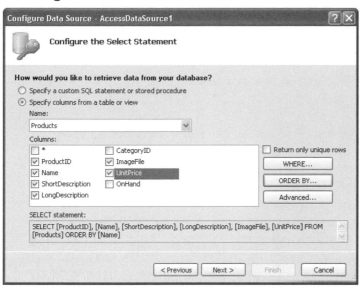

The aspx code for an Access data source control

```
<asp:AccessDataSource ID="AccessDataSource1" runat="server"
    DataFile="~/App_Data/Halloween.mdb"
    SelectCommand="SELECT [ProductID], [Name], [ShortDescription],
        [LongDescription], [ImageFile], [UnitPrice]
        FROM [Products] ORDER BY [Name]">
</asp:AccessDataSource>
```

Description

- The Configure Data Source wizard is similar to the Data Adapter Configuration wizard in Visual Studio 2002/2003. It lets you create a query using SQL. You can specify the SELECT statement for the query directly or you can let the wizard construct the SELECT statement for you from your specifications.

- You can click the WHERE button to specify one or more conditions that will be used to select the records.

- You can click the ORDER BY button to specify a sort order for the records.

- You can click the Advanced button to include INSERT, UPDATE, and DELETE statements for the data source.

Figure 2-10 How to configure an Access data source

How to bind a drop-down list to a data source

Once you've created a data source, you can bind a drop-down list to it as shown in figure 2-11. To start, select the Choose Data Source command from the smart tag menu for the drop-down list. Then, when the Data Source Configuration Wizard is displayed, choose the data source in the first drop-down list. In this figure, I chose AccessDataSource1, the data source that I created in the previous figures.

Next, select the column that provides the data you want displayed in the drop-down list. The column that you select here is used for the drop-down list's DataTextField property. In this figure, I chose the Name column so the drop-down list displays the name of each product in the data source.

Finally, select the column that you want to use as the value of the item selected by the user. The column you select here is used for the list's DataValueField property, and the value of that column can be retrieved by using the list's SelectedValue property. In this figure, I selected the ProductID column. As a result, the program can use the SelectedValue property to determine the ID of the product selected by the user.

The Data Source Configuration Wizard dialog box

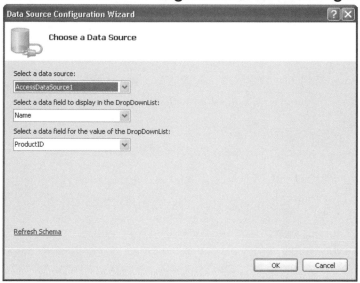

The aspx code for a drop-down list that's bound to a data source

```
<asp:DropDownList ID="ddlProducts" Runat="server" Width="150px"
    AutoPostBack="True"
    DataSourceID="AccessDataSource1"
    DataTextField="Name"
    DataValueField="ProductID" >
</asp:DropDownList>
```

Attributes for binding a drop-down list

Attribute	Description
DataSourceID	The ID of the data source that the drop-down list should be bound to.
DataTextField	The name of the data source field that should be displayed in the drop-down list.
DataValueField	The name of the data source field whose value should be returned by the SelectedValue property of the drop-down list.

Description

- You can bind a drop-down list to a data source so the list automatically displays data retrieved by the data source.
- You can use the Data Source Configuration Wizard dialog box to configure the data binding for a drop-down list. To display this dialog box, select the Choose Data Source command from the list's smart tag menu.
- Alternatively, you can use the Properties window or edit the aspx code directly to set the data binding attributes for a drop-down list.

Figure 2-11   How to bind a drop-down list to a data source

How to add code to an ASP.NET 2.0 page

As in previous versions, the preferred way to write code for an ASP.NET 2.0 application is to use code-behind files. The topics that follow show you how to do that using Visual Studio 2005.

How to use the Code Editor

To create and edit the Visual Basic code for an ASP.NET 2.0 application, you use the Code Editor shown in figure 2-12. For the most part, this editor works the same as it did in previous versions of Visual Studio.

As in previous versions, you can open a code file for editing by double-clicking the file in the Solution Explorer. Then, you can use the drop-down lists at the top of the Code Editor to create the event procedures the form requires. In addition, you can type any other procedures you need directly into the Code Editor.

You can also create a procedure to handle the Page Load event by double-clicking the page in the Web Forms Designer. This opens the code-behind file and creates an empty procedure to handle the event. Similarly, you can create an event procedure for a control's default event by double-clicking the control in the Web Forms Designer. For example, if you double-click a button control, Visual Studio 2005 creates an empty procedure to handle the button's Click event.

With Visual Studio 2005, you can also create event procedures for controls using the Events button in the Properties window. This technique is particularly useful for creating event procedures for control events other than the default event. To use this technique, select the control in the Web Forms Designer. Then, click the Events button in the Properties window to display a list of all the events that can be raised for the control. When you double-click on the event you want to handle, Visual Studio creates an empty procedure that you can code to handle the event.

As in previous versions, the Visual Studio 2005 Code Editor has several powerful features that can help you code more quickly and accurately. One of the most useful of these features is IntelliSense, which anticipates what you're typing and displays completion lists. If, for example, you type an object name and a period, Visual Studio displays a list of the members that are available for that object.

Visual Studio 2005 also includes a new feature called *code snippets* that takes IntelliSense a step further by offering to insert short segments of code rather than just completing the word you were typing. The Code Snippets feature is described in the next figure.

A project with the Code Editor window displayed

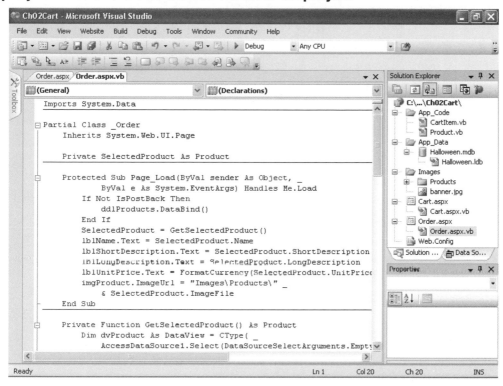

Description

- The Code Editor works essentially the same as it did in previous versions of Visual Studio. To open a Code Editor window, double-click a VB file (.aspx.vb or .vb) in the Solution Explorer. Or, double-click the page or a control in the Web Forms Designer.

- When you double-click a page, the Web Forms Designer generates a procedure to handle the Load event of the page. When you double-click a control, it generates a procedure to handle the default event of the control.

- To create a procedure to handle an event other than Page Load or a default control event, select an object and an event from the drop-down lists at the top of the Code Editor window.

- You can also create an event procedure for a control using the Events button in the Properties window (the one with the lightening bolt on it). To do that, select the control in the Web Forms Designer, click the Events button, and then double-click the event you want to create an event procedure for.

Figure 2-12   How to use the Code Editor

How to use code snippets

Figure 2-13 shows you how to use *code snippets*, a new feature of Visual Studio 2005. A code snippet is a short section of code that's stored in a library and can be quickly inserted into a source file. When the code snippet is inserted, Visual Studio maintains the correct indentation and highlights any sections of the snippet that contain generic code that you should modify.

Visual Studio 2005 comes with a library of basic snippets that automatically create Visual Basic statements and structures for you. For example, there's a snippet that creates a basic If statement, a snippet that creates a For Each...Next loop, and a snippet that creates a Try...Catch statement. These snippets are stored in XML format. If you find that you like working with snippets, you can download additional snippets from the web, and you can create your own snippets. (For more information about that, please refer to Visual Studio's help.)

The first example in this figure shows how to insert a snippet using the Insert Snippet shortcut menu. First, right click in the source file at the spot where you want to insert the snippet and choose the Insert Snippet command. Then, double-click the category that contains the snippet you want to insert. In this example, I selected the Visual Basic Language category. Finally, double-click the snippet from the list that's displayed. That will cause the snippet to be inserted into your code with one or more parts highlighted. These are the parts that you should replace with your own code.

Because each snippet in the snippet library has a shortcut name, the fastest way to insert a snippet is to use this shortcut name, as shown in the second example in this figure. Here, you type the snippet's shortcut name, then press the Tab key. If, for example, you type the word *if* and press the Tab key, the snippet that creates a basic If statement will be inserted. Note that this works only if there's at least one space between the end of the shortcut name and the beginning of any other code on the same line. Because of that, you'll typically enter a shortcut name on a blank line.

How to insert a code snippet

Step 1: Right-click and choose the Insert Snippet command

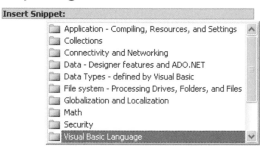

Step 2: Double-click the category that contains the snippet you want to insert

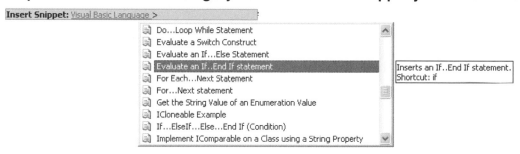

Step 3: Double-click the snippet to insert it

```
If True Then
     ' Add code to execute if condition is True.
End If
```

How to use shortcuts to insert code snippets

Step 1: Type the shortcut name of the snippet

```
if
```

Step 2: Press the Tab key to expand the snippet

```
If True Then
     ' Add code to execute if condition is True.
End If
```

Description

- *Code snippets* are a new feature of Visual Studio 2005 that let you insert previously written sections of code.

- After you insert a snippet, you must replace the highlighted sections of code with your own code. For example, you should replace the word *true* in the if snippet shown above with the condition you want to use in the if statement. You should also replace the comment with the code you want executed if the condition is true.

- You can find out what code snippets are available and add your own code snippets to the library by choosing the Tools→Code Snippets Manager command.

Figure 2-13   How to use code snippets

Two new ASP.NET 2.0 programming techniques

The Shopping Cart application presented in this chapter uses two programming techniques that are new to ASP.NET 2.0. First, it uses cross-page posting so a button on one page can post directly to another page. Second, it uses code that directly accesses the data retrieved by a data source.

How to use cross-page posting

ASP.NET 1.x applications commonly use either Response.Redirect or Server.Transfer to display a different web page from the one that was posted. Both of those features still work, but ASP.NET 2.0 introduces a new way to display a different page, called *cross-page posting*. This new feature is described in figure 2-14.

To use cross-page posting, you specify the URL of another page in the PostBackUrl property of a Button control. Then, when the user clicks the button, an HTTP Post message that contains the URL specified by the PostBackUrl property is sent back to the server. As a result, the PostBackUrl page is loaded and executed instead of the page that was originally displayed.

For example, the Go to Cart button on the Order page uses cross-page posting to go to the Cart page. As a result, the PostBackUrl property of this button is set to Cart.aspx. Then, when the user clicks the Go to Cart button, ASP.NET loads and executes the Cart.aspx page instead of the Order.aspx page.

If the user enters data into one or more controls on a page that uses cross-page posting, you can use the PreviousPage property to retrieve the data entered by the user. As the code example in this figure shows, you should first check to make sure that the PreviousPage property isn't null. If it isn't, you can use the FindControl method to retrieve the value of the Text property for a control on the previous page.

Because of the extra programming required to retrieve data entered by the user, cross-page posting is best used when no user input needs to be processed. For instance, since no data needs to be processed when the user clicks the Go to Cart button, I used cross-page posting instead of Response.Redirect or Server.Transfer. However, I used Response.Redirect for the Add to Cart button on the Order page so I could easily retrieve the selected product and the quantity entered by the user.

The PostBackUrl property of the Button control

Property	Description
PostBackUrl	Specifies the URL of the page that should be requested when the user clicks the button.

The Page class

Property	Description
PreviousPage	Returns a Page object that represents the previous page.

Method	Description
FindControl(String id)	Returns the control with the specified id. If the control is a text box, you can cast it to TextBox, then use the Text property to access the data entered by the user.

The aspx code for a button that posts to a different page

```
<asp:Button ID="btnCart" runat="server" Text="Go to Cart"
    CausesValidation="False" PostBackUrl="~/Cart.aspx" />
```

Code that retrieves data from the previous page

```
Protected Sub Page_Load(ByVal sender As Object, _
        ByVal e As System.EventArgs) Handles Me.Load
    If Not PreviousPage Is Nothing Then
        lblQuantity.Text = _
            CType(PreviousPage.FindControl("txtQuantity"), TextBox).Text
    End If
End Sub
```

Description

- *Cross-page posting* lets you specify that when the user clicks a button, a different page should be requested instead of the current page.

- When you post back to another page, the previous page is available via the PreviousPage property. Then, you can use the FindControl method to retrieve data entered by the user.

- Although the Server.Transfer and Response.Redirect methods are still available, cross-page posting is more efficient than these methods. However, cross-page posting makes it more difficult to retrieve data from the original page.

- If you don't need to retrieve data from the original page, cross-page posting is clearly better than the Server.Transfer or Response.Redirect methods.

Figure 2-14   How to use cross-page posting

How to use Visual Basic code to get data from a data source

For the Shopping Cart application to work, it must retrieve the data for the product selected by the user from the drop-down list. Although there are several ways to do that, none of them are easy. One way is to create a second data source that queries the database again to retrieve the data for the selected product, and then use a special type of ASP.NET web control called a DetailsView control that is bound to this second data source. You'll learn how to do that in Chapter 6.

A simpler way, though, is to write code that retrieves the product data from the existing Access data source. That's the technique that the Shopping Cart application uses, and it's presented in figure 2-15. Although this technique isn't difficult, you must contend with the classes, methods, and properties that are summarized in this figure.

The code example in this figure shows how to retrieve data from a row that matches the ProductID value returned by the SelectedValue property of the drop-down list. First, you use the Select method of the AccessDataSource class with the Empty argument to retrieve all of the rows from the underlying Access database. Because the return type of this method is IEnumerable, you must explicitly cast the returned object to a DataView object so you can use the methods of that class.

Once you have the rows in a DataView object, you can use the RowFilter property to filter the rows so only the row selected by the user is available. To do that, you build a simple *filter expression* that lists the column name and value. For example, ProductID='ABC' filters the data view so only rows whose ProductID column contains ABC are included.

Once you've filtered the DataView object so only the selected row is available, you can use two indexes to retrieve the data for a column. The first index identifies a row. Since only one row will match a specific ProductID, the filtered Data View object will have only one row, and you can specify 0 for its row index. This row is returned as a DataRowView object. Then, you can specify the index of the column you want to retrieve from the row, either as a string that provides the column name or as the index position of the column. In this example, column names are used for the columns that need to be retrieved. (Although using an index value is a little more efficient, specifying the column name makes the code more understandable.)

Once you establish the row and column index for each value, all that remains is to cast this value to the appropriate type. In this example, all of the columns except the UnitPrice column are cast to strings, and the UnitPrice column is cast to a decimal type. Please note that all six of the values that are retrieved are stored in the Product object that's instantiated by the third statement in this example. Also note that all of the casting in this example is done explicitly. Although that isn't required, a warning is displayed if you try to perform a narrowing conversion using an implicit cast. Because of that, I recommend you always use an explicit cast to perform a narrowing conversion.

The Select method of the AccessDataSource class

Method	Description
IEnumerable Select(selectOptions)	Returns an IEnumerable object that contains the rows retrieved from the underlying Access database. To get all the rows, the selectOptions parameter should be DataSourceSelectArguments.Empty.

The DataView class

Property	Description
string RowFilter	A string that is used to filter the rows retrieved from the Access database.

Indexer	Description
(int index)	Returns a DataRowView object for the specified row. This property is the indexer for the DataView class.

The DataRowView class

Indexer	Description
(int index)	Returns the value of the column at the specified index position as an object.
(string name)	Returns the value of the column with the specified name as an object.

Code that gets product information for the selected product

```
Dim dvProduct As DataView = CType( _
    AccessDataSource1.Select(DataSourceSelectArguments.Empty), DataView)
dvProduct.RowFilter = "ProductID = '" & ddlProducts.SelectedValue & "'"
Dim Product As New Product
Product.ProductID = dvProduct(0)("ProductID").ToString
Product.Name = dvProduct(0)("Name").ToString
Product.ShortDescription = dvProduct(0)("ShortDescription").ToString
Product.LongDescription = dvProduct(0)("LongDescription").ToString
Product.UnitPrice = CDec(dvProduct(0)("UnitPrice"))
Product.ImageFile = dvProduct(0)("ImageFile").ToString
```

Description

- The Select method of the AccessDataSource class returns a DataView object that contains the rows retrieved from the Access database. Because the return type of this method is IEnumerable, you must explicitly cast the returned object to a DataView.

- The RowFilter property of the DataView class lets you filter rows in the data view based on a criteria string.

- You can use the indexer of the DataView class to return a specific row as a DataRowView object. Then, you can use the indexer of the DataRowView class to return the value of a specified column. The indexer for the column can be an integer that represents the column's position in the row or a string that represents the name of the column.

Figure 2-15   How to use Visual Basic code to get data from a data source

The code for the Shopping Cart application

Now that you've learned the skills for developing a basic ASP.NET 2.0 application, you're ready to see all the aspx and Visual Basic code for the Shopping Cart application. Because you should be able to follow it without much trouble, I'll keep the descriptions to a minimum.

The code for the Product and CartItem classes

Figure 2-16 shows the Visual Basic code for the Product and CartItem classes. The Product class, which represents a product, has public fields for each of the columns in the Products table except CategoryID and OnHand.

The CartItem class, which represents one item in the shopping cart, has two public fields that hold the Product object and quantity for each item. In addition, the Display method returns a string that formats this data so it can be displayed in one line of the list box on the Cart page.

The aspx code for the Order page

Figure 2-17 shows the aspx code for the Order page, which is shown in its rendered form in figure 2-1. Since all of the code for this page is generated by the Web Forms Designer, you don't have to code any of it. To make it easier to follow this code, I highlighted the start tag and ID attribute for each of the server controls that appear on this page.

The first group of four controls defines an image that's used for the banner, a label with the text "Please select a product:", a drop-down list named ddlProducts, and the Access data source that the drop-down list is bound to. Here, the AutoPostBack attribute for the drop-down list is set to True so the page will be posted back to the server when the user selects a product. In addition, the DataSourceID, DataTextField, and DataValueField attributes specify how the drop-down list is bound to the Access data source.

The second group of server controls displays product information using several labels and an image control. A table is used to manage the layout of these controls so the image can be displayed to the right of the labels.

The third group of server controls defines a label with the text "Quantity:" followed by a text box named txtQuantity. Then, two validator controls provide data validation for the text box. Notice that both specify txtQuantity in the ControlToValidate attribute and Dynamic in the Display attribute.

The last group of controls for this page are the two buttons. The second button, named btnCart, uses the PostBackUrl property to indicate that when the user clicks the button, the Cart.aspx page should be requested rather than the Order.aspx page. Since the CausesValidation attribute is set to False, the validation controls for the txtQuantity text box won't be executed when the button is clicked.

The code for the Product class

```
Imports Microsoft.VisualBasic

Public Class Product
    Public ProductID As String
    Public Name As String
    Public ShortDescription As String
    Public LongDescription As String
    Public UnitPrice As Decimal
    Public ImageFile As String
End Class
```

The code for the CartItem class

```
Imports Microsoft.VisualBasic

Public Class CartItem
    Public Product As Product
    Public Quantity As Integer

    Public Function Display() As String
        Return Product.Name & " (" & Quantity.ToString() _
            & " at " & FormatCurrency(Product.UnitPrice) & " each)"

    End Function
End Class
```

Description

- The Product class represents a product.
- The CartItem class represents a product that the user has added to the shopping cart plus the quantity ordered.

Figure 2-16   The code for the Product and CartItem classes

The aspx code for the Order page (Order.aspx)   **Page 1**

```
<%@ Page Language="VB" AutoEventWireup="false" CodeFile="Order.aspx.vb"
Inherits="Order" %>

<!DOCTYPE html PUBLIC "-//W3C//DTD XHTML 1.1//EN"
"http://www.w3.org/TR/xhtml11/DTD/xhtml11.dtd">

<html xmlns="http://www.w3.org/1999/xhtml" >
<head runat="server">
    <title>Murach's ASP.NET 2.0 Upgrader's Guide: Chapter 2 Shopping Cart
    Application</title>
</head>
<body>
    <form id="form1" runat="server">
    <div>
        <asp:Image ID="Image1" runat="server"
            ImageUrl="~/Images/banner.jpg" /><br /><br />
        <asp:Label ID="Label1" runat="server"
            Text="Please select a product:"></asp:Label>
        <asp:DropDownList ID="ddlProducts" runat="server" Width = "150px"
            DataSourceID="AccessDataSource1" DataTextField="Name"
            DataValueField="ProductID" AutoPostBack="True">
        </asp:DropDownList>
        <asp:AccessDataSource ID="AccessDataSource1" runat="server"
            DataFile="~/App_Data/Halloween.mdb"
            SelectCommand="SELECT [ProductID], [Name], [ShortDescription],
                [LongDescription], [ImageFile], [UnitPrice]
                FROM [Products] ORDER BY [Name]">
        </asp:AccessDataSource>
        <br />
        <table>
            <tr >
                <td style="width: 250px; height: 22px">
                    <asp:Label ID="lblName" runat="server"
                        Font-Bold=false Font-Size=Larger>
                    </asp:Label>
                </td>
                <td style="width: 20px" rowspan=4>
                </td>
                <td rowspan=4 valign=top>
                    <asp:Image ID="imgProduct" runat="server" Height=200 />
                </td>
            </tr>
            <tr>
                <td style="width: 250px">
                    <asp:Label ID="lblShortDescription" runat="server">
                    </asp:Label>
                </td>
            </tr>
```

Description

- The Order.aspx page displays a drop-down list that is bound to an Access data source.

- A table is used to specify the layout of the labels and image controls that display information about the product selected by the user.

Figure 2-17   The aspx code for the Order page (part 1 of 2)

The aspx code for the Order page (Order.aspx)   **Page 2**

```
            <tr>
                <td style="width: 250px">
                    <asp:Label ID="lblLongDescription" runat="server">
                    </asp:Label>
                </td>
            </tr>
            <tr>
                <td style="width: 250px">
                    <asp:Label ID="lblUnitPrice" runat="server"
                        Font-Bold=true Font-Size=Larger>
                    </asp:Label>
                    <asp:Label ID="Label2" runat="server" Text="each"
                        Font-Bold=true Font-Size=Larger>
                    </asp:Label>
                </td>
            </tr>
        </table>
        <br />
        <asp:Label ID="Label3" runat="server" Text="Quantity:"
            Width="80px" BorderWidth = "0px"></asp:Label>
        <asp:TextBox ID="txtQuantity" runat="server" Width="80px">
        </asp:TextBox>
        <asp:RequiredFieldValidator ID="RequiredFieldValidator1"
            runat="server" ControlToValidate="txtQuantity" Display="Dynamic"
            ErrorMessage="Quantity is a required field.">
        </asp:RequiredFieldValidator>
        <asp:CompareValidator ID="CompareValidator1" runat="server"
            ControlToValidate="txtQuantity" Display="Dynamic"
            ErrorMessage="Quantity must be greater than zero."
            Operator="GreaterThan" Type="Integer"
            ValueToCompare="0"></asp:CompareValidator><br /><br />
        <asp:Button ID="btnAdd" runat="server" Text="Add to Cart" /> 
        <asp:Button ID="btnCart" runat="server" CausesValidation="False"
            PostBackUrl="~/Cart.aspx" Text="Go to Cart" />
    </div>
    </form>
</body>
</html>
```

Description

- The txtQuantity text box lets the user enter the order quantity of the selected item. A RequiredFieldValidator and a CompareValidator are used to ensure that the user enters valid data in this text box.

- The btnCart button uses cross-page posting to post to the Cart.aspx page.

Figure 2-17   The aspx code for the Order page (part 2 of 2)

The Visual Basic code for the Order page

Figure 2-18 presents the code for the Order page's code-behind file, Order.aspx.vb. This code starts by declaring a module-level variable that will hold a Product object that represents the item that the user has selected from the drop-down list. This object is instantiated by the third statement in the GetSelectedProduct procedure that's called from the Page_Load procedure.

The Page_Load procedure starts by calling the DataBind method of the drop-down list if the page is being loaded for the first time (IsPostBack isn't true), which means that the data for the data source hasn't been retrieved yet. Then, this procedure calls the GetSelectedProduct procedure, which gets the data for the selected product from the Access data source and returns a Product object. That object is then stored in the SelectedProduct variable. Finally, this procedure formats the labels and the Image control to display the data for the selected product. At that point, the Order page is sent back to the user's browser.

For many applications, you don't need to call the DataBind method in the Page_Load procedure when you use data binding. Instead, you let ASP.NET automatically bind any data-bound controls. Unfortunately, this automatic data binding doesn't occur until after the Page_Load procedure and any handlers for control events have been executed. In this case, because the GetSelectedProduct procedure won't work unless the drop-down list has already been bound, I had to call the DataBind method to force the data binding to occur earlier than it normally would.

The code-behind file for the Order page (Order.aspx.vb)   Page 1

```vb
Imports System.Data

Partial Class Order
    Inherits System.Web.UI.Page

    Private SelectedProduct As Product

    Protected Sub Page_Load(ByVal sender As Object, _
            ByVal e As System.EventArgs) Handles Me.Load
        If Not IsPostBack Then
            ddlProducts.DataBind()
        End If
        SelectedProduct = Me.GetSelectedProduct()
        lblName.Text = SelectedProduct.Name
        lblShortDescription.Text = SelectedProduct.ShortDescription
        lblLongDescription.Text = SelectedProduct.LongDescription
        lblUnitPrice.Text = FormatCurrency(SelectedProduct.UnitPrice)
        imgProduct.ImageUrl = "Images\Products\" _
            & SelectedProduct.ImageFile
    End Sub

    Private Function GetSelectedProduct() As Product
        Dim dvProduct As DataView = CType(AccessDataSource1.Select( _
            DataSourceSelectArguments.Empty), DataView)
        dvProduct.RowFilter = "ProductID = '" _
            & ddlProducts.SelectedValue & "'"
        Dim Product As New Product
        Product.ProductID = dvProduct(0)("ProductID").ToString
        Product.Name = dvProduct(0)("Name").ToString
        Product.ShortDescription = dvProduct(0)("ShortDescription").ToString
        Product.LongDescription = dvProduct(0)("LongDescription").ToString
        Product.UnitPrice = CDec(dvProduct(0)("UnitPrice"))
        Product.ImageFile = dvProduct(0)("ImageFile").ToString
        Return Product
    End Function
End Function
```

Description

- The Page_Load procedure binds the drop-down list if the page is not being posted back to itself. Then, it calls the GetSelectedProduct procedure to get a Product object for the selected product. Finally, it sets the Label and Image controls to display the information for the selected product.

- The GetSelectedProduct procedure extracts the data for the selected product from the data source. Then, it uses this data to create a Product object.

Figure 2-18   The code-behind file for the Order page (part 1 of 2)

If the user clicks the Add to Cart button, the btnAdd_Click procedure is executed. It starts by creating a new instance of the CartItem class named CartItem. Next, it sets the item's Product field to the Product object that's stored in the SelectedProduct variable, and it sets the Quantity field to the value entered by the user. Then, it calls the AddToCart procedure to add the CartItem object to the user's shopping cart. Finally, it uses Response.Redirect to go to the Cart.aspx page.

The AddToCart procedure declares a SortedList variable named Cart and calls the GetCart procedure to retrieve the shopping cart from Session state. If you look at the GetCart procedure, you'll see that it first checks to see if a Session state item named "cart" is equal to Nothing. If it is, which means that a cart hasn't yet been created for the current user, a new shopping cart is created and added to Session state. Then, the GetCart procedure returns the shopping cart to the AddToCart procedure.

After the shopping cart list has been returned, the AddToCart procedure determines whether the list already contains an entry for the selected product. To do that, it uses the ContainsKey method of a SortedList object to look for a cart entry with the product ID of the product. If an entry is found with this product ID, the quantity the user entered is added to the existing quantity for this item. Otherwise, the Add method for the SortedList object that represents the shopping cart is used to add the cart item to the shopping cart with the product's ID as the key.

The code-behind file for the Order page (Order.aspx.vb)   **Page 2**

```vb
    Protected Sub btnAdd_Click(ByVal sender As Object, _
            ByVal e As System.EventArgs) Handles btnAdd.Click
        If Page.IsValid Then
            Dim CartItem As New CartItem
            CartItem.Product = SelectedProduct
            CartItem.Quantity = CType(txtQuantity.Text, Integer)
            Me.AddToCart(CartItem)
            Response.Redirect("Cart.aspx")
        End If
    End Sub

    Private Sub AddToCart(ByVal CartItem As CartItem)
        Dim Cart As SortedList = GetCart()
        Dim sProductID As String = SelectedProduct.ProductID
        If Cart.ContainsKey(sProductID) Then
            CartItem = CType(Cart(sProductID), CartItem)
            CartItem.Quantity += CType(txtQuantity.Text, Integer)
        Else
            Cart.Add(sProductID, CartItem)
        End If
    End Sub

    Private Function GetCart() As SortedList
        If Session("cart") Is Nothing Then
            Session.Add("cart", New SortedList)
        End If
        Return CType(Session("cart"), SortedList)

    End Function
End Class
```

Description

- The btnAdd_Click procedure is called when the user clicks the Add button. It creates a CartItem object, then calls the AddToCart procedure to add the item to the shopping cart.

- The AddToCart procedure calls GetCart to get the shopping cart from session state. Then, it checks to see if the shopping cart already contains an item for the selected product. If so, the item's quantity is incremented. If not, the CartItem object is added to the shopping cart.

- The GetCart procedure retrieves the shopping cart from session state. If session state doesn't contain a cart, a cart is created and added to session state.

Figure 2-18   The code-behind file for the Order page (part 2 of 2)

The aspx code for the Cart page

Figure 2-19 shows the HTML code for the second page of the Shopping Cart application, Cart.aspx, which is rendered in figure 2-2. Once again, I've high-lighted the start of each tag that defines a server control.

Here, the shopping cart is a ListBox control within an HTML table that allows the Remove and Empty buttons to be displayed to the right of the list box. The Continue button uses the PostBackUrl attribute to return to the Order.aspx page. And the lblMessage label is used to display a message when the user clicks the Check Out button. Like the Order page, this page also contains an image control that defines the image that's displayed in the banner.

The Visual Basic code for the Cart page

Figure 2-20 presents the code-behind file for the Cart page. This code starts by declaring a module-level variable that will hold the SortedList object for the shopping cart. Then, each time the page is loaded, the Page_Load procedure calls the GetCart procedure to retrieve the shopping cart from session state and store it in this variable.

If the page is being loaded for the first time, the Page_Load procedure also calls the DisplayCart procedure. This procedure starts by clearing the list box that will display the shopping cart items. Then, it uses a For Each...Next loop to add an item to the list box for each item in the shopping cart list.

To understand this loop, remember that each item in a sorted list is a DictionaryEntry object that consists of a key and a value. Here, the key is the product ID, the value is a CartItem object, and the first line in the body of the loop uses the Value property to retrieve the CartItem object for that entry. How-ever, because the Value property returns an Object type, it must be explicitly cast to CartItem to assign the value to the CartItem variable.

If the user clicks the Remove button, the btnRemove_Click procedure is executed. This procedure begins by making sure that an item in the shopping cart list box is selected and that the cart contains at least one item. If so, the selected item is deleted from the shopping cart. Then, the DisplayCart procedure is called to add the cart items to the list box again, but without the deleted item.

If the user clicks the Empty button, the btnEmpty_Click procedure is ex-ecuted. This procedure clears the shopping cart and the shopping cart list box. Please note, though, that instead of clearing the list box by calling the Items.Clear method, this procedure could call the DisplayCart procedure. Similarly, the btnRemove_Click procedure could use the Items.Remove method of the list box to remove the item at the selected index instead of calling the DisplayCart procedure. This just shows that there is usually more than one way that proce-dures like these can be coded.

Note that there is no procedure for the Click event of the Continue button. That's because the Continue button uses the PostBackUrl property to post di-rectly to the Order.aspx page. As a result, the Cart page isn't executed if the user clicks the Continue button.

The aspx code for the Cart page (Cart.aspx)

```
<%@ Page Language="VB" AutoEventWireup="false" CodeFile="Cart.aspx.vb"
Inherits="Cart" %>

<!DOCTYPE html PUBLIC "-//W3C//DTD XHTML 1.1//EN"
"http://www.w3.org/TR/xhtml11/DTD/xhtml11.dtd">

<html xmlns="http://www.w3.org/1999/xhtml" >
<head runat="server">
    <title>Murach's ASP.NET 2.0 Upgrader's Guide: Chapter 2 Shopping Cart
    Application</title>
</head>
<body>
    <form id="form1" runat="server">
    <div>
        <asp:Image ID="Image1" runat="server"
            ImageUrl="~/Images/banner.jpg" /><br /><br />
        Your shopping cart:<br />
        <table style="width: 500px" cellspacing=0
                cellpadding=0 border=0>
            <tr>
                <td style="width: 286px; height: 153px">
                    <asp:ListBox ID="lstCart" runat="server"
                        Width=267px Height=135px></asp:ListBox>
                </td>
                <td style="height: 153px">
                    <asp:Button ID="btnRemove" runat="server"
                        Width=100px Text="Remove Item" /><br /><br />
                    <asp:Button ID="btnEmpty" runat="server"
                        Width=100px Text="Empty Cart" />
                </td>
            </tr>
        </table>
        <br />
        <asp:Button ID="btnContinue" runat="server"
            PostBackUrl="~/Order.aspx" Text="Continue Shopping" /> 
        <asp:Button ID="btnCheckOut" runat="server" Text="Check Out" /><br />
        <br />
        <asp:Label ID="lblMessage" runat="server"></asp:Label>
    </div>
    </form>
</body>
</html>
```

Description

- The Cart.aspx page uses a list box to display the shopping cart.
- The btnContinue button uses cross-page posting to post back to the Order.aspx page.

Figure 2-19   The aspx code for the Cart page

The code-behind file for the Cart page (Cart.aspx.vb)   **Page 1**

```
Partial Class Cart
    Inherits System.Web.UI.Page

    Private Cart As SortedList

    Protected Sub Page_Load(ByVal sender As Object, _
            ByVal e As System.EventArgs) Handles Me.Load
        Cart = GetCart()
        If Not IsPostBack Then
            Me.DisplayCart()
        End If
    End Sub

    Private Function GetCart() As SortedList
        If Session("cart") Is Nothing Then
            Session.Add("cart", New SortedList)
        End If
        Return CType(Session("cart"), SortedList)
    End Function

    Private Sub DisplayCart()
        lstCart.Items.Clear()
        Dim CartItem As CartItem
        Dim CartEntry As DictionaryEntry
        For Each CartEntry In Cart
            CartItem = CType(CartEntry.Value, CartItem)
            lstCart.Items.Add(CartItem.Display)
        Next
    End Sub
End Sub
```

Description

- The Page_Load procedure calls the GetCart procedure to get the shopping cart. Then, if IsPostBack is false, it calls the DisplayCart procedure to add the shopping cart items to the list box.

- The GetCart procedure retrieves the sorted list for the shopping cart from session state. But if session state doesn't contain a cart, a cart is created and added to session state.

Figure 2-20   The code-behind file for the Cart page (part 1 of 2)

The code-behind file for the Cart page (Cart.aspx.vb)   Page 2

```
    Protected Sub btnRemove_Click(ByVal sender As Object, _
            ByVal e As System.EventArgs) Handles btnRemove.Click
        If lstCart.SelectedIndex > -1 And Cart.Count > 0 Then
            Cart.RemoveAt(lstCart.SelectedIndex)
            Me.DisplayCart()
        End If
    End Sub

    Protected Sub btnEmpty_Click(ByVal sender As Object, _
            ByVal e As System.EventArgs) Handles btnEmpty.Click
        Cart.Clear()
        lstCart.Items.Clear()
        lblMessage.Text = ""
    End Sub

    Protected Sub btnCheckOut_Click(ByVal sender As Object, _
            ByVal e As System.EventArgs) Handles btnCheckOut.Click
        lblMessage.Text = "Sorry, that function hasn't been implemented yet."
    End Sub
End Class
```

Description

- The btnRemove_Click procedure is called when the user clicks the Remove Item button. It removes the selected item, then calls the DisplayCart procedure to redisplay the shopping cart.

- The btnEmpty_Cart procedure is called when the user clicks the Empty Cart item. It clears the sorted list for the shopping cart as well as the list box.

- The btnCheckOut_Click procedure is called when the user clicks the Check Out button. It displays a message to indicate that the check out function hasn't been implemented yet.

- There isn't any procedure for the Click event of the Continue Shopping button because it uses cross-page posting to go to the Order page.

Figure 2-20   The code-behind file for the Cart page (part 2 of 2)

How to run an ASP.NET 2.0 application

After you design the forms and develop the code for a web application, you need to run it to be sure it works properly. Then, if you discover any errors in the application, you can debug it, correct the errors, and run it again.

How to use the development server

When you run a file-system web site by using one of the techniques in figure 2-21, Visual Studio 2005 automatically launches the built-in ASP.NET 2.0 development server. Although this server is fine for the initial testing of an ASP.NET web site, it has several limitations that are summarized in this figure.

The most significant of these limitations is that it always runs under the current user's security context, but your own user account probably has stronger security privileges than the account IIS runs ASP.NET applications under. As a result, when you move the application to a real web server, you may have to contend with security issues that weren't apparent when you tested with the development server, especially if you access files or databases located in folders outside of the application's folder structure.

How to run a file-system web site with IIS

Once you've thoroughly tested and debugged an application using the built-in development server, you'll want to test it with IIS to make sure it works properly.

The first step is to create a *virtual directory* in IIS for the application. This is simply a directory name within IIS that is mapped to the directory on your hard drive that actually contains the files for the web site. To create a virtual directory, you use the IIS management console, which you can reach from the Administrative Tools icon in the Control Panel. Then, you use the New→Virtual Directory command to create a virtual directory that maps to the folder that contains your web site.

Once you've created a virtual directory for an ASP.NET application, you can run the application by opening a browser window and entering a URL for the application's start page. If, for example, you created a virtual directory named Ch02Cart for the Shopping Cart application, you would enter //localhost/Ch02Cart/Order.aspx in the browser's address box to run the Order page of the application.

The dialog box for the ASP.NET Development Server

Three ways to run a file-system web site from the development server

- Click the Start Debugging button in the Standard toolbar
- Press F5
- Choose the Debug→Start command

Limitations of the development server

- Can serve pages only to the local computer.
- Runs in the current user's security context, so it doesn't accurately test security issues.
- Does not include an SMTP server, so it can't be used to test email applications.
- Uses a randomly chosen port rather than the standard HTTP port 80.

How to create an IIS Virtual Directory for a file-system web site

- Open the Control Panel, double-click Administrative Tools, then double-click Internet Information Services. This opens the IIS management console.
- Use the tree to locate the Default Web Site node, right-click Default Web Site, and choose New→Virtual Directory. Then, use the Virtual Directory Creation Wizard to create a virtual directory for the application.

How to run a file-system web site with IIS

- Open the browser you want to use to test the application, and enter //localhost/ followed by the virtual directory you created for the application and the starting page. For example, //localhost/Ch02Cart/Order.aspx.

Description

- When you run a file-system web application, Visual Studio 2005 starts its built-in web server, called the ASP.NET Development Server, to run the application.
- If you have IIS installed on your computer, you can use it to test your web site instead of the built-in web server. But you must first create a virtual directory for the web site.

Figure 2-21   How to run an ASP.NET 2.0 web application

Perspective

The purpose of this chapter has been to help you get started with Visual Studio 2005 and ASP.NET 2.0. That's why this chapter has introduced you to the new features of Visual Studio as well as some of the new ASP.NET 2.0 features like data sources and cross-page posting. If you've had much experience with earlier versions of ASP.NET, you should now be ready to learn how to use the major new features of ASP.NET 2.0.

If you had any trouble following the Visual Basic code for the Shopping Cart application, though, you may be interested in our Visual Basic book, *Murach's Beginning Visual Basic .NET*. It will quickly get you up to speed with the Visual Basic language and many of the .NET classes, like the SortedList class. It is also a terrific on-the-job reference.

Terms

web site
file-system web site
smart tag menu
data source
code snippet
cross-page posting
virtual directory

3

How to use master pages

A master page makes it easy for you to create pages that have common elements such as banners and navigation menus. That's why it is one of the most important new features of ASP.NET 2.0. In fact, you may decide that you're going to use one master page for every group of pages that you develop.

How to create master pages

A *master page* is a page that provides a framework within which the content from other pages can be displayed. Master pages make it easy to include banners, navigation menus, and other elements on all of the pages in an application. In the topics that follow, you'll learn how to create master pages in your ASP.NET applications.

An introduction to master pages

Figure 3-1 shows the basics of how master pages work. As you can see, the page that's actually sent to the browser is created by combining elements from a master page and a *content page*. The content page provides the content that's unique to each page in the application, while the master page provides the elements that are common to all pages. In this example, the master page (MasterPage.master) provides a banner at the top of each page, a simple navigation menu at the side of each page, and a message that indicates how many days remain until Halloween at the bottom of each page.

In addition, the master page contains a *content placeholder* that indicates where the content from each content page should be displayed. In this example, the content page is the Order.aspx page, and its content is displayed in the content placeholder in the central portion of the master page.

Notice that the name of the content page is Order.aspx, the same as the Order page that you saw in chapter 2. In other words, when you use master pages, the individual pages of your web application become the content pages. You'll learn how to create content pages or convert existing ASP.NET pages to content pages in figure 3-6.

The Cart application with a master page

Master page (MasterPage.master)

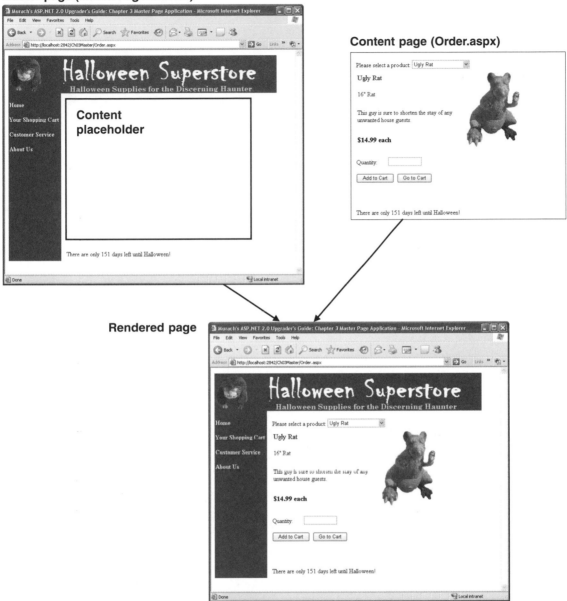

Content page (Order.aspx)

Rendered page

Description

- A *master page* provides a framework in which the content of each page on a web site is presented. Master pages make it easy to create pages that have a consistent look.

- The pages that provide the content that's displayed in a master page are called *content pages*.

- The content of each content page is displayed in the master page's *content placeholder*.

Figure 3-1   An application that uses a master page

How to create a master page

As figure 3-2 shows, you create a master page by using the Website→Add New Item command. Master Page is listed as one of the templates in the Add New Item dialog box. Select this template, select Visual Basic as the language, and click Add to create the master page. The default name for a master page is MasterPage.master.

The master page created from the template includes a ContentPlaceHolder control that will contain the content page, but nothing else. You'll learn more about the ContentPlaceHolder control in the next figure. For now, just realize that it marks the location on the rendered page where the content from the content page will be displayed.

You can develop the master page by adding elements outside of the ContentPlaceHolder control. For example, to create the master page in figure 3-1, you add an image for a banner above the placeholder, navigation links to the left of the placeholder, and a label to display the days remaining until Halloween below the placeholder. Typically, you'll use an HTML table to specify the layout of these elements.

Note that an application can contain more than one master page. This allows you to create an application that has two or more sections with distinct page layouts. For example, you may want to use one master page for all of the content pages in the online shopping section of a web site, and another master page for the content pages in the customer service section.

In addition, you should realize that a master page can have more than one content placeholder. This lets you create a page layout that has custom content in two or more different areas of the page. To create an additional content placeholder, you simply drag the ContentPlaceHolder control from the Standard tab of the Toolbox onto the master page and give it a unique ID.

A new master page in Design view

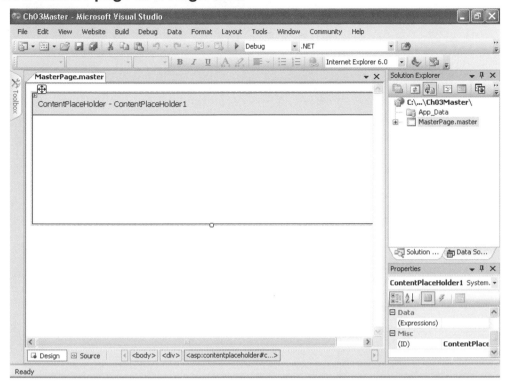

Description

- To add a master page to a project, choose the Website→Add New Item command. Then, in the Add New Item dialog box, select Master Page from the list of templates, specify the name of the master page you want to create in the Name text box (the default is Master Page.master), and select the programming language. Then, click Add.

- The content placeholder appears as a control in the Web Forms Designer. Although you can change the position of the content placeholder, you can't edit its contents from the master page. Instead, you add content to the master page by creating content pages as described later in this chapter.

- Any elements you add to the master page outside of the content placeholder will appear on every content page that uses the master page.

- Although most master pages have just one content placeholder, you can create more than one content placeholder if you need to. In that case, each placeholder displays a portion of the content of each content page.

- An application can have more than one master page, and each content page specifies which master page should be used to display the content page.

- The aspx file for a master page uses the extension .master. The code-behind file uses .master.vb.

Figure 3-2   How to create a master page

The aspx code for a new master page

The listing at the top of figure 3-3 shows the aspx code that's generated when you create a master page using the Master Page template. As you can see, this code is similar to the aspx code generated for a regular ASP.NET web page, with two important differences.

First, instead of a Page directive, the code begins with a Master directive. This indicates that the file contains a master page rather than a regular ASP.NET page. Second, the Div element that normally contains the content for the page now contains a ContentPlaceHolder control.

Notice that the master page file is itself a well-formed HTML document with Html, Head, and Body elements. The Body element includes a Form element, which in turn contains the ContentPlaceHolder control. Any elements you add to the master page should appear within the Form element, but outside of the ContentPlaceHolder control.

The aspx code for a new master page

```
<%@ Master Language="VB" CodeFile="MasterPage.master.vb" Inherits="MasterPage" %>

<!DOCTYPE html PUBLIC "-//W3C//DTD XHTML 1.1//EN" "http://www.w3.org/TR/xhtml11/
DTD/xhtml11.dtd">

<html xmlns="http://www.w3.org/1999/xhtml" >
<head runat="server">
    <title>Untitled Page</title>
</head>
<body>
    <form id="form1" runat="server">
    <div>
        <asp:contentplaceholder id="ContentPlaceHolder1" runat="server">
        </asp:contentplaceholder>
    </div>
    </form>
</body>
</html>
```

Attributes of the Master page directive

Attribute	Description
Language	Specifies the language used for any code required by the page.
CodeFile	Specifies the name of the code-behind file.
Inherits	Specifies the name of the page class defined in the code-behind file.

Attributes of the ContentPlaceHolder control

Attribute	Description
ID	Specifies the name of the content placeholder.
Runat	Specifies that the control is a server-side control.

Description

- A master page must begin with a Master page directive and should include at least one ContentPlaceHolder control.

- Any HTML or aspx elements that you add to the master page will be displayed on every page that uses the master page along with the ContentPlaceHolder control.

Figure 3-3   The aspx code for a new master page

The aspx code for the Halloween Store master page

Figure 3-4 shows the complete aspx code for the master page in figure 3-1. Although this listing fills the entire page, there's nothing complex about it. So you shouldn't have any trouble understanding its elements.

The banner at the top of the page is displayed using an Image control. After the banner, a table element controls the layout of the rest of the page. The first row of this table specifies a height of 400 pixels. It has three cells. The first cell contains a simple navigation menu built using <a> tags. The background color for this cell is set to red. The second cell is a small (10 pixel) spacer cell that gives some space between the navigation menu and the content. And the third cell contains the content placeholder.

The second row defines the footer that appears at the bottom of the page. It also has three cells, each the same width as the cells in the first row. However, the height of this row is set to 25 pixels. The third cell in this row contains a label control named lblMessage. This label will be used to display the number of days that remain until Halloween.

The aspx code for the master page

```
<%@ Master Language="VB" CodeFile="MasterPage.master.vb" Inherits="MasterPage" %>

<!DOCTYPE html PUBLIC "-//W3C//DTD XHTML 1.1//EN"
"http://www.w3.org/TR/xhtml11/DTD/xhtml11.dtd">

<html xmlns="http://www.w3.org/1999/xhtml" >
<head runat="server">
    <title>Murach's ASP.NET 2.0 Upgrader's Guide: Chapter 3 Master Page
Application</title>
</head>
<body>
    <form id="form1" runat="server">
    <asp:Image ID="Image1" runat="server" ImageUrl="~/Images/banner.jpg" /><br />
    <table cellpadding="2" cellspacing="0">
      <tr height="400">
        <td style="width: 157px" valign="top" bordercolor="red" bgcolor="red">
            <br />
            <a href="Order.aspx">
                <span style="color: #ffffff"><b>Home</b></span>
            </a><br /><br />
            <a href="Cart.aspx">
                <span style="color: #ffffff"><b>Your Shopping Cart</b></span>
            </a><br /><br />
            <a href="Service.aspx">
                <span style="color: #ffffff"><b>Customer Service</b></span>
            </a><br /><br />
            <a href="About.aspx">
                <span style="color: #ffffff"><b>About Us</b></span>
            </a></td>
        <td style="width: 10px"></td>
        <td style="width: 704px" valign="top">
            <asp:contentplaceholder id="Main" runat="server">
            </asp:contentplaceholder>
        </td>
      </tr>
      <tr height="25">
        <td bgcolor="red" bordercolor="red"
            style="width: 153px" valign="top"></td>
        <td style="width: 10px"></td>
        <td style="width: 704px" valign="top">
            <asp:Label ID="lblMessage" runat="server"></asp:Label>
        </td>
      </tr>
    </table>
    </form>
</body>
</html>
```

Description

- Most master pages include elements like banners and navigation controls.
- It's common to use tables to provide the layout for the elements on the master page, including the content placeholder.

Figure 3-4   The aspx code for the Halloween Store master page

The code-behind file for the master page

Master pages have events just like regular ASP.NET pages. So it's important to realize that most of these events are raised *after* the corresponding events for the content page are raised. For example, the Load event for the master page will be processed after the Load event for the content page. Likewise, any control events for the content page are processed before any control events for the master page. Note, however, that both the content page and the master page Load events are processed before any of the control events are processed.

Figure 3-5 shows the code-behind file for the master page in figure 3-4. This code-behind file includes a Page_Load procedure that's executed when the master page loads. As you can see, this procedure calls a procedure named DaysUntilHalloween, which calculates and returns the number of days remaining until October 31. Then, an appropriate message is assigned to the Text property of the lblMessage label.

The code-behind file for the master page

```
Partial Class MasterPage
    Inherits System.Web.UI.MasterPage

    Protected Sub Page_Load(ByVal sender As Object, _
            ByVal e As System.EventArgs) Handles Me.Load
        Dim iDaysUntil As Integer = DaysUntilHalloween()
        If iDaysUntil = 0 Then
            lblMessage.Text = "Happy Halloween!"
        ElseIf iDaysUntil = 1 Then
            lblMessage.Text = "Tomorrow is Halloween!"
        Else
            lblMessage.Text = "There are only " & iDaysUntil _
                & " days left until Halloween!"
        End If
    End Sub

    Private Function DaysUntilHalloween() As Integer
        Dim dtmHalloween As Date = New DateTime(DateTime.Today.Year, 10, 31)
        If DateTime.Today > dtmHalloween Then
            dtmHalloween.AddYears(1)
        End If
        Dim tsTimeUntil As TimeSpan = dtmHalloween - DateTime.Today
        Return tsTimeUntil.Days
    End Function

End Class
```

Description

- Master pages have events just like regular ASP.NET pages. For this master page, the Load event is used to display the number of days remaining until Halloween.

- Most events for the content page are raised before the corresponding events for the master page. For example, the Load event for the content page is raised before the Load event for the master page. Similarly, events for controls in the content page are raised before events for controls in the master page.

Figure 3-5   The code-behind file for the master page

How to create and develop content pages

Once you create a master page, you can create and develop the content pages for the master page. The topics that follow show how.

How to create a content page

Figure 3-6 shows how to create a content page. In short, you use the same procedure to create a content page that you use to create a regular page, but you check the Select a Master Page check box. Then, you can choose the master page you want to use for the content page from the Select a Master Page dialog box that's displayed.

Alternatively, you can select the master page you want to use in the Solution Explorer. Then, choose the Website→Add Content Page command. This creates a content page for the selected master page. Note that when you use this technique, the content page is automatically named Default.

The code example in this figure shows the code that's generated when you create a new content page for the master page shown in figure 3-4. This code is quite different from the code that's generated when you create a regular ASP.NET page. Although the Page directive includes the same information as a regular ASP.NET page, it also includes a MasterPageFile attribute that specifies the master page you selected. And the rest of the content page is completely different from a normal ASP.NET page.

Before I describe the other differences, you should know that the title you specify in the Title attribute of the Page directive of a content page overrides any title you specify in the master page. That way, you can display a different title for each content page. If you want to use the same title for each content page, however, you can specify the title in the master page and then delete the Title attribute from the content pages.

Unlike normal ASP.NET pages, content pages don't include a Doctype directive or any structural HTML elements such as html, head, body, or form. That's because those elements are provided by the master page. Instead, the content page includes an ASP.NET Content element that indicates which content placeholder the page should be displayed in. Then, you place the content that you want to display on the page between the start and end tags of this element.

This figure also includes a procedure for converting a regular page to a content page. You'll need to follow this procedure if you start a web site without using master pages, and later decide to use master pages. Unfortunately, though, Visual Studio doesn't provide a way to automatically do this. As a result, you'll have to manually edit each of the pages to add the MasterPageFile attribute to the Page directive, remove the Doctype directive and structural HTML elements (Html, Head, Body, and Form), and add a Content element.

The aspx code for a new page that uses the master page in figure 3-4

```
<%@ Page Language="VB" MasterPageFile="~/MasterPage.master"
    AutoEventWireup="false" CodeFile="Order.aspx.vb"
    Inherits="Order" Title="Untitled Page" %>

<asp:Content ID="Content1" ContentPlaceHolderID="Main" Runat="Server">
</asp:Content>
```

How to create a new content page

- One way is to choose the Website→Add New Item command. Then, select Web Form from the list of templates, enter the name for the form, check the Select a Master Page check box, and click Add. When the Select a Master Page dialog box appears, select the master page you want and click OK.

- Another way is to select the master page in the Solution Explorer, then choose the Website→Add Content Page command.

How to convert a regular ASP.NET page to a content page

- First, add a MasterPageFile attribute to the Page directive that specifies the URL of the master page. Next, replace the Div element that contains the actual content of the page with a Content element as shown above. Then, delete everything that's outside this Content element except for the Page directive.

Two other ways to specify the master page

In the web.config file

```
<system.web>
    .
    <pages masterPageFile="MasterPage.master" />
    .
</system.web>
```

In the Page_PreInit procedure

```
Protected Sub Page_PreInit(ByVal sender As Object, _
        ByVal e As System.EventArgs) Handles Me.PreInit
    MasterPageFile = "MasterPage.master"
End Sub
```

Description

- The Page directive in the aspx code for a content page includes a MasterPageFile attribute that specifies the name of the master page.

- The aspx code for a content page includes a Content element that indicates the ID of the content placeholder where the content for the page should be displayed. Any content you create for the page should be placed between the start and end tags for this element.

- You can also specify the master page in the web.config file or in the Page_PreInit procedure. However, the Web Forms Designer doesn't support either of these techniques, so you won't be able to view the content page in Design view.

Figure 3-6   How to create a content page

Because this conversion procedure is error prone, it pays to use master pages for all but the simplest of applications, even if each master page contains only a content placeholder. Then, when you're ready to provide a consistent look to the pages within the application, you can enhance the master pages.

This figure also shows two other ways to specify which master page is used with a content page. First, you can add a <pages> element to the web.config file with a MasterPageFile attribute that specifies the master page to be used with all pages that don't specify a master file. Second, you can specify the master page at runtime by setting the MasterPageFile attribute of the page in the Page_PreInit procedure. Note, however, that the Web Forms Designer doesn't support either of these techniques. If you use them, then, you won't be able to view or edit your content pages in Design view.

How to add content to a page

Figure 3-7 shows how a content page appears in Design view. As you can see, the master page is displayed, but it is dimmed, and you can't edit any of the master page elements from this view. However, you can click in the Content control, and then edit the content of the page by adding text or dragging controls from the Toolbox. Later, when you switch to Source view, any elements that you've added will appear between the Content element's start and end tags.

If you work with a master page that has more than one content placeholder, there will be a separate Content control for each placeholder. Then, you can edit the contents for each of those controls.

A content page in Design View

Description

- When you display a content page in Design view, the elements from the master page are dimly displayed so you can see how they will affect the final appearance of the page.
- To add the content for a page, click the content placeholder. Then, you can type text or use the toolbox to drag controls into the content area of the page. Any text or other elements you add will be placed between the start and end tags of the Content element in the aspx file.

Note

- If you can't edit the contents of the placeholder, click the Smart Tag icon in the upper-right corner of the placeholder and choose Create Custom Content from the menu that appears. This is sometimes necessary, probably due to a bug in Visual Studio.

Figure 3-7   How to add content to a page

How to access master page controls from a content page

In many applications, you need to access one or more of the controls in a master page from one of the application's content pages. For example, the master page shown earlier in this chapter has a label in the footer area that normally displays the number of days remaining until Halloween. But what if you want to display other information in this label when certain content pages are displayed?

For example, when the user is shopping for products with the Order.aspx page, you may want to display the number of items currently in the shopping cart instead of the number of days left until Halloween. To do that, you can expose a master page control as a public property, and then access the property from the content page.

How to expose a master page control as a public property

The easiest way to access a control on a master page from a content page is to create a public property that provides access to the control. Figure 3-8 illustrates a code-behind file for a master page that shows you how to do that.

First, you create a public property in the master page that identifies the control you want to be able to access. In this case, the property is a Label type, and the property is named MessageLabel. Then, you code get and set procedures for the property. Here, the get procedure returns the lblMessage label, and the set procedure assigns the property value to lblMessage.

Please notice that I also added another If statement to the Page_Load procedure for the master page. Now, the lblMessage label is set to the number of days left until Halloween only if the value of the label's Text property is empty. That way, if the content page has assigned a value to this label in its Page_Load procedure, the master page's Page_Load procedure won't overwrite the value. This works because the content page's Page_Load procedure is called before the master page's Page_Load procedure.

The code-behind file for a master page that provides a public property

```
Partial Class MasterPage
    Inherits System.Web.UI.MasterPage

    Public Property MessageLabel() As Label
        Get
            Return lblMessage
        End Get
        Set(ByVal value As Label)
            lblMessage = value
        End Set
    End Property

    Protected Sub Page_Load(ByVal sender As Object, _
            ByVal e As System.EventArgs) Handles Me.Load
        If lblMessage.Text = "" Then
            Dim iDaysUntil As Integer = DaysUntilHalloween()
            If iDaysUntil = 0 Then
                lblMessage.Text = "Happy Halloween!"
            ElseIf iDaysUntil = 1 Then
                lblMessage.Text = "Tomorrow is Halloween!"
            Else
                lblMessage.Text = "There are only " & iDaysUntil _
                    & " days left until Halloween!"
            End If
        End If
    End Sub

    Private Function DaysUntilHalloween() As Integer
        Dim dtmHalloween As Date = New DateTime(DateTime.Today.Year, 10, 31)
        If DateTime.Today > dtmHalloween Then
            dtmHalloween.AddYears(1)
        End If
        Dim tsTimeUntil As TimeSpan = dtmHalloween - DateTime.Today
        Return tsTimeUntil.Days
    End Function

End Class
```

Description

- A content page can access a control in the master page if you expose the control as a public property in the master page. To do that, you code a property procedure with get and set procedures.

Figure 3-8   How to expose a master page control as a public property

How to access a public property of the master page from a content page

Figure 3-9 shows how you can access a public property in a master page from a content page. As you can see in the top part of this figure, you use the MasterType directive in the aspx file of the content page to specify the name of the type used for the master page. The value you name in this directive specifies the type of the object returned by the content page's Master property. So in this example, the Master property will return an object of type MasterPage. If you look at the class declaration in the previous figure, you'll see that MasterPage is the name of the class that defines the master page.

The second part of this figure shows two procedures from the code-behind file for the Order.aspx content page. As you can see, the Page_Load procedure calls a procedure named DisplayCartMessage. This procedure determines the number of items currently in the shopping cart and sets the Text property of the label exposed by the master page's MessageLabel property accordingly. But note that no value is assigned to the message label if the shopping cart is empty. In that case, the Page_Load procedure for the master page will set the label to the number of days remaining until Halloween.

Although using the MasterType directive in the content page's aspx file makes it easier to access the properties of the master page, you should realize that this directive isn't necessary. If you don't specify the MasterType directive, the Master property will return an object of type Master. You can then cast this object to the actual type of your master page to access any properties you've created.

For example, you could use code like this to assign text to the MessageLabel property:

```
If Cart.Count = 1 Then
    CType(Me.Master, MasterPage).MessageLabel.Text _
        = "There is one item in your cart."
ElseIf Cart.Count > 1 Then
    CType(Me.Master, MasterPage).MessageLabel.Text _
        = "There are " & Cart.Count & " items in your cart."
End If
```

Here, the Master object is cast to MasterPage so its MessageLabel property can be accessed. The purpose of the MasterType directive is to avoid this awkward casting.

A portion of the Order.aspx page

```
<%@ Page Language="VB" MasterPageFile="~/MasterPage.master"
AutoEventWireup="false" CodeFile="Order.aspx.vb"
Inherits="Order" %>

<%@ MasterType TypeName="MasterPage" %>

<asp:Content ID="Content1" ContentPlaceHolderID="Main" Runat="server">
.
.
.
</asp:Content>
```

Two procedures from the code-behind file for the Order.aspx page

```
Protected Sub Page_Load(ByVal sender As Object, _
        ByVal e As System.EventArgs) Handles Me.Load
    If Not IsPostBack Then
        ddlProducts.DataBind()
        Me.DisplayCartMessage()
    End If
    SelectedProduct = GetSelectedProduct()
    lblName.Text = SelectedProduct.Name
    lblShortDescription.Text = SelectedProduct.ShortDescription
    lblLongDescription.Text = SelectedProduct.LongDescription
    lblUnitPrice.Text = FormatCurrency(SelectedProduct.UnitPrice)
    imgProduct.ImageUrl = "Images\Products\" _
        & SelectedProduct.ImageFile
End Sub

Private Sub DisplayCartMessage()
    Dim Cart As SortedList = CType(Session("cart"), SortedList)
    If Not Cart Is Nothing Then
        If Cart.Count = 1 Then
            Me.Master.MessageLabel.Text _
                = "There is one item in your cart."
        ElseIf Cart.Count > 1 Then
            Me.Master.MessageLabel.Text _
                = "There are " & Cart.Count & " items in your cart."
        End If
    End If
End Sub
```

Description

- The MasterType directive in an aspx file specifies the name of the master page type. If you include this directive in a content page, you can use the Master property in the code-behind file to access the exposed property of the master page.

Figure 3-9   How to access a public property of the master page from a content page

How to use nested master pages

In some web applications, particularly large ones, one or more sections of the web site may have common formatting elements in addition to the elements that apply to the entire site. In that case, you can use nested master pages as described in the following topics.

How nested master pages work

Figure 3-10 shows how *nested master pages* might be used in the Halloween Store application. Here, a portion of the web site is devoted to presenting do-it-yourself project instructions that show the user how to create home-made Halloween decorations and props. In addition to the other elements from the master page, each of the pages in this section of the web site has an additional banner that displays the text "Do-It-Yourself Projects."

To create this additional banner, a second master page named ProjectsMaster.master is used. The content page (in this example, Tombstone.aspx) specifies that its master page is ProjectsMaster.master. Like any other master page, the ProjectsMaster master page includes a content placeholder. However, unlike regular master pages, the ProjectsMaster master page also includes a Master directive that specifies the application's main master page, MasterPage.master. Thus, ProjectsMaster.master is nested within MasterPage.master. As you can see, elements from all three pages— MasterPage.master, ProjectsMaster.master, and Tombstone.aspx—are combined to create the final page that's sent to the browser.

A master page that's nested within another master page is called a *child master*, and the master page it's nested in is called a *parent master*. Note that a parent master can also be a child master. In other words, you can nest master pages more than one level deep. However, few applications require more than one level of nesting.

An application with nested master pages

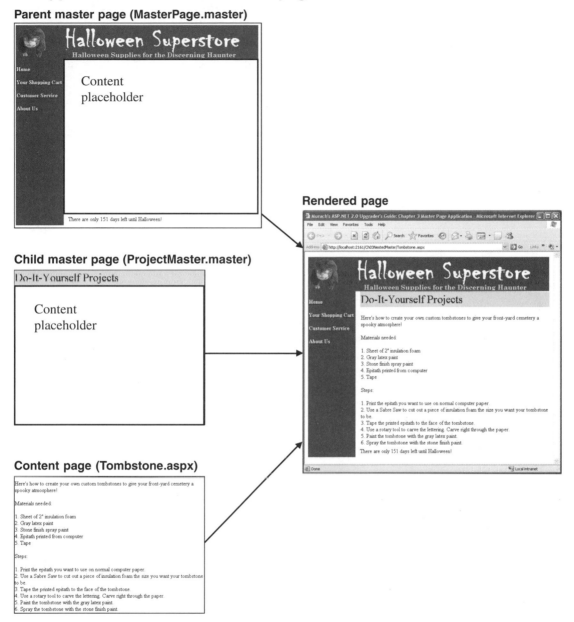

Parent master page (MasterPage.master)

Child master page (ProjectMaster.master)

Rendered page

Content page (Tombstone.aspx)

Description

- Master pages can be nested. This lets you create elements that are common to all pages of a web site and other elements that are common to a subset of pages within the site.

- When you nest master pages, the content placeholder of one master page, called the *parent master*, holds another master page, called the *child master*.

Figure 3-10   How nested master pages work

How to create nested master pages

Unfortunately, Visual Studio 2005 doesn't support nested master pages in Design view. Microsoft has indicated that nested master pages may be supported in design view in a future version of Visual Studio. But until then, you'll have to work in Source view to create nested master pages and the content pages that use them. This is described in figure 3-11.

Note that no special coding is required to create a parent master page. As a result, the MasterPage.master page that was shown earlier in this chapter will work fine as a parent master page.

To create a child master page, first use the Add New Item command to add a new item to the web site and choose Master Page as the template for the new item. Then, in Source view, delete all the generated code except for the Master directive and the ContentPlaceHolder element. Change the ID attribute of the ContentPlaceHolder element as appropriate. In this figure, the ID of this element is set to Project.

Next, add a MasterPageFile attribute to the Master page directive. The value of the MasterPageFile attribute should be the name of the page you want to use as the parent master page.

Finally, add a Content element to the master page so that it contains the ContentPlaceHolder element. The ContentPlaceHolderID attribute of the Content element should name the ContentPlaceHolder element in the parent master page. In this example, the ContentPlaceHolderID attribute specifies Main as the name of the content placeholder. If you look back to figure 3-4, you'll see that Main is the name of the content placeholder in MasterPage.master.

Once you've created a child master page, you can create a content page as shown in the second code example in this figure. Here, the MasterPageFile attribute for the Page directive specifies the name of the child master page (ProjectsMaster.master). In addition, the ContentPlaceHolderID attribute of the Content element specifies Project, which matches the ID attribute of the ContentPlaceHolder element in ProjectsMaster.master.

Frankly, the lack of Design view support for nested master pages is a major impediment to their use. So if your application requires nested master pages, be prepared to do most of your development work without the benefit of Design view.

A child master page (ProjectsMaster.aspx)

```
<%@ Master Language="VB" CodeFile="ProjectsMaster.master.vb"
Inherits="ProjectsMaster" MasterPageFile="~/MasterPage.master"%>

<asp:Content runat=server ContentPlaceHolderID=Main>
    <table border=0 cellpadding=2 cellspacing=0>
        <tr>
            <td height=40 bgcolor=gainsboro>
                <span style="font-size: 24pt">Do-It-Yourself Projects</span>
            </td>
        </tr>
        <tr>
            <td valign=top>
                <asp:contentplaceholder id="Project" runat="server">
                </asp:contentplaceholder>
            </td>
        </tr>
    </table>
</asp:Content>
```

A content page that uses a child master (Tombstone.aspx)

```
<%@ Page Language="VB" MasterPageFile="~/ProjectsMaster.master"
AutoEventWireup="false" CodeFile="Tombstone.aspx.vb" Inherits="Tombstone" %>

<asp:Content ID="Content1" ContentPlaceHolderID="Project" Runat="Server"><br />
    Here's how to create your own custom tombstones to give your front-yard
cemetery a spooky atmosphere!<br /><br />
    Materials needed:<br /><br />
    1. Sheet of 2" insulation foam<br />
    2. Gray latex paint<br />
    3. Stone finish spray paint<br />
    4. Epitath printed from computer<br />
    5. Tape<br /><br />
    Steps:<br /><br />
    1. Print the epitath you want to use on normal computer paper.<br />
    2. Use a Sabre Saw to cut out a piece of insulation foam the size you want
your tombstone to be.<br />
    3. Tape the printed epitath to the face of the tombstone.<br />
    4. Use a rotary tool to carve the lettering. Carve right through the
paper.<br />
    5. Paint the tombstone with the gray latex paint.<br />
    6. Spray the tombstone with the stone finish paint.
</asp:Content>
```

Description

- Because the Web Forms Designer doesn't support nested master pages, you have to work in Source view to create child masters and content pages that use a child master.

- To create a child master page, add a MasterPageFile attribute to the Master page directive of a master page. Then, delete the rest of the generated code except for the ContentPlaceHolder element, and create a Content element that includes the ContentPlaceHolder element.

- To create a content page that uses a child master, specify the child master in the content page's MasterPageFile element. Then, add a Content element with the content for the page, and set the ContentPlaceHolderID attribute to the ID of the child master's content place-holder.

Figure 3-11   How to create nested master pages

Perspective

I hope this chapter has illustrated the power of master pages. In fact, I recommend that you use master pages for all but the simplest applications, even if you start out with nothing in your master pages but placeholders. Then, when you're ready to provide a professional look to your content pages, you can enhance the master pages, which will also enhance all of your content pages.

The alternative is to convert regular content pages so they use the master pages that you develop later on. But as figure 3-6 shows, that's a time-consuming and error-prone procedure. How much better it is to think ahead.

New terms

master page
content page
content placeholder
nested master pages
parent master
child master

Section 2

ASP.NET 2.0 data access

In this section, you'll learn how to use the new data access features of ASP.NET 2.0. That includes the use of the new data source controls, as well as the new data controls that can be bound to data sources. As you will see, these features make database programming much easier than it was with earlier versions of ASP.NET.

In chapter 4, you'll start by learning how to use two of the new types of data sources for creating simple applications: the SQL and the XML data sources. In chapter 5, you'll learn how to use the new GridView control to create more complex applications. In chapter 6, you'll learn how to use the new DetailsView and FormView controls. And in chapter 7, you'll learn how to use the new object data source to build 3-layer applications. Because all four chapters present substantial new features, you'll want to read all of these chapters in sequence.

4

How to use SQL and XML data sources

The data source controls are one of the most important new features of ASP.NET 2.0. In this chapter, you'll learn how to use the SqlDataSource control, which lets you access data from a SQL Server database with little or no programming. You'll also learn how to use the XmlDataSource control, which lets you access XML data.

An application that uses the new data access features

In chapter 2, you were introduced to a simple application that used an Access data source. Now, I want to introduce a simple ASP.NET 2.0 application that uses two SQL data sources. After you learn how this application works, you'll see how it is implemented with two XML data sources.

The Product List application

Figure 4-1 shows a simple one-page application that demonstrates the use of two SQL data sources. The drop-down list at the top of the page is bound to a SQL data source that gets the categories for the products that the company offers. Then, when the user selects a category from this list, the products for the selected category are retrieved from a second SQL data source, which is bound to a Repeater control that's below the drop-down list. As a result, the products are displayed in the Repeater control.

Since this application relies entirely on the data binding that's established in the Web Forms Designer, the code-behind file for this application contains no Visual Basic code. That illustrates one of the major improvements in ASP.NET 2.0: the amount of database handling code that you have to write for a typical database application is drastically reduced. In fact, even complicated applications that insert, update, and delete database data can often be written with little or no code.

That's not to say that most ASP.NET database applications are code-free. In chapters 5 and 6, for example, you'll see applications that require database handling code. In particular, these applications require code to detect database errors and concurrency violations and display appropriate error messages. Also, as you'll learn in chapter 7, you can use object data sources to build 3-layer applications that require extensive amounts of database handling code.

Before we move on, I want you to know that I used the Repeater control for this application because I didn't want to introduce any of the new 2.0 data controls in this chapter. In the next chapter, though, you'll learn how to use the new GridView control, which is specifically designed to display lists like this.

The Product List application displayed in a web browser

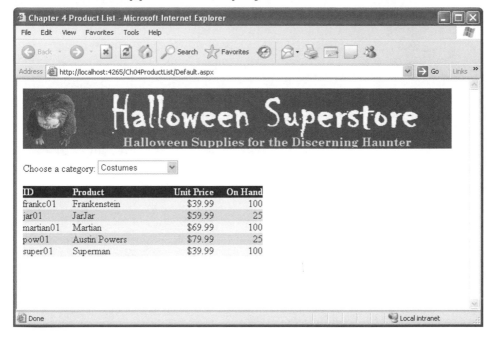

Description

- The Product List application uses two SqlDataSource controls to get category and product data from a SQL Server database and display it in two bound controls.
- The drop-down list near the top of the form displays the product categories. This control is bound to the first data source control.
- The Repeater control, which is bound to the second data source control, displays the data for the products that are in the category that's selected in the drop-down list.
- This application requires no Visual Basic code in the code-behind file.

Figure 4-1   The Product List application

The design of the Halloween database

Figure 4-2 shows the design of the Halloween database that's used in the application presented in this chapter and throughout this book. The purpose of the Halloween database is to track orders placed at an online Halloween products store. To do that, the database must track not only invoices, but also products and customers. Although this database may seem complicated, its design is actually much simpler than most databases you'll encounter when you work on real world database applications.

The Products and Categories tables work together to store information about the products offered by the Halloween store. The Categories table has just three columns: CategoryID, ShortName, and LongName. The CategoryID column is a 10-character code that uniquely identifies each category. The ShortName and LongName columns provide two different descriptions of the category that the application can use, depending on how much room is available to display the category information.

The Products table contains one row for each product. Its primary key is the ProductID column. The Name, ShortDescription, and LongDescription columns provide descriptive information about the product. The CategoryID column relates the product to a category. The ImageFile column provides the name of a separate image file that depicts the product. This column specifies just the name of each image file, not the complete path. The image files are stored in a directory named Images beneath the application's root directory, so the application knows where to find them.

The Products and Categories tables are the only ones you need to worry about for the application presented in this chapter. However, the other tables will be used by other applications presented later in this book. So although you don't need to use those tables now, you may want to refer back to this figure later.

The Invoices table contains one row for each order placed by the company's customers. The primary key for this table is the InvoiceNumber column, which is an identity column. As a result, invoice numbers are generated automatically by SQL Server whenever a new invoice is created.

The LineItems table contains the line item details for each invoice. The primary key for this table is a combination of the InvoiceNumber and ProductID columns. The InvoiceNumber column relates each line item to an invoice, and the ProductID column relates each line item to a product. As a result, each invoice can have only one line item for a given product.

The Customers table contains a row for each customer who has purchased from the Halloween Store. The primary key for this table is the customer's email address. The other columns in this table contain the customer's name, address, and phone number.

Finally, the InvoiceData table contains a single column that defines the sales tax rate that's applied to taxable orders. Note that this table doesn't have any relationships to any other tables in the database.

The tables that make up the Halloween database

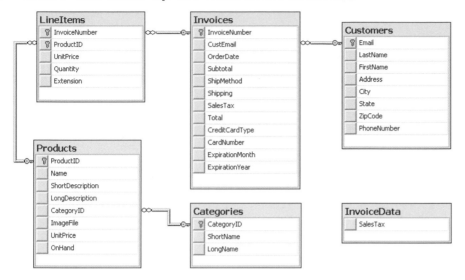

Description

- The Categories table contains a row for each product category. Its primary key is CategoryID, a 10-character code that identifies each category.

- The Products table contains a row for each product. Its primary key is ProductID, a 10-character code that identifies each product. CategoryID is a foreign key that relates each product to a row in the Categories table.

- The Customers table contains a row for each customer. Its primary key is Email, which identifies each customer by his or her email address.

- The Invoices table contains a row for each invoice. Its primary key is InvoiceNumber, an identity field that's generated automatically when a new invoice is created. CustEmail is a foreign key that relates each invoice to a row in the Customers table.

- The LineItems table contains one row for each line item of each invoice. Its primary key is a combination of InvoiceNumber and ProductID. InvoiceNumber is a foreign key that relates each line item to an invoice, and ProductID is a foreign key that relates each line item to a product.

- The InvoiceData table contains a single row that has a single data item, which represents the current sales tax rate.

- The relationships between the tables in this diagram appear as links, where the endpoints indicate the type of relationship. A key indicates the "one" side of a relationship, and the infinity symbol (∞) indicates the "many" side.

Figure 4-2   The design of the Halloween database

How to use a SQL data source

In chapter 2, you learned the basics of using the AccessDataSource control to get data from an Access data source. Now, in the topics that follow, you'll learn how to use a SqlDataSource control to get data from a SQL Server database, which can be referred to as a *SQL data source*.

How to create a SQL data source

Figure 4-3 shows how to create a SQL data source. As you will see, this process is similar to the one for creating an Access data source. To get the process started, you can drag a SqlDataSource control onto the form you're developing.

Since a data source control isn't displayed on the page when the application is run, it doesn't matter where you drop this control. But it does make sense to place it near the control that it will be bound to. Once you've got the data source control on the form, you can use its smart tag menu to run the Configure Data Source command, which brings you to the dialog box in the next figure.

You can also create a SQL data source using the Choose Data Source command in the smart tag menu of a bindable control. The exact technique for doing that varies depending on the control you're binding. For a drop-down list, you select the Choose Data Source command to start the Data Source Configuration Wizard. Then, you can choose New Data Source from the drop-down list in the first dialog box that's displayed and click OK. That displays the dialog box shown in this figure. From this dialog box, you can select the Database icon and click OK, which drops the data source control onto the form next to the bindable control and brings you to the dialog box in the next figure.

The technique for creating a SQL data source from a Repeater control is similar. The only difference is that the Choose Data Source command in the control's smart tag menu includes a drop-down list that lets you select New Data Source. When you do that, the Data Source Configuration Wizard dialog box shown in this figure is displayed just as it is for a drop-down list.

The starting dialog box of the Data Source Configuration Wizard

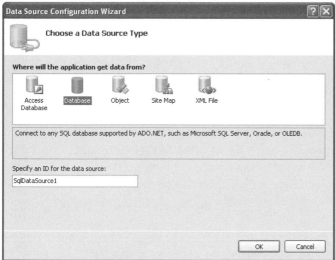

Aspx code generated for a basic SqlDataSource control

```
<asp:SqlDataSource ID="SqlDataSource1" runat="server"
    ConnectionString="<%$ ConnectionStrings:HalloweenConnectionString %>"
    SelectCommand="SELECT [CategoryID], [LongName] FROM [Categories]
        ORDER BY [LongName]">
</asp:SqlDataSource>
```

Basic SqlDataSource control attributes

Attribute	Description
ID	The ID for the SqlDataSource control.
Runat	Must specify "server."
ConnectionString	The connection string. In most cases, you should use a <%$ expression to specify the name of a connection string saved in the web.config file (see figure 4-5).
ProviderName	The name of the provider used to access the database. Values can be System.Data.Odbc, System.Data.Oledb, System.Data.OracleClient, or System.Data.SqlClient. The default is System.Data.SqlClient.
SelectCommand	The SQL SELECT statement executed by the data source to retrieve data.

Description

- To create a *SQL data source*, drag the SqlDataSource control from the Data tab of the Toolbox onto the form. Then, choose Configure Data Source from the control's smart tag menu and proceed from there.

- You can also create a SQL data source using the Choose Data Source command in the smart tag menu of a bindable control. When you use this command, the dialog box shown above is displayed. Then, you can select the Database icon and proceed from there.

- Once the SqlDataSource control has been configured, you can bind controls to it so they get their data from the SQL data source.

Figure 4-3 How to create a SQL data source

How to define the connection

The first step in configuring a SqlDataSource control is to create the connection for the data source, as shown in figure 4-4. From this dialog box, you can select an existing connection (one you've already created for this project or for another project), or you can click the New Connection button to display the Add Connection dialog box. This dialog box helps you identify the database that you want to access and provide the information you need to access it.

In the Add Connection dialog box, you select the name of the server that contains the database you want to access, enter the information that's required to log on to the server, and select the name of the database you want to access. How you do that, though, varies depending on whether you're using the SQL Server Express Edition on your own PC or whether you're using a database that resides on a database server.

If you're using SQL Server Express on your own PC and you've installed it and attached the Halloween database to it as described in the appendix, you can type localhost\sqlexpress for the server name. Alternatively, you can select the server name from the drop-down list, which will include your computer name like this: ANNEPC\SQLEXPRESS. If you will be porting your applications from one computer to another, though, it's best to use localhost. That way, you won't have to change the server name to refer to the correct computer.

For the logon information, you can click on the Use Windows Authentication option. Then, SQL Server Express will use the login name and password that you use for your computer as the name and password for the database too. As a result, you won't need to provide a separate user name and password in this dialog box. Last, you select the name of the database that you want to connect to. When you're done, you can click on the Test Connection button to be sure that the connection works.

In contrast, if you're using a database on a server computer, you need to get the connection information from the network or database administrator. That will include the server name, logon information, and database name. Once you establish a connection to a database, you can use that connection for all of the other applications that use that database.

The dialog boxes for defining a connection

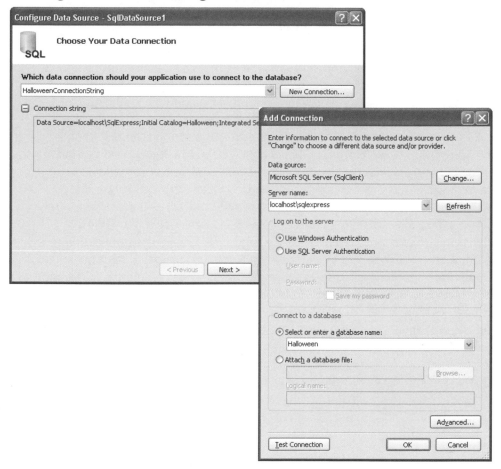

Description

- The Configure Data Source dialog box asks you to identify the data connection for the database you want to use. If you've previously created a connection for that database, you can select it from the drop-down list. To see the connection string for that connection, click the + button below the drop-down list.

- To create a new connection, click the New Connection button to display the Add Connection dialog box. Then, enter the name of the database server in the Server Name text box or select it from the drop-down list. For SQL Server Express, you can use localhost\sqlexpress as the server name.

- After you enter the server name, select the authentication mode you want to use (we recommend Windows Authentication). Then, select the database you want to connect to from the Select or Enter a Database Name drop-down list.

- To be sure that the connection is configured properly, you can click the Test Connection button.

Figure 4-4   How to define the connection

How to save the connection string in the web.config file

Although you can hard-code connection strings into your programs, it's much better to store connection strings in the application's web.config file. That way, if you move the database to another server or make some other change that affects the connection string, you won't have to recompile the application. Instead, you can simply change the connection string in the web.config file.

As figure 4-5 shows, ASP.NET 2.0 can store connection strings in the web.config file automatically if you check the Yes box in the next step of the wizard. That way, you don't have to manually edit the web.config file or write code to retrieve the connection string. When you select this check box, the connection string will automatically be saved with the name that you supply.

This figure also shows the entries made in the web.config file when a connection string is saved. Here, the web.config file has a connectionStrings element that contains an add element for each connection string. In the example, the connection string is named HalloweenConnectionString. And the connection string refers to a database named Halloween on the server named localhost\sqlexpress.

Last, this figure shows how the aspx code that's generated for a data source can refer to the connection string by name. Here, the shaded portion of the example shows the value of the ConnectionString attribute. As you can see, it begins with the word ConnectionStrings followed by a colon and the name of the connection string you want to use. Note that this code is automatically generated by the Data Source Configuration Wizard, so you don't have to write this code yourself.

The dialog box for saving the connection string in the web.config file

The ConnectionStrings section of the web.config file

```
<connectionStrings>
    <add name="HalloweenConnectionString"
        connectionString="Data Source=localhost\sqlexpress;
        Initial Catalog=Halloween;Integrated Security=True"
        providerName="System.Data.SqlClient" />
</connectionStrings>
```

Aspx code that refers to a connection string in the web.config file

```
<asp:SqlDataSource ID="SqlDataSource1" runat="server"
    ConnectionString="<%$ ConnectionStrings:HalloweenConnectionString %>"
    SelectCommand="SELECT [CategoryID], [LongName] FROM [Categories]
        ORDER BY [LongName]">
</asp:SqlDataSource>
```

Description

- ASP.NET 2.0 applications can store connection strings in the web.config file.
- If you choose to save the connection string in the web.config file, the ConnectionString attribute of the data source control will include a special code that retrieves the connection string from the web.config file.
- If you choose not to save the connection string in the web.config file, the ConnectionString attribute of the data source control will specify the actual connection string.
- We recommend that you always save the connection string in the web.config file. Then, if the location of the database changes, you can change the connection string in the web.config file rather than in each page that uses the connection.

Figure 4-5   How to save the connection string in the web.config file

How to configure the SELECT statement

Figure 4-6 shows how to configure the SELECT statement for a data source as you proceed through the steps of the wizard. In the first dialog box, you can specify a custom SQL statement or stored procedure, or you can choose the columns for the query from a single table or view.

To select columns from a table, use the Name drop-down list to select the table you want to select the columns from. Then, check each of the columns you want to retrieve in the Columns list box. In this figure, I chose the Products table and selected four columns: ProductID, Name, UnitPrice, and OnHand.

As you check the columns in the list box, the wizard creates a SELECT statement that's shown in the text box at the bottom of the dialog box. In this case, the SELECT statement indicates that the data source will retrieve the ProductID, Name, UnitPrice, and OnHand columns from the Products table.

The buttons to the right of the Columns list box let you specify additional options for selecting data. If, for example, you want to sort the data that's retrieved, you can click on the ORDER BY button to display a dialog box that lets you select up to three sort columns. If you want to select specific types of records, you can click on the WHERE button to display the dialog box that's described in the next figure. And if you want to use an advanced feature, you can click on the Advanced button to display the dialog box that's described in figure 4-14.

When you finish specifying the data you want the data source to retrieve, click Next. This takes you to a page that includes a Test Query button. If you click this button, the wizard immediately retrieves the data that you specified. You can then look over this data to make sure the query retrieves the data you expected. If it doesn't, click the Back button and adjust the query as needed.

The second dialog box in this figure is the one that you use to specify a custom SQL statement or stored procedure. As you can see, this dialog box includes tabs that also let you enter UPDATE, INSERT, and DELETE statements for the data source. You can also click on the Query Builder button to open the Query Builder, which lets you visually create advanced SELECT statements that include joins and other features. You'll learn more about the Query Builder in figure 4-9.

The dialog box for defining the SELECT statement

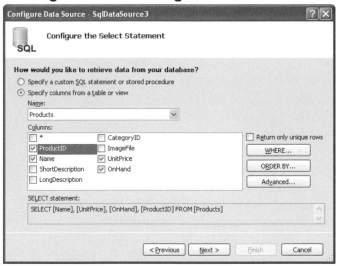

The dialog box for entering a custom SELECT statement

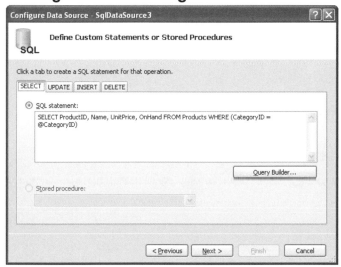

Description

- To configure the SELECT statement, you choose whether you want to use custom SQL statements or specify the columns from a table or view in the database.
- If you choose to select the columns from a table or view, you can choose the table and columns you want retrieved. You can click the ORDER BY button to specify how the records should be sorted. And you can click the WHERE button to specify the selection criteria as shown in figure 4-7.
- If you choose to use custom SQL statements, the next dialog box lets you enter the SQL statements or click the Query Builder button to build the query as shown in figure 4-9.

Figure 4-6   How to configure the SELECT statement

How to create a WHERE clause

If you click on the WHERE button shown in the first dialog box in figure 4-6, the Add WHERE Clause dialog box in figure 4-7 is displayed. It lets you create a WHERE clause and parameters for the SELECT statement.

A WHERE clause is made up of one or more conditions that limit the rows retrieved by the SELECT statement. To create these conditions, the Add WHERE Clause dialog box lets you compare the values in the columns of a database table with several different types of data, including a literal value, the value of another control on the page, the value of a query string passed via the page's URL, a profile property (see chapter 10), or a cookie.

For example, the SELECT statement for the data source that's bound to the Repeater control in the Product List application uses a WHERE clause that compares the CategoryID column in the Products table with the category selected from the drop-down list. To create this WHERE clause, select CategoryID in the Column drop-down list, the equals operator in the Operator drop-down list, and Control in the Source drop-down list. Next, select ddlCategory in the Control ID drop-down list. When you do, the SelectedValue property of the control is automatically selected. Then, when you click on the Add button, this condition is shown in the WHERE clause section of the dialog box.

The Add WHERE Clause dialog box

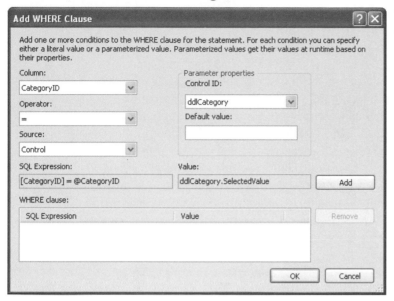

The WHERE clause section after a condition has been added

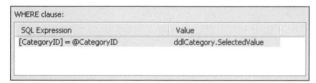

Description

- The Add WHERE Clause dialog box lets you specify a WHERE clause for the SELECT statement.

- The WHERE clause consists of one or more conditions that you construct by using the controls in this dialog box. To create a condition, you select the column you want to compare, the operator you want to use for the comparison, and the source of the data to use for the comparison. Then, you must click Add to add the condition to the list of WHERE clause conditions.

- The source of the data for the comparison can be a literal value, the value of another control on the form, a cookie, an HTML form field, a profile property, a query string in the URL for the page, or a value stored in session state.

Remember

- After you select the column, operator, and source for the comparison, be sure to click the Add button to add the condition to the generated WHERE clause. Otherwise, the condition won't be added to the WHERE clause.

Figure 4-7   How to create a WHERE clause

How select parameters work

When you create a WHERE clause as described in the previous figure, the wizard creates one or more *select parameters* that provide the values used by the WHERE clause. Figure 4-8 shows how these select parameters work. As you can see, each SqlDataSource control that includes select parameters is defined by a SqlDataSource element that includes a child element named SelectParameters. Then, this element contains a child element for each of the parameters used by the SELECT statement.

The select parameters themselves are defined by one of the elements listed in the first table. Each of these elements specifies a parameter whose value is obtained from a different type of source. For example, if the parameter's value is obtained from a form control, this *control parameter* is defined by a ControlParameter element. Similarly, the QueryStringParameter element defines a parameter whose value comes from a query string in the URL that's used for the page.

The second table in this figure lists the attributes used by the ControlParameter element to define a parameter whose value comes from a form control. As you can see, these attributes provide the name of the parameter, the SQL data type used for the parameter, the ID of the form control that provides the value, and the name of the property used to obtain the value.

The code example at the top of this figure shows the aspx code generated for the second SqlDataSource control used by the Product List application. Here, the SELECT statement uses one parameter named CategoryID. This parameter is defined by a ControlParameter element whose Name attribute is set to CategoryID. The SQL data type for this parameter is String, and the parameter's value is obtained from the SelectedValue property of the form control whose ID is ddlCategory.

Please note that the code in this example is generated by the Web Forms Designer when you configure the data source using the Data Source Configuration Wizard. As a result, you don't have to write this code yourself.

The aspx code for a SqlDataSource that includes a select parameter

```
<asp:SqlDataSource
    ConnectionString="<%$ ConnectionStrings:HalloweenConnectionString %>"
    ID="SqlDataSource2" runat="server"
    SelectCommand="SELECT [ProductID], [Name], [UnitPrice], [OnHand]
        FROM [Products]
        WHERE ([CategoryID] = @CategoryID)
        ORDER BY [ProductID]">
    <SelectParameters>
        <asp:ControlParameter Name="CategoryID" Type="String"
            ControlID="ddlCategory" PropertyName="SelectedValue" />
    </SelectParameters>
</asp:SqlDataSource>
```

Elements used to define select parameters

Element	Description
SelectParameters	A container that contains a child element for each parameter used by the data source's SELECT statement.
ControlParameter	Defines a parameter that gets its value from a control on the page.
QueryStringParameter	Defines a parameter that gets its value from a query string in the URL used to request the page.
FormParameter	Defines a parameter that gets its value from an HTML form field.
SessionParameter	Defines a parameter that gets its value from an item in session state.
ProfileParameter	Defines a parameter that gets its value from a property of the user's profile.
CookieParameter	Defines a parameter that gets its value from a cookie.

The ControlParameter element

Attribute	Description
Name	The parameter name.
Type	The SQL data type of the parameter.
ControlID	The ID of the web form control that supplies the value for the parameter.
PropertyName	The name of the property from the web form control that supplies the value for the parameter.

Description

- The SelectParameters element defines the *select parameters* that are used by the SELECT statement of a data source. The aspx code that defines these parameters is generated automatically when you use the Add WHERE Clause dialog box to create parameters.

- A *control parameter* is a parameter whose value is obtained from another control on a web form, such as the value selected by a drop-down list. Control parameters are defined by the ControlParameter element.

- Once you understand how to use control parameters, you shouldn't have any trouble learning how to use the other types of parameters on your own.

Figure 4-8   How select parameters work

How to use the Query Builder

You may have used the *Query Builder* with previous versions of Visual Studio. If so, you'll be glad to know that the Query Builder is still available, although it's a little harder to get to now. The topics that follow explain how to use it.

How to create a SELECT statement with the Query Builder

To use the Query Builder, you tell the wizard that you want to specify a custom SQL statement or stored procedure in the first dialog box shown in figure 4-6. Then, when the next dialog box appears, you click the Query Builder button to display the dialog box shown in figure 4-9.

When the Query Builder window opens, the Add Table dialog box is displayed. This dialog box, which isn't shown in this figure, lists all of the tables and views in the database that the data source is connected to. You can use this dialog box to add one or more tables to the *diagram pane* of the Query Builder window so you can use them in your query. In this figure, for example, the Products table has been added to the diagram pane.

In the *grid pane*, which appears beneath the diagram pane, you can see the columns that will be included in the query. To add columns to this pane, you just check the boxes before the column names in the diagram pane. You can also enter an expression in the Column column of the grid pane to create a calculated column, and you can enter a name in the Alias column to give the calculated column a name.

Once the columns have been added to the grid pane, you can use the Sort Type column to identify any columns that should be used to sort the returned rows and the Sort Order column to give the order of precedence for the sort if more than one column is identified. The Query Builder uses these specifications to build the ORDER BY clause for the SELECT statement.

You can use the Filter column to establish the criteria to be used to select the rows that will be retrieved by the query. For the query in this figure, a parameter named @CategoryID is specified for the CategoryID column. As a result, only the products whose CategoryID field matches the value of the @CategoryID parameter will be retrieved.

The Query Builder dialog box

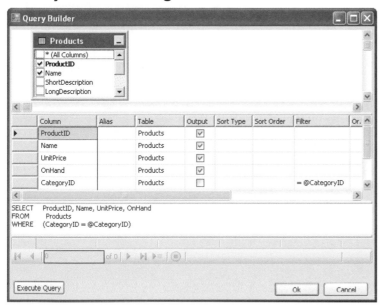

Description

- The *Query Builder* is displayed if you choose to enter a custom SELECT statement, and then click the Query Builder button in the dialog box that follows.
- The Query Builder lets you build a SELECT statement by choosing columns from one or more tables and views and specifying the sort order and filter criteria for each column.
- When you first start the Query Builder, a dialog box is displayed that lets you select the database tables you want to include in the query. Each table you select is displayed in the *diagram pane* at the top of the Query Builder window.
- If you add two related tables to the diagram pane, the Query Builder automatically joins the two tables by including a JOIN phrase in the FROM clause. You can also create a join by dragging a column from one table to a column in another table.
- To include a column from a table, use the check box that appears next to the column in the diagram. This adds the column to the *grid pane* that appears beneath the diagram pane. Then, you can specify any sorting or filtering requirements for the column.
- You can use a parameter in an expression in the Filter column to create a parameterized query. If you use one or more parameters in the query, the Data Source Configuration Wizard lets you specify the source of the parameter values, as described in figure 4-10.

Figure 4-9   How to create a SELECT statement with the Query Builder

How to define the parameters

If you specify one or more parameters when you create a SELECT statement with the Query Builder, the next dialog box lets you define those parameters as shown in figure 4-10. Here, the list box on the left side of the dialog box lists each of the parameters you created in the Query Builder. To define the source for one of these parameters, you select the parameter in this list box. Then, you can use the controls on the right side of the dialog box to select the parameter's source.

In this example, the source of the CategoryID parameter is set to the SelectedValue property of the control named ddlCategory. When I selected the ddlCategory control, the SelectedValue property was selected by default. If you want to use a different property as the source for a parameter, however, you can click the Show Advanced Properties link to display a list of the parameter properties. Then, you can set the PropertyName property to the control property you want to use.

The dialog box for defining parameters

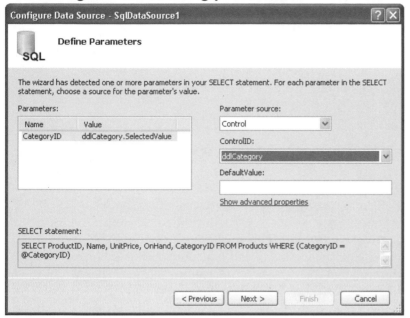

Parameter sources

Source	Description
Control	The parameter's value comes from a control on the page.
QueryString	The parameter's value comes from a query string in the URL used to request the page.
Form	The parameter's value comes from an HTML form field.
Session	The parameter's value comes from an item in session state.
Profile	The parameter's value comes from a property of the user's profile.
Cookie	The parameter's value comes from a cookie.

Description

- If you specify one or more parameters when you use the Query Builder to define a SELECT statement, the next dialog box lets you define those parameters.
- To define a parameter, you specify the source of the value for each parameter.

Figure 4-10   How to define the parameters

How to use data binding

Once you've configured a data source control, you can bind it to a web form control to automatically display the data retrieved by the data source on the page. In the following topics, you'll learn how to bind a data source to a list control and how to code data binding expressions for controls like a Repeater control.

How to bind a list control to a data source

A *list control* is a web control that inherits the ListControl class. The first table in figure 4-11 lists the five types of list controls provided by ASP.NET 2.0. These controls display the data retrieved by a data source in a simple list form.

The second table in this figure shows the three attributes you use to bind a list control to a data source. The DataSourceID attribute provides the ID of the data source. The DataTextField attribute provides the name of the data source field that's displayed in the list. And the DataValueField attribute provides the name of the data source field that is returned by the SelectedValue property when the user selects an item from the list.

You can set these properties manually by using the Properties window or by directly editing the aspx code. Or, you can use the Data Source Configuration Wizard shown at the top of this figure to set these properties. To do that, display the smart tag menu for the list and select Choose Data Source. Then, use the wizard's controls to set the data source, display field, and value field.

The code example in this figure shows a drop-down list that's bound to a data source named SqlDataSource1. The field named LongName provides the values that are displayed in the drop-down list, and the field named CategoryID supplies the value that's returned by the SelectedValue property when the user selects an item from the list.

The Data Source Configuration Wizard for binding a drop-down list

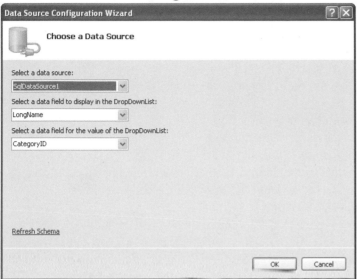

ASP.NET list controls

Control	Description
DropDownList	A drop-down list.
ListBox	A list box.
BulletedList	A bulleted list.
CheckBoxList	A list of check boxes.
RadioButtonList	A list of radio buttons.

List control attributes for data binding

Attribute	Description
DataSourceID	The ID of the data source to bind the list to.
DataTextField	The name of the data source field that should be displayed in the list.
DataValueField	The name of the data source field whose value should be returned by the SelectedValue property of the list.

The aspx code for a drop-down list that's bound to a SQL data source

```
<asp:DropDownList ID="ddlCategory" runat="server"
    AutoPostBack="True" Width="130px"
    DataSourceID="SqlDataSource1"
    DataTextField="LongName"
    DataValueField="CategoryID" />
```

Description

- You can use the Data Source Configuration Wizard to select the data source, the data field to display in the list, and the data value to return for the selected item.

Figure 4-11   How to bind a list control to a data source

How to use the ASP.NET 2.0 Eval and Bind methods to bind data

Figure 4-12 shows how you can use ASP.NET 2.0's Eval and Bind methods to bind data to any control that uses templates and specifies a data source. In the application presented in this chapter, these binding techniques are used for the Repeater control.

This figure starts by showing how you can use the Eval method of the DataBinder class in binding expressions. This method was available in ASP.NET 1.x, so it isn't a new feature. To use it, you code at least two parameters. The first specifies the source of the data, while the second one provides the name of the property to be bound. An optional third parameter provides a format string that's used to format the data.

However, as this figure shows, ASP.NET 2.0 provides a new Eval method that you can call in a control that's bound to a data source. This new Eval method doesn't require that you specify the data source. Instead, it assumes that the data source is specified by the containing control's DataSourceID attribute. In addition, you don't have to explicitly refer to the DataBinder class to use this method. In the next figure, you'll get a better idea of how this works.

ASP.NET 2.0 also provides a new feature called *two-way binding* that's implemented by the Bind method. This method is similar to the Eval method, but it's used to bind controls that are used for both input and output. Although the application in this chapter doesn't use two-way binding, chapter 6 presents an application that does use it.

The ASP.NET 1.x DataBinder.Eval method

Syntax

```
<%# DataBinder.Eval(Object, Name [,FormatString]) %>
```

Examples

```
<%# DataBinder.Eval(Container, "DataItem.Name") %>
<%# DataBinder.Eval(Container, "DataItem.UnitPrice", "{0:c}") %>
```

The ASP.NET 2.0 Eval method

Syntax

```
<%# Eval(Name [,FormatString]) %>
```

Examples

```
<%# Eval("Name") %>
<%# Eval("UnitPrice", "{0:c}") %>
```

The ASP.NET 2.0 Bind method

Syntax

```
<%# Bind(Name [,FormatString]) %>
```

Examples

```
<%# Bind("Name") %>
<%# Bind("UnitPrice", "{0:c}") %>
```

Description

- ASP.NET 2.0 includes a new Eval method that provides a simplified syntax for data binding expressions. It also provides for a format expression that's applied to the bound data.

- The Eval method can only be used in controls that specify a data source, such as a Repeater or DataList control.

- The Bind method is similar to the Eval method, but it provides for *two-way binding*. In other words, it can be used to bind input fields as well as output fields.

Figure 4-12   How to use the ASP.NET 2.0 Eval and Bind methods to bind data

The aspx file for the Product List application

To show you how everything that you've learned works together, figure 4-13 presents the complete aspx code for the Product List application of figure 4-1. To make it easier for you to follow this code, I've shaded parts of the data source controls and the controls they're bound to. Because this application relies entirely on the data binding declared in this aspx file, it doesn't require any Visual Basic code at all.

The first control is the drop-down list that's bound to the first SqlDataSource control, SqlDataSource1. Here, the AutoPostBack attribute for the drop-down list is set to True so the page is automatically posted back to the server when the user selects a category.

The second control is the first SqlDataSource control, which uses this SELECT statement to get the required data:

```
SELECT [CategoryID], [LongName] FROM [Categories]
    ORDER BY [LongName]
```

As a result, this data source gets the CategoryID and LongName fields for each row in the Categories table and sorts the result based on the LongName field. Then, these fields are used by the drop-down list that's bound to this data source.

The third control is a Repeater control that's bound to the second SqlDataSource control, SqlDataSource2. Since the Repeater control isn't new with ASP.NET 2.0, this book doesn't present it in detail, but you should be able to figure out how it works by looking at the definitions for the four templates that are used to render the data as an HTML table. The HeaderTemplate provides the starting element for the table as well as a row of headings. The ItemTemplate and AlternatingItemTemplate define alternating table rows that display the data in the rows that are retrieved by the data source. And the FooterTemplate completes the table. Incidentally, the only difference between the row templates is the background color.

Note that the table data elements in these templates use the Eval method to display the right data source. As I explained earlier, these methods assume that the data is coming from the data source that the Repeater control is bound to. Although you can use the properties of a Repeater control to generate the starting code for the templates, you will normally want to modify that code. And you always need to code the Eval methods.

The fourth control, SqlDataSource2, uses this SELECT statement:

```
SELECT [ProductID], [Name], [UnitPrice], [OnHand]
    FROM [Products]
    WHERE ([CategoryID] = @CategoryID)
    ORDER BY [ProductID]
```

Here, the WHERE clause specifies that only those rows whose CategoryID field equals the value of the CategoryID parameter should be retrieved. To make this work, the ControlParameter element specifies that the value of the CategoryID parameter is obtained from the SelectedValue property of the ddlCategory control.

Default.aspx (ProductList application)

```
<body>
    <form id="form1" runat="server">
    <div>
        <asp:Image ID="Image1" runat="server"
            ImageUrl="~/Images/banner.jpg" /><br /><br />Choose a category:
        <asp:DropDownList ID="ddlCategory" runat="server"
            AutoPostBack="True" Width="130px" DataSourceID="SqlDataSource1"
            DataTextField="LongName" DataValueField="CategoryID">
        </asp:DropDownList>
        <asp:SqlDataSource ID="SqlDataSource1" runat="server"
            ConnectionString="<%$ ConnectionStrings:HalloweenConnectionString %>"
            SelectCommand="SELECT [CategoryID], [LongName] FROM [Categories]
                ORDER BY [LongName]">
        </asp:SqlDataSource><br /><br />
        <asp:Repeater ID="Repeater1" runat="server"
            DataSourceID="SqlDataSource2">
            <HeaderTemplate>
                <table cellpadding="0" cellspacing="0">
                  <tr bgcolor="Black" style="color: white">
                    <td width="80"><b>ID</b></td>
                    <td width="150"><b>Product</b></td>
                    <td width="80" align="right"><b>Unit Price</b></td>
                    <td width="80" align="right"><b>On Hand</b></td>
                  </tr>
            </HeaderTemplate>
            <ItemTemplate>
                <tr bgcolor="WhiteSmoke">
                  <td><%# Eval("ProductID") %></td>
                  <td><%# Eval("Name") %></td>
                  <td align="right"><%# Eval("UnitPrice", "{0:c}") %></td>
                  <td align="right"><%# Eval("OnHand") %></td>
                </tr>
            </ItemTemplate>
            <AlternatingItemTemplate>
                <tr bgcolor="Gainsboro">
                  <td><%# Eval("ProductID") %></td>
                  <td><%# Eval("Name") %></td>
                  <td align="right"><%# Eval("UnitPrice", "{0:c}") %></td>
                  <td align="right"><%# Eval("OnHand") %></td>
                </tr>
            </AlternatingItemTemplate>
            <FooterTemplate>
                </table>
            </FooterTemplate></asp:Repeater>
        <asp:SqlDataSource ID="SqlDataSource2" runat="server"
            ConnectionString="<%$ ConnectionStrings:HalloweenConnectionString %>"
            SelectCommand="SELECT [ProductID], [Name], [UnitPrice], [OnHand]
                FROM [Products]
                WHERE ([CategoryID] = @CategoryID)
                ORDER BY [ProductID]">
            <SelectParameters>
                <asp:ControlParameter  Name="CategoryID" Type="String"
                    ControlID="ddlCategory" PropertyName="SelectedValue"  />
            </SelectParameters>
        </asp:SqlDataSource>
    </div>
    </form>
</body>
```

Figure 4-13   The aspx file for the Product List application

How to use the advanced features of a SQL data source

The SqlDataSource control provides several advanced features that you may want to use in your applications. These features are explained in the topics that follow.

How to create a data source that can update the database

Much like ADO.NET 1.x data adapters, a SQL data source can include INSERT, UPDATE, and DELETE statements that let you automatically update the underlying database based on changes made by the user to bound data controls. To automatically generate these statements, you can check the first box in the dialog box shown in figure 4-14, which is displayed when you click on the Advanced button in the first dialog box shown in figure 4-6. You can also check the box for optimistic concurrency, which enhances the generated statements so they check whether updated or deleted rows have changed since the data source retrieved the original data.

The code in this figure shows the aspx elements that are generated when you request INSERT, UPDATE, and DELETE statements without using optimistic concurrency. Here, the InsertCommand, UpdateCommand, and DeleteCommand attributes provide the statements, and the InsertParameters, UpdateParameters, and DeleteParameters child elements define the parameters used by these commands. Because optimistic concurrency isn't used, these commands will update the database whether or not the data has changed since it was originally retrieved, which could lead to corrupt data.

If you check the Use Optimistic Concurrency check box, though, the update and delete commands will include WHERE clauses that compare the value of each column with the value originally retrieved. Because these values are passed as parameters, the generated aspx code will also include additional elements that define these parameters. Then, if the value of any column has changed since it was originally retrieved, the update or delete operation will be refused, and your application needs to provide code that handles that situation. You'll see how that works in chapter 5.

The Advanced SQL Generation Options dialog box

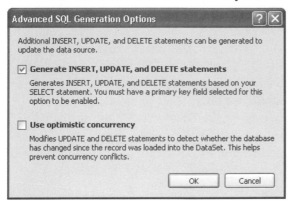

The aspx code for a SqlDataSource that uses action queries

```
<asp:SqlDataSource ID="SqlDataSource1" runat="server"
    ConnectionString="<%$ ConnectionStrings:HalloweenConnectionString %>"
    SelectCommand="SELECT [ShortName], [CategoryID] FROM [Categories]"
    InsertCommand="INSERT INTO [Categories] ([ShortName], [CategoryID])
                VALUES (@ShortName, @CategoryID)"
    UpdateCommand="UPDATE [Categories] SET [ShortName] = @ShortName
                WHERE [CategoryID] = @original_CategoryID"
    DeleteCommand="DELETE FROM [Categories]
                WHERE [CategoryID] = @original_CategoryID" >

    <DeleteParameters>
        <asp:Parameter Name="original_CategoryID" Type="String" />
    </DeleteParameters>

    <UpdateParameters>
        <asp:Parameter Name="ShortName" Type="String" />
        <asp:Parameter Name="original_CategoryID" Type="String" />
    </UpdateParameters>

    <InsertParameters>
        <asp:Parameter Name="ShortName" Type="String" />
        <asp:Parameter Name="CategoryID" Type="String" />
    </InsertParameters>

</asp:SqlDataSource>
```

Description

- To automatically generate INSERT, UPDATE, and DELETE statements for a data source, check the first box in the dialog box that you get by clicking on the Advanced button in the first dialog box in figure 4-6. To generate enhanced versions of these statements that use optimistic concurrency, check the second box too.

- The InsertCommand, UpdateCommand, and DeleteCommand attributes in the aspx code define the INSERT, UPDATE, and DELETE statements used by a data source. If these statements require parameters, the InsertParameters, UpdateParameters, and DeleteParameters elements specify those parameters.

Figure 4-14   How to create a SQL data source that can update the database

How to change the data source mode

As you may know, ADO.NET provides two basic ways to retrieve data from a database. You can either retrieve the data into a dataset, which retains a copy of the data in memory so it can be accessed multiple times and updated if necessary. Or, you can retrieve the data using a data reader, which lets you retrieve the data in forward-only, read-only fashion.

In figure 4-15, you can see how you can use the DataSourceMode attribute to set the mode for a SQL data source. If the data will be read just once and not updated, you can usually improve the application's performance by changing this attribute to DataReader mode. Otherwise, you can leave it at the default DataSet mode.

How to use caching

ASP.NET's caching feature lets you save the data retrieved by a data source in cache memory on the server. That way, the next time the data needs to be retrieved, the cached data is used instead of getting it from the database again. Since this reduces database access, it often improves an application's overall performance.

In ASP.NET 1.x, you had to write code that explicitly saved and retrieved the data in cache memory. But with ASP.NET 2.0, you can automatically cache data retrieved as shown in figure 4-15.

To enable caching, you simply set the EnableCaching attribute for a SQL data source to True. Then, you can use the CacheDuration attribute to specify how long data should be kept in the cache. If, for example, the cached data rarely changes, you can set a long cache duration value such as 30 minutes or more. Or, if the data changes frequently, you can set a short cache duration value, perhaps just a few seconds.

But what if the data in the database changes before the duration expires? To prevent the application from using the wrong data, you can use a new feature of ASP.NET 2.0, which is presented next.

The DataSourceMode attribute

Attribute	Description
DataSourceMode	DataSet or DataReader. The default is DataSet, but you can specify DataReader if the data source is read-only.

A SqlDataSource control that uses a data reader

```
<asp:SqlDataSource ID="SqlDataSource1" runat="server"
    ConnectionString="<%$ ConnectionStrings:HalloweenConnectionString %>"
    DataSourceMode="DataReader"
    SelectCommand="SELECT [CategoryID], [LongName]
        FROM [Categories]
        ORDER BY [LongName]"
</asp:SqlDataSource>
```

SqlDataSource attributes for caching

Attribute	Description
EnableCaching	A Boolean value that indicates whether caching is enabled for the data source. The default is False.
CacheDuration	The length of time in seconds that the cached data should be saved in cache storage.
CacheExpirationPolicy	If this attribute is set to Absolute, the cache duration timer is started from the first time the data is retrieved. If this attribute is set to Sliding, the cache duration timer is reset to zero each time the data is retrieved.
CacheKeyDependency	A string that provides a key value associated with the cached data. If you provide a key for the cached data, you can use the key value to programmatically expire the cached data at any time.

A SqlDataSource control that uses caching

```
<asp:SqlDataSource ID="SqlDataSource1" runat="server"
    ConnectionString="<%$ ConnectionStrings:HalloweenConnectionString %>"
    EnableCaching="True" CacheDuration="60"
    SelectCommand="SELECT [CategoryID], [LongName]
        FROM [Categories]
        ORDER BY [LongName]"
</asp:SqlDataSource>
```

Description

- The DataSourceMode attribute lets you specify that data should be retrieved using a data reader rather than a dataset. For read-only data, a data reader is usually more efficient.
- The data source caching attributes let you specify that data should be stored in cache storage for a specified period of time. For data that changes infrequently, caching can improve performance.

Figure 4-15   How to change the data source mode and use caching

How to create and use a SQL cache dependency

SQL cache dependency is a new feature of ASP.NET 2.0 that lets you cache data, but ensure that the cached data is automatically updated if the database table from which the data is retrieved changes. For example, you can set up a SQL cache dependency that caches the data retrieved from a Category table, but retrieves the data from the database if the contents of the Categories table changes. Figure 4-16 shows how to do that.

The first step is to prepare the database for using the SQL cache dependency feature. For a production database, this will probably be done by a database administrator. But for a test database, you may need to do it yourself. To do so, open a command prompt by choosing Start→All Programs→Microsoft Visual Studio 2005→Visual Studio Tools→Visual Studio 2005 Command Prompt. Then, issue the two aspnet_regsql commands shown at the top of this figure. The first one enables SQL cache dependencies for the database. The second one enables a SQL cache dependency for a specific table. Note that you need to provide the computer name and server name for your SQL Server instance whenever you use this command.

Once you've enabled the SQL cache dependency feature, the next step is to modify the web.config file so it includes a <caching> element as shown in this figure. Here, the <add> element provides the name of a database (Halloween), the name of a connection string (HalloweenConnectionString), and a poll time that specifies how often the database should be checked for changes (5000 milliseconds).

The last step is to add a SqlCacheDependency attribute to the SqlDataSource element for the data source. The value of this attribute should be the database name specified in the web.config file (in this case, Halloween), followed by a colon and the name of the table. If necessary, you can create a dependency based on two or more tables by listing two or more database:table specifications, separated with semi-colons.

Keep in mind that whenever you use cached data, there is a chance that a user will view data that is out of date. Although creating a cache dependency minimizes this possibility, it doesn't eliminate this possibility. And, of course, there is a performance price to be paid if you use cache dependencies because they require system resources. This just means that when you set the poll time for a cache dependency, you must balance the need for having up-to-date data with the performance impact of frequently polling the database for changes.

The ASPNET_REGSQL command

To enable SQL cache dependency for a database

```
aspnet_regsql -S server -E -d database -ed
```

To enable SQL cache dependency for a table

```
aspnet_regsql -S server -E -t table -d database -et
```

Typical commands to enable a cache dependency for the Categories table

```
aspnet_regsql -S localhost\sqlexpress -E -d Halloween -ed
aspnet_regsql -S localhost\sqlexpress -E -t Categories -d Halloween -et
```

The <caching> element in a web.config file for SQL cache dependency

```
<system.web>
...
    <caching>
        <sqlCacheDependency enabled="true">
            <databases>
                <add name="Halloween"
                    connectionStringName="HalloweenConnectionString"
                    pollTime="5000" />
            </databases>
        </sqlCacheDependency>
    </caching>

</system.web>
```

A SqlDataSource with a cache dependency

```
<asp:SqlDataSource ID="SqlDataSource1" runat="server"
    ConnectionString="<%$ ConnectionStrings:HalloweenConnectionString %>"
    SelectCommand="SELECT [CategoryID], [LongName] FROM [Categories]
        ORDER BY [LongName]"
    EnableCaching="True" SqlCacheDependency="Halloween:Categories">
</asp:SqlDataSource>
```

Description

- A *SQL cache dependency* lets you specify that cached data should become invalid if the contents of a database table changes.

- To use SQL cache dependency, you must first issue two aspnet_regsql commands to enable cache dependencies for both the database and the table. To run these commands, choose Start→All Programs→Microsoft Visual Studio 2005→Visual Studio Tools→Visual Studio 2005 Command Prompt. Then, use a CD command to switch to c:\Windows\Microsoft.NET\Framework\v2.0.xxxxx, where *xxxxx* is the .NET build number, before issuing the commands.

- You must also add a <caching> element to the <system.web> section of the web.config file. The <caching> element should contain a <databases> element, which in turn contains an <add> element that provides a database name, a connection string, and the frequency in milliseconds with which the database should be checked for changes.

- You can then use the SqlCacheDependency attribute in the SqlDataSource element of an aspx file to specify that cached data should be invalidated if a specified table changes.

Figure 4-16   How to create and use a SQL cache dependency

How to use an XML data source

Besides the new SqlDataSource control, ASP.NET 2.0 provides three other data source controls. The first of these controls is the AccessDataSource control, which you learned about in chapter 2. This control is actually a specialized version of the SqlDataSource control. In fact, the AccessDataSource class inherits the SqlDataSource class. The second data source control is the ObjectDataSource control, which is described in detail in chapter 7.

That leaves the XmlDataSource control, which lets you bind directly to XML data. In recent years, XML data has become a popular alternative to relational databases, especially for web applications. For example, web services commonly use XML to exchange information. And web feeds, which provide frequently updated information such as news stories or blog updates, almost always use XML. The topics that follow introduce you to the use of XML data sources with ASP.NET 2.0.

XML files that contain category and product data

Figure 4-17 presents two simple XML files that contain the same information that's provided by the Categories and Products tables in the Halloween database. Later in this chapter, you'll see a version of the Product List application that uses these XML files rather than the database to display category and product information.

The Categories.xml file consists of two simple elements. The root element, <Categories>, contains one or more <Category> elements. Each <Category> element includes two attributes: ID, which provides the category ID, and LongName, which provides the name of the category. (To keep this data simple, I omitted the short name, but it could be added as a third attribute.)

The Products.xml file has a slightly more complicated structure. Its root element (Products) contains one or more <Product> elements. Then, each <Product> element has four attributes: ID, Category, Name, and ImageFile. In addition, each <Product> element has four child elements: <ShortDescription>, <LongDescription>, <UnitPrice>, and <OnHand>.

Because this structure makes the Products.xml file too long to show in its entirety, this figure just shows the <Product> element for two products. You can assume, however, that the complete Products.xml file contains all of the Product elements.

The Categories.xml file

```
<?xml version="1.0" encoding="utf-8" ?>
<Categories>
  <Category ID="costumes" LongName="Costumes" />
  <Category ID="fx" LongName="Special Effects" />
  <Category ID="masks" LongName="Masks" />
  <Category ID="props" LongName="Props" />
</Categories>
```

A portion of the Products.xml file

```
<?xml version="1.0" encoding="utf-8" ?>
<Products>
  <Product ID="bl01" Category="fx" Name="Black Light (24in)"
    ImageFile="blacklight01.jpg">
    <ShortDescription>24-in Black Light</ShortDescription>
    <LongDescription>
      Create that creepy glow-in-the-dark effect with this powerful black light.
    </LongDescription>
    <UnitPrice>24.99</UnitPrice>
    <OnHand>200</OnHand>
  </Product>
  <Product ID="cat01" Category="props" Name="Deranged Cat"
    ImageFile="cat01.jpg">
    <ShortDescription>20" Ugly Cat</ShortDescription>
    <LongDescription>
      This is one ugly cat.
    </LongDescription>
    <UnitPrice>19.99</UnitPrice>
    <OnHand>45</OnHand>
  </Product>
  .
  .
  .
</Products>
```

Description

- The Categories.xml file contains the data for the categories of products sold by the Halloween store. The root element (<Categories>) contains one or more <Category> elements, each of which has attributes named ID and LongName.

- The Products.xml file contains product data. The root element (<Products>) contains one or more <Product> elements, each of which has attributes named ID, Category, Name, and ImageFile. In addition, each <Product> element contains <ShortDescription>, <LongDescription>, <UnitPrice>, and <OnHand> child elements that provide the short description, long description, unit price, and on-hand data for each product.

- This figure shows only a portion of the complete Products.xml file.

Figure 4-17   XML files that contain category and product data

How to create an XML data source

Figure 4-18 shows how you can create an *XML data source*. As with the SqlDataSource and other data source controls, there are two ways to get started. One is to drag the XmlDataSource control from the Data tab of the Toolbox to the page and proceed from there. The other is to create the control you want to bind the XML data source to, select the Choose Data Source command from that control's smart tag menu, and proceed from there.

The Data Source Configuration Wizard for an XmlDataSource asks for just three items of information. First, you must use the DataFile attribute to provide a path to the XML data. In this example, the XML data comes from a file in the application's App_Data folder, but you can also provide a URL for the XML file location. For example, you can create an XML data source that reads the news from reuters.com by specifying http://www.microsite.reuters.com/rss/topNews as the data file.

Second, you can use the TransformFile attribute to provide an optional XML style sheet file (XST). This lets you change the format of the incoming XML into a format more suitable for your application. For more information, use a web search page to search for "XML style sheets."

Third, you can use the XPath attribute to provide an XPath expression that filters the data in the XML file so only certain elements are retrieved. The most common XPath expression selects the child elements that are immediately beneath the root element, so the root element itself isn't processed. For example, the XPath expression in this figure selects the Category elements. For more information about XPath expressions, see the next figure.

The Configure Data Source dialog box for an XML data source

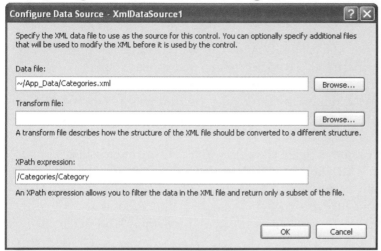

A typical XmlDataSource control

```
<asp:XmlDataSource ID="XmlDataSource1" runat="server"
    DataFile="~/App_Data/Categories.xml"
    XPath="/Categories/Category">
</asp:XmlDataSource>
```

Basic attributes for an XmlDataSource control

Attribute	Description
ID	The ID for the control.
Runat	Must specify "server."
DataFile	The path to the XML file.
TransformFile	The path to an optional XST (XML style sheet file) that's used to transform the contents of the XML data before it's processed by the data source.
XPath	An XPath expression that filters the data used by the data source. For more information about XPath expressions, see figure 4-19.

Description

- To create an *XML data source*, drag the XmlDataSource icon from the Data tab of the Toolbox onto the form, select Configure Data Source from the control's smart tag menu, and proceed from there. Or, use the Choose Data Source command in the smart tag menu of a bindable control to display the dialog box in figure 4-3, select the XML File icon, and proceed from there.

- Use the DataFile attribute to specify the path to the XML data file. The value of this attribute can be a file path that points to a disk file or a URL that points to any source of XML data.

Figure 4-18   How to create an XML data source

How to use XPath expressions for data sources and data binding

Figure 4-19 describes how you can use *XPath expressions* to filter data in an XML data source. You can specify an XPath expression in the Data Source Configuration Wizard when you create an XML data source. You can also change the XPath expression at runtime by setting the data source's XPath property. And finally, you can use the XPath method as an alternative to the Eval method in a data binding expression.

The first set of examples in this figure show how to use XPath expressions in the XPath attribute of an XML data source. The first example selects all of the <Product> elements within the <Products> element. The next two examples show how you can specify an attribute value. In example 2, the <Product> element with an ID attribute equal to "bl01" is selected. In example 3, all of the products with Category attributes equal to "props" are selected.

The second set of examples show how you can use XPath expressions for data binding. Here, the expression in example 1 binds to the <OnHand> element. The expression in example 2 binds to the <UnitPrice> element and uses a formatting expression to format the output. And the expression in example 3 binds to an attribute named Name.

Examples of XPath expressions for selecting data

Example 1: Select all <Product> elements

```
/Products/Product
```

Example 2: Select a specific <Product> element

```
/Products/Product[@ID="bl01"]
```

Example 3: Select all <Product> elements for the props category

```
/Products/Product[@Category="props"]
```

A procedure that sets the XPath property of an XML data source

```
Private Sub SetPath()
    XmlDataSource2.XPath = "/Products/Product[@Category='" _
        & ddlCategory.SelectedValue & "']"
End Sub
```

The syntax of an XPath expression for data binding

```
<%# XPath(XPathString [,FormatString] )%>
```

Examples of XPath expressions for data binding

Example 1: Bind to element content

```
<%# XPath("OnHand") %>
```

Example 2: Bind to element content with formatting

```
<%# XPath("UnitPrice", "{0:c}") %>
```

Example 3: Bind to an attribute value

```
<%# XPath("@Name") %>
```

Description

- An *XPath expression* lets you select elements of an XML file based on either the element name or the value of a specific element or attribute.
- You can use an XPath expression to filter the elements that are processed by the XML data source. To change the XPath expression at runtime, use the XPath property of the data source.
- You can also use an XPath expression for binding by calling the XPath method.
- An XPath expression that begins with a slash starts at the root of the XML document. (The root of the document is a hypothetical document node that's immediately above the document's root element.)
- You can use brackets [ ] to add filter expressions that specify element or attribute values.
- Attribute names begin with the @ symbol.

Figure 4-19   How to use XPath expressions for data sources and data binding

The aspx file for the XML version of the Product List application

To help you understand how this all works together, figure 4-20 shows the aspx file for an XML version of the Product List application that was presented earlier in this chapter. This version of the application looks exactly like the SqlDataSource version, but it gets its data from the XML files listed in figure 4-17 rather than from a SQL Server database. As a result, it uses XmlDataSource controls rather than SqlDataSource controls to retrieve the data that's bound to the drop-down list and Repeater controls.

Because much of this listing is identical to the SqlDataSource version that you saw in figure 4-13, I've highlighted just the differences. First, notice that the drop-down list is bound to an XmlDataSource named XmlDataSource1. This data source specifies the Categories.xml file as its XML file. Also, its XPath attribute is set to /Categories/Category so just the <Category> elements are selected. As a result, the drop-down list will display the LongName attribute of each <Category> element in the Categories.xml file.

The Repeater control requires two changes to work with the XML data source. First, the DataSourceID property specifies the name of the second XmlDataSource control. Second, the templates use XPath expressions instead of Eval methods to get the required data from the XML data source.

Finally, the second XmlDataSource control specifies the Products.xml file as its input file. Its XPath attribute is set to retrieve all of the <Product> elements.

Default.aspx (XmlProductList application)

```
<body>
    <form id="form1" runat="server">
    <div>
        <asp:Image ID="Image1" runat="server"
            ImageUrl="~/Images/banner.jpg" /><br /><br />Choose a category:
        <asp:DropDownList ID="ddlCategory" runat="server"
            AutoPostBack="True" Width="130px" DataSourceID="XmlDataSource1"
            DataTextField="LongName" DataValueField="ID">
        </asp:DropDownList>
        <asp:XmlDataSource ID="XmlDataSource1" runat="server"
            DataFile="~/App_Data/Categories.xml"
            XPath="/Categories/Category">
        </asp:XmlDataSource><br /><br />
        <asp:Repeater ID="Repeater1" runat="server"
            DataSourceID="XmlDataSource2">
            <HeaderTemplate>
                <table cellpadding="0" cellspacing="0">
                  <tr bgcolor="Black" style="color: white">
                    <td width="80"><b>ID</b></td>
                    <td width="150"><b>Product</b></td>
                    <td width="80" align="right"><b>Unit Price</b></td>
                    <td width="80" align="right"><b>On Hand</b></td>
                  </tr>
            </HeaderTemplate>
            <ItemTemplate>
                <tr bgcolor="WhiteSmoke">
                  <td><%# XPath("@ID") %></td>
                  <td><%# XPath("@Name") %></td>
                  <td align="right"><%# XPath("UnitPrice", "{0:c}") %></td>
                  <td align="right"><%# XPath("OnHand") %></td>
                </tr>
            </ItemTemplate>
            <AlternatingItemTemplate>
                <tr bgcolor="Gainsboro">
                  <td><%# XPath("@ID") %></td>
                  <td><%# XPath("@Name") %></td>
                  <td align="right"><%# XPath("UnitPrice", "{0:c}") %></td>
                  <td align="right"><%# XPath("OnHand") %></td>
                </tr>
            </AlternatingItemTemplate>
            <FooterTemplate>
                </table>
            </FooterTemplate></asp:Repeater>
        <asp:XmlDataSource ID="XmlDataSource2" runat="server"
            DataFile="~/App_Data/Products.xml"
            XPath="/Products/Product">
        </asp:XmlDataSource>
    </div>
    </form>
</body>
```

Figure 4-20   The aspx file for the XML version of the Product List application

The code-behind file for the XML version of the Product List application

Figure 4-21 shows the code-behind file for the XML version of the Product List application. As you can see, this file requires just three procedures. First, the Page_Load procedure is executed when the page is loaded. The first time this page is loaded, this procedure calls the DataBind method for the drop-down list to force the drop-down list to bind to the XML file.

Then, the Page_Load procedure calls the SetPath procedure. This procedure sets the XPath property of the second XML data source to filter the products so that just those products whose Category attribute matches the CategoryID value selected in the drop-down list are displayed in the Repeater control. That way, the Repeater control will display the right data the first time the page is requested.

Please note that the Page_Load procedure must bind the drop-down list before it calls the SetPath procedure. If it didn't, the drop-down list wouldn't be populated, so the SelectedValue property that's used by the SetPath procedure wouldn't be set. As a result, the Repeater control would be rendered without any data in it the first time the page is requested.

The ddlCategory_SelectedIndexChanged procedure is called whenever the user changes the selection in the drop-down list. It just calls the SetPath procedure to set the XPath property for the second XML data source to the selected category so only the products in that category will be displayed in the Repeater control.

Default.aspx.vb (XmlProductList application)

```
Partial Class _Default
    Inherits System.Web.UI.Page

    Protected Sub Page_Load(ByVal sender As Object, _
            ByVal e As System.EventArgs) Handles Me.Load
        If Not IsPostBack Then
            ddlCategory.DataBind()
            Me.SetPath()
        End If
    End Sub

    Protected Sub ddlCategory_SelectedIndexChanged( _
            ByVal sender As Object, ByVal e As System.EventArgs) _
            Handles ddlCategory.SelectedIndexChanged
        Me.SetPath()
    End Sub

    Private Sub SetPath()
        XmlDataSource2.XPath = "/Products/Product[@Category='" _
            & ddlCategory.SelectedValue & "']"
    End Sub
End Class
```

Figure 4-21   The code-behind file for the XML version of the Product List application

Perspective

In this chapter, you've learned how to use two of ASP.NET 2.0's new data source controls, SqlDataSource and XmlDataSource. However, we've only scratched the surface of what data sources can do. As you will see, the real power of data sources lies in what they can do in combination with composite data controls like GridView, DetailsView, and FormView. As a result, all this chapter has really done is set the foundation for what you'll learn in chapters 5 and 6.

I also want to point out what many developers feel is a weakness of the data source controls, especially the SqlDataSource control. Because this control can directly specify the SQL statements used to access and update a database, it violates one of the basic principles of good application design. That is, that the code that's used to manage the application's user interface should be separated from the code that's used to access the application's database and perform its business logic. Clearly, when you use the SqlDataSource control, the database code is mixed with the presentation code.

Fortunately, ASP.NET 2.0 provides several ways to minimize or eliminate this problem. First, the SqlDataSource control can use stored procedures rather than actual SQL statements. That way, the SQL statements that access and update the database are placed in the database itself, separate from the presentation code. Second, you can use ObjectDataSource controls rather than SqlDataSource controls. When you use ObjectDataSource controls, you can create and use separate database access classes, so the database access code isn't in the aspx file at all. In chapter 7, you'll learn how that works.

Terms

SQL data source
select parameter
control parameter
Query Builder
diagram pane
grid pane
two-way binding
SQL cache dependency
XML data source
XPath expression

5

How to use the GridView control

In this chapter, you'll learn how to use the new GridView control. This control lets you display the data from a data source in the rows and columns of a table. It includes many advanced features, such as automatic paging and sorting. It lets you update and delete data with minimal Visual Basic code. And its appearance is fully customizable.

An introduction to the GridView control

The GridView control is one of the most powerful user interface controls available in ASP.NET 2.0. The following topics provide a general introduction to this control and compare it with its ASP.NET 1.x predecessor, the DataGrid control.

How the GridView control works

As figure 5-1 shows, the GridView control displays data provided by a data source in a row and column format. In fact, the GridView control renders its data as an HTML table with one Tr element for each row in the data source, and one Td element for each field in the data source.

The GridView control at the top of this figure displays the data from the Categories table of the Halloween database. Here, the first three columns of the control display the data from the three columns of the table.

The other two columns of this control display buttons that the user can click to edit or delete a row. In this example, the user has clicked the Edit button for the masks row, which placed that row into edit mode. In this mode, text boxes are displayed in place of the labels for the short and long name columns, the Edit button is replaced by Update and Cancel buttons, and the Delete button is removed.

The table in this figure lists some of the basic attributes of the GridView control, and the aspx code in this figure is the code that creates the GridView control above it. By default, this control automatically creates columns for each of the fields in the data source. But you'll almost always want to override that behavior by setting the AutoGenerateColumns attribute to False. Then, you can provide a Columns element to define your own columns. The Columns element, in turn, contains the child elements that define the columns to be displayed. In this code example, the Columns element includes three BoundField elements and two CommandField elements. Notice also that the three BoundField elements contain ItemStyle elements that define the styles used to display the data in the columns.

Most of the aspx code for a GridView control is created automatically by Visual Studio when you drag the control from the Toolbox onto the form and when you use the configuration wizard to configure the data source. However, you commonly work with the aspx code directly so you can have more control over the appearance and behavior of this control.

A GridView control that provides for updating a table

ID	Short Name	Long Name		
costumes	Costumes	Costumes	[Edit]	[Delete]
fx	FX	Special Effects	[Edit]	[Delete]
masks	[Masks]	[Masks]	[Update] [Cancel]	
props	Props	Props	[Edit]	[Delete]

The code for the GridView control shown above

```
<asp:GridView ID="GridView1" runat="server" AutoGenerateColumns="False"
        DataSourceID="SqlDataSource1" DataKeyNames="CategoryID" >
    <Columns>
        <asp:BoundField DataField="CategoryID" HeaderText="ID"
                    ReadOnly="True" SortExpression="CategoryID">
            <ItemStyle Width="100px" />
        </asp:BoundField>
        <asp:BoundField DataField="ShortName" HeaderText="Short Name"
                    SortExpression="ShortName">
            <ItemStyle Width="150px" />
        </asp:BoundField>
        <asp:BoundField DataField="LongName" HeaderText="Long Name"
                    SortExpression="LongName">
            <ItemStyle Width="200px" />
        </asp:BoundField>
        <asp:CommandField ButtonType="Button" ShowEditButton="True"
                    CausesValidation="False" />
        <asp:CommandField ButtonType="Button" ShowDeleteButton="True"
                    CausesValidation="False" />
    </Columns>
</asp:GridView>
```

Basic attributes of the GridView control

Element	Description
ID	The ID of the control.
Runat	Must specify "server."
DataSourceID	The ID of the data source to bind to.
DataKeyNames	The names of the primary key fields separated by commas.
AutoGenerateColumns	Specifies whether the control's columns should be automatically generated.
SelectedIndex	Specifies the row to be initially selected.

Description

- The GridView control displays data from a data source in row and column format. The data is rendered as an HTML table.
- To create a GridView control, drag the GridView icon from the Data tab of the Toolbox.
- To bind a GridView control to a data source, use the smart tag menu's Choose Data Source command.

Figure 5-1   How the GridView control works

How the GridView and DataGrid controls compare

As I've already mentioned, the GridView control is a replacement for the ASP.NET 1.x DataGrid control, and the two controls are similar. However, as figure 5-2 points out, there are some important differences between these two controls.

For starters, the GridView control can be bound to the new data source controls. So if you want to take advantage of the data source controls, you'll have to use the GridView control instead of the DataGrid control.

The GridView control also improves several features that were available with the DataGrid control but required a lot of custom code to implement. For example, the GridView control supports in-place editing with little or no code. In contrast, you had to write a lot of code to implement in-place editing with the DataGrid control. Similarly, the GridView control supports sorting and paging with no additional code.

Another important difference is that the GridView control supports more events than were supported by the DataGrid control. In particular, the GridView control raises events both before and after changes are made to the data source. For example, an event named RowUpdating is raised before any changes to a row are committed to the data source, and an event named RowUpdated is raised after the update has been made. This means you can handle these events in your code-behind file to provide customized processing. (For more information about row events, see figure 5-11.)

For compatibility purposes, the DataGrid control is still supported. However, it no longer appears in the Toolbox, and you shouldn't use it in new ASP.NET 2.0 applications.

The GridView and DataGrid controls compared

Feature	DataGrid	GridView
Data binding	Can bind to an ADO.NET dataset, data reader, or any collection that implements IEnumerable.	Can also bind to the new data source controls.
In-place updating	Requires extensive code to place the DataGrid into edit mode and update the underlying dataset.	Requires little code. Usually, the only required code is to handle database update errors.
Sorting	Supports sorting, but requires code to handle the SortCommand event and re-bind the DataGrid based on the new sort order.	Supports sorting with no additional code required.
Paging	Supports paging, but requires code to handle the PageIndexChanged event and re-bind the DataGrid based on the new page index.	Supports paging with no additional code required. In addition, you can completely customize the appearance of the paging controls.
Event model	Events are raised at key points, such as when data is bound or a button is clicked.	New events are fired both before and after database updates occur.

Description

- The GridView control is similar to the ASP.NET 1.x DataGrid control, but provides new features and drastically reduces the amount of code required to implement features such as in-place editing, sorting, and paging.

- The DataGrid control is still available, but isn't present in the Toolbox. You should use the GridView control for all new ASP.NET 2.0 applications.

Figure 5-2   How the GridView and DataGrid controls compare

How to customize the GridView control

The GridView control provides many options that let you customize its appearance and behavior. In the following topics, you'll learn how to define fields, customize the contents and appearance of those fields, enable sorting, and provide for custom paging.

How to define the fields in a GridView control

By default, a GridView control displays one column for each field in the data source. If that's not what you want, you can choose Edit Columns from the control's smart tag menu to display the Fields dialog box shown in figure 5-3. Then, you can use this dialog box to delete fields you don't want to display, change the order of the fields, add additional fields like command buttons, and adjust the properties of the fields.

The Available Fields list box lists all of the available sources for GridView fields, while the Selected Fields list box shows the fields that have already been added to the GridView control. To add an additional field to the GridView control, select the field you want to add in the Available Fields list box and click Add. To change the properties for a field, select the field in the Selected Fields list, and use the Properties list.

The table in this figure lists some of the properties you're most likely to want to change. For example, the HeaderText property determines the text displayed for the field's header row, and the ItemStyle.Width property sets the width for the field.

The Fields dialog box

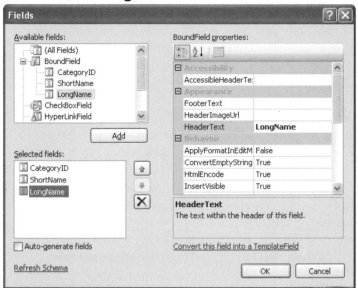

Commonly used field properties

Property	Description
ConvertEmptyStringToNull	If True (the default), empty strings are treated as nulls when data is updated in the database. Set this property to False if the underlying database field doesn't allow nulls.
DataField	For a bound column, the name of the field in the underlying data source that the field should be bound to.
DataFormatString	A format string used to format the data. For example, use {0:c} to format a decimal value as currency.
HeaderText	The text that's displayed in the header row for the field.
ItemStyle.Width	The width of the field.
NullDisplayText	The text that's displayed if the data field is null.
ReadOnly	True if the field is used for display only.
ShowHeader	True if the header should be displayed for this field.

Description

- By default, the GridView control displays one column for each field in the data source.
- To define the fields that you want to display in the GridView control, display the Fields dialog box by selecting the Edit Columns command in the control's smart tag menu.
- You can also add columns by choosing the Add New Column command from the smart tag menu. This technique is illustrated for the DetailsView control in the next chapter, but it works just as well for the GridView control.

Figure 5-3   How to define the fields in a GridView control

Elements used to create and format fields

As figure 5-4 shows, the GridView control uses several different types of child elements to create and format its fields. The first element listed here is the Columns element, which defines the collection of columns that are displayed by the control. This element should be placed between the start and end tags for the GridView control.

Between the start and end tags for the Columns element, you can place any combination of the remaining elements listed in the first table in this figure. For example, to create a column that's bound to a field from the data source, you use the BoundField element.

The second table in this figure lists the various types of style elements you can use with a GridView control to set the formatting used for different parts of the control. Some of these elements are used as child elements of the column elements. For example, the ItemStyle element is used in the code example in this figure to set the width for the Category ID column. The other style elements in this example are used to set the foreground and background colors for different types of rows displayed by the GridView control.

Note that you don't have to create all of these elements yourself. These elements are created automatically when you use the Fields dialog box as described in the previous figure or when you apply an AutoFormat to the GridView control.

Column field elements

Element	Description
<Columns>	The columns that are displayed by a GridView control.
<asp:BoundField>	A field bound to a data source field.
<asp:ButtonField>	A field that displays a button.
<asp:CheckBoxField>	A field that displays a check box.
<asp:CommandField>	A field that contains Select, Edit, Delete, Update, or Cancel buttons.
<asp:HyperlinkField>	A field that displays a hyperlink.
<asp:ImageField>	A field that displays an image.
<asp:TemplateField>	Lets you create a column with custom content.

Style elements

Element	Description
<AlternatingItemStyle>	The style for alternating data rows.
<EditRowStyle>	The style used when the row is being edited.
<EmptyDataRowStyle>	The style used when the data source is empty.
<FooterStyle>	The style used to format the footer row.
<HeaderStyle>	The style used to format the header row.
<ItemStyle>	The style used for an individual field.
<PagerStyle>	The style used to format the GridView's pager row.
<RowStyle>	The style used for data rows.
<SelectedRowStyle>	The style used when the row is selected.

The aspx code for a control that uses field and style elements

```
<asp:GridView ID="GridView1" runat="server" AutoGenerateColumns="False"
    DataKeyNames="CategoryID" DataSourceID="SqlDataSource1">
  <Columns>
    <asp:BoundField DataField="CategoryID" HeaderText="ID" readOnly="true" >
      <ItemStyle Width="100px" />
    </asp:BoundField>
      .
      .
      .
  </Columns>
  <HeaderStyle BackColor="LightGray" ForeColor="White"
            Font-Bold="True" />
  <RowStyle BackColor="White" ForeColor="Black" />
  <SelectedRowStyle BackColor="Gray" ForeColor="White"
                Font-Bold="True" />
  <FooterStyle BackColor="LightGray" ForeColor="Blue" />
  <PagerStyle BackColor="LightGray" ForeColor="Blue"
            HorizontalAlign="Center" />
</asp:GridView>
```

Description

- The GridView control uses several child elements to define the column fields in a row and the styles used to format the data.

Figure 5-4   Elements used to create and format fields

How to enable sorting

The GridView control has a built-in ability to let the user sort the rows based on any or all of the columns displayed by the control. As figure 5-5 shows, all you have to do to enable sorting is set the AllowSorting attribute to True and provide a SortExpression attribute for each column you want to allow sorting for. When sorting is enabled for a column, the user can sort the data by clicking the column header.

Note that a SortExpression attribute is automatically generated for each column that you create with the Fields dialog box. As a result, instead of adding SortExpression attributes for the columns you want to allow sorting for, you must remove the SortExpression attributes for the columns you don't want to allow sorting for. You can use the Fields dialog box to do that by clearing the SortExpression properties. Or, you can use the HTML Editor to delete the SortExpression attributes.

The code example in this figure allows sorting for three of the five fields displayed by the GridView control. For the first two fields, the SortExpression attribute simply duplicates the name of the data source field the column is bound to. If, for example, the user clicks the header of the ProductID column, the data is sorted on the ProductID field.

In some cases, though, you may want the sort expression to be based on two or more columns. To do that, you just use commas to separate the sort field names. In this example, the sort expression for the Category ID column is "CategoryID, Name". That way, any rows with the same Category ID will be sorted by the Name column.

It's important to note that the GridView control doesn't actually do the sorting. Instead, it relies on the underlying data source to sort the data. As a result, sorting will only work if the data source provides for sorting. For a SqlDataSource or AccessDataSource, this means that you need to use the default DataSet mode. This also means that you can't use an XmlDataSource for sorting because it doesn't provide for it.

A GridView control with sorting enabled

ID	Name	Category	Unit Price	On Hand
frankc01	Frankenstein	costumes	$39.99	100
jar01	JarJar	costumes	$59.99	25
martian01	Martian	costumes	$69.99	100
pow01	Austin Powers	costumes	$79.99	25
super01	Superman	costumes	$39.99	100
bl01	Black light (24")	fx	$24.99	200
fog01	Fog Machine	fx	$34.99	100
fogj01	Fog Juice (1qt)	fx	$9.99	500
skullfog01	Skull Fogger	fx	$39.95	50
str01	Mini-strobe	fx	$13.99	200
cool01	Cool Ghoul	masks	$69.99	25
fred01	Freddie	masks	$29.99	50

The aspx code for the control shown above

```
<asp:GridView ID="GridView1" runat="server" AllowSorting="True"
        AutoGenerateColumns="False" DataKeyNames="ProductID"
        DataSourceID="SqlDataSource1">
    <Columns>
        <asp:BoundField DataField="ProductID" HeaderText="ID"
            ReadOnly="True" SortExpression="ProductID">
            <HeaderStyle HorizontalAlign="Left"  />
            <ItemStyle Width="75px" />
        </asp:BoundField>
        <asp:BoundField DataField="Name" HeaderText="Name"
            SortExpression="Name">
            <HeaderStyle HorizontalAlign="Left" />
            <ItemStyle Width="200px" />
        </asp:BoundField>
        <asp:BoundField DataField="CategoryID" HeaderText="Category"
            SortExpression="CategoryID, Name" />
        <asp:BoundField DataField="UnitPrice" DataFormatString="{0:c}"
            HeaderText="Unit Price">
            <ItemStyle Width="85px" HorizontalAlign="Right" />
            <HeaderStyle HorizontalAlign="Right"  />
        </asp:BoundField>
        <asp:BoundField DataField="OnHand" HeaderText="On Hand">
            <ItemStyle Width="85px" HorizontalAlign="Right" />
            <HeaderStyle HorizontalAlign="Right"  />
        </asp:BoundField>
    </Columns>
    <HeaderStyle BackColor="LightGray" />
</asp:GridView>
```

Description

- To enable sorting, set the AllowSorting attribute to True. Then, add a SortExpression attribute to each column you want to allow sorting for.

- For sorting to work, the data source must be set to DataSet mode.

Figure 5-5   How to enable sorting

How to enable paging

Paging refers to the ability of the GridView control to display bound data one page at a time, along with paging controls that let the user select which page of data to display next. Although the old DataGrid control provided some basic support for paging, you had to write a lot of code to support it. But as figure 5-6 shows, the GridView control lets you enable paging simply by setting AllowPaging to True.

When you enable paging, an additional row is displayed at the bottom of the GridView control to display the paging controls. If you want, you can provide a PagerStyle element to control how this row is formatted. In the example in this figure, the PagerStyle element specifies that the background color for the pager row should be light gray and the pager controls should be horizontally centered.

Unlike sorting, the GridView control doesn't delegate the paging function to the underlying data source. However, paging works only for data sources that are in DataSet mode, which means that you can't use paging with an XmlDataSource control.

A GridView control with paging enabled

ID	Name	Category	Unit Price	On Hand
arm01	Severed Arm	props	$19.99	200
bl01	Black light (24")	fx	$24.99	200
cat01	Deranged Cat	props	$19.99	45
cool01	Cool Ghoul	masks	$69.99	25
fog01	Fog Machine	fx	$34.99	100
fogj01	Fog Juice (1qt)	fx	$9.99	500
frankc01	Frankenstein	costumes	$39.99	100
fred01	Freddie	masks	$29.99	50
head01	Shrunken Head	props	$29.99	100
head02	Severed Head	props	$29.99	100

1 2 3

The code for the GridView control shown above

```
<asp:GridView ID="GridView1" runat="server" AllowPaging="True"
    AutoGenerateColumns="False" DataKeyNames="ProductID"
    DataSourceID="SqlDataSource1">
    <Columns>
        <asp:BoundField DataField="ProductID" HeaderText="ID"
            ReadOnly="True">
            <HeaderStyle HorizontalAlign="Left" />
            <ItemStyle Width="75px" />
        </asp:BoundField>
        <asp:BoundField DataField="Name" HeaderText="Name">
            <HeaderStyle HorizontalAlign="Left" />
            <ItemStyle Width="200px" />
        </asp:BoundField>
        <asp:BoundField DataField="CategoryID" HeaderText="Category" />
        <asp:BoundField DataField="UnitPrice" DataFormatString="{0:c}"
            HeaderText="Unit Price">
            <ItemStyle Width="85px" HorizontalAlign="Right" />
            <HeaderStyle HorizontalAlign="Right" />
        </asp:BoundField>
        <asp:BoundField DataField="OnHand" HeaderText="On Hand">
            <ItemStyle Width="85px" HorizontalAlign="Right" />
            <HeaderStyle HorizontalAlign="Right" />
        </asp:BoundField>
    </Columns>
    <HeaderStyle BackColor="LightGray" />
    <PagerStyle BackColor="LightGray" HorizontalAlign="Center" />
</asp:GridView>
```

Description

- To enable *paging*, set the AllowPaging attribute to True. Then, add a PagerStyle element to define the appearance of the pager controls. You can also add a PagerSettings element as described in the next figure to customize the way paging works.

- For paging to work, the data source must be set to DataSet mode.

Figure 5-6   How to enable paging

How to customize paging

Figure 5-7 shows how you can customize the way paging works with a GridView control. To start, the two attributes in the first table let you enable paging and specify the number of data rows that will be displayed on each page. The default setting for the second attribute is 10, which is an appropriate value for most GridView controls.

You can also customize the appearance of the pager area by including a PagerSettings element between the start and end tags of a GridView control. Then, you can use the attributes in the second table for the customization. The most important of these attributes is Mode, which determines what types of controls are displayed in the pager area. If, for example, you set the mode to NextPrevious, only Next and Previous buttons will be displayed.

If you specify Numeric or NumericFirstLast for the Mode attribute, individual page numbers are displayed in the pager area so the user can go directly to any of the listed pages. You can then use the PageButtonCount attribute to specify how many of these page numbers should be displayed in the pager area. Note that if you specify NumericFirstLast, the first and last buttons are displayed only if the total number of pages exceeds the value you specify for the PageButtonCount attribute and the first or last page number isn't displayed.

The remaining attributes in this table let you control the text or image that's displayed for the various buttons. By default, the values for the First, Previous, Next, and Last buttons use less-than and greater-than signs, but the example shows how you can change the text for these buttons.

Attributes of the GridView element that affect paging

Attribute	Description
AllowPaging	Set to True to enable paging.
PageSize	Specifies the number of rows to display on each page.

Attributes of the PagerSettings element

Attribute	Description
FirstPageImageUrl	The URL of an image file used to display the first page button.
FirstPageText	The text to display for the first page button. The default is <<, which displays as <<.
LastPageImageUrl	The URL of an image file used to display the last page button.
LastPageText	The text to display for the last page button. The default is >>, which displays as >>.
Mode	Controls what buttons are displayed in the pager area. You can specify NextPrevious, NextPreviousFirstLast, Numeric, or NumericFirstLast.
NextPageImageUrl	The URL of an image file used to display the next page button.
NextPageText	The text to display for the next page button. The default is >, which displays as >.
PageButtonCount	The number of page buttons to display if the Mode is set to Numeric or NumericFirstLast.
PreviousPageImageUrl	The URL of an image file used to display the previous page button.
PreviousPageText	The text to display for the previous page button. The default is <, which displays as <.
Position	The location of the pager area. You can specify Top, Bottom, or TopAndBottom.
Visible	Set to False to hide the pager controls.

Example

A PagerSettings element

```
<PagerSettings Mode="NextPreviousFirstLast"
            NextPageText="Next" PreviousPageText="Prev"
            FirstPageText="First" LastPageText="Last" />
```

The resulting pager area

First Prev Next Last

Description

- You can use the PageSize attribute of the GridView element to specify the number of pages to display on each page.
- You can also add a PagerSettings element to control the appearance of the pager area.

Figure 5-7   How to customize paging

A list application that uses a GridView control

Now that you've learned the basics of working with a GridView control, the following topics present the design and code for an application that uses a GridView control to list the rows of a data source. As you'll see, this application provides for sorting and paging and doesn't require a single line of Visual Basic code.

The Product List application

Figure 5-8 presents the Product List application. Here, the data from the Products table of the Halloween database is displayed in a GridView control. The data is displayed 8 rows at a time, and numeric page buttons are displayed at the bottom of the GridView control so the user can navigate from page to page. In addition, the user can sort the data by clicking the column headings for the ID, Name, and Category columns.

The Product List application

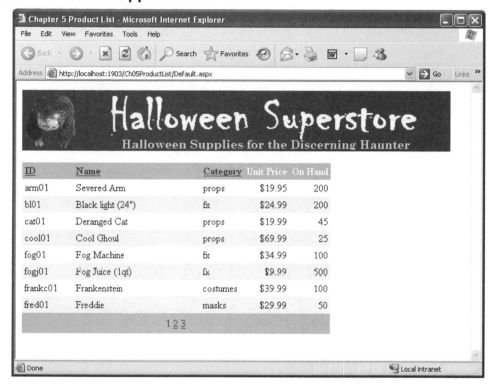

Description

- The Product List application uses a GridView control to display a list of all the products in the Products table. The GridView control is bound to a SqlDataSource control that works in DataSet mode.

- Sorting is enabled for the first three columns. That way, the user can sort the product data by ID, Name, or Category.

- Paging is enabled with 8 products displayed on each page.

Figure 5-8   The Product List application

The aspx file

Figure 5-9 shows the aspx code for this application, which is stored in the Default.aspx file. Because no code-behind procedures are needed, the code-behind file isn't shown.

Because you've already been introduced to all of the code in the aspx file, you should be able to follow it without much trouble. So I'll just point out a few highlights.

The Columns element contains five BoundField child elements that define the fields displayed by the grid. All five columns are retrieved from the SQL data source. The first three of these BoundField elements include the SortExpression attribute to allow sorting. The ItemStyle elements for the first two fields set the width of the fields, and the ItemStyle elements for the last two fields set the alignment to right. Otherwise, the default formatting is used for the five fields.

A PagerStyle element is used to center the pager buttons in the pager area. Then, a PagerSettings element is used to specify the types of pager controls to display.

Finally, the SqlDataSource control uses this Select statement to retrieve data from the Halloween database:

```
SELECT [ProductID], [Name], [CategoryID],
    [UnitPrice], [OnHand] FROM [Products] ORDER BY [ProductID]
```

Because the DataSourceMode attribute isn't set, the default of DataSet mode is used, which means that sorting and paging can be enabled.

The Default.aspx file

```
<%@ Page Language="VB" AutoEventWireup="false" CodeFile="Default.aspx.vb"
Inherits="_Default" %>

<!DOCTYPE html PUBLIC "-//W3C//DTD XHTML 1.1//EN"
"http://www.w3.org/TR/xhtml11/DTD/xhtml11.dtd">

<html xmlns="http://www.w3.org/1999/xhtml" >
<head runat="server">
    <title>Chapter 5 Product List</title>
</head>
<body>
    <form id="form1" runat="server">
    <div>
        <asp:Image ID="Image1" runat="server" ImageUrl="~/Images/banner.jpg" />
        <br /><br />
        <asp:GridView ID="GridView1" runat="server"
            AllowSorting="True"
            AllowPaging="True" PageSize="8"
            DataKeyNames="ProductID" DataSourceID="SqlDataSource1"
            AutoGenerateColumns="False"
            CellPadding="4" GridLines="None" ForeColor="Black">
            <Columns>
                <asp:BoundField DataField="ProductID" HeaderText="ID"
                    ReadOnly="True" SortExpression="ProductID">
                    <HeaderStyle HorizontalAlign="Left" />
                    <ItemStyle Width="75px" />
                </asp:BoundField>
                <asp:BoundField DataField="Name" HeaderText="Name"
                    SortExpression="Name">
                    <HeaderStyle HorizontalAlign="Left" />
                    <ItemStyle Width="200px" />
                </asp:BoundField>
                <asp:BoundField DataField="CategoryID" HeaderText="Category"
                    SortExpression="CategoryID, Name" />
                <asp:BoundField DataField="UnitPrice" DataFormatString="{0:c}"
                    HeaderText="Unit Price">
                    <ItemStyle HorizontalAlign="Right" />
                </asp:BoundField>
                <asp:BoundField DataField="OnHand" HeaderText="On Hand">
                    <ItemStyle HorizontalAlign="Right" />
                </asp:BoundField>
            </Columns>
            <HeaderStyle BackColor="Silver" Font-Bold="True"
                ForeColor="White" />
            <RowStyle BackColor="White" ForeColor="Black" />
            <AlternatingRowStyle BackColor="WhiteSmoke" ForeColor="Black" />
            <FooterStyle BackColor="Silver" Font-Bold="True" ForeColor="White" />
            <PagerStyle BackColor="Silver" ForeColor="Blue"
                HorizontalAlign="Center" />
            <PagerSettings Mode="NumericFirstLast" />
        </asp:GridView>
        <asp:SqlDataSource ID="SqlDataSource1" runat="server"
            ConnectionString="<%$ ConnectionStrings:HalloweenConnection %>"
            SelectCommand="SELECT [ProductID], [Name], [CategoryID],
                [UnitPrice], [OnHand] FROM [Products] ORDER BY [ProductID]">
        </asp:SqlDataSource>
    </div>
    </form>
</body>
</html>
```

Figure 5-9   The aspx file of the Product List application

How to update GridView data

Another impressive feature of the GridView control is its ability to update data in the underlying data source with little additional code. Before you can set that up, though, you must configure the data source with Update, Delete, and Insert statements, as described in the last chapter. Once you've done that, you can set up a GridView control so it calls the Update and Delete statements, which you'll learn how to do next.

How to work with command fields

A *command field* is a GridView column that contains one or more command buttons. As figure 5-10 shows, there are five different command buttons that you can include in each row of a GridView control. Please note, however, that the Update and Cancel buttons are displayed only when a user clicks the Edit button to edit a row.

When the user clicks a Delete button, the GridView control calls the data source control's Delete method, which deletes the selected row from the underlying database. Then, the GridView control redisplays the data without the deleted row.

When the user clicks the Edit button, the GridView control places the selected row in *edit mode*. In this mode, the labels used to display each bound field are replaced by text boxes so the user can enter changes. Also, the row is formatted using the style attributes provided by the EditRowStyle element. Finally, the Edit button itself is replaced by Update and Cancel buttons. Then, if the user clicks the Update button, any changes are sent back to the data source, which in turn updates the underlying database. But if the user clicks Cancel, any changes made by the user are discarded and the original values are redisplayed.

The Select button lets the user select a row. Then, the selected row is displayed with the settings in the SelectedRowStyle element. Also, the SelectedIndex and SelectedRow properties are updated to reflect the selected row. The Select button is most often used in combination with the FormView or DetailsView controls to create pages that show the details for an item selected from the GridView control. You'll learn how this works in chapter 6.

The two tables in this figure show the attributes of a CommandField element. For instance, you can set the ShowEditButton attribute to True to display an Edit button in a command field. And you can use the EditText attribute to set the text that's displayed on that button.

Although a single command field can display more than one button, it's common to create separate command fields for Select, Edit, and Delete buttons. Also, because the Update and Cancel buttons will appear together in a command field that displays an Edit button when the user clicks the Edit button, it's uncommon to create separate command fields that display these buttons.

As a general rule, you should set the CausesValidation attribute to False for most command fields. If you don't, validation will be triggered when the user clicks a command button. However, because the Select, Edit, Cancel, and Delete

The Fields dialog box for working with a command field

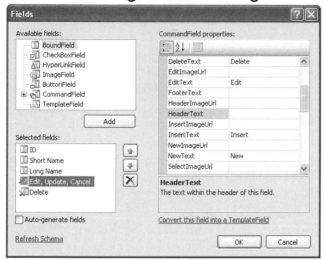

Typical code to define command fields

```
<asp:CommandField ButtonType="Button" ShowEditButton="True"
    CausesValidation="False" />
<asp:CommandField ButtonType="Button" ShowDeleteButton="True"
    CausesValidation="False" />
```

Attributes of the CommandField element

Attribute	Explanation
ButtonType	Specifies the type of button displayed in the command field. Valid options are Button, Link, or Image.
CausesValidation	Specifics whether validation should be performed if the user clicks the button.
ValidationGroup	Specifies the name of the group to be validated if CausesValidation is True.

Attributes that show buttons and set the text or images they display

Button	Show	Text	Image
Cancel	ShowCancelButton	CancelText	CancelImage
Delete	ShowDeleteButton	DeleteText	DeleteImage
Edit	ShowEditButton	EditText	EditImage
Select	ShowSelectButton	SelectText	SelectImage
Update	n/a	UpdateText	UpdateImage

Description

- A *command field* adds buttons that let the user edit, delete, or select data in a GridView control.

- The CommandField element also provides for an Insert button, but the GridView control doesn't directly support insert operations.

Figure 5-10   How to work with command fields

buttons don't cause any input data to be sent to the server, there's no reason to invoke data validation. On the other hand, you can use validation controls with the Update button, and you'll learn how to do that with template controls later in this chapter.

How to use events raised by the GridView control

Although the GridView control provides many features automatically, you still must write some code to handle such things as data validation, database exceptions, and concurrency errors. As figure 5-11 shows, most of this code will be in the form of event handlers that respond to one or more of the events raised by the GridView control.

If you look at the list of events in the table in this figure, you'll see that several of them come in pairs, with one event raised before an action is taken and the other after the action completes. For example, when the user clicks the Delete button in a GridView row, two events are raised. The RowDeleting event is raised before the row is deleted, and the RowDeleted event is raised after the row has been deleted.

The most common reason to handle the before-action events is to provide data validation. For example, when the user clicks the Update button, you can handle the RowUpdating event to make sure the user has entered correct data. If not, you can set the e argument's Cancel property to True to cancel the update.

In contrast, the after-action events give you an opportunity to make sure the database operation completed successfully. In most applications, you should test for two conditions. First, you should check for any database exceptions by checking the Exception property of the e argument. If this property isn't nothing, an exception has occurred and you can notify the user with an appropriate error message.

Second, if optimistic concurrency is used, you should check to see if a concurrency violation has occurred. To do that, you can check the AffectedRows property of the e argument. If this property is zero, which means no rows have been changed, you can assume a concurrency error has occurred and notify the user with an appropriate error message.

When you use optimistic concurrency, remember that the WHERE clause in an UPDATE or DELETE statement tries to find a record that has the same values as when the record was originally retrieved. If that record can't be found, which means that another user has updated one of the fields, the update or delete operation never takes place so no records are affected.

When you try to update a record, one of the most common exceptions is caused by an attempt to store a null value in a database field that doesn't allow null values. This occurs when the user doesn't enter a value in one of the fields that's being updated. In this case, you can display an appropriate error message and set the e argument's ExceptionHandled property to True to suppress further processing of the exception. You can also set the KeepInEditMode property to True to leave the GridView control in edit mode. This is illustrated by the event procedure that's coded in this figure.

Events raised by the GridView control

Event	Raised when ...
RowCancelingEdit	The Cancel button of a row in edit mode is clicked.
RowDataBound	Data binding completes for a row.
RowDeleted	A row has been deleted.
RowDeleting	A row is about to be deleted.
RowEditing	A row is about to be edited.
RowUpdated	A row has been updated.
RowUpdating	A row is about to be updated.
SelectedIndexChanged	A row has been selected.
SelectedIndexChanging	A row is about to be selected.

An event handler for the RowUpdated event

```
Protected Sub GridView1_RowUpdated(ByVal sender As Object,_
        ByVal e As System.Web.UI.WebControls.GridViewUpdatedEventArgs) _
        Handles GridView1.RowUpdated
    If e.Exception IsNot Nothing Then
        lblError.Text = "Invalid data. Please correct and try again."
        e.ExceptionHandled = True
        e.KeepInEditMode = True
    ElseIf e.AffectedRows = 0 Then
        lblError.Text = "Another user updated that category. " _
                    & "Please try again."
    End If
End Sub
```

Description

- The GridView control raises various events that can be handled when data is updated.

- The RowUpdating and RowDeleting events are often used for data validation. You can cancel the update or delete operation by setting the e argument's Cancel property to True.

- You can handle the RowUpdated and RowDeleted events to ensure that the row was successfully updated or deleted.

- To determine if a SQL exception has occurred, check the Exception property of the e argument. If an exception has occurred, the most likely cause is a null value for a field that doesn't accept nulls. To suppress the exception, you can set the ExceptionHandled property to True. And to keep the control in edit mode, you can set the KeepInEditMode property to True.

- To determine how many rows were updated or deleted, check the AffectedRows property of the e argument. If this property is zero and an exception has *not* been thrown, the most likely cause is a concurrency error.

Figure 5-11   How to use events raised by the GridView control

How to insert a row in a GridView control

You may have noticed that although the GridView control lets you update and delete records, it has no provision for inserting new rows. When you use the GridView control in concert with a FormView or DetailsView control, though, you can provide for insert operations with a minimum of code. You'll learn how to do that in chapter 6. Another alternative is to create a page that lets you insert data into a GridView control by using the techniques described in figure 5-12.

To provide for insertions, you must first create a set of input controls such as text boxes in which the user can enter data for the row to be inserted. Next, you must provide a button that the user can click to start the insertion. Then, in the event handler for this button, you can set the insert parameter values to the values entered by the user and call the data source's Insert method to add the new record.

This is illustrated by the code in this figure. Here, if the insertion is successful, the contents of the text boxes are cleared. But if an exception is thrown, an error message is displayed. This message indicates that the new record has a primary key that's already in use, which is the most common cause of an exception during an insert operation.

Methods and properties of the SqlDataSource class for inserting rows

Method	Description
Insert	Executes the Insert command defined for the data source.

Property	Description
InsertCommand	The Insert command to be executed.
InsertParameters["name"].DefaultValue	The value of a parameter used by the Insert command.

Code that uses a SqlDataSource control to insert a row

```
Protected Sub btnAdd_Click(ByVal sender As Object, _
        ByVal e As System.EventArgs) Handles btnAdd.Click
    SqlDataSource1.InsertParameters("CategoryID").DefaultValue _
        = txtID.Text
    SqlDataSource1.InsertParameters("ShortName").DefaultValue _
        = txtShortName.Text
    SqlDataSource1.InsertParameters("LongName").DefaultValue _
        = txtLongName.Text
    Try
        SqlDataSource1.Insert()
        txtID.Text = ""
        txtShortName.Text = ""
        txtLongName.Text = ""
    Catch ex As Exception
        lblError.Text = "A category with that ID already exists."
    End Try
End Sub
```

Description

- The GridView control doesn't support insert operations, but you can use the GridView's data source to insert rows into the database. When you do, the new row will automatically be shown in the GridView control.

- To provide for inserts, the page should include controls such as text boxes for the user to enter data and a button that the user can click to insert the data.

- To use a SqlDataSource control to insert a database row, first set the DefaultValue property of each insert parameter to the value you want to insert. Then, call the Insert method.

- The Insert method may throw a SqlException if a SQL error occurs. The most likely cause of the exception is a primary key constraint violation.

Figure 5-12   How to insert a row in a GridView control

A maintenance application that uses a GridView control

To give you a better idea of how you can use a GridView control to update, delete, and insert data, the following topics present an application that maintains the Categories table in the Halloween database.

The Category Maintenance application

Figure 5-13 introduces you to the Category Maintenance application. It lets the user update, delete, and insert rows in the Categories table of the Halloween database. Here, a GridView control is used to display the rows in the Categories database along with Edit and Delete buttons. In this figure, the user has clicked the Edit button for the third data row, placing that row in edit mode.

Beneath the GridView control, three text boxes let the user enter data for a new category. Then, if the user clicks the Add New Category button, the data entered in these text boxes is used to add a category record to the database. Although it isn't apparent from this figure, required field validators are used for each text box. Also, there's a label control beneath the GridView control that's used to display error messages when an update, delete, or insert operation fails.

The Category Maintenance application

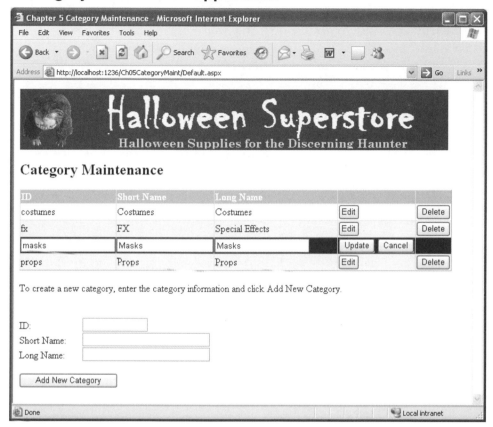

Description

- The Category Maintenance application uses a GridView control to let the user update or delete rows in the Categories table.

- To edit a category, the user clicks the Edit button. This places the GridView control into edit mode. The user can then change the ID, Short Name, or Long Name and click Update. Or, the user can click Cancel to leave edit mode.

- To delete a category, the user clicks the Delete button.

- The user can add a category to the table by entering data into the text boxes beneath the GridView control and clicking the Add New Category button.

- If the user attempts to update or add a record with a field that is blank, an error message is displayed. In addition, an error message is displayed if the user tries to insert a category with an ID that's already in use.

Figure 5-13   The Category Maintenance application

The aspx file

Figure 5-14 shows the complete aspx listing for this application. Since most of this code has already been introduced, I'll just point out a few highlights.

Part 1 of this figure shows the aspx code for the GridView control. It specifies that the data source is SqlDataSource1 and the primary key for the data is CategoryID. The five columns defined in the Columns element display the three fields from the data source, an Edit button, and a Delete button.

Part 2 of this figure shows the SqlDataSource control. Note that this data source specifies CompareAllValues for the ConflictDetection attribute, which means that optimistic concurrency checking will be done. As a result, these are the statements that are used to retrieve, delete, update, and insert category rows:

```
SELECT [CategoryID], [ShortName], [LongName]
    FROM [Categories]

DELETE FROM [Categories]
    WHERE [CategoryID] = @original_CategoryID
      AND [ShortName] = @original_ShortName
      AND [LongName] = @original_LongName

UPDATE [Categories]
    SET [ShortName] = @ShortName,
        [LongName] = @LongName
    WHERE [CategoryID] = @original_CategoryID
      AND [ShortName] = @original_ShortName
      AND [LongName] = @original_LongName

INSERT INTO [Categories]
    ([CategoryID], [ShortName], [LongName])
    VALUES (@CategoryID, @ShortName, @LongName)"
```

Here, the WHERE clauses implement optimistic concurrency by looking for records that have the values originally retrieved. Then, the DeleteParameters, UpdateParameters, and InsertParameters elements in the aspx code define the parameters used by these statements.

Finally, part 3 of this figure shows the input controls used to enter the data for a new category. As you can see, each text box is validated by a required field validator that makes sure the user has entered data for the field. Then, when the user clicks the Add New Category button, the btnAdd_Click procedure is called to insert the category row.

The Default.aspx file   **Page 1**

```
<%@ Page Language="VB" AutoEventWireup="false" CodeFile="Default.aspx.vb"
Inherits="_Default" %>

<!DOCTYPE html PUBLIC "-//W3C//DTD XHTML 1.1//EN"
"http://www.w3.org/TR/xhtml11/DTD/xhtml11.dtd">

<html xmlns="http://www.w3.org/1999/xhtml" >
<head runat="server">
    <title>Chapter 5 Category Maintenance</title>
</head>
<body>
    <form id="form1" runat="server">
    <div>
        <asp:Image ID="Image1" runat="server" ImageUrl="~/Images/banner.jpg" />
        <br /><br />
        <h2>Category Maintenance</h2>
        <asp:GridView ID="GridView1" runat="server"
            AutoGenerateColumns="False" DataKeyNames="CategoryID"
            DataSourceID="SqlDataSource1" ForeColor="Black">
            <Columns>
                <asp:BoundField DataField="CategoryID" HeaderText="ID">
                    <HeaderStyle HorizontalAlign="Left" />
                    <ItemStyle Width="100px" />
                </asp:BoundField>
                <asp:BoundField DataField="ShortName" HeaderText="Short Name">
                    <HeaderStyle HorizontalAlign="Left" />
                    <ItemStyle Width="150px" />
                </asp:BoundField>
                <asp:BoundField DataField="LongName" HeaderText="Long Name">
                    <HeaderStyle HorizontalAlign="Left" />
                    <ItemStyle Width="200px" />
                </asp:BoundField>
                <asp:CommandField ButtonType="Button" ShowEditButton="True"
                    CausesValidation="False" />
                <asp:CommandField ButtonType="Button" ShowDeleteButton="True"
                    CausesValidation="False" />
            </Columns>
            <HeaderStyle BackColor="Silver" Font-Bold="True"
                ForeColor="White" />
            <RowStyle BackColor="White" ForeColor="Black" />
            <AlternatingRowStyle BackColor="WhiteSmoke" ForeColor="Black" />
            <EditRowStyle BackColor="Blue" ForeColor="White" />
        </asp:GridView>
```

Notes

- The GridView control is bound to the data source SqlDataSource1.
- The Columns element includes child elements that define five columns. Three are for the bound fields, the other two for the command buttons.

Figure 5-14   The aspx file of the Category Maintenance application (part 1 of 3)

The Default.aspx file   **Page 2**

```
<asp:SqlDataSource ID="SqlDataSource1" runat="server"
    ConflictDetection="CompareAllValues"
    ConnectionString="<%$ ConnectionStrings:HalloweenConnection %>"
    SelectCommand="SELECT [CategoryID], [ShortName], [LongName]
        FROM [Categories]"
    DeleteCommand="DELETE FROM [Categories]
        WHERE [CategoryID] = @original_CategoryID
          AND [ShortName] = @original_ShortName
          AND [LongName] = @original_LongName"
    UpdateCommand="UPDATE [Categories] SET [ShortName] = @ShortName,
        [LongName] = @LongName
        WHERE [CategoryID] = @original_CategoryID
          AND [ShortName] = @original_ShortName
          AND [LongName] = @original_LongName"
    InsertCommand="INSERT INTO [Categories]
        ([CategoryID], [ShortName], [LongName])
        VALUES (@CategoryID, @ShortName, @LongName)">
    <DeleteParameters>
        <asp:Parameter Name="original_CategoryID" Type="String" />
        <asp:Parameter Name="original_ShortName" Type="String" />
        <asp:Parameter Name="original_LongName" Type="String" />
    </DeleteParameters>
    <UpdateParameters>
        <asp:Parameter Name="ShortName" Type="String" />
        <asp:Parameter Name="LongName" Type="String" />
        <asp:Parameter Name="original_CategoryID" Type="String" />
        <asp:Parameter Name="original_ShortName" Type="String" />
        <asp:Parameter Name="original_LongName" Type="String" />
    </UpdateParameters>
    <InsertParameters>
        <asp:Parameter Name="CategoryID" Type="String" />
        <asp:Parameter Name="ShortName" Type="String" />
        <asp:Parameter Name="LongName" Type="String" />
    </InsertParameters>
</asp:SqlDataSource><br />
```

Notes

- The SELECT statement retrieves all rows in the Categories table.
- The WHERE clauses in the DELETE and UPDATE statements provide for optimistic concurrency.

Figure 5-14   The aspx file of the Category Maintenance application (part 2 of 3)

The Default.aspx file   **Page 3**

```
            To create a new category, enter the category information
            and click Add New Category.<br />
            <asp:Label ID="lblError" runat="server" EnableViewState="False"
                ForeColor="Red"></asp:Label><br /><br />
            <asp:Label ID="Label1" runat="server" BorderStyle="None" Text="ID:"
                Width="100px"></asp:Label>
            <asp:TextBox ID="txtID" runat="server" EnableViewState="False"
                Width="100px"></asp:TextBox>
            <asp:RequiredFieldValidator ID="RequiredFieldValidator1" runat="server"
                ControlToValidate="txtID" ErrorMessage="ID is a required field.">
            </asp:RequiredFieldValidator><br />
            <asp:Label ID="Label2" runat="server" BorderStyle="None"
                Text="Short Name:" Width="100px"></asp:Label>
            <asp:TextBox ID="txtShortName" runat="server" EnableViewState="False"
                Width="200px"></asp:TextBox>
            <asp:RequiredFieldValidator ID="RequiredFieldValidator2" runat="server"
                ControlToValidate="txtShortName"
                ErrorMessage="Short Name is a required field.">
            </asp:RequiredFieldValidator><br />
            <asp:Label ID="Label3" runat="server" BorderStyle="None"
                Text="Long Name:" Width="100px"></asp:Label>
            <asp:TextBox ID="txtLongName" runat="server" EnableViewState="False"
                Width="200px"></asp:TextBox>
            <asp:RequiredFieldValidator ID="RequiredFieldValidator3" runat="server"
                ControlToValidate="txtLongName"
                ErrorMessage="Long Name is a required field.">
            </asp:RequiredFieldValidator><br /><br />
            <asp:Button ID="btnAdd" runat="server" Text="Add New Category" />
        </div>
        </form>
</body>
</html>
```

Notes

- The text boxes are used to enter data for a new row.
- The required field validators ensure that the user enters data in each field of a new record.

Figure 5-14   The aspx file of the Category Maintenance application (part 3 of 3)

The code-behind file

Although it would be nice if you could create a robust database application without writing any Visual Basic code, you must still write code to insert data into a GridView control and to catch and handle any database or concurrency errors that might occur. Figure 5-15 shows this code for the Category Maintenance application.

As you can see, this code-behind file consists of just three procedures. The first, btnAdd_Click, sets the value of the three insert parameters to the values entered by the user. Then, it calls the Insert method of the data source control. If an exception is thrown, an appropriate error message is displayed.

The second procedure, GridView1_RowUpdated, is called after a row has been updated. This procedure checks the Exception property of the e argument to determine if an exception has been thrown. If so, an error message is displayed, the ExceptionHandled property is set to True to suppress the exception, and the KeepInEditMode property is set to True to leave the GridView control in edit mode. If an exception hasn't occurred, the e argument's AffectedRows property is checked. If it's zero, it means that a concurrency error has occurred and an appropriate message is displayed.

The third procedure, GridView1_RowDeleted, is called after a row has been deleted. This procedure checks the e argument's AffectedRows property and displays an appropriate error message if a concurrency error has occurred.

The Default.aspx.vb file

```
Partial Class _Default
    Inherits System.Web.UI.Page

    Protected Sub btnAdd_Click(ByVal sender As Object, _
            ByVal e As System.EventArgs) Handles btnAdd.Click
        SqlDataSource1.InsertParameters("CategoryID").DefaultValue _
            = txtID.Text
        SqlDataSource1.InsertParameters("ShortName").DefaultValue _
            = txtShortName.Text
        SqlDataSource1.InsertParameters("LongName").DefaultValue _
            = txtLongName.Text
        Try
            SqlDataSource1.Insert()
            txtID.Text = ""
            txtShortName.Text = ""
            txtLongName.Text = ""
        Catch ex As Exception
            lblError.Text = "A category with that ID already exists."
        End Try
    End Sub

    Protected Sub GridView1_RowUpdated(ByVal sender As Object, _
            ByVal e As System.Web.UI.WebControls.GridViewUpdatedEventArgs) _
            Handles GridView1.RowUpdated
        If e.Exception IsNot Nothing Then
            lblError.Text = "Invalid data. Please correct and try again."
            e.ExceptionHandled = True
            e.KeepInEditMode = True
        ElseIf e.AffectedRows = 0 Then
            lblError.Text = "Another user updated that category. " _
                            & "Please try again."
        End If
    End Sub

    Protected Sub GridView1_RowDeleted(ByVal sender As Object, _
            ByVal e As System.Web.UI.WebControls.GridViewDeletedEventArgs) _
            Handles GridView1.RowDeleted
        If e.AffectedRows = 0 Then
            lblError.Text = "Another user updated that category. " _
                            & "Please try again."
        End If
    End Sub
End Class
```

Figure 5-15   The code-behind file of the Category Maintenance application

How to work with template fields

Although using bound fields is a convenient way to include bound data in a GridView control, the most flexible way is to use template fields. A *template field* is simply a field that provides one or more templates that are used to render the column. You can include anything you want in these templates, including labels or text boxes, data binding expressions, and validation controls. In fact, including validation controls for editable GridView controls is one of the main reasons for using template fields.

How to create template fields

Figure 5-16 shows how to create template fields. The easiest way to do that is to first create a regular bound field. Then, click the Convert This Field into a TemplateField link in the Fields dialog box. This changes the BoundField element to a TemplateField element and, more importantly, generates ItemTemplate and EditItemTemplate elements that include labels and text boxes with appropriate binding expressions. In particular, each EditItemTemplate element includes a text box that uses the new Bind method to implement two-way binding (please see figure 4-12 for more information about this method).

Once you've converted the bound field to a template, you can edit the template to add any additional elements you want to include, such as validation controls. In the code example in this figure, you can see that I added a RequiredFieldValidator control to the EditItem template for the CategoryID field. That way, the user must enter data into the txtGridCategory text box. I also changed the names of the label and the text field generated for the EditItem template from their defaults (Label1 and TextBox1) to lblGridCategory and txtGridCategory.

You can also edit the templates from Design view. To do that, choose Edit Templates from the GridView control's smart tag menu. This places the control in template editing mode, as shown at the top of this figure. In this mode, you can use the smart tag menu to select the template you want to edit. Then, you can use the Web Forms Designer to add controls and other elements to the template. To leave template editing mode, you choose End Template Editing from the smart tag menu.

How to edit templates

GridView templates

Element	Description
<AlternatingItemTemplate>	The template used for alternate rows.
<EditItemTemplate>	The template used when the row is being edited.
<FooterTemplate>	The template used for the footer row.
<HeaderTemplate>	The template used for the header row.
<ItemTemplate>	The template used for an individual field.

A template field that includes a validation control

```
<asp:TemplateField HeaderText="ID">
    <ItemTemplate>
        <asp:Label ID="lblGridCategory" runat="server"
            Text='<%# Bind("CategoryID") %>'></asp:Label>
    </ItemTemplate>
    <EditItemTemplate>
        <asp:TextBox ID="txtGridCategory" runat="server"
            Text='<%# Bind("CategoryID") %>'></asp:TextBox>
        <asp:RequiredFieldValidator runat="server"
            ID="RequiredFieldValidator4"
            ControlToValidate="txtGridCategory"
            ErrorMessage="ID is a required field."
            ValidationGroup="Edit">*</asp:RequiredFieldValidator>
    </EditItemTemplate>
    <HeaderStyle HorizontalAlign="Left" />
    <ItemStyle Width="100px" />
</asp:TemplateField>
```

Description

- *Template fields* provide more control over the appearance of the columns in a GridView control. A common reason for using template fields is to add validation controls.

- To create a template field, first use the Fields dialog box to create a bound field. Then, click the Convert This Field into a TemplateField link.

- To edit a template, choose Edit Templates from the smart tag menu for the GridView control. Then, select the template you want to edit in the smart tag menu and edit the template by adding text or other controls. You may also want to change the names of the labels and text fields that were generated when you converted to a template field. When you're finished, choose End Template Editing in the smart tag menu.

Figure 5-16   How to create template fields

The template version of the Category Maintenance application

Figure 5-17 shows a version of the Category Maintenance application that uses templates instead of bound fields in the GridView control. Then, each edit template includes a required field validator. In addition, the page uses a validation summary control to display any error messages that are generated by the required field validators.

The aspx code for the template version

Figure 5-18 shows the aspx code for the template version of the Category Maintenance application. Because most of this file is similar to the file shown in figure 5-14, this figure shows only the portions that are different. In particular, it shows the code for the GridView control and the ValidationSummary control. Because you've already been introduced to most of this code, I'll just point out a few highlights.

First, the GridView control uses template fields that include required field validators to validate the text box input fields. What's interesting here is that I used the ValidationGroup attribute of the new *validation group* feature of ASP.NET 2.0 to assign each validator to a group named Edit. Then, in the CommandField element for the Edit button, the CausesValidation attribute is set to True and the ValidationGroup attribute is set to Edit. As a result, just the validators that belong to the Edit group will be invoked when this button is clicked.

Second, the ErrorMessage attribute of each of the Edit validators provides the error message that's displayed in the ValidationSummary control. For this control, you can see that the ValidationGroup is set to Edit so the right messages will be displayed. Note, however, that the text that's displayed by a validator when an error is detected is the content that appears between the validator's start and end tags. In this case, the text for each validator is simply an asterisk so an asterisk will appear to the right of each field in the GridView control. If you look closely at the screen in the last figure, you can see that these asterisks are displayed in white on the dark column dividers.

Please note that there is one other difference between this version of the application and the previous version that isn't shown in this figure. Because this version uses a validation group for the validators in the GridView control, it must also use a validation group for the validators that are outside of the GridView control. As a result, the three validators for the text boxes as well as the Add New Category button all have a ValidationGroup attribute that assigns them to the New group.

The Category Maintenance application with template fields

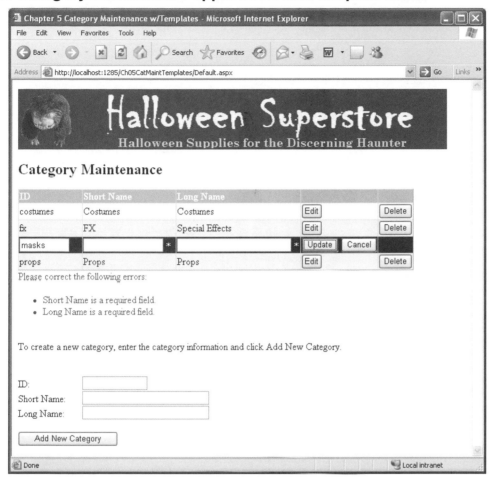

Description

- This version of the Category Maintenance application uses template fields in the GridView control, and the edit template for each field includes a required field validator.

- A ValidationSummary control is used to display the error messages generated by the required field validators.

Figure 5-17   The template version of the Category Maintenance application

The Default.aspx file   Page 1

```
<asp:GridView ID="GridView1" runat="server"
    AutoGenerateColumns="False" DataKeyNames="CategoryID"
    DataSourceID="SqlDataSource1" ForeColor="Black">
    <Columns>
        <asp:TemplateField HeaderText="ID">
            <ItemTemplate>
                <asp:Label id="lblGridCategory" runat="server"
                    Text='<%# Bind("CategoryID") %>'></asp:Label>
            </ItemTemplate>
            <EditItemTemplate>
                <asp:TextBox ID="txtGridCategory" runat="server"
                    width = "75px" Text='<%# Bind("CategoryID") %>'>
                </asp:TextBox>
                <asp:RequiredFieldValidator
                    ID="RequiredFieldValidator4" runat="server"
                    ControlToValidate="txtGridCategory"
                    ErrorMessage="ID is a required field."
                    ValidationGroup="Edit">*</asp:RequiredFieldValidator>
                </EditItemTemplate>
            <HeaderStyle HorizontalAlign="Left" />
            <ItemStyle Width="100px" />
        </asp:TemplateField>
        <asp:TemplateField HeaderText="Short Name">
            <ItemTemplate>
                <asp:Label ID="lblGridShortName" runat="server"
                    Text='<%# Bind("ShortName") %>'></asp:Label>
            </ItemTemplate>
            <EditItemTemplate>
                <asp:TextBox ID="txtGridShortName" runat="server"
                    width = "125px" Text='<%# Bind("ShortName") %>'>
                </asp:TextBox>
                <asp:RequiredFieldValidator
                    ID="RequiredFieldValidator5" runat="server"
                    ControlToValidate="txtGridShortName"
                    ErrorMessage="Short Name is a required field."
                    ValidationGroup="Edit">*</asp:RequiredFieldValidator>
            </EditItemTemplate>
            <HeaderStyle HorizontalAlign="Left" />
            <ItemStyle Width="150px" />
        </asp:TemplateField>
```

Figure 5-18   The aspx code for the template version of the Category Maintenance application (part 1 of 2)

The Default.aspx file   **Page 2**

```
        <asp:TemplateField HeaderText="Long Name">
            <ItemTemplate>
                <asp:Label ID="lblGridLongName" runat="server"
                    Text='<%# Bind("LongName") %>'></asp:Label>
            </ItemTemplate>
            <EditItemTemplate>
                <asp:TextBox ID="txtGridLongName" runat="server"
                    width = "180px" Text='<%# Bind("LongName") %>'>
                </asp:TextBox>
                <asp:RequiredFieldValidator
                    ID="RequiredFieldValidator6" runat="server"
                    ControlToValidate="txtGridLongName"
                    ErrorMessage="Long Name is a required field."
                    ValidationGroup="Edit">*</asp:RequiredFieldValidator>
            </EditItemTemplate>
            <HeaderStyle HorizontalAlign="Left" />
            <ItemStyle Width="200px" />
        </asp:TemplateField>
        <asp:CommandField ButtonType="Button" ShowEditButton="True"
            CausesValidation="True" ValidationGroup="Edit" />
        <asp:CommandField ButtonType="Button" ShowDeleteButton="True"
            CausesValidation="False" />
    </Columns>
    <HeaderStyle BackColor="Silver" Font-Bold="True"
        ForeColor="White" />
    <RowStyle BackColor="White" ForeColor="Black" />
    <AlternatingRowStyle BackColor="WhiteSmoke" ForeColor="Black" />
    <EditRowStyle BackColor="Blue" ForeColor="White" />
</asp:GridView>
  .
  .
  .
<asp:ValidationSummary ID="ValidationSummary1" runat="server"
    HeaderText="Please correct the following errors:"
    ValidationGroup="Edit"/>
  .
  .
  .
```

Description

- This figure shows the aspx code for just the GridView control and the ValidationSummary control. The other elements are identical to the listing in figure 5-13.

- The three template fields include required field validators, which are assigned to a *validation group* named Edit. This group is also referenced in the code for the Edit button and the ValidationSummary control so only the validators in this group are included. Validation groups like this one are a new feature of ASP.NET 2.0.

Figure 5-18   The aspx code for the template version of the Category Maintenance application (part 2 of 2)

Perspective

The GridView control is widely heralded as one of the most significant improvements of ASP.NET 2.0, and rightfully so. This control is ideal for any application that displays a list of items retrieved from a database, and nearly all applications have that need. For instance, the Shopping Cart application of chapter 2 can easily be implemented with a GridView control if the database is enhanced so it supports shopping cart items. The GridView control is also ideal for displaying search results, such as product searches for an online catalog or document searches in an online customer support site.

In spite of the promise of code-free programming, though, you still have to write and test code if you want to create bulletproof applications. In particular, you must often write code to deal with data validation, exception handling, and concurrency errors. Even so, the amount of code you must write is much less than what you had to write with the DataGrid control of ASP.NET 1.x.

In the next chapter, you'll build on your knowledge of the GridView control by learning how to use it in combination with the new FormView and DetailsView controls. Both are designed to display the details for an item that's selected from a GridView control or a list control. And the combination of a GridView control and a FormView or DetailsView control can be powerful.

Terms

paging
command field
edit mode
template field
validation group

6

How to use the DetailsView and FormView controls

In this chapter, you'll learn how to use the new DetailsView and FormView controls. Although both of these controls are designed to work with the GridView control to display the details of the item selected in that control, they can also be used on their own or in combination with other types of list controls such as drop-down lists or list boxes.

How to use the DetailsView control

The following topics present the basics of working with the DetailsView control. Note that much of what you'll learn in these topics applies to the FormView control as well.

An introduction to the DetailsView control

As figure 6-1 shows, the DetailsView control is designed to display the data for a single item of a data source. To use this control effectively, you must provide some way for the user to select which data item to display. The most common way to do that is to use the DetailsView control in combination with another control such as a GridView control or a drop-down list. At the top of this figure, you can see how the DetailsView control works with a drop-down list, and you'll see how it works with a GridView control later in this chapter.

Alternatively, you can enable paging for the DetailsView control to allow the user to select the data item to be displayed. Then, a row of paging controls appears at the bottom of the DetailsView control to allow the user to select the item. You'll learn how this works in figure 6-4.

As the code example in this figure shows, you use the DataSourceID attribute to specify the data source that a DetailsView control should be bound to. Then, the Fields element contains a set of child elements that define the individual fields to be displayed by the DetailsView control. This is similar to the way the Columns element for a GridView control works. To edit the fields in the Fields element, you can choose Edit Fields from the smart tag menu of the DetailsView control.

A DetailsView control can be displayed in one of three modes. In ReadOnly mode, the data for the current data source row is displayed but can't be modified. In Edit mode, the user can modify the data for the current row. And in Insert mode, the user can enter data that will be inserted into the data source as a new row.

A DetailsView control that displays data for a selected product

Choose a product:	Skull Fogger

Product ID:	skullfog01
Name:	Skull Fogger
Short Description:	2,800 Cubic Foot Fogger
Long Description:	This fogger puts out a whopping 2,800 cubic feet of fog per minute. Comes with a 10-foot remote control.
Category ID:	fx
Image File:	skullfog01.jpg
Unit Price:	39.9500
On Hand:	50

The code for the DetailsView control shown above

```
<asp:DetailsView ID="DetailsView1" runat="server" AutoGenerateRows="False"
    DataKeyNames="ProductID" DataSourceID="SqlDataSource2"
    ForeColor="Black" GridLines="Horizontal" Width="400px">
    <Fields>
        <asp:BoundField DataField="ProductID" HeaderText="Product ID:" >
            <HeaderStyle Width="150 px" />
            <ItemStyle Width="250px" />
        </asp:BoundField>
        <asp:BoundField DataField="Name" HeaderText="Name:" />
        <asp:BoundField DataField="ShortDescription"
            HeaderText="Short Description:"/>
        <asp:BoundField DataField="LongDescription"
            HeaderText="Long Description:"/>
        <asp:BoundField DataField="CategoryID" HeaderText="Category ID:"/>
        <asp:BoundField DataField="ImageFile" HeaderText="Image File:"/>
        <asp:BoundField DataField="UnitPrice" HeaderText="Unit Price:"/>
        <asp:BoundField DataField="OnHand" HeaderText="On Hand:"/>
    </Fields>
</asp:DetailsView>
```

Three modes of the DetailsView control

Mode	Description
ReadOnly	Used to display an item from the data source.
Edit	Used to edit an item in the data source.
Insert	Used to insert a new item into a data source.

Description

- The DetailsView control displays data for a single row of a data source. It is usually used in combination with a drop-down list or GridView control that is used to select the item to be displayed.
- The DetailsView element includes a Fields element that contains a BoundField element for each field retrieved from the data source.
- You can edit the fields collection by choosing Edit Fields from the smart tag menu of a DetailsView control.

Figure 6-1   An introduction to the DetailsView control

Attributes and child elements for the DetailsView control

The tables in figure 6-2 list the attributes and child elements you can use to declare a DetailsView control. The first table lists the attributes you're most likely to use for this control. You can use the DataKeyNames attribute to list the names of the primary key fields for the data source. And you'll usually set the AutoGenerateRows attribute to False to prevent the DetailsView control from automatically generating data fields. That way, you can define the data fields you want to appear in the DetailsView control by using the Fields element.

By the way, there are many other attributes you can use on the DetailsView element to specify the control's layout and formatting. For example, you can include attributes like Height, Width, BackColor, and ForeColor. To see all of the attributes that are available, you can use the HTML Editor's IntelliSense feature.

The second table in this figure lists the child elements that you can use between the start and end tags of the DetailsView element. Most of these elements provide styles and templates that control the formatting for the different parts of the DetailsView control.

The Fields element can contain any of the child elements listed in the third table of this figure. These elements describe the individual data fields that are displayed by the DetailsView control. You can use the HTML Editor to create these elements manually. You can use the Fields dialog box as described in the previous chapter by choosing Edit Fields from the smart tag menu. Or, you can use the Add Field dialog box as described in the next figure.

Although this figure doesn't show it, the child elements in the third table can themselves include child elements to specify formatting information. For example, you can include HeaderStyle and ItemStyle as child elements of a BoundField element to control the formatting for the header and item sections of a bound field. Here again, you can use the HTML Editor's IntelliSense feature to see what child elements are available and what attributes they support.

DetailsView control attributes

Attribute	Description
AllowPaging	Set to True to allow paging.
AutoGenerateRows	If True, a row is automatically generated for each field in the data source. If False, you must define the rows in the Fields element.
DataKeyNames	A list of field names that form the primary key for the data source.
DataSourceID	The ID of the data source to bind the DetailsView control to.
DefaultMode	Sets the initial mode of the DetailsView control. Valid options are Edit, Insert, or ReadOnly.
ID	The ID of this control.
Runat	Must specify "server".

DetailsView child elements

Element	Description
AlternatingItemStyle	The style used for alternate rows.
CommandRowStyle	The style used for command rows.
EditRowStyle	The style used for data rows in Edit mode.
EmptyDataRowStyle	The style used for data rows when the data source is empty.
EmptyDataTemplate	The template used when the data source is empty.
Fields	The fields that are displayed by a DetailsView control.
FooterStyle	The style used for the footer row.
FooterTemplate	The template used for the footer row.
HeaderStyle	The style used for the header row.
HeaderTemplate	The template used for the header row.
InsertRowStyle	The style used for data rows in Insert mode.
PagerSettings	The settings used to control the pager row.
PagerStyle	The style used for the pager row.
PagerTemplate	The template used for the pager row.
RowStyle	The style used for data rows in ReadOnly mode.

Fields child elements

Element	Description
BoundField	A field bound to a data source field.
ButtonField	A field that displays a button.
CheckBoxField	A field that displays a check box.
CommandField	A field that contains command buttons.
HyperlinkField	A field that displays a hyperlink.
ImageField	A field that displays an image.
TemplateField	A column with custom content.

Figure 6-2   Attributes and child elements for the DetailsView control

How to add fields to a DetailsView control

Figure 6-3 shows how to add fields to a DetailsView control by using the Add Field dialog box. To display this dialog box, choose Add Field from the control's smart tag menu. Next, select the type of field you want to add. Then, set any other settings required by the field. If, for example, you select BoundField as the field type, you'll need to enter the text to display as a heading and identify the data source field you want to bind to.

Each time you use the Add Field dialog box, a child element is added to the Fields element of the DetailsView control. As you can see in the code example in this figure, each BoundField element includes a ReadOnly attribute that's set to True as well as a SortExpression attribute. However, since the sort expression is only meaningful if you enable paging, you can safely delete this attribute if you're not using paging.

Remember that by default the DetailsView control automatically generates a bound field for each field in the data source. You can prevent that, though, by setting the AutoGenerateRows attribute to False. Then, you'll have complete control over the fields that are displayed in the DetailsView control.

The Add Field dialog box

Code generated by the Add Field dialog box

```
<asp:BoundField DataField="ProductID" HeaderText="Product ID:"
    ReadOnly="True" SortExpression="ProductID" />
```

Description

- The DetailsView control supports the same field types as the GridView control.

- You can add a field to a DetailsView control by choosing Add Field from the smart tag menu. Then, you can use the Add Field dialog box to add the field.

- You can also choose Edit Fields from the smart tag menu to bring up the Fields dialog box that's shown in figure 5-3 of chapter 5.

- By default, the DetailsView control will automatically generate a field for each field in the data source. To prevent this, set the AutoGenerateRows attribute for the control to False.

Figure 6-3   How to add fields to a DetailsView control

How to enable paging

Like the GridView control, the DetailsView control supports paging. As figure 6-4 shows, a row of paging controls is displayed at the bottom of the DetailsView control when you set the AllowPaging attribute to True. Then, you can specify the paging mode by including a PagerSettings element, and you can include PagerStyle and PagerTemplate elements to specify the appearance of the pager controls.

Note that if the data source contains more than a few dozen items, paging isn't a practical way to provide for navigation. In most cases, then, a DetailsView control is associated with a list control that is used to select the item to be displayed. You'll learn how to create pages that work this way in the next figure.

A DetailsView control that allows paging

ProductID	bl01
Name	Black light (24")
Short Description:	24" black light
Long Description:	Create that creepy glow-in-the-dark effect with this powerful black light.
Category ID:	fx
Image File:	blacklight01.jpg
Unit Price:	24.9900
On Hand:	200

<< < > >>

The code for the DetailsView control shown above

```
<asp:DetailsView ID="DetailsView1" runat="server" AllowPaging="True"
    AutoGenerateRows="False"
    DataKeyNames="ProductID" DataSourceID="SqlDataSource1"
    Height="50px" Width="420px">
    <PagerSettings Mode="NextPreviousFirstLast" />
    <Fields>
        <asp:BoundField DataField="ProductID" HeaderText="ProductID"
            ReadOnly="True">
            <HeaderStyle Width="150px" />
            <ItemStyle Width="300px" />
        </asp:BoundField>
        <asp:BoundField DataField="Name" HeaderText="Name:" />
        <asp:BoundField DataField="ShortDescription"
            HeaderText="Short Description:" />
        <asp:BoundField DataField="LongDescription"
            HeaderText="Long Description:" />
        <asp:BoundField DataField="CategoryID"
            HeaderText="Category ID: " />
        <asp:BoundField DataField="ImageFile" HeaderText="Image File:" />
        <asp:BoundField DataField="UnitPrice" HeaderText="Unit Price:" />
        <asp:BoundField DataField="OnHand" HeaderText="On Hand:" />
    </Fields>
</asp:DetailsView>
```

Description

- The DetailsView control supports paging. Then, you can move from one item to the next by using the paging controls. This works much the same as it does for a GridView control, except that data from only one row is displayed at a time.

- For more information about paging, please refer to figure 5-7 in chapter 5.

Figure 6-4   How to enable paging

How to create a Master/Detail page

As figure 6-5 shows, a *Master/Detail page* is a page that displays a list of data items from a data source along with the details for one of the items selected from the list. The list of items can be displayed by any list control that allows the user to select an item, including a drop-down list or a GridView control. Then, you can use a DetailsView control to display the details for the selected item. The page shown in figure 6-1 is an example of a Master/Detail page in which the master list is displayed as a drop-down list and a DetailsView control is used to display the details for the selected item.

A Master/Detail page typically uses two data sources. The first retrieves the items to be displayed by the list control. For efficiency's sake, this data source should retrieve only the data columns necessary to display the list. For example, the data source for the drop-down list in figure 6-1 only needs to retrieve the ProductName and ProductID columns from the Products table in the Halloween database.

The second data source provides the data for the selected item. It usually uses a parameter to specify which row should be retrieved from the database. In the example in this figure, the data source uses a parameter that's bound to the drop-down list. That way, this data source automatically retrieves the data for the product that's selected by the drop-down list.

A Master/Detail page must contain:

- A list control, such as a drop-down list or a GridView control, that lets the user choose an item to display.
- A data source that retrieves all of the items to be displayed in the list. The list control should be bound to this data source.
- A DetailsView control that displays data for the item selected by the user.
- A data source that retrieves the data for the item selected by the user. The DetailsView control should be bound to this data source. To retrieve the selected item, this data source can use a parameter that's bound to the SelectedValue property of the list control.

A SqlDataSource control with a parameter that's bound to a list box

```
<asp:SqlDataSource ID="SqlDataSource2" runat="server"
    ConnectionString="<%$ ConnectionStrings:HalloweenConnection %>"
    SelectCommand="SELECT [ProductID], [Name], [ShortDescription],
        [LongDescription], [CategoryID], [ImageFile], [UnitPrice], [OnHand]
        FROM [Products]
        WHERE ([ProductID] = @ProductID)">
    <SelectParameters>
        <asp:ControlParameter ControlID="ddlProducts" Name="ProductID"
            PropertyName="SelectedValue" Type="String" />
    </SelectParameters>
</asp:SqlDataSource>
```

Description

- A *Master/Detail page* is a page that displays a list of items from a database along with the details of one item from the list. The DetailsView control is often used to display the details portion of a Master/Detail page.
- The list portion of a Master/Detail page can be displayed by any list control, including a drop-down list or a GridView control.
- A Master/Detail page usually includes two data sources, one for the master list and the other for the DetailsView control.

Figure 6-5   How to create a Master/Detail page

How to update DetailsView data

Besides displaying data for a specific item from a data source, you can also use a DetailsView control to edit, insert, and delete items. You'll learn how to do that in the following topics.

An introduction to command buttons

Much like the GridView control, the DetailsView control uses command buttons to let the user edit and delete data. Thus, the DetailsView control provides Edit, Delete, Update, and Cancel buttons. In addition, the DetailsView control lets the user insert data so it provides for two more buttons. The New button places the DetailsView control into Insert mode, and the Insert button accepts the data entered by the user and writes it to the data source. These command buttons are summarized in figure 6-6.

There are two ways to provide the command buttons for a DetailsView control. The easiest way is to use the AutoGenerate*xxx*Button attributes, listed in the second table and illustrated in the code example. However, when you use these attributes, you have no control over the appearance of the buttons. For that, you must use command fields as described in the next figure.

A DetailsView control with automatically generated command buttons

Product ID:	arm01
Name:	Severed Arm
Short Description:	Bloody Severed Arm
Long Description:	A severed arm, complete with protruding bones and lots of blood.
Category ID:	props
Image File:	arm01.jpg
Unit Price:	$19.95
On Hand:	200

Edit Delete New

Command buttons

Button	Description
Edit	Places the DetailsView control in Edit mode.
Delete	Deletes the current item and leaves the DetailsView control in ReadOnly mode.
New	Places the DetailsView control in Insert mode.
Update	Displayed only in Edit mode. Updates the data source, then returns to ReadOnly mode.
Insert	Displayed only in Insert mode. Inserts the data, then returns to ReadOnly mode.
Cancel	Displayed in Edit or Insert mode. Cancels the operation and returns to ReadOnly mode.

Attributes that generate command buttons

Attribute	Description
AutoGenerateDeleteButton	Generates a Delete button.
AutoGenerateEditButton	Generates an Edit button.
AutoGenerateInsertButton	Generates a New button.

A DetailsView element that automatically generates command buttons

```
<asp:DetailsView ID="DetailsView1" runat="server"
    DataSourceID="SqlDataSource2" DataKeyNames="ProductID"
    AutoGenerateRows="False"
    AutoGenerateDeleteButton="True"
    AutoGenerateEditButton="True"
    AutoGenerateInsertButton="True">
```

Description

- The DetailsView control supports six different command buttons.
- You can use the AutoGenerateDeleteButton, AutoGenerateEditButton, and AutoGenerateInsertButton attributes to automatically generate command buttons.
- To customize command button appearance, use command fields instead of automatically generated buttons, as described in the next figure.

Figure 6-6   An introduction to command buttons

How to add command buttons

Like the GridView control, the DetailsView control lets you use CommandField elements to specify the command buttons that should be displayed by the control. One way to do that is to use the Add Field dialog box shown in figure 6-7 to add a command field to a DetailsView control. Of course, you can also use the Edit Fields dialog box to add command fields, or you can use the HTML Editor to code the CommandField element manually.

When you select CommandField as the field type, four check boxes appear that let you select which command buttons you want to show in the command field. In addition, a drop-down list lets you choose whether the command buttons should be displayed as buttons or hyperlinks.

Note that the CommandField element includes attributes that let you specify the text or image to be displayed and whether the button causes validation. For more information about using these attributes, please refer back to chapter 5.

The Add Field dialog box for adding a command field

Code generated by the above dialog box

```
<asp:CommandField ButtonType="Button"
    ShowDeleteButton="True"
    ShowEditButton="True"
    ShowInsertButton="True" />
```

Description

- You can add command buttons to a DetailsView control to let the user update, insert, and delete data.

- The command buttons for a DetailsView control are similar to the command buttons for a GridView control. However, the DetailsView control doesn't provide a Select button, and it does provide New and Insert buttons. For more information about command buttons, please refer to figure 5-10 in chapter 5.

- To display the Add Field dialog box, choose Add Fields from the smart tag menu of the DetailsView control.

Figure 6-7   How to add command buttons

How to handle DetailsView events

Figure 6-8 lists the events that are raised by the DetailsView control. As you can see, these events are similar to the events raised by the GridView control. Most of these events come in pairs, one that's raised before an operation occurs, and another that's raised after the operation completes. For example, the ItemDeleting event is raised before an item is deleted, and the ItemDeleted event is raised after an item has been deleted.

As with the GridView control, the most common reason to handle the before events for the DetailsView control is to provide data validation. For example, when the user clicks the Update button, you can handle the ItemUpdating event to make sure the user has entered correct data. Then, you can set the e argument's Cancel property to True if the user hasn't entered correct data. This cancels the update.

The after-action events let you check that database operations have completed successfully. To do that, you need to check for two types of errors. First, you should check for database exceptions by testing the Exception property of the e argument. If it isn't nothing, a database exception has occurred. Then, you should display an appropriate error message to let the user know about the problem.

If the data source uses optimistic concurrency, you should also check to make sure there hasn't been a concurrency error. You can do that by testing the AffectedRows property of the e argument. If a concurrency error has occurred, this property will be set to zero meaning that no rows have been changed. Then, you can display an appropriate error message.

The ItemUpdated event shown in this figure ends by calling the DataBind method for the drop-down list control. This is necessary because view state is enabled for this control. As a result, this control will continue to display the old data unless you call its DataBind method to refresh its data. If view state were disabled for this control, the DataBind call wouldn't be necessary.

Note that there is a bug in the way ASP.NET 2.0 data sources handle optimistic concurrency when null values are involved. For more information about this bug and how to work around it, see the next figure.

Events raised by the DetailsView control

Event	Description
ItemCommand	Raised when a button is clicked.
ItemCreated	Raised when an item is created.
DataBound	Raised when data binding completes for an item.
ItemDeleted	Raised when an item has been deleted.
ItemDeleting	Raised when an item is about to be deleted.
ItemInserted	Raised when an item has been inserted.
ItemInserting	Raised when an item is about to be inserted.
ItemUpdated	Raised when an item has been updated.
ItemUpdating	Raised when an item is about to be updated.
PageIndexChanged	Raised when the index of the displayed item has changed.
PageIndexChanging	Raised when the index of the displayed item is about to change.

An event handler for the ItemUpdated event

```
Protected Sub DetailsView1_ItemUpdated(ByVal sender As Object, _
        ByVal e As System.Web.UI.WebControls.DetailsViewUpdatedEventArgs) _
        Handles DetailsView1.ItemUpdated
    If e.Exception IsNot Nothing Then
        lblError.Text = "Invalid data. Please correct and try again."
        e.ExceptionHandled = True
    ElseIf e.AffectedRows = 0 Then
        lblError.Text = "Another user has updated that product. " _
            & "Please try again."
    End If
    ddlProducts.DataBind()
End Sub
```

Description

- Like the GridView control, the DetailsView control raises events that can be handled when data is updated. At the minimum, you should use these events to test for database exceptions and concurrency errors.

- To determine if a SQL exception has occurred, test the Exception property of the e argument. If an exception has occurred, you can set the ExceptionHandled property to True to suppress the exception. You can also set the KeepInEditMode property to True to keep the DetailsView control in edit mode.

- If the AffectedRows property of the e argument is zero and an exception has not been thrown, a concurrency error has probably occurred.

- If the DetailsView control is used on a Master/Detail page, you should call the DataBind method of the master list control after a successful insert, update, or delete.

Figure 6-8   How to handle DetailsView events

How to fix the optimistic concurrency bug

Optimistic concurrency works by using a Where clause that compares each column in the database row with the values saved when the row was originally retrieved. If that row can't be found, it means that another user has updated the row and changed one of the columns. Then, the row isn't updated or deleted.

Unfortunately, there's a bug in the way ASP.NET 2.0 generates the Where clauses for columns that allow nulls. This bug, along with a workaround for it, is described in figure 6-9. In short, the problem is that when a database column allows nulls, the comparisons generated for the Where clauses don't work. That's because SQL defines the result of an equal comparison between a null and a null as False. (Since a null represents an unknown value, no value–even another null–can be considered equal to a null.)

The Halloween database illustrates this problem because it allows nulls for the ImageFile column in the Products table. But look at the Where clause that's generated for the first Delete statement in this figure:

```
[ImageFile] = @original_ImageFile
```

In this case, if the original value of the ImageFile column is null, this comparison will never test True, so the row will never be deleted.

The workaround to this bug is to modify the generated Delete and Update statements for any database table that allows nulls in any of its columns. For the ImageFile column, you can modify the Delete statement so it looks like this:

```
( [ImageFile] = @original_ImageFile
  OR [ImageFile] IS NULL AND @original_ImageFile IS NULL )
```

Then, the comparison will test true if both the ImageFile column and the @original_ImageFile parameter are null.

A generated Delete statement that handles concurrency errors

```
DELETE FROM [Products]
      WHERE [ProductID] = @original_ProductID
        AND [Name] = @original_Name
        AND [ShortDescription] = @original_ShortDescription
        AND [LongDescription] = @original_LongDescription
        AND [CategoryID] = @original_CategoryID
        AND [ImageFile] = @original_ImageFile
        AND [UnitPrice] = @original_UnitPrice
        AND [OnHand] = @original_OnHand"
```

How to modify the Delete statement for a column that allows nulls

```
DELETE FROM [Products]
      WHERE [ProductID] = @original_ProductID
        AND [Name] = @original_Name
        AND [ShortDescription] = @original_ShortDescription
        AND [LongDescription] = @original_LongDescription
        AND [CategoryID] = @original_CategoryID
        AND ( [ImageFile] = @original_ImageFile
         OR ImageFile IS NULL AND @original_ImageFile IS NULL )
        AND [UnitPrice] = @original_UnitPrice
        AND [OnHand] = @original_OnHand"
```

Description

- When you select optimistic concurrency for a data source in the Data Source Configuration Wizard, the wizard adds code to the Update and Delete statements that prevents concurrency errors.

- Unfortunately, the generated code for Update and Delete statements doesn't work properly for database columns that allow nulls because two nulls aren't treated as equal.

- To fix this error, you can edit the Update and Delete statements so they include an Is Null test for each column that allows nulls.

Known bug

- This is a known bug in the last Beta release for ASP.NET 2.0. However, it probably won't be fixed in the actual release of this product.

Figure 6-9   How to fix the optimistic concurrency bug

The Product Maintenance application

The following topics present an application that uses a GridView and a DetailsView control in a Master/Detail page to maintain the Products table in the Halloween database. As you'll see, this application uses most of the features of the DetailsView control that have been presented in this chapter.

The operation of the application

Figure 6-10 shows the operation of the Product Maintenance application. This application uses a GridView control to list the product records on the left side of the page. This control uses paging to allow the user to scroll through the entire Products table.

When the user clicks the Select button for a product, the details for that product are displayed in the DetailsView control on the right side of the page. Then, the user can use the Edit or Delete buttons to edit or delete the selected product. The user can also click the New button to insert a new product.

The aspx file

Figure 6-11 shows the complete Default.aspx file for the Product Maintenance application. This file uses a table to control the overall layout of the page. In part 1, you can see the GridView control that displays the products as well as the data source for this control. Notice that the SelectedIndex attribute of the GridView control is set to 0. That way, the information for the first product will be displayed in the DetailsView control when the page is first displayed.

The DetailsView control is shown in parts 2 and 3 of the listing. Here, the DetailsView element includes the attributes that control the overall appearance of the control. I generated most of these attributes by applying an AutoFormat to the DetailsView control, then editing the attributes to change the colors. You can also see that the AutoFormat added HeaderStyle and ItemStyle attributes to each of the BoundField elements in the Fields collection. And you can see that I added a CommandField element to provide the Edit, Delete, and Insert buttons.

Note that this DetailsView control doesn't provide for data validation for insert and update operations. Instead, it relies on the data source to throw database exceptions if the user tries to enter incorrect data. To provide data validation in Input or Edit mode, you could convert the bound fields to template fields and add data validators as shown in figure 5-16 in chapter 5.

The rest of this listing is filled mostly with the data source that the DetailsView control is bound to. This data source includes Delete, Insert, and Update commands that use optimistic concurrency. If you look at the Where clauses for the Delete and Update commands, you can see the modifications that I made to correctly handle nulls for the ImageFile column.

The Product Maintenance application

Description

- The Product Maintenance application uses a GridView and a DetailsView control to let the user update the data in the Products table.

- To select a product, the user locates the product in the GridView control and clicks the Select button. This displays the details for the product in the DetailsView control. Then, the user can click the Edit button to change the product data or the Delete button to delete the product.

- To add a new product to the database, the user clicks the New button in the DetailsView control. Then, the user can enter the data for the new product and click the Insert button.

Figure 6-10   The Product Maintenance application

The Default.aspx file   Page 1

```
<%@ Page Language="VB" AutoEventWireup="false" CodeFile="Default.aspx.vb"
Inherits="_Default" %>

<!DOCTYPE html PUBLIC "-//W3C//DTD XHTML 1.1//EN"
"http://www.w3.org/TR/xhtml11/DTD/xhtml11.dtd">

<html xmlns="http://www.w3.org/1999/xhtml" >
<head runat="server">
    <title>Chapter 5 Product List</title>
</head>
<body>
  <form id="form1" runat="server">
  <div>
    <asp:Image ID="Image1" runat="server" ImageUrl="~/Images/banner.jpg" />
    <br /><br />
    <table>
      <tr>
        <td width="300px" valign="top">
          <asp:GridView ID="GridView1" runat="server"
              AllowSorting="True" AllowPaging="True"
              DataKeyNames="ProductID" DataSourceID="SqlDataSource1"
              AutoGenerateColumns="False" SelectedIndex="0"
              CellPadding="4" GridLines="None" ForeColor="Black" >
            <Columns>
              <asp:BoundField DataField="ProductID" HeaderText="ID"
                  ReadOnly="True">
                <HeaderStyle HorizontalAlign="Left" />
                <ItemStyle Width="75px" />
              </asp:BoundField>
              <asp:BoundField DataField="Name" HeaderText="Name">
                <HeaderStyle HorizontalAlign="Left" />
                <ItemStyle Width="200px" />
              </asp:BoundField>
              <asp:BoundField DataField="CategoryID" HeaderText="Category" />
              <asp:CommandField ButtonType="Button" ShowSelectButton="True" />
            </Columns>
            <HeaderStyle BackColor="Silver" Font-Bold="True"
                ForeColor="White" />
            <RowStyle BackColor="White" ForeColor="Black" />
            <AlternatingRowStyle BackColor="WhiteSmoke" ForeColor="Black" />
            <FooterStyle BackColor="Silver" Font-Bold="True"
                ForeColor="White" />
            <PagerStyle BackColor="Silver" ForeColor="Blue"
                HorizontalAlign="Center" />
          </asp:GridView>

          <asp:SqlDataSource ID="SqlDataSource1" runat="server"
              ConnectionString="<%$ ConnectionStrings:HalloweenConnection %>"
              SelectCommand="SELECT [ProductID], [Name], [CategoryID]
                  FROM [Products] ORDER BY [ProductID]">
          </asp:SqlDataSource>
        </td>
```

Figure 6-11   The aspx file for the Product Maintenance application (part 1 of 4)

The Default.aspx file   **Page 2**

```
<td width="400px" valign="top">
  <asp:DetailsView ID="DetailsView1" runat="server"
      DataSourceID="SqlDataSource2"  DataKeyNames="ProductID"
      Height="50px" Width="400px" AutoGenerateRows="False"
      BackColor="White" BorderColor="White" BorderStyle="Ridge"
      BorderWidth="2px" CellPadding="3" CellSpacing="1"
      GridLines="None">
    <RowStyle BackColor="#DEDFDE" ForeColor="Black" />
    <Fields>
      <asp:BoundField DataField="ProductID"
          HeaderText="Product ID:"
          ReadOnly="True" SortExpression="ProductID">
        <HeaderStyle HorizontalAlign="Left" Width="150px" />
        <ItemStyle Width="250px" />
      </asp:BoundField>
      <asp:BoundField DataField="Name" HeaderText="Name:">
        <HeaderStyle HorizontalAlign="Left" Width="150px" />
        <ItemStyle Width="250px" />
      </asp:BoundField>
      <asp:BoundField DataField="ShortDescription"
          HeaderText="Short Description:">
        <HeaderStyle HorizontalAlign="Left" Width="150px" />
        <ItemStyle Width="250px" />
      </asp:BoundField>
      <asp:BoundField DataField="LongDescription"
          HeaderText="Long Description:">
        <HeaderStyle HorizontalAlign="Left" Width="150px" />
        <ItemStyle Width="250px" />
      </asp:BoundField>
      <asp:BoundField DataField="CategoryID"
          HeaderText="Category ID:">
        <HeaderStyle HorizontalAlign="Left" Width="150px" />
        <ItemStyle Width="250px" />
      </asp:BoundField>
      <asp:BoundField DataField="ImageFile"
          HeaderText="Image File:" SortExpression="ImageFile">
        <HeaderStyle HorizontalAlign="Left" Width="150px" />
        <ItemStyle Width="250px" />
      </asp:BoundField>
      <asp:BoundField DataField="UnitPrice"
          HeaderText="Unit Price:" >
        <HeaderStyle HorizontalAlign="Left" Width="150px" />
        <ItemStyle Width="250px" />
      </asp:BoundField>
      <asp:BoundField DataField="OnHand" HeaderText="On Hand:">
        <HeaderStyle HorizontalAlign="Left" Width="150px" />
        <ItemStyle Width="250px" />
      </asp:BoundField>
```

Figure 6-11   The aspx file for the Product Maintenance application (part 2 of 4)

The Default.aspx file   Page 3

```
                <asp:CommandField ButtonType="Button"
                    ShowDeleteButton="True"
                    ShowEditButton="True"
                    ShowInsertButton="True" />
            </Fields>
            <HeaderStyle BackColor="Silver" Font-Bold="True"
                ForeColor="Black" />
            <EditRowStyle BackColor="Blue" Font-Bold="True"
                ForeColor="White" />
        </asp:DetailsView>

        <asp:SqlDataSource ID="SqlDataSource2" runat="server"
            ConflictDetection="CompareAllValues"
            ConnectionString="<%$ ConnectionStrings:HalloweenConnection %>"
            SelectCommand="SELECT [ProductID], [Name], [ShortDescription],
                    [LongDescription], [CategoryID], [ImageFile],
                    [UnitPrice], [OnHand]
                FROM [Products]
                WHERE (([ProductID] = @ProductID)"
            DeleteCommand="DELETE FROM [Products]
                WHERE [ProductID] = @original_ProductID
                    AND [Name] = @original_Name
                    AND [ShortDescription] = @original_ShortDescription
                    AND [LongDescription] = @original_LongDescription
                    AND [CategoryID] = @original_CategoryID
                    AND ( [ImageFile] = @original_ImageFile
                     OR ImageFile IS NULL AND @original_ImageFile IS NULL )
                    AND [UnitPrice] = @original_UnitPrice
                    AND [OnHand] = @original_OnHand"
            InsertCommand="INSERT INTO [Products] ([ProductID], [Name],
                    [ShortDescription], [LongDescription], [CategoryID],
                    [ImageFile], [UnitPrice], [OnHand])
                VALUES (@ProductID, @Name, @ShortDescription,
                        @LongDescription, @CategoryID, @ImageFile,
                        @UnitPrice, @OnHand)"
            UpdateCommand="UPDATE [Products] SET [Name] = @Name,
                    [ShortDescription] = @ShortDescription,
                    [LongDescription] = @LongDescription,
                    [CategoryID] = @CategoryID,
                    [ImageFile] = @ImageFile,
                    [UnitPrice] = @UnitPrice,
                    [OnHand] = @OnHand
                WHERE [ProductID] = @original_ProductID
                    AND [Name] = @original_Name
                    AND [ShortDescription] = @original_ShortDescription
                    AND [LongDescription] = @original_LongDescription
                    AND [CategoryID] = @original_CategoryID
                    AND ( [ImageFile] = @original_ImageFile
                     OR ImageFile IS NULL AND @original_ImageFile IS NULL )
                    AND [UnitPrice] = @original_UnitPrice
                    AND [OnHand] = @original_OnHand">
```

Figure 6-11   The aspx file for the Product Maintenance application (part 3 of 4)

The Default.aspx file   **Page 4**

```
            <SelectParameters>
              <asp:ControlParameter ControlID="GridView1" Name="ProductID"
                 PropertyName="SelectedValue" Type="String" />
            </SelectParameters>
            <DeleteParameters>
              <asp:Parameter Name="original_ProductID" Type="String" />
              <asp:Parameter Name="original_Name" Type="String" />
              <asp:Parameter Name="original_ShortDescription" Type="String" />
              <asp:Parameter Name="original_LongDescription" Type="String" />
              <asp:Parameter Name="original_CategoryID" Type="String" />
              <asp:Parameter Name="original_ImageFile" Type="String" />
              <asp:Parameter Name="original_UnitPrice" Type="Decimal" />
              <asp:Parameter Name="original_OnHand" Type="Int32" />
            </DeleteParameters>
            <UpdateParameters>
              <asp:Parameter Name="Name" Type="String" />
              <asp:Parameter Name="ShortDescription" Type="String" />
              <asp:Parameter Name="LongDescription" Type="String" />
              <asp:Parameter Name="CategoryID" Type="String" />
              <asp:Parameter Name="ImageFile" Type="String" />
              <asp:Parameter Name="UnitPrice" Type="Decimal" />
              <asp:Parameter Name="OnHand" Type="Int32" />
              <asp:Parameter Name="original_ProductID" Type="String" />
              <asp:Parameter Name="original_Name" Type="String" />
              <asp:Parameter Name="original_ShortDescription" Type="String" />
              <asp:Parameter Name="original_LongDescription" Type="String" />
              <asp:Parameter Name="original_CategoryID" Type="String" />
              <asp:Parameter Name="original_ImageFile" Type="String" />
              <asp:Parameter Name="original_UnitPrice" Type="Decimal" />
              <asp:Parameter Name="original_OnHand" Type="Int32" />
            </UpdateParameters>
            <InsertParameters>
              <asp:Parameter Name="ProductID" Type="String" />
              <asp:Parameter Name="Name" Type="String" />
              <asp:Parameter Name="ShortDescription" Type="String" />
              <asp:Parameter Name="LongDescription" Type="String" />
              <asp:Parameter Name="CategoryID" Type="String" />
              <asp:Parameter Name="ImageFile" Type="String" />
              <asp:Parameter Name="UnitPrice" Type="Decimal" />
              <asp:Parameter Name="OnHand" Type="Int32" />
            </InsertParameters>
          </asp:SqlDataSource><br />

          <asp:Label ID = "lblError" runat="server" ForeColor="Red"
             EnableViewState="False"></asp:Label>
        </td>
      </tr>
    </table>
  </div>
  </form>
</body>
</html>
```

Figure 6-11   The aspx file for the Product Maintenance application (part 4 of 4)

The code-behind file

Figure 6-12 shows the code-behind file for the Default page of the Product Maintenance application. Even though this application provides complete maintenance for the Products table, only four procedures are required. These procedures respond to events raised by the DetailsView control. The first three handle database exceptions and concurrency errors for updates, deletions, and insertions.

Note that the error-handling code for the insert procedure is simpler than the error-handling code for the update and delete procedures. That's because optimistic concurrency doesn't apply to insert operations. As a result, there's no need to check the AffectedRows property to see if a concurrency error has occurred.

The last procedure, DetailsView1_ItemDeleting, handles a problem that can occur when you apply a format to a bound field. In this case, the currency format is applied to the unit price field. Because this application uses optimistic concurrency, the original values of each field are passed to the Delete statement as parameters to make sure that another user hasn't changed the product row since it was retrieved. Unfortunately, the DetailsView control sets the value of the unit price parameter to its formatted value, which includes the currency symbol. If you allow this value to be passed on to the Delete statement, an exception will be thrown because the parameter value is in the wrong format.

Before the Delete statement is executed, then, the DetailsView1_ItemDeleting procedure is called. This procedure removes the currency symbol from the parameter value so the value will be passed to the Delete statement in the correct format. Note that a similar procedure isn't required when you update a row because the DetailsView control doesn't use the format string in Edit mode by default.

The Default.aspx.vb file

```vb
Partial Class _Default
    Inherits System.Web.UI.Page

    Protected Sub DetailsView1_ItemUpdated(ByVal sender As Object, _
            ByVal e As System.Web.UI.WebControls.DetailsViewUpdatedEventArgs) _
            Handles DetailsView1.ItemUpdated
        If e.Exception IsNot Nothing Then
            lblError.Text = "Invalid data. Please correct and try again."
            e.ExceptionHandled = True
        ElseIf e.AffectedRows = 0 Then
            lblError.Text = "Another user has updated that product. " _
                & "Please try again."
        End If
        GridView1.DataBind()
    End Sub

    Protected Sub DetailsView1_ItemDeleted(ByVal sender As Object, _
            ByVal e As System.Web.UI.WebControls.DetailsViewDeletedEventArgs) _
            Handles DetailsView1.ItemDeleted
        If e.Exception IsNot Nothing Then
            lblError.Text = "A database error has occurred. " _
                & "Please try again."
            e.ExceptionHandled = True
        ElseIf e.AffectedRows = 0 Then
            lblError.Text = "Another user has updated that product. " _
                & "Please try again."
        End If
        GridView1.DataBind()
    End Sub

    Protected Sub DetailsView1_ItemInserted(ByVal sender As Object, _
            ByVal e As System.Web.UI.WebControls.DetailsViewInsertedEventArgs) _
            Handles DetailsView1.ItemInserted
        If e.Exception IsNot Nothing Then
            lblError.Text = "Invalid data. Please correct and try again."
            e.ExceptionHandled = True
        End If
        GridView1.DataBind()
    End Sub

    Protected Sub DetailsView1_ItemDeleting(ByVal sender As Object, _
            ByVal e As System.Web.UI.WebControls.DetailsViewDeleteEventArgs) _
            Handles DetailsView1.ItemDeleting
        e.Values("UnitPrice") _
            = e.Values("UnitPrice").ToString().Substring(1);

    End Sub

End Class
```

Figure 6-12   The code-behind file for the Product Maintenance application

How to use the FormView control

Besides the DetailsView control, ASP.NET 2.0 also provides a new FormView control. Like the DetailsView control, the FormView control is designed to display data for a single item from a data source. However, as you'll see in the following topics, the FormView control uses a different approach to displaying its data.

An introduction to the FormView control

Figure 6-13 presents an introduction to the FormView control. Although the FormView control is similar to the DetailsView control, it differs in several key ways. Most importantly, the FormView control isn't restricted by the HTML table layout of the DetailsView control, in which each field in the data source is rendered as a table row. Instead, the FormView control uses templates to specify how the data item is rendered. This gives you complete control over the layout of the data.

Another important difference is that the FormView control doesn't include a Fields collection like the DetailsView control. As a result, data binding for a FormView control is done with binding expressions rather than BoundField elements.

The easiest way to create a FormView control is to drag the FormView control icon from the Toolbox onto the page. Then, you can use the smart tag menu to bind the FormView control to a data source. When you do that, the Web Forms Designer will automatically create the FormView control's templates for you, as shown in the first image in this figure.

You can then edit the templates to achieve the layout you want. To do that, choose Edit Templates from the smart tag menu. This places the control in Template Editing mode, as shown in the second image in this figure. The drop-down list in this figure shows the various templates that are used by the FormView control. For most applications, you'll use just the Item, EditItem, InsertItem, and EmptyData templates.

A FormView control after a data source has been assigned

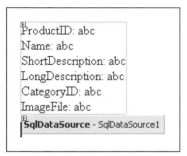

A FormView control in Template Editing mode

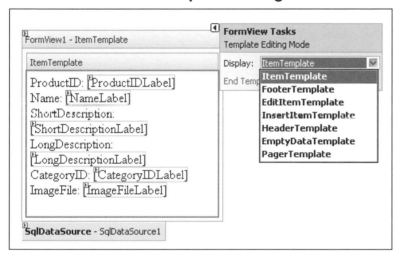

How the FormView control differs from the DetailsView control

- The DetailsView control is easier to work with, but the FormView control provides more formatting and layout options.
- The DetailsView control renders each data source item as a table row, but the FormView control uses a template to render each item.
- The DetailsView control uses BoundField elements to define bound data fields, but the FormView control uses data binding expressions in its templates to display bound data.

Description

- A FormView control is similar to a DetailsView control, but it uses templates that give you more control over how its data is displayed.
- To create a FormView control, you drag its icon from the Data tab of the Toolbox onto the page, and you assign a data source to the control. Then, you edit the control's templates so the data is displayed the way you want.

Figure 6-13 An introduction to the FormView control

How to work with the item template

When you use the Web Forms Designer to create a FormView control and bind it to a data source, the Web Forms Designer automatically generates basic templates for the FormView control. For instance, the code in figure 6-14 shows a typical ItemTemplate that has been generated. As you can see, it consists of a literal header and a label control for each field in the data source. The Text attribute of each label control uses either the ASP.NET 2.0 Bind or Eval method for data binding.

To control the format and layout of the item data, you can edit the item template. In fact, it's common to include an HTML table in the item template to control the layout of the individual fields in the template. You'll see an example of this later in this chapter.

Note that if the data source includes Update, Delete, and Insert commands, the item template will include command buttons that let the user edit, delete, or add new rows. Although these buttons are created as link buttons, you can easily change them to regular buttons or image buttons.

The item template generated for a FormView control

```
<asp:FormView ID="FormView1" runat="server" DataKeyNames="ProductID"
    DataSourceID="SqlDataSource1">
    <ItemTemplate>
        ProductID:
        <asp:Label ID="ProductIDLabel" runat="server"
            Text='<%# Eval("ProductID") %>'></asp:Label><br />
        Name:
        <asp:Label ID="NameLabel" runat="server"
            Text='<%# Bind("Name") %>'></asp:Label><br />
        ShortDescription:
        <asp:Label ID="ShortDescriptionLabel" runat="server"
            Text='<%# Bind("ShortDescription") %>'></asp:Label><br />
        LongDescription:
        <asp:Label ID="LongDescriptionLabel" runat="server"
            Text='<%# Bind("LongDescription") %>'></asp:Label><br />
        CategoryID:
        <asp:Label ID="CategoryIDLabel" runat="server"
            Text='<%# Bind("CategoryID") %>'></asp:Label><br />
        ImageFile:
        <asp:Label ID="ImageFileLabel" runat="server"
            Text='<%# Bind("ImageFile") %>'></asp:Label><br />
    </ItemTemplate>
    .
    .
    .
</asp:FormView>
```

Description

- When you bind a FormView control to a data source, templates are created with heading text, bound labels, and text boxes for each field in the data source.

- The item template is rendered whenever the FormView control is bound in ReadOnly mode.

- The generated templates use the new Eval and Bind methods to create binding expressions for each of the fields in the data source (see figure 4-12 in chapter 4).

- If the data source includes Update, Delete, and Insert statements, the generated item template will include Edit, Delete, and New buttons.

- The Web Forms Designer also generates an EditItemTemplate and an InsertItemTemplate, even if the data source doesn't include an Update or Insert statement. For more information, see the next figure.

- You can add a table to a generated template to control the layout of the data that's rendered for that template.

Figure 6-14   How to work with the item template

How to work with the edit item and insert item templates

As figure 6-15 shows, the Web Forms Designer also generates an edit item and insert item template when you bind it to a data source. These templates are generated even if the data source doesn't have an Update or Insert command. As a result, you can delete these templates if your application doesn't allow for edits and inserts. Although this figure only shows an edit item template, the insert item template is similar.

One drawback to using the FormView control is that once you edit the item template so the data is arranged the way you want, you must provide similar layout code in both the edit item template and the insert item template. If, for example, you create a table in the item template to arrange the fields in a certain way, you'll need to create similar tables in the edit item and insert item templates so the layout is the same in all three templates. And if you later decide to change that layout, you'll have to make the change to all three templates. Unfortunately, there's no escaping this duplication of effort.

A generated edit item template as displayed in a browser window

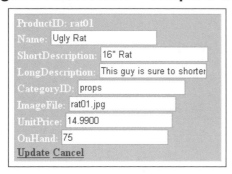

The code for the edit item template shown above

```
<EditItemTemplate>
    ProductID:
    <asp:Label ID="ProductIDLabel1" runat="server"
        Text='<%# Eval("ProductID") %>'></asp:Label><br />
    Name:
    <asp:TextBox ID="NameTextBox" runat="server" Text='<%# Bind("Name") %>'>
    </asp:TextBox><br />
    ShortDescription:
    <asp:TextBox ID="ShortDescriptionTextBox" runat="server"
        Text='<%# Bind("ShortDescription") %>'>
    </asp:TextBox><br />
    .
    .
    .
    .
    .
    .
```

> The code generated for the LongDescription, CategoryID, ImageFile, UnitPrice, and OnHand fields is similar to the code generated for the ShortDescription field.

```
    <asp:LinkButton ID="UpdateButton" runat="server" CausesValidation="True"
        CommandName="Update" Text="Update">
    </asp:LinkButton>
    <asp:LinkButton ID="UpdateCancelButton" runat="server"
        CausesValidation="False" CommandName="Cancel" Text="Cancel">
    </asp:LinkButton>
</EditItemTemplate>
```

Description

- The edit item template determines how the FormView control is rendered in Edit mode. It includes a text box for each bound field in the data source. The Text attribute for each text box uses a binding expression that binds the text box to its data source field.

- The edit item template also includes Update and Cancel buttons.

- The insert item template is similar to the edit item template. It determines how the FormView control is rendered in Insert mode.

Figure 6-15   How to work with the edit item and insert item templates

A Shopping Cart application that uses a FormView control

To show the versatility of the FormView control, the following topics present a version of the Order page from the Shopping Cart application that was originally presented in chapter 2. That version of the application used simple label and image controls to display the information for the product selected by the user. Because data binding didn't work for those controls, Visual Basic code was required in the Page_Load procedure to set the values of the label and image controls. In contrast, this new version of the application takes advantage of the data binding ability of the FormView control, so no Page_Load procedure is required.

Because this application doesn't allow the user to update, delete, or insert product information, it doesn't illustrate the use the edit item or insert item templates or the use of command buttons with a FormView control. If you want to see an application that does use those features, though, you can download a FormView version of the Product Maintenance application from our web site, www.murach.com.

The operation of the application

To refresh your memory, figure 6-16 shows the Order page displayed by the Shopping Cart application. As you can see, this page lets the user select a product from a drop-down list. When the user selects a product, the page displays the name, description, price, and an image of the selected product. Then, the user can order the product by entering a quantity and clicking the Add to Cart button.

This time, the product information is displayed within a FormView control, and the item template includes a simple HTML table that displays the text information on the left and the image on the right. This demonstrates the layout flexibility of the FormView control. With a DetailsView control, it wouldn't be possible to display the image to the right of the text data, because the DetailsView control displays each field of the data source in a separate table row.

The Order page as viewed in the Web Forms Designer

Description

- This is the Shopping Cart application that was originally presented in chapter 2, but this time it's implemented with a FormView control that displays the data for the selected product.
- The ItemTemplate for the FormView control includes an HTML table with cells that contain labels that are bound to the fields in the data source. It also includes an Image control whose ImageUrl property is bound to the ImageFile field in the data source.

Figure 6-16   The Shopping Cart application with a FormView control

The aspx file for the Order page

Figure 6-17 shows the aspx file for the Order page of the Shopping Cart application. Here, the FormView control includes an item template that uses a table to format the data for the selected product. This table has four rows, each with three columns. The first column contains the labels that present the name, short description, long description, and price for the selected product. The second column (which spans all four rows) is a small spacer column to provide some space between the text and the image. And the third column (which also spans all four rows) contains the image control that displays the product's image.

Note that although the Web Forms Designer generated the edit item and insert item templates, this application doesn't use them. As a result, I deleted those templates so they wouldn't clutter the listing.

There are two interesting things to notice about the format strings used in the binding expressions on this page. First, the format string used to bind the image control is this: "Images\Products\{0}". Since the ImageFile column in the Products table contains just the name of the image file for each product, not its complete path, this formatting expression prefixes the file name with the path \Images\Products\ so the image file can be located.

Second, the format string used in the binding expression that displays the unit price is this: "{c:0} each". As a result, the price is displayed in currency format, followed by the word "each."

The code-behind file for the Order page

Figure 6-18 shows the code-behind file for the Order page. This code is almost identical to the code for the original version of this program that was presented back in chapter 2. In fact, there are only two substantial differences. First, this version doesn't include a Page_Load procedure because it doesn't need to do any data binding.

Second, the GetSelectedProduct procedure in this version is simpler than the one in the original version. Because the new application uses two data sources, a select parameter can be used to retrieve the selected product in the second data source. Then, because the second data source retrieves just a single row, a row filter isn't required. Instead, the index value 0 is used to retrieve data from the first and only row of the data source.

The Order.aspx file   **Page 1**

```
<%@ Page Language="VB" AutoEventWireup="false" CodeFile="Order.aspx.vb"
Inherits="Order" %>

<!DOCTYPE html PUBLIC "-//W3C//DTD XHTML 1.1//EN"
"http://www.w3.org/TR/xhtml11/DTD/xhtml11.dtd">

<html xmlns="http://www.w3.org/1999/xhtml" >
<head runat="server">
    <title>Chapter 6 Shopping Cart w/FormView</title>
</head>
<body>
    <form id="form1" runat="server">
    <div>
        <asp:Image ID="Image1" runat="server"
            ImageUrl="~/Images/banner.jpg" /><br /><br />
        <asp:Label ID="Label1" runat="server"
            Text="Please select a product:"></asp:Label>
        <asp:DropDownList ID="ddlProducts" runat="server" Width="150px"
            AutoPostBack="True" DataSourceID="SqlDataSource1"
            DataTextField="Name" DataValueField="ProductID">
        </asp:DropDownList>
        <asp:SqlDataSource ID="SqlDataSource1" runat="server"
            ConnectionString="<%$ ConnectionStrings:HalloweenConnection %>"
            SelectCommand="SELECT [ProductID], [Name] FROM [Products]
                ORDER BY [Name]">
        </asp:SqlDataSource>
        <br />
        <asp:FormView ID="FormView1" runat="server"
            DataSourceID="SqlDataSource2">
          <ItemTemplate>
            <table>
              <tr>
                <td style="height: 22px" width="250">
                  <asp:Label ID="lblName" runat="server"
                      Font-Bold="True" Font-Size="Larger"
                      Text='<%# Bind("Name") %>' >
                  </asp:Label>
                </td>
                <td rowspan="4" valign="top" width="20"></td>
                <td rowspan="4" valign="top">
                  <asp:Image ID="imgProduct" runat="server" Height="200px"
                      ImageUrl='<%# Bind("ImageFile", "Images\Products\{0}") %>' />
                </td>
              </tr>
              <tr>
                <td width="250">
                  <asp:Label ID="lblShortDescription" runat="server"
                      Text='<%# Bind("ShortDescription") %>'>
                  </asp:Label>
                </td>
              </tr>
```

Figure 6-17   The aspx file for the Order page of the Shopping Cart application (part 1 of 2)

```
              <tr>
                <td width="250">
                  <asp:Label ID="lblLongDescription" runat="server"
                      Text='<%# Bind("LongDescription") %>'>
                  </asp:Label>
                </td>
              </tr>
              <tr>
                <td width="250">
                  <asp:Label ID="lblUnitPrice" runat="server"
                      Font-Bold="True" Font-Size="Larger"
                      Text='<%# Bind("UnitPrice", "{0:c} each") %>'>
                  </asp:Label>
                </td>
              </tr>
            </table>
          </ItemTemplate>
        </asp:FormView>
        <asp:SqlDataSource ID="SqlDataSource2" runat="server"
            ConnectionString="<%$ ConnectionStrings:HalloweenConnection %>"
            SelectCommand="SELECT [ProductID], [Name], [ShortDescription],
                [LongDescription], [ImageFile], [UnitPrice]
                FROM [Products]
                WHERE ([ProductID] = @ProductID)">
            <SelectParameters>
                <asp:ControlParameter ControlID="ddlProducts" Name="ProductID"
                    PropertyName="SelectedValue" Type="String" />
            </SelectParameters>
        </asp:SqlDataSource><br />
        <asp:Label ID="Label2" runat="server" BorderWidth="0px" Text="Quantity:"
            Width="80px"></asp:Label>
        <asp:TextBox ID="txtQuantity" runat="server" Width="80px"></asp:TextBox>
        <asp:RequiredFieldValidator
            ID="RequiredFieldValidator1" runat="server"
            ControlToValidate="txtQuantity" Display="Dynamic"
            ErrorMessage="Quantity is a required field.">
        </asp:RequiredFieldValidator>
        <asp:CompareValidator ID="CompareValidator1" runat="server"
            ControlToValidate="txtQuantity" Display="Dynamic"
            ErrorMessage="Quantity must be greater than zero."
            Operator="GreaterThan" ValueToCompare="0">
        </asp:CompareValidator><br /><br />
        <asp:Button ID="btnAdd" runat="server" Text="Add to Cart" /> 
        <asp:Button ID="Button1" runat="server"  Text="Go to Cart"
            CausesValidation="False" PostBackUrl="~/Cart.aspx" />
    </div>
    </form>
</body>
</html>
```

Figure 6-17   The aspx file for the Order page of the Shopping Cart application (part 2 of 2)

The Order.aspx.vb file

```
Imports System.Data

Partial Class Order
    Inherits System.Web.UI.Page

    Protected Sub btnAdd_Click(ByVal sender As Object, _
            ByVal e As System.EventArgs) Handles btnAdd.Click
        If Page.IsValid Then
            Dim CartItem As New CartItem
            CartItem.Product = GetSelectedProduct()
            CartItem.Quantity = CType(txtQuantity.Text, Integer)
            Me.AddToCart(CartItem)
            Response.Redirect("Cart.aspx")
        End If
    End Sub

    Private Function GetSelectedProduct() As Product
        Dim dvProduct As DataView = CType( _
            SqlDataSource2.Select(DataSourceSelectArguments.Empty), DataView)
        Dim Product As New Product
        Product.ProductID = dvProduct(0)("ProductID").ToString
        Product.Name = dvProduct(0)("Name").ToString
        Product.ShortDescription = dvProduct(0)("ShortDescription").ToString
        Product.LongDescription = dvProduct(0)("LongDescription").ToString
        Product.UnitPrice = CDec(dvProduct(0)("UnitPrice"))
        Product.ImageFile = dvProduct(0)("ImageFile").ToString
        Return Product
    End Function

    Private Sub AddToCart(ByVal CartItem As CartItem)
        Dim Cart As SortedList = GetCart()
        Dim sProductID As String = CartItem.Product.ProductID
        If Cart.ContainsKey(sProductID) Then
            CartItem = CType(Cart(sProductID), CartItem)
            CartItem.Quantity += CType(txtQuantity.Text, Integer)
        Else
            Cart.Add(sProductID, CartItem)
        End If
    End Sub

    Private Function GetCart() As SortedList
        If Session("cart") Is Nothing Then
            Session.Add("cart", New SortedList)
        End If
        Return CType(Session("cart"), SortedList)
    End Function

End Class
```

Figure 6-18   The code-behind file for the Order page of the Shopping Cart application

Perspective

The DetailsView and FormView controls are ideal for any application that displays bound data one record at a time. The choice of whether to use a DetailsView or a FormView control depends mostly on how much control you want over the layout of the data. If you want to present a simple list of fields, choose the DetailsView control because it can automatically present data in that format. But if you need more control over the data layout, choose the FormView control.

Up to this point, all of the database applications presented in this book have relied heavily on data binding and declarative code, using Visual Basic code only for data validation and exception handling. However, ASP.NET 2.0 also has powerful new features for working with data access classes written with custom code. In the next chapter, then, you'll learn how the new ObjectDataSource control lets you use data bound controls such as the GridView, DetailsView, and FormView controls with custom data access classes.

Terms

Master/Detail page

7

How to use
object data sources

In this chapter, you'll learn how to use object data sources as an alternative to the Access, SQL, and XML data sources that you've already learned about. The benefit of using object data sources is that they let you use a three-layer design in which the data access code is kept in data access classes. This lets you separate the presentation code from the data access code, but still lets you use the data binding features of ASP.NET 2.0.

An introduction to object data sources

The following topics introduce you to object data sources and the 3-layer architecture that they let you implement.

How 3-layer applications work in ASP.NET 2.0

As you probably know, most development experts recommend a *3-layer architecture* for web applications that separates the presentation, business rules, and data access components of the application. The *presentation layer* includes the web pages that define the user interface. The *middle layer* includes the classes that manage the data access for those objects, and it may also include classes that implement business rules such as data validation requirements or discount policies. The *database layer* consists of the database itself.

Unfortunately, using the 3-layer architecture in previous versions of ASP.NET meant that you couldn't take advantage of ASP.NET's powerful data binding features. That's because data binding with ASP.NET 1.x required that you place the data access components in the application's presentation layer.

But now, as figure 7-1 shows, ASP.NET 2.0 addresses that problem by providing *object data sources*. To make that work, the ObjectDataSource control serves as an interface between the data-bound controls in the presentation layer and the *data access classes* in the middle layer. This means that you can use data binding in the presentation layer without placing the data access code in that layer.

When you use an ObjectDataSource control, you must create a data access class to handle the data access for the control. This class provides at least one method that retrieves data from the database and returns it in a form that the ObjectDataSource control can handle. It can also provide methods to insert, update, and delete data. The data access class should be placed in the application's App_Code folder.

When you code a data access class, you can use any techniques you want to access the database. In this chapter, for example, you'll see data access classes that use the ADO.NET classes that were introduced with .NET 1.0. These classes can be used to get data from a SQL Server database, from other types of databases such as Oracle or MySQL databases, or from other sources such as XML or plain text files.

If you have already developed data access classes for the database used by your application, you may be able to use those classes with an object data source. Often, though, it's better to develop the data access classes specifically for the ObjectDataSource controls that you're going to use. That way, you can design each class so it works as efficiently as possible.

Incidentally, Microsoft uses both the term *business object class* and the term *data object class* to refer to a class that provides data access for an object data source. In this chapter, though, I used the term *data access class* for this type of class because if you use shared methods to provide the data access functions, an object is never instantiated from the class.

The 3-layer architecture in ASP.NET 2.0

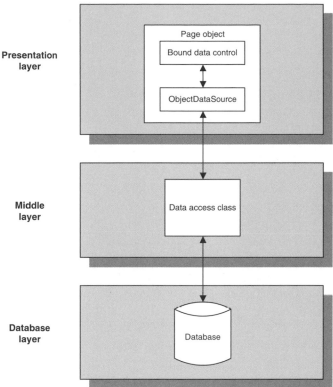

The three layers

- The **presentation layer** consists of the ASP.NET 2.0 pages that manage the appearance of the application. This layer can include bound data controls and ObjectDataSource objects that bind the data controls to the data.

- The **middle layer** contains the *data access classes* that manage the data access for the application. This layer can also contain business objects that represent business entities such as customers, products, or employees and that implement business rules such as credit and discount policies.

- The **database layer** consists of the database that contains the data for the application. Ideally, the SQL statements that do the database access should be saved in stored procedures within the database, but the SQL statements are often stored in the data access classes.

Description

- An *object data source* is implemented by the new ObjectDataSource control, which lets you use data binding with the *3-layer architecture* for a database application.

- An object data source is similar to a SQL data source. However, instead of directly accessing a database, the object data source gets its data through a data access class that handles the details of database access.

Figure 7-1   How 3-layer applications work in ASP.NET 2.0

Also, you may be accustomed to using the term *3-tier architecture* for the *3-layer architecture* that's described in figure 7-1. Because some people use *3-tier* to refer to an architecture that puts the 3 layers on three different physical devices, though, I've used the term *3-layer* in this chapter. Although you could put each of the 3 layers on 3 separate devices, you don't have to.

How to use the ObjectDataSource control

Figure 7-2 presents the basics of working with the ObjectDataSource control. The image at the top of this figure shows how an ObjectDataSource control that's bound to a drop-down list appears in the Web Forms Designer. Then, the first code example shows the aspx code for the drop-down list and the ObjectDataSource it's bound to. As with any other data source, you can add an object data source to a web page by dragging it from the Toolbox in Design view or by entering the aspx code for the ObjectDataSource element in Source view.

In the first code example, you can see that the drop-down list is bound to the object data source just as if it were bound to a SQL data source. The only difference is that the DataSourceID attribute provides the ID of an object data source rather than a SQL data source. You can also see that the code for the ObjectDataSource control has just two attributes besides the required ID and runat attributes. The TypeName attribute provides the name of the data access class, and the SelectMethod attribute provides the name of the method used to retrieve the data. In this case, the data access class is ProductDB and the select method is GetAllCategories.

The second code example in this figure shows the GetAllCategories method of the ProductDB data access class. This method uses straightforward ADO.NET code to retrieve category rows from the Categories table and return a data reader that can be used to read the category rows. Notice, though, that the return type for this method is IEnumerable. Because the SqlDataReader class implements the IEnumerable interface, a data reader is a valid return object for this method. (You'll learn more about the return types that are acceptable for a select method in figure 7-8.)

A drop-down list bound to an ObjectDataSource

The code for the drop-down list and the ObjectDataSource

```
<asp:DropDownList ID="ddlCategories" runat="server" AutoPostBack="True"
    DataSourceID="ObjectDataSource1"
    DataTextField="ShortName"
    DataValueField="CategoryID">
</asp:DropDownList>
<asp:ObjectDataSource ID="ObjectDataSource1" runat="server"
    TypeName="ProductDB"
    SelectMethod="GetAllCategories">
</asp:ObjectDataSource>
```

The GetAllCategories method of the ProductDB class

```
<DataObjectMethod(DataObjectMethodType.Select)> _
Public Shared Function GetAllCategories() As IEnumerable
    Dim sel As String = "SELECT CategoryID, ShortName " _
        & "FROM Categories ORDER BY ShortName"
    Dim cmd As SqlCommand = _
        New SqlCommand(sel, New SqlConnection(GetConnectionString()))
    cmd.Connection.Open()
    Return cmd.ExecuteReader(CommandBehavior.CloseConnection)
End Function
```

Basic attributes of the ObjectDataSource control

Attribute	Description
ID	The ID of the control.
Runat	Must specify "server."
TypeName	The name of the data access class.
SelectMethod	The name of the method that retrieves the data.
UpdateMethod	The name of the method that updates the data.
DeleteMethod	The name of the method that deletes the data.
InsertMethod	The name of the method that inserts the data.
DataObjectTypeName	The name of an aggregate data type used to pass parameter values. For more information, see figures 7-15 and 7-16.
ConflictDetection	Specifies how concurrency conflicts will be detected. CompareAllValues uses optimistic concurrency checking. OverwriteValues, which is the default, does no concurrency checking. For more information, see figure 7-17.

Description

- The ObjectDataSource control specifies the name of the data access class and the methods used to select, update, delete, and insert data.

Figure 7-2   How to use the ObjectDataSource control

How to configure an ObjectDataSource control

Figure 7-3 shows how you can use the Data Source Configuration Wizard to configure an object data source control. As you can see, the first step of the wizard lets you choose the business object that will be associated with this object data source. The selection you make here will be used in the TypeName attribute of the ObjectDataSource control. (Notice that Microsoft refers to the data access class as a *business object* in this wizard. In other contexts, though, Microsoft refers to the data access class as a *data object* or a *data component*.)

The drop-down list in the first step of the wizard lists all of the classes that are available in the App_Code folder. If you check the "Show Only Data Components" box, only those classes that identify themselves as data components will be listed. In figure 7-10, you'll learn how to mark classes this way.

When you select a data object class and click Next, the Define Data Methods step of the configuration wizard is displayed. Here, you can select the method you want to use to retrieve data for the object data source. The one you select is specified in the SelectMethod attribute of the ObjectDataSource control. (In this step, the wizard uses a new .NET 2.0 feature called *reflection* to determine all of the available methods, and you'll learn more about reflection in a moment.)

If you select a select method that requires parameters, the Define Parameters step lets you specify the source for each of the required parameters. Then, the wizard generates the elements that define the parameters required by the ObjectDataSource control.

As you can see in this figure, the Data Source Configuration Wizard also provides tabs that let you specify the methods for update, insert, and delete operations. Later in this chapter, you'll see an application that uses these methods. But for now, I'll just focus on how you can use an ObjectDataSource control to retrieve data.

The Data Source Configuration Wizard

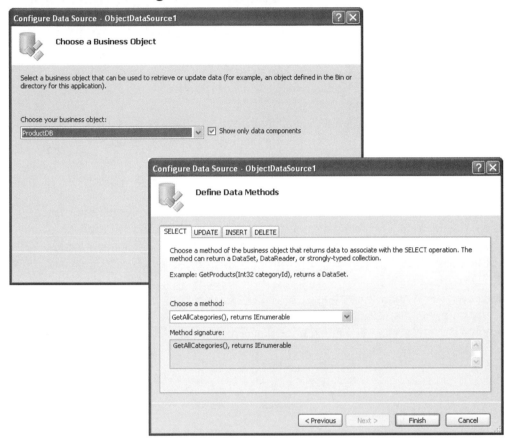

Description

- You can use the Data Source Configuration Wizard to configure an ObjectDataSource control by choosing Configure Data Source from its smart tag menu.

- The Choose a Business Object step of the wizard lets you select the data access class you want to use.

- The Define Data Methods step of the wizard includes tabs that let you choose the methods you want to use for Select, Update, Insert, and Delete operations.

- If you choose a method that requires parameters, a Define Parameters step will appear. This step will let you choose the source of each parameter required by the method. For example, you can specify that a drop-down list should be used as the source for a parameter.

Figure 7-3   How to configure an ObjectDataSource control

A Product List application

To illustrate the basics of working with the ObjectDataSource control, figure 7-4 presents a Product List application. This application is identical in appearance to the Product List application that was presented in chapter 4. However, instead of using SqlDataSource controls to retrieve the data, it uses ObjectDataSource controls.

This figure also lists the methods that are provided by the data access class named ProductDB that is used by this application. The first method, GetAllCategories, returns an IEnumerable object (actually, a data reader) that contains the data for all of the categories in the Categories table. This data includes just the category ID and short name for each category.

The second method, GetProductsByCategory, returns an IEnumerable object (again, a data reader) that includes all of the products in the Products table that have the category ID that's supplied by a parameter. This parameter will be bound to the SelectedValue property of the drop-down list. As a result, the ID of the category selected by the user will be passed to the GetProductsByCategory method.

This application illustrates how the use of object data sources lets you separate the presentation code from the data access code. As you will see, all of the presentation code is in the aspx file. And all of the data access code is in the data access class that's named ProductDB.

The Product List application

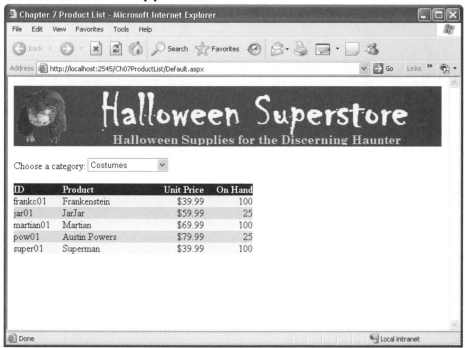

Methods of the ProductDB class

Method	Description
GetAllCategories() As IEnumerable	Returns an IEnumerable object with the ID and short name of all the categories in the Categories table.
GetProductsByCategory(CategoryID As String) As IEnumerable	Returns an IEnumerable object with the ID, name, category ID, unit price, and on-hand quantity for all products in the Products table for the specified category.

Description

- The Category drop-down list is bound to an ObjectDataSource control that receives a list of categories from the Categories table.

- The Repeater control is bound to a second ObjectDataSource control that uses a parameterized query to retrieve the products for a selected category. The CategoryID for the parameter is taken from the SelectedValue property of the drop-down list.

- Both ObjectDataSource controls use a data access class named ProductDB that contains the shared methods that return a list of categories and the products for a specific category.

Figure 7-4   The Product List application

The aspx file

Figure 7-5 shows the body of the Default.aspx page for the Product List application. If you compare this listing with the listing shown in figure 4-13, you'll discover that the only difference is that the SqlDataSource elements have been replaced by ObjectDataSource elements. In other words, the code for the drop-down list and Repeater controls is identical whether the application uses a SQL data source or an object data source.

In the first ObjectDataSource control, the TypeName attribute specifies ProductDB, and the SelectMethod attribute specifies GetAllCategories. As a result, the GetAllCategories method in the ProductDB data access class will be called to retrieve the category data when the drop-down list is bound.

In the second ObjectDataSource control, a ControlParameter element within the SelectParameters element is used to declare the CategoryID parameter. This parameter is bound to the SelectedValue property of the drop-down list.

Because this application relies entirely on declarative data binding, there is no code-behind file for this page. As a result, the only Visual Basic code for this application is in the ProductDB class, which is presented in the next figure.

The body of the Default.aspx file

```
<body>
    <form id="form1" runat="server">
    <div>
        <asp:Image ID="Image1" runat="server"
            ImageUrl="~/Images/banner.jpg" /><br /><br />
        Choose a category:
        <asp:DropDownList ID="ddlCategory" runat="server" AutoPostBack="True"
            DataSourceID="ObjectDataSource1" DataTextField="LongName"
            DataValueField="CategoryID" Width="130px">
        </asp:DropDownList>
        <asp:ObjectDataSource ID="ObjectDataSource1" runat="server"
            TypeName="ProductDB"
            SelectMethod="GetAllCategories">
        </asp:ObjectDataSource><br /><br />
        <asp:Repeater ID="Repeater1" runat="server"
            DataSourceID="ObjectDataSource2">
            <HeaderTemplate>
                <table cellpadding="0" cellspacing="0">
                  <tr bgcolor="Black" style="color: white">
                    <td width="80"><b>ID</b></td>
                    <td width="150"><b>Product</b></td>
                    <td width="80" align="right"><b>Unit Price</b></td>
                    <td width="80" align="right"><b>On Hand</b></td></tr>
            </HeaderTemplate>
            <ItemTemplate>
                <tr bgcolor="WhiteSmoke">
                  <td><%# Eval("ProductID") %></td>
                  <td><%# Eval("Name") %></td>
                  <td align="right"><%# Eval("UnitPrice", "{0:c}") %></td>
                  <td align="right"><%# Eval("OnHand") %></td></tr>
            </ItemTemplate>
            <AlternatingItemTemplate>
                <tr bgcolor="Gainsboro">
                  <td><%# Eval("ProductID") %></td>
                  <td><%# Eval("Name") %></td>
                  <td align="right"><%# Eval("UnitPrice", "{0:c}") %></td>
                  <td align="right"><%# Eval("OnHand") %></td></tr>
            </AlternatingItemTemplate>
            <FooterTemplate>
                </table>
            </FooterTemplate></asp:Repeater>
        <asp:ObjectDataSource ID="ObjectDataSource2" runat="server"
            TypeName="ProductDB"
            SelectMethod="GetProductsByCategory" >
            <SelectParameters>
                <asp:ControlParameter ControlID="ddlCategory"
                    Name="CategoryID" PropertyName="SelectedValue"
                    Type="String" />
            </SelectParameters>
        </asp:ObjectDataSource>
    </div>
    </form>
</body>
```

Figure 7-5   The aspx file for the Product List application

The ProductDB class

Figure 7-6 presents the Visual Basic code for the ProductDB class. To create this class, I used the Website→Add New Item command to add a class file to the App_Code folder. Then, I added the code for the public GetAllCategories and GetProductsByCategory methods. I also created a private method named GetConnectionString. This method is used by both of the public methods to retrieve the connection string for the Halloween database.

Before I explain the details of how these methods work, I want to point out the DataObject and DataObjectMethod attributes that appear in this class. These attributes are used to identify the class and methods as data objects, and you'll learn how to use them in figure 7-10. For now, just realize that they're used by the Data Source Configuration Wizard to determine which classes and methods to display when you configure an object data source.

The GetAllCategories method uses a standard ADO.NET SqlCommand object to retrieve data from the Halloween database using this Select statement:

```
SELECT CategoryID, LongName
FROM Categories
ORDER BY LongName
```

The SqlCommand object is instantiated using a string that contains the above Select statement and the connection string returned by the GetConnectionString method. Then, the command is opened by calling the connection's Open method. Finally, the ExecuteReader method is called, which returns a data reader that contains the requested data.

The GetProductsByCategory method is slightly more complicated because it uses a parameter in its Select statement:

```
SELECT ProductID, Name, CategoryID,
    UnitPrice, OnHand
FROM Products
WHERE CategoryID = @CategoryID
ORDER BY ProductID
```

Here again, a SqlCommand object is created using this Select statement and the connection string returned from the GetConnectionString method. Then, a parameter named CategoryID is added to the command's Parameters collection before the connection is opened and the command is executed so it returns a data reader with the requested data.

The GetConnectionString method uses the ConfigurationManager class to retrieve the connection string named "HalloweenConnection" from the web.config file. As a result, the connection string for the Halloween database must be stored in web.config. To refresh your memory about how to store it, please refer to figure 4-5 in chapter 4.

The ProductDB class

```
Imports Microsoft.VisualBasic
Imports System.ComponentModel
Imports System.Data
Imports System.Data.SqlClient

<DataObject(True)> _
Public Class ProductDB

    <DataObjectMethod(DataObjectMethodType.Select)> _
    Public Shared Function GetAllCategories() As IEnumerable
        Dim sel As String = "SELECT CategoryID, LongName " _
            & "FROM Categories ORDER BY LongName"
        Dim cmd As SqlCommand = _
            New SqlCommand(sel, New SqlConnection(GetConnectionString()))
        cmd.Connection.Open()
        Return cmd.ExecuteReader(CommandBehavior.CloseConnection)

    End Function

    <DataObjectMethod(DataObjectMethodType.Select)> _
    Public Shared Function GetProductsByCategory(ByVal CategoryID As String) _
            As IEnumerable
        Dim sel As String = "SELECT ProductID, Name, CategoryID, " _
            & "UnitPrice, OnHand " _
            & "FROM Products " _
            & "WHERE CategoryID = @CategoryID " _
            & "ORDER BY ProductID"
        Dim cmd As SqlCommand = _
            New SqlCommand(sel, New SqlConnection(GetConnectionString()))
        cmd.Parameters.AddWithValue("CategoryID", CategoryID)
        cmd.Connection.Open()
        Return cmd.ExecuteReader(CommandBehavior.CloseConnection)

    End Function

    Private Shared Function GetConnectionString() As String
        Return ConfigurationManager.ConnectionStrings _
            ("HalloweenConnection").ConnectionString
    End Function

End Class
```

Note

- The DataObject and DataObjectMethod attributes are described in figure 7-10.

Figure 7-6   The ProductDB class for the Product List application

How to create a data access class

The most challenging aspect of using object data sources is developing the data access classes that they require. So the topics that follow explain how to design and implement these classes.

How to design a data access class

As figure 7-7 shows, the data access class used by an ObjectDataSource control can have four different types of methods that are used to select, insert, update, and delete data. You can use any method names that you want for these methods, and you can design the class so that it has more than one of each of these types of methods. For example, the ProductDB class used in the previous figure has two select methods that are named GetAllCategories and GetCategoriesByProduct.

The data access methods can be shared methods or instance methods. If you define them as instance methods, the ObjectDataSource control will create an instance of the data access class before it calls the method, and then destroy the object after the method has been executed. For this to work, the data access class must provide a parameterless constructor. In Visual Basic, though, a parameterless constructor is provided by default if the class has no constructors.

Because creating and destroying a data access object can be time consuming, I suggest that you use shared methods for the select, insert, update, and delete methods whenever possible. That way, the ObjectDataSource control won't have to create an instance of the data access class when it calls one of the data access methods.

Although you provide the name of the methods called by the ObjectDataSource control by using the SelectMethod, InsertMethod, UpdateMethod, and DeleteMethod attributes, the ObjectDataSource control needs more than just the method names to know what methods to call. In addition, the ObjectDataSource control needs to know what parameters those methods are designed to accept. Because the parameters aren't specified at design time, the ObjectDataSource control must determine them at runtime. To do that, it uses a .NET feature called *reflection*.

In case you haven't encountered reflection before, it's a .NET feature that provides information about compiled classes at runtime. For example, reflection can determine what methods are provided by a particular class. In addition, it can determine what parameters each method requires and the type returned by the method.

The ObjectDataSource control uses reflection to determine the parameters that are expected by the data access class methods. That way, the ObjectDataSource control can pass the correct parameters when it calls the select, insert, update, or delete method. It also uses reflection to determine the return type of each data access class method. As you'll see in the next figure, this lets you design a select method that can return the selected data in a variety of forms.

Types of methods in a data access class

Method type	Description
Select	Retrieves data from a database and returns it as an IEnumerable object or a dataset.
Insert	Inserts data for one row into the underlying database. The values are passed via parameters.
Update	Updates the data for one row in the underlying database. The values are passed via parameters.
Delete	Deletes a row from the underlying database. The key or keys for the row to be deleted are passed via parameters.

How an object data source determines which method to call

- The name of the method used for select, insert, update, and delete operations is specified by the SelectMethod, InsertMethod, UpdateMethod, or DeleteMethod attribute.
- The ObjectDataSource control determines what parameters need to be passed to the data access class methods based on the data fields to be inserted, updated, or deleted.
- The ObjectDataSource control then uses reflection to determine the parameter signatures for the insert, update, and delete methods provided by the data access class.
- At runtime, if the class doesn't provide a method with the correct name and parameters, an exception is thrown.

Description

- A data access class can declare public methods that select, insert, update, and delete data. These methods can be instance methods or shared methods.
- You can use any method names you want for the select, insert, update, and delete methods.
- If the select, insert, update, and delete methods are shared methods, the methods can be used without creating an instance of the data access class.
- If the select, insert, update, and delete methods are instance methods, an instance of the data access class must be created and destroyed for each data access operation. In this case, the data access class should provide a parameterless constructor.
- You can use parameters to pass selection criteria or other data to the select, insert, update, and delete methods. For more information, see figure 7-9.
- *Reflection* is a .NET feature that provides information about compiled classes and methods at runtime.

Figure 7-7   How to design a data access class

How to create a select method

Figure 7-8 shows how to design and code a select method that can be used with an ObjectDataSource control. The table at the top of this figure lists the four different types of values that a select method can return. The simplest is the IEnumerable interface, which can return a data reader because a data reader implements the IEnumerable interface. Also, the IEnumerable object can be a strongly-typed collection that's created by using an aggregate data type and the new generics feature. You'll learn more about this later in this chapter.

The select method can also return a DataTable or DataSet object. Because a dataset can contain more than one table, the ObjectDataSource control simply uses the first table in the dataset. As a result, you must design the select method so the first table in the dataset contains the data you want to access.

The main advantage of returning a dataset rather than a table is that the ObjectDataSource can cache a dataset. Then, to enable caching, you can set the EnableCaching attribute to True for the ObjectDataSource control. In that case, the select method will be called only the first time the data is requested. For more information on caching, which works the same as it does for a SqlDataSource control, please refer back to chapter 4.

You can also pass parameters to the select method. But if you do, you should provide a SelectParameters collection for the ObjectDataSource control. Then, you can use a ControlParameter element to bind a parameter to a control such as a listbox or a textbox. You saw an example of this in figure 7-5.

Allowable return types for a select method

Return type	Description
IEnumerable	A collection such as an ArrayList or HashTable or a strongly-typed generic collection such as System.Collections.Generic.List. (Because the DataReader class implements IEnumerable, the select method can also return a data reader.)
DataTable	If the select method returns a data table, the ObjectDataSource automatically extracts a data view from the table and uses the view for data binding.
DataSet	If the select method returns a dataset, the ObjectDataSource extracts a data view from the first data table in the dataset and uses the view for data binding. When the object data source returns a dataset, it can also use caching.
Object	If the select method returns a single object, the ObjectDataSource wraps the object in an IEnumerable collection with just one item, then does the data binding as if the method returned an IEnumerable.

A select method that returns a data reader

```
Public Shared Function GetAllCategories() As IEnumerable
    Dim sel As String = "SELECT CategoryID, LongName " _
        & "FROM Categories ORDER BY LongName"
    Dim cmd As SqlCommand = _
        New SqlCommand(sel, New SqlConnection(GetConnectionString()))
    cmd.Connection.Open()
    Return cmd.ExecuteReader(CommandBehavior.CloseConnection)
End Function
```

A select method that returns a dataset

```
Public Shared Function GetAllCategories() As DataSet
    Dim sel As String = "SELECT CategoryID, LongName " _
        & "FROM Categories ORDER BY LongName"
    Dim da As SqlDataAdapter = New SqlDataAdapter(sel, GetConnectionString)
    Dim dsCategories As DataSet = New DataSet
    da.Fill(dsCategories, "Categories")
    Return dsCategories
End Function
```

Description

- The select method returns data retrieved from the underlying database.

- The select method can return the data in several forms, including a data reader or a dataset.

- If the select method returns a dataset, the object data source can cache the data.

- The select method can also return a strongly-typed collection using Visual Basic's new generics feature. For more information, see figure 7-18.

- If the select method accepts parameters, the parameters must be declared within the SelectParameters collection of the ObjectDataSource control. Within this collection, you can use the ControlParameter element to declare a parameter that's bound to another control on the page.

Figure 7-8   How to create a select method

How to create update, delete, and insert methods

Besides select methods, the data access class used by an object data source can provide methods that update, delete, and insert data in the underlying database. Figure 7-9 presents some guidelines that you should follow when you create these methods.

Undoubtedly the most difficult aspect of working with object data sources is determining how the parameters for update, delete, and insert methods are passed to them from the data source. The reason for this difficulty is that these parameters aren't determined until runtime. Then, the ObjectDataSource control creates a collection of parameters that are passed to the data access class method based on several factors, including (1) the bound fields that are used by the control that the object data source is bound to, (2) the DataKeyNames attribute of the bound control, (3) whether the object data source uses optimistic concurrency checking, and (4) whether the key fields are read-only or updatable.

Once the ObjectDataSource control has determined what parameters need to be passed, it uses the new reflection feature to determine whether the data access class has a method that accepts the required parameters. If so, the method is called using these parameters. If not, an exception is thrown. This means that you must anticipate the parameters that will be passed to your method so you can code them correctly. Fortunately, though, if you guess wrong, you can use the message displayed by the exception that occurs to determine what parameters were expected and then correct your code.

If the object data source is bound to a GridView, DetailsView, or FormView control, the parameter names are determined by the DataField attributes of the BoundField elements that are used to create the bound data fields. As a result, the parameter names you use in your data access class methods must be the same as the names you use on the DataField attributes.

Note, however, that the order of the parameters doesn't matter. Instead, the object data source control uses reflection to determine the names and order of the parameters expected by the data access methods. Then, when it calls those methods, the object data source passes the parameters in the expected order.

The most confusing aspect of how the ObjectDataSource generates parameters has to do with the cases that require two sets of values to be passed to an update method. That happens if you use optimistic concurrency or if the primary key field is updatable. For optimistic concurrency, both values are needed so the update statement can make sure the data hasn't been changed before it applies the update. And if optimistic concurrency isn't used but the key field is updatable, the update statement needs the original key value so it can properly retrieve the record to be updated.

In either case, the original parameter values are passed by parameters that use the data field name prefixed by "original_". For example, the new value of a field named ShortName is passed via a parameter named ShortName, but the original value is passed via a parameter named original_ShortName.

Similarly, the name of the parameter that's passed to a delete statement depends on whether the primary key field is read-only or updatable when

A typical Update method

```
Public Shared Sub UpdateCategory(ByVal CategoryID As String, _
        ByVal ShortName As String, ByVal LongName As String)
    Dim up As String = "UPDATE Categories " _
        & "SET ShortName = @ShortName, " _
        & "LongName = @LongName " _
        & "WHERE CategoryID = @CategoryID"
    Dim cmd As SqlCommand = _
        New SqlCommand(up, New SqlConnection(GetConnectionString))
    cmd.Parameters.AddWithValue("CategoryID", CategoryID)
    cmd.Parameters.AddWithValue("ShortName", ShortName)
    cmd.Parameters.AddWithValue("LongName", LongName)
    cmd.Connection.Open()
    cmd.ExecuteNonQuery()
End Sub
```

How parameters are generated

- Parameters are automatically generated when an ObjectDataSource is bound to a GridView or other list control.

- One parameter is generated for each BoundField column using the name specified in the DataField attribute.

- If the ObjectDataSource control uses optimistic concurrency, an original_*datafield* parameter is also generated for each BoundField column when you call the update method.

- If optimistic concurrency isn't used but the key field of the data source is updatable, the key value of the record to be updated is passed via the original_*datafield* parameter.

- The parameter passed to the delete method is always the original_*datafield* parameter.

- If you want, you can control the names used for the original value parameters by setting the OldValuesParameterFormatString attribute. The default is "original_{0}" if optimistic concurrency is enabled or if the key field is updatable. Otherwise, the default is "{0}".

Description

- To properly design an update, delete, or insert method, you must be aware of how the ObjectDataSource control generates the parameters passed to these methods.

- Although the order in which the parameters appear in your update, delete, and insert methods doesn't matter, your parameter names must match the names generated by the ObjectDataSource control.

- If your methods don't use the parameter names that the object data source expects, you can use the exception messages that occur at runtime to correct your parameter names.

Figure 7-9   How to create update, delete, and insert methods

optimistic concurrency isn't used. If the key field is read-only and optimistic concurrency isn't used, the parameter name is simply the key field name. But if optimistic concurrency is used or if the key field is updatable, the delete method's parameter will begin with original_.

Incidentally, the names of the original value parameters are determined by a format string that's specified in the OldValuesParameterFormatString attribute. If optimistic concurrency isn't used and if the primary key field is read-only, the default value of this attribute is "{0}", which doesn't modify the parameter names. But if optimistic concurrency is used or if the key field is updatable, the default value for this attribute is "original_{0}", which provides different names for the original value parameters. Although you can change this format string so it uses different naming conventions, you shouldn't need to do that unless you're using the ObjectDataSource control with an existing data access class that uses some other naming convention for the parameters that pass the original values.

How to use attributes to mark a data access class

Figure 7-10 shows how you can use Visual Basic *attributes* to identify a data access class and its methods. In case you haven't worked with attributes before, they are simply a way to provide declarative information for classes, methods, properties, and so on. Although some of these attributes have meaning at runtime, the attributes in this figure are used at design time. In particular, the Data Source Configuration Wizard uses these attributes to determine which classes in the App_Code folder are data access classes and which methods in the data access class are select, insert, update, and delete methods.

Note, however, that you don't need to use these attributes. The only reason to use them is to help the Data Source Configuration Wizard recognize the data access classes and methods. If you haven't marked your data access classes with these attributes, you can still access them from the wizard by clearing the Show Only Data Components checkbox in the Choose a Business Object step of the wizard (see figure 7-3).

Attributes for marking data access classes

To mark an element as...	Use this attribute...
A data object class	`<DataObject(true)>`
A Select method	`<DataObjectMethod(DataObjectMethodType.Select)>`
An Insert method	`<DataObjectMethod(DataObjectMethodType.Insert)>`
An Update method	`<DataObjectMethod(DataObjectMethodType.Update)>`
A Delete method	`<DataObjectMethod(DataObjectMethodType.Delete)>`

A marked data access class

```vb
Imports Microsoft.VisualBasic
Imports System.ComponentModel
Imports System.Data
Imports System.Data.SqlClient

<DataObject(True)> _
Public Class ProductDB

    <DataObjectMethod(DataObjectMethodType.Select)> _
    Public Shared Function GetAllCategories() As IEnumerable
        Dim sel As String = "SELECT CategoryID, LongName " _
            & "FROM Categories ORDER BY LongName"
        Dim cmd As SqlCommand = _
            New SqlCommand(sel, New SqlConnection(GetConnectionString()))
        cmd.Connection.Open()
        Return cmd.ExecuteReader(CommandBehavior.CloseConnection)
    End Function

End Class
```

Description

- You can use DataObject and DataObjectMethod attributes to mark data access classes and methods. Visual Studio uses these attributes to determine which classes and methods to list in the drop-down boxes of the Data Source Configuration Wizard.

- The DataObject and DataObjectMethod attributes are in the System.ComponentModel namespace.

Figure 7-10   How to use attributes to mark a data access class

A Category Maintenance application

To give you a better idea of how you can use an object data source to update, delete, and insert data, the following topics present an application that maintains the Categories table in the Halloween database. This application is a variation of the Category Maintenance application that was presented in chapter 5.

The design of the Category Maintenance application

Figure 7-11 presents the design for this version of the Category Maintenance application. It uses a GridView control to let the user update and delete category records and a DetailsView control below the GridView control to insert new category records. Both the GridView and DetailsView controls are bound to a single ObjectDataSource control. But the DetailsView control is used only in insert mode so it isn't used to display, update, or delete existing category records.

The table in this figure shows the public methods that are provided by the CategoryDB class. These four methods provide the select, update, delete, and insert functions. Since all of these methods are defined as shared, an instance of the CategoryDB class doesn't have to be created to access the database.

To keep this application simple, it doesn't use optimistic concurrency. That way, it's easy to figure out what parameters are required by the methods in the data access class. However, the next application in this chapter does use optimistic concurrency so you can see what that entails.

The aspx file

The two parts of figure 7-12 show the Default.aspx file for this application. In part 1, you can see the aspx code for the GridView control that displays the category rows. Its Columns collection includes three BoundField columns, named CategoryID, ShortName, and LongName.

In part 2, you can see the aspx code for the ObjectDataSource control. It names CategoryDB as the data access class, then provides the names of the select, insert, update, and delete methods that will be used to access the data.

Notice that I also set the OldValuesParameterFormatString attribute for this data source to {0}. In the final release version of ASP.NET 2.0, this will be the default setting for this attribute, so this line won't be necessary. However, in the Beta 2 version that we used to develop this application, the default was "original_{0}". So without this line of code, the CategoryID parameter that's sent to the DeleteCategory and UpdateCategory methods of the CategoryDB class would be named original_CategoryID.

You can also see the aspx code for the DetailsView control in part 2. Here, I set the DefaultMode attribute to Insert so this control is always displayed in Insert mode.

The Category Maintenance application

Methods of the CategoryDB class

Method type	Signature
select	`Public Shared Function GetCategories() As IEnumerable`
update	`Public Shared Sub UpdateCategory(ByVal CategoryID As String, _` `        ByVal ShortName As String, ByVal LongName As String)`
delete	`Public Shared Sub DeleteCategory(By Val CategoryID As String)`
insert	`Public Shared Sub InsertCategory(ByVal CategoryID As String, _` `        ByVal ShortName As String, ByVal LongName As String)`

Description

- The GridView and DetailsView controls are bound to an ObjectDataSource control that accesses the Categories table of the Halloween database.
- The data access class named CategoryDB provides the select, insert, update, and delete methods.
- This version of the application doesn't provide concurrency checking.

Figure 7-11   The Category Maintenance application

The Default.aspx file

```
<%@ Page Language="VB" AutoEventWireup="false" CodeFile="Default.aspx.vb"
Inherits="_Default" %>

<!DOCTYPE html PUBLIC "-//W3C//DTD XHTML 1.1//EN"
"http://www.w3.org/TR/xhtml11/DTD/xhtml11.dtd">

<html xmlns="http://www.w3.org/1999/xhtml" >
<head runat="server">
    <title>Chapter 7 Category Maintenance</title>
</head>
<body>
    <form id="form1" runat="server">
    <div>
        <asp:Image ID="Image1" runat="server" ImageUrl="~/Images/banner.jpg" />
        <br /><br /><h2>Category Maintenance</h2>
        <asp:GridView ID="GridView1" runat="server"
            DataSourceID="ObjectDataSource1" DataKeyNames="CategoryID"
            AutoGenerateColumns="False" ForeColor="Black" >
            <Columns>
                <asp:BoundField DataField="CategoryID" ReadOnly="True"
                    HeaderText="Category ID" >
                    <ItemStyle Width="100px" />
                </asp:BoundField>
                <asp:BoundField DataField="ShortName" HeaderText="Short Name" >
                    <ItemStyle Width="150px" />
                </asp:BoundField>
                <asp:BoundField DataField="LongName" HeaderText="Long Name" >
                    <ItemStyle Width="200px" />
                </asp:BoundField>
                <asp:CommandField ButtonType="Button" ShowEditButton="True" />
                <asp:CommandField ButtonType="Button" ShowDeleteButton="True" />
            </Columns>
            <HeaderStyle BackColor="Silver" Font-Bold="True"
                ForeColor="White" />
            <RowStyle BackColor="White" ForeColor="Black" />
            <AlternatingRowStyle BackColor="WhiteSmoke" ForeColor="Black" />
            <EditRowStyle BackColor="Blue" ForeColor="White" />
        </asp:GridView>
```

Note

- If you use the designer to bind fields defined by an object data source to controls like the GridView control, you should realize that the fields won't be listed by name. That's because the fields are defined in the data access class and not directly in the data source. Because of that, you'll have to enter the names of the fields you want to bind manually.

Figure 7-12   The aspx file of the Category Maintenance application (part 1 of 2)

The Default.aspx file   **Page 2**

```
<asp:ObjectDataSource ID="ObjectDataSource1" runat="server"
    TypeName="CategoryDB"
    SelectMethod="GetCategories"
    InsertMethod="InsertCategory"
    DeleteMethod="DeleteCategory"
    UpdateMethod="UpdateCategory"
    OldValuesParameterFormatString="{0}" >
    <DeleteParameters>
        <asp:Parameter Name="CategoryID" Type="String" />
    </DeleteParameters>
    <UpdateParameters>
        <asp:Parameter Name="CategoryID" Type="String" />
        <asp:Parameter Name="ShortName" Type="String" />
        <asp:Parameter Name="LongName" Type="String" />
    </UpdateParameters>
    <InsertParameters>
        <asp:Parameter Name="CategoryID" Type="String" />
        <asp:Parameter Name="ShortName" Type="String" />
        <asp:Parameter Name="LongName" Type="String" />
    </InsertParameters>
</asp:ObjectDataSource><br />

<asp:Label ID="lblError" runat="server" EnableViewState="False"
    ForeColor="Red">
</asp:Label><br />
To create a new category, enter the category information
and click Insert.<br /><br />

<asp:DetailsView ID="DetailsView1" runat="server"
    AutoGenerateRows="False" DataSourceID="ObjectDataSource1"
    DefaultMode="Insert" Height="50px" Width="300px"
    GridLines="None" BorderStyle="None" CellSpacing="5" >
    <Fields>
        <asp:BoundField DataField="CategoryID"
            HeaderText="Category ID:" />
        <asp:BoundField DataField="ShortName"
            HeaderText="Short Name:" />
        <asp:BoundField DataField="LongName"
            HeaderText="Long Name:" />
        <asp:CommandField ButtonType="Button"
            ShowInsertButton="True" />
    </Fields>
</asp:DetailsView>
</div>
</form>
</body>
</html>
```

Figure 7-12   The aspx file of the Category Maintenance application (part 2 of 2)

The code-behind file

Figure 7-13 shows the code-behind file for the Default.aspx page of the Category Maintenance application. This file consists of just three procedures that handle the exceptions that might be raised when the object data source's update, delete, or insert methods are called.

The first procedure is called after a row has been updated. This procedure checks the Exception property of the e argument to determine if an exception has been thrown. If so, an error message is displayed, the ExceptionHandled property is set to True to suppress the exception, and the KeepInEditMode property is set to True to leave the GridView control in edit mode.

The other two procedures are similar. GridView1_RowDeleted is called after a row has been deleted, and DetailView1_ItemInserted is called after a row has been inserted. Both procedures check for exceptions and display appropriate error messages.

The CategoryDB class

The two parts of figure 7-14 present the CategoryDB class that's used as the data access class for this application. This class uses the DataObject and DataObjectMethodType attributes to mark the class as a data object class and to mark the methods as data object methods.

The four public methods in this class use standard ADO.NET commands to access the database. Since this code is straightforward, you shouldn't have any trouble understanding how they work. So I won't describe them in detail here.

The private GetConnectionString method is called by each of the four public methods to get the connection string for the Halloween database. This connection string is stored in the web.config file.

The Default.aspx.vb file

```vb
Partial Class _Default
    Inherits System.Web.UI.Page

    Protected Sub GridView1_RowUpdated(ByVal sender As Object, _
            ByVal e As System.Web.UI.WebControls.GridViewUpdatedEventArgs) _
            Handles GridView1.RowUpdated
        If e.Exception IsNot Nothing Then
            lblError.Text = "Invalid data. Please correct and try again."
            e.ExceptionHandled = True
            e.KeepInEditMode = True
        End If
    End Sub

    Protected Sub GridView1_RowDeleted(ByVal sender As Object, _
            ByVal e As System.Web.UI.WebControls.GridViewDeletedEventArgs) _
            Handles GridView1.RowDeleted
        If e.Exception IsNot Nothing Then
            lblError.Text = "The category cound not be deleted."
            e.ExceptionHandled = True
        End If
    End Sub

    Protected Sub DetailsView1_ItemInserted(ByVal sender As Object, _
            ByVal e As System.Web.UI.WebControls.DetailsViewInsertedEventArgs) _
            Handles DetailsView1.ItemInserted
        If e.Exception IsNot Nothing Then
            lblError.Text = "Invalid data. Please correct and try again."
            e.ExceptionHandled = True
        End If
    End Sub

End Class
```

Figure 7-13   The code-behind file for the Category Maintenance application

The CategoryDB.vb file

```vb
Imports Microsoft.VisualBasic
Imports System.Data
Imports System.Data.SqlClient
Imports System.ComponentModel

<DataObject(True)> _
Public Class CategoryDB

    <DataObjectMethod(DataObjectMethodType.Select)> _
    Public Shared Function GetCategories() As IEnumerable
        Dim sel As String = "SELECT CategoryID, ShortName, LongName " _
            & "FROM Categories ORDER BY ShortName"
        Dim cmd As SqlCommand = _
            New SqlCommand(sel, New SqlConnection(GetConnectionString))
        cmd.Connection.Open()
        Return cmd.ExecuteReader(CommandBehavior.CloseConnection)
    End Function

    Private Shared Function GetConnectionString() As String
        Return ConfigurationManager.ConnectionStrings _
            ("HalloweenConnection").ConnectionString
    End Function

    <DataObjectMethod(DataObjectMethodType.Insert)> _
    Public Shared Sub InsertCategory(ByVal CategoryID As String, _
            ByVal ShortName As String, ByVal LongName As String)
        Dim ins As String = "INSERT INTO Categories " _
            & "(CategoryID, ShortName, LongName) " _
            & "VALUES(@CategoryID, @ShortName, @LongName)"
        Dim cmd As SqlCommand = _
            New SqlCommand(ins, New SqlConnection(GetConnectionString))
        cmd.Parameters.AddWithValue("CategoryID", CategoryID)
        cmd.Parameters.AddWithValue("ShortName", ShortName)
        cmd.Parameters.AddWithValue("LongName", LongName)
        cmd.Connection.Open()
        cmd.ExecuteNonQuery()
    End Sub
```

Figure 7-14   The CategoryDB class for the Category Maintenance application (part 1 of 2)

The CategoryDB.vb file   Page 2

```vb
<DataObjectMethod(DataObjectMethodType.Delete)> _
Public Shared Sub DeleteCategory(ByVal CategoryID As String)
    Dim del As String = "DELETE FROM Categories " _
        & "WHERE CategoryID = @CategoryID"
    Dim cmd As SqlCommand = _
        New SqlCommand(del, New SqlConnection(GetConnectionString))
    cmd.Parameters.AddWithValue("CategoryID", CategoryID)
    cmd.Connection.Open()
    cmd.ExecuteNonQuery()
End Sub

<DataObjectMethod(DataObjectMethodType.Update)> _
Public Shared Sub UpdateCategory(ByVal CategoryID As String, _
        ByVal ShortName As String, ByVal LongName As String)
    Dim up As String = "UPDATE Categories " _
        & "SET ShortName = @ShortName, " _
        & "LongName = @LongName " _
        & "WHERE CategoryID = @CategoryID"
    Dim cmd As SqlCommand = _
        New SqlCommand(up, New SqlConnection(GetConnectionString))
    cmd.Parameters.AddWithValue("CategoryID", CategoryID)
    cmd.Parameters.AddWithValue("ShortName", ShortName)
    cmd.Parameters.AddWithValue("LongName", LongName)
    cmd.Connection.Open()
    cmd.ExecuteNonQuery()
End Sub

End Class
```

Figure 7-14   The CategoryDB class for the Category Maintenance application (part 2 of 2)

How to use aggregate data types and detect concurrency errors

The Category Maintenance application that you've just seen updates only three fields in the underlying database. But imagine if the application needed to update 25 fields. Then, if the application used optimistic concurrency, the update method would require 50 parameters: 25 for the new data and 25 more for the original data.

To reduce the number of parameters that need to be passed to the methods in your data access classes, the ObjectDataSource control is designed to work with aggregate data types, which you'll learn how to use next. Along the way, you'll also learn how to check for concurrency errors when you use an object data source.

How to create an aggregate data type

As figure 7-15 shows, an *aggregate data type* is simply a class that provides properties that correspond to the parameters that would otherwise have to be sent separately to a method of a data access class. In the example in this figure, I created a class named Category that provides properties named CategoryID, ShortName, and LongName. Then, instead of passing these three parameters separately to the data access class methods, the ObjectDataSource control can be configured to pass an instance of the Category class as a single parameter.

There are only two rules you need to follow when you create a class for an aggregate data type. First, you must provide a parameterless constructor that the ObjectDataSource class uses to create an instance of the aggregate class. Actually, if this is the only constructor for the class, you can omit it and Visual Basic will provide a parameterless constructor for you. However, it's a good idea to explicitly code the parameterless constructor. That way, if you later add another constructor (for example, one that accepts the CategoryID, ShortName, and LongName as parameters), the parameterless constructor will still be available.

Second, you must provide a property for each data field used by the data source. These properties must provide both get and set accessors and must use the names specified by the DataField attributes of the BoundField controls. In this case, CategoryID, ShortName, and LongName are the property names.

The Category class

```
Public Class Category
    Private sCategoryID As String
    Private sShortName As String
    Private sLongName As String

    Public Sub New()

    End Sub

    Public Property CategoryID() As String
        Get
            Return sCategoryID
        End Get
        Set(ByVal value As String)
            sCategoryID = value
        End Set
    End Property

    Public Property ShortName() As String
        Get
            Return sShortName
        End Get
        Set(ByVal value As String)
            sShortName = value
        End Set
    End Property

    Public Property LongName() As String
        Get
            Return sLongName
        End Get
        Set(ByVal value As String)
            sLongName = value
        End Set
    End Property

End Class
```

Description

- An *aggregate data type* is a class that provides properties that would otherwise be passed separately to the methods of a data access class. This reduces the number of parameters that are passed to the data access methods.

- An aggregate data type should have a parameterless constructor and a property with both a get and set accessor for each data field used by the data source.

- If the ObjectDataSource is bound to a GridView, DetailsView, or FormView control, the property names must match the DataField properties of the BoundField elements that define each bound column.

Figure 7-15   How to create an aggregate data type

How to use an aggregate data type

The code in figure 7-16 shows how you can declare an ObjectDataSource control that uses an aggregate data type. To do that, you provide the name of the class for the aggregate data type in the DataObjectTypeName attribute.

Of course, you must also adjust the methods of the data access class so they accept aggregate data types as their parameters instead of individual data field parameters. As this figure indicates, the parameters passed to these methods depend on whether the object data source uses optimistic concurrency. If optimistic concurrency isn't used, the insert, update, and delete methods are passed a single instance of the aggregate data type. For the delete method, though, only the data key properties will be set and all other properties will be null.

If you use optimistic concurrency, the parameters are more complicated. For an insert or delete, a single instance of the aggregate data type is passed. But for an update, two instances of the aggregate data type are passed. The first contains the changed data, and the second contains the original data. Then, the update method can use the original data to determine whether the data has been modified by another user before the update is applied.

An ObjectDataSource control that uses an aggregate data type

```
<asp:ObjectDataSource ID="ObjectDataSource1" runat="server"
    TypeName="CategoryDB" DataObjectTypeName="Category"
    SelectMethod="GetCategories"
    InsertMethod="InsertCategory"
    UpdateMethod="UpdateCategory"
    DeleteMethod="DeleteCategory" >
</asp:ObjectDataSource>
```

How parameters are passed when you use an aggregate data type

If optimistic concurrency isn't used:

- The insert, update, and delete methods are passed a single parameter of the type specified in the DataObjectTypeName attribute.
- For the delete method, only the properties that represent the data keys will be set. The other properties will be null.

If optimistic concurrency is used:

- The insert method is passed a single parameter of the type specified in the DataObjectTypeName attribute.
- The update method is passed two parameters, both of the type specified in the DataObjectTypeName attribute. The first contains the data to be updated, the second contains the original data.
- The delete method is passed a single parameter of the type specified in the DataObjectTypeName attribute. All of its properties are set.

Description

- You use the DataObjectTypeName attribute of the ObjectDataSource control to specify the name of an aggregate data type.
- The parameters passed to the insert, update, and delete methods depend on whether optimistic concurrency is specified for the ObjectDataSource control.

Figure 7-16   How to use an aggregate data type

How to check for concurrency errors

As figure 7-17 shows, you can use optimistic concurrency with an ObjectDataSource control by setting the ConflictDetection attribute to CompareAllValues. However, checking for concurrency errors when you use an object data source is more complicated than it is when you use a SQL data source. That's because the object data source has no built-in way to determine if the update or delete method has actually detected a concurrency error. However, the object data source does pass the parameters that you need for detecting concurrency errors in your code-behind files.

There are several techniques you can use to determine when concurrency errors have occurred. One is to write the update and delete methods so they throw an exception if a concurrency error occurs. Then, the RowUpdated and RowDeleted events can test the e.Exception property to determine if this exception has been thrown.

Another approach is to write the update and delete methods so they return an integer value that represents the number of rows affected by the update or delete. This method is similar to the way the SqlDataSource control detects concurrency violations. Unfortunately, the ObjectDataSource control doesn't automatically update the e.AffectedRows property that's available in the Updated and Deleted event handlers for a bound data control. As a result, you must provide an event handler for the ObjectDataSource control to set these properties.

As the second example in this figure shows, you can retrieve the return value from the update or delete method by using the ReturnValue property in an Updated or Deleted event handler for an object data source. Since this value is returned as an Object, you have to convert it to an integer before you can assign it to the AffectedRows property.

Once you've set the AffectedRows property, the third example in this figure shows how you can use this property to check for a concurrency error in the RowUpdated event of a GridView control. If the value of this property is zero, a concurrency error has occurred.

If you find the second and third examples confusing, keep in mind that the second example handles the Updated event for the ObjectDataSource control, but the third code example handles the RowUpdated event for the GridView control. As a result, the e argument for these two event handlers is defined by two different classes. For the object data source, the e argument is defined by the ObjectDataSourceStatusEventArgs class. This class includes a property named ReturnValue that's automatically set to the value returned by the update or delete method. It also includes an AffectedRows property that's set to zero by default.

In contrast, the e argument for the RowUpdated event of the GridView control is defined by the GridViewUpdatedEventArgs class. This class also defines an AffectedRows property. Then, the value you assign to the AffectedRows property in the Updated event handler for the object data source is passed forward to the RowUpdated event handler for the GridView control, where it can be tested to determine if a concurrency error has occurred.

Incidentally, I like this way of handling concurrency errors with object data sources because the code for the RowUpdated event handler of a bound control is

An ObjectDataSource control that uses optimistic concurrency

```
<asp:ObjectDataSource ID="ObjectDataSource1" runat="server"
    TypeName="CategoryDB" DataObjectTypeName="Category"
    ConflictDetection="CompareAllValues"
    SelectMethod="GetCategories"
    InsertMethod="InsertCategory"
    UpdateMethod="UpdateCategory"
    DeleteMethod="DeleteCategory" >
</asp:ObjectDataSource>
```

An Updated procedure for an ObjectDataSource control that sets the AffectedRows property

```
Protected Sub ObjectDataSource1_Updated(ByVal sender As Object, _
    ByVal e As System.Web.UI.WebControls.ObjectDataSourceStatusEventArgs) _
        Handles ObjectDataSource1.Updated
    e.AffectedRows = CType(e.ReturnValue, Integer)
End Sub
```

A RowUpdated procedure for a GridView control that checks for concurrency errors

```
Protected Sub GridView1_RowUpdated(ByVal sender As Object, _
        ByVal e As System.Web.UI.WebControls.GridViewUpdatedEventArgs) _
        Handles GridView1.RowUpdated
    If e.Exception IsNot Nothing Then
        lblError.Text = "Invalid data. Please correct and try again."
        e.ExceptionHandled = True
        e.KeepInEditMode = True
    ElseIf e.AffectedRows = 0 Then
        lblError.Text = "Another user has updated that category. " _
            & "Please try again."
    End If
End Sub
```

Description

- When you use optimistic concurrency with an ObjectDataSource control, the update and delete methods usually return the number of rows affected by the update or delete operation as a return value.
- You must handle the Updated and Deleted events for the ObjectDataSource control to store the number of rows affected by the update or delete operation in the AffectedRows property. Then, you can test for concurrency errors in the RowUpdated and RowDeleted events of a GridView or other bound control.

Figure 7-17   How to check for concurrency errors

the same as it is when you use a SQL data source. To make that work, you just have to set the AffectedRows property of the e argument in the event handlers for your object data source.

How to use the generics feature to return a typed list

So far, you've seen how you can use an aggregate data type in an update, delete, or insert method. But you can also use aggregate data types in select methods. The easiest way to do that is to use a new feature of .NET 2.0 called *generics* along with the new List class. As figure 7-18 shows, the generics feature and the List class let you create a select method that returns a *strongly-typed collection*, which is a collection that can hold objects of a specific type.

The List class lets you create a *generic list*. This type of list is similar to an array list, but it can only contain objects of a certain type. When you declare a generic list, you declare the type of objects it can contain. For example, the code shown in this figure includes a list of the Category type, which is the aggregrate data type shown in figure 7-15. As a result, this list can hold only Category objects. If you try to add any other type of object to the list, an exception will be thrown.

When you specify an aggregate data type in the DataObjectTypeName attribute of an object data source, you can use select methods that return generic lists that specify the aggregate type. For example, the GetCategories method in this figure is a select method that returns a list of Category objects. This method uses standard ADO.NET classes to get a data reader that contains the category information. Then, it uses a Do While loop to read each category from the data reader, create a Category object, and add the Category object to the generic list. This list is used as the select method's return value.

A method that returns a list of Category objects

```
Public Shared Function GetCategories() As List(Of Category)
    Dim sel As String = "SELECT CategoryID, ShortName, LongName " _
        & "FROM Categories ORDER BY ShortName"
    Dim cmd As SqlCommand = _
        New SqlCommand(sel, New SqlConnection(GetConnectionString))
    cmd.Connection.Open()
    Dim dr As SqlDataReader = _
        cmd.ExecuteReader(CommandBehavior.CloseConnection)
    Dim catList As New List(Of Category)
    Do While dr.Read
        Dim c As Category = New Category
        c.CategoryID = dr("CategoryID").ToString
        c.ShortName = dr("ShortName").ToString
        c.LongName = dr("LongName").ToString
        catList.Add(c)
    Loop
    dr.Close()
    Return catList
End Function
```

The syntax for creating a generic List collection

```
Dim|Private|Public|Static listname As New List(Of Type)
```

Description

- *Generics* refers to a new feature of Visual Basic 2.0 that lets you create strongly-typed collections. A *strongly-typed collection* is a collection that can hold only objects of a certain type.

- The select method can return a strongly-typed collection that contains objects of the type specified by the DataObjectTypeName attribute. For example, a select method can return a list of Category objects.

- Version 2.0 of the .NET Framework includes several new collection classes that are designed to work with the generics feature. For example, the List class is a generic version of the ArrayList class.

- To declare a variable that refers to a List, you specify the List class name, followed by the Of keyword and the type in parentheses. Then, the list can contain objects only of the type you specify.

Note

- The List class is found in the System.Collections.Generic namespace. You need to provide an Imports statement for this namespace if you want to use the List class.

Figure 7-18   How to use the generics feature to return a typed list

A Category Maintenance application that uses an aggregate class

Now that you've seen the basics of how aggregate data types work and how to check for concurrency errors when you use object data sources, the following topics present another version of the Category Maintenance application. If you want to review the user interface for this application, please refer to figure 7-11. But this time, the application uses an aggregate data type and concurrency checking.

This version of the application uses the Category class that's shown in figure 7-15. Also, since the Default.apsx file is almost identical to the file shown in figure 7-12, I won't repeat it here. The only difference is that the aspx code for the ObjectDataSource control is replaced by the code at the top of figure 7-17.

The code-behind file

Figure 7-19 shows the code-behind file for this application. This file is similar to the code-behind file for the previous version of this application. However, because this application checks for concurrency errors, it provides Updated and Deleted event handlers for the object data source. Both of these handlers get the value returned by the corresponding method in the data access class (the number of rows affected by the update or delete operation), and set the AffectedRows property of the e argument to that value.

The AffectedRows property is then passed to the corresponding event handlers for the GridView control, RowUpdated and RowDeleted. As a result, these handlers can test the value of this property and display appropriate messages if the value is zero, which means that the operation wasn't successful.

The CategoryDB class

The two parts of figure 7-20 show the CategoryDB class used for this application. As you can see, the GetCategories method has been modified so it returns a generic list of Category objects. Similarly, the InsertCategory, UpdateCategory, and DeleteCategory methods have been modified so they accept Category objects rather than individual data field parameters.

What's interesting is the way concurrency checking is done in the update and delete methods. First, the Update and Delete statements are coded with Where clauses that use the original values of the fields to make sure the row to be deleted or updated hasn't been changed by another user since it was retrieved. Second, the original values are included in the parameters collection for the delete command, and both the original values and the new values are included in the parameters collection for the update command. Third, both methods return an integer value that represents the number of rows affected by the command.

The Default.aspx.vb file for an application that uses an aggregate class

```
Partial Class _Default
    Inherits System.Web.UI.Page

    Protected Sub ObjectDataSource1_Updated(ByVal sender As Object, _
        ByVal e As System.Web.UI.WebControls.ObjectDataSourceStatusEventArgs) _
            Handles ObjectDataSource1.Updated
        e.AffectedRows = CType(e.ReturnValue, Integer)
    End Sub

    Protected Sub GridView1_RowUpdated(ByVal sender As Object, _
            ByVal e As System.Web.UI.WebControls.GridViewUpdatedEventArgs) _
            Handles GridView1.RowUpdated
        If e.Exception IsNot Nothing Then
            lblError.Text = "Invalid data. Please correct and try again."
            e.ExceptionHandled = True
            e.KeepInEditMode = True
        ElseIf e.AffectedRows = 0 Then
            lblError.Text = "Another user has updated that category. " _
                & "Please try again."
        End If
    End Sub

    Protected Sub ObjectDataSource1_Deleted(ByVal sender As Object, _
        ByVal e As System.Web.UI.WebControls.ObjectDataSourceStatusEventArgs) _
            Handles ObjectDataSource1.Deleted
        e.AffectedRows = CType(e.ReturnValue, Integer)
    End Sub

    Protected Sub GridView1_RowDeleted(ByVal sender As Object, _
            ByVal e As System.Web.UI.WebControls.GridViewDeletedEventArgs) _
            Handles GridView1.RowDeleted
        If e.Exception IsNot Nothing Then
            lblError.Text = "The category cound not be deleted."
            e.ExceptionHandled = True
        ElseIf e.AffectedRows = 0 Then
            lblError.Text = "Another user has updated that category. " _
                & "Please try again."
        End If
    End Sub

    Protected Sub DetailsView1_ItemInserted(ByVal sender As Object, _
            ByVal e As System.Web.UI.WebControls.DetailsViewInsertedEventArgs) _
            Handles DetailsView1.ItemInserted
        If e.Exception IsNot Nothing Then
            lblError.Text = "Invalid data. Please correct and try again."
            e.ExceptionHandled = True
        End If
    End Sub

End Class
```

Figure 7-19   The code-behind file for an application that uses an aggregate class

The CategoryDB.vb file with an aggregate data type

```vb
Imports Microsoft.VisualBasic
Imports System.Data
Imports System.Data.SqlClient
Imports System.ComponentModel
Imports System.Collections.Generic

<DataObject(True)> _
Public Class CategoryDB

    <DataObjectMethod(DataObjectMethodType.Select)> _
    Public Shared Function GetCategories() As List(Of Category)
        Dim sel As String = "SELECT CategoryID, ShortName, LongName " _
            & "FROM Categories ORDER BY ShortName"
        Dim cmd As SqlCommand = _
            New SqlCommand(sel, New SqlConnection(GetConnectionString))
        cmd.Connection.Open()
        Dim dr As SqlDataReader = _
            cmd.ExecuteReader(CommandBehavior.CloseConnection)
        Dim catList As New List(Of Category)
        Do While dr.Read
            Dim c As Category = New Category
            c.CategoryID = dr("CategoryID").ToString
            c.ShortName = dr("ShortName").ToString
            c.LongName = dr("LongName").ToString
            catList.Add(c)
        Loop
        dr.Close()
        Return catList
    End Function

    Private Shared Function GetConnectionString() As String
        Return ConfigurationManager.ConnectionStrings _
            ("HalloweenConnection").ConnectionString
    End Function

    <DataObjectMethod(DataObjectMethodType.Insert)> _
    Public Shared Sub InsertCategory(ByVal Category As Category)
        Dim ins As String = "INSERT INTO Categories " _
            & "(CategoryID, ShortName, LongName) " _
            & "VALUES(@CategoryID, @ShortName, @LongName)"
        Dim cmd As SqlCommand = _
            New SqlCommand(ins, New SqlConnection(GetConnectionString))
        cmd.Parameters.AddWithValue("CategoryID", Category.CategoryID)
        cmd.Parameters.AddWithValue("ShortName", Category.ShortName)
        cmd.Parameters.AddWithValue("LongName", Category.LongName)
        cmd.Connection.Open()
        cmd.ExecuteNonQuery()
    End Sub
```

Figure 7-20   The CategoryDB class with an aggregate data type (part 1 of 2)

The CategoryDB.vb file with an aggregate data type   Part 2

```vb
<DataObjectMethod(DataObjectMethodType.Delete)> _
Public Shared Function DeleteCategory(ByVal Category As Category) _
        As Integer
    Dim del As String = "DELETE FROM Categories " _
        & "WHERE CategoryID = @original_CategoryID " _
        & "   AND ShortName = @original_CategoryID " _
        & "   AND LongName = @original_CategoryID"
    Dim cmd As SqlCommand = _
        New SqlCommand(del, New SqlConnection(GetConnectionString))
    cmd.Parameters.AddWithValue("original_CategoryID", _
        Category.CategoryID)
    cmd.Parameters.AddWithValue("original_ShortName", _
        Category.ShortName)
    cmd.Parameters.AddWithValue("original_LongName", _
        Category.LongName)
    cmd.Connection.Open()
    Dim i As Integer = cmd.ExecuteNonQuery()
    cmd.Connection.Close()
    Return i
End Function

<DataObjectMethod(DataObjectMethodType.Update)> _
Public Shared Function UpdateCategory(ByVal Category As Category, _
        ByVal original_Category As Category) As Integer
    Dim up As String = "UPDATE Categories " _
        & "SET ShortName = @ShortName, " _
        & "LongName = @LongName " _
        & "WHERE CategoryID = @original_CategoryID " _
        & "   AND ShortName = @original_ShortName " _
        & "   AND LongName = @original_LongName"
    Dim cmd As SqlCommand = _
        New SqlCommand(up, New SqlConnection(GetConnectionString))
    cmd.Parameters.AddWithValue("CategoryID", Category.CategoryID)
    cmd.Parameters.AddWithValue("ShortName", Category.ShortName)
    cmd.Parameters.AddWithValue("LongName", Category.LongName)
    cmd.Parameters.AddWithValue("original_CategoryID", _
        original_Category.CategoryID)
    cmd.Parameters.AddWithValue("original_ShortName", _
        original_Category.ShortName)
    cmd.Parameters.AddWithValue("original_LongName", _
        original_Category.LongName)
    cmd.Connection.Open()
    Dim i As Integer = cmd.ExecuteNonQuery()
    cmd.Connection.Close()
    Return i
End Function

End Class
```

Figure 7-20   The CategoryDB class with an aggregate data type (part 2 of 2)

Perspective

In this chapter, you've learned the basics of working with object data sources, one of the major new features of ASP.NET 2.0. Many ASP.NET experts are excited about this feature because it provides a way to take advantage of the time-saving data binding features of ASP.NET without sacrificing the basic principle of separating presentation code from data access code.

However, it remains to be seen how well the object data sources will deliver on their promise because of two shortcomings. First, this feature's reliance on reflection means that it must resolve method calls at runtime rather than at compile time, which adds overhead (albeit small) to every data access. Second, the way this feature uses parameters often leaves developers guessing at what parameters the ObjectDataSource control is going to pass to your data access methods, which makes it more difficult to code and test them.

Terms

3-layer architecture
presentation layer
middle layer
database layer
object data source
data access class
business object class
data object class
3-tier architecture
reflection
Visual Basic attribute
aggregate data type
generics
generic list
strongly-typed collection

Section 3

New ASP.NET 2.0 features

In this section, you'll learn how to use all of the other new features of ASP.NET 2.0 that you were introduced to in chapter 1. That includes site navigation, login controls, profiles, and other features that you're likely to want to use in your web applications.

As much as possible, each of the chapters in this section is designed as an independent module. That means that you can read the chapters in whatever sequence you prefer. So if you're interested in the new login controls, go directly to chapter 9. Or if you're interested in themes, go directly to chapter 12. Before you're done, though, you should read all of the chapters in this section because all of the new features are useful for some applications.

8

How to use the site navigation features

The new site navigation features make it easy for users to navigate to the various pages in your site. These features are valuable for both small and large web sites. This chapter shows you how to get the most from these features.

An introduction to site navigation

ASP.NET's *site navigation* features are designed to simplify the task of creating menus and other navigation features that let users find their way around your web site. To implement that, ASP.NET provides a site map data source control and three navigation controls: TreeView, Menu, and SiteMapPath. The following topics introduce you to these controls.

An introduction to the navigation controls

Figure 8-1 shows a page from an ASP.NET 2.0 application called the Navigation application. This application is a variation of the Halloween Store application that's been shown throughout this book, but with navigation features added to the master page as well as a new page that displays a complete site map for the application. All three of the new ASP.NET 2.0 navigation controls are illustrated on this page.

The TreeView control displays the pages in a web site in a tree structure that's similar to a directory tree displayed by the Windows Explorer. The user can expand or collapse a node by clicking the + or − icon that appears next to each node that has children. This control is most useful when you want to give users a complete view of the pages in a web site.

The Menu control creates dynamic menus that expand when you hover the mouse over a menu item that contains subitems. For example, if you were to hover the mouse over the Projects item in the menu in this figure, a submenu listing Costumes, Static Props, and Animated Props would appear.

The SiteMapPath control displays a list of links that lead from the web site's home page to the current page. This makes it easy for the user to quickly return to the home page or to a parent of the current page.

The TreeView and the Menu controls must be used with a SiteMapDataSource, which binds the controls to a file named web.sitemap. This file contains XML that defines the structure of the pages that make up the web site. You'll learn how to create the web.sitemap file in the next two figures.

In most cases, you'll use either the Menu or the SiteMapPath control and possibly a TreeView control in a master page. That way, these navigation controls will be available from any page in the web site. If the site contains a large number of pages, though, you may want to use a separate Site Map page that includes a TreeView control. Then, the user can use the Site Map page to quickly locate any page within the web site.

A page with three site navigation controls

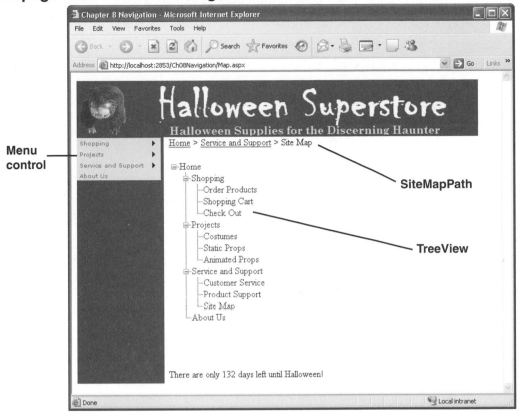

Menu control

SiteMapPath

TreeView

ASP.NET navigation controls

Control	Description
TreeView	Provides a hierarchical view of the site's structure. The user can click + or – icons next to each node to expand or collapse the node. Must be bound to a SiteMapDataSource control. Located in the Navigation tab of the Toolbox.
Menu	Creates a horizontal or vertical menu. Must be bound to a SiteMapDataSource control. Located in the Navigation tab of the Toolbox.
SiteMapPath	Displays a list of links from the application's root page (the home page) to the current page. Doesn't need to be bound to a SiteMapDataSource control. Located in the Navigation tab of the Toolbox.
SiteMapDataSource	Connects a navigation control to the site hierarchy specified by the web.sitemap file. Located in the Data tab of the Toolbox.

Description

- ASP.NET 2.0 provides three user-interface controls and a data source control designed to let the user navigate the pages in a web site.

- The navigation structure of a web site is defined by an XML file named web.sitemap located in the application's root folder. You must create this file before you can work with the navigation controls.

Figure 8-1   An introduction to site navigation

How to create a web.sitemap file

Before you can use one of the site navigation controls, you must create a web.sitemap file in the application's root directory. This file uses XML tags to define the hierarchical structure of the pages that make up the application.

As figure 8-2 shows, you can add a web.sitemap file to an application by choosing the Website→Add New Item command and selecting Site Map from the list of templates. Then, you use the Code Editor to edit the contents of this file. The web.sitemap file can contain two types of XML elements: siteMap and siteMapNode.

The siteMap element is the root element for the XML file and should occur only once in the file. You usually don't need to modify this element.

In contrast, you need to create a siteMapNode element for each page in the web site that you want to include in the navigation controls. In the siteMapNode element, you specify the url of the page (relative to the application's root folder); the page title that's displayed as the link in the menu, tree, or map path; and a description of the page.

To indicate the hierarchy of the pages in the site map, you nest the siteMapNode elements. The file should contain just one top-level siteMapNode element that represents the site's home page. Then, additional elements can be nested between the start and end tags for the home-page siteMapNode.

An important rule you must follow when you create the sitemap file is that each siteMapNode element must have a unique url attribute. That means each page in the web site can appear only once in the site map.

Another important point is that you don't have to include all of the pages in the web site in the sitemap file. Instead, you should only include those pages that you want to make available via the site's navigation controls. If, for example, the site uses a two-page checkout process, you may not want to include the second check out page in the sitemap file. That way, the user will be able to access the first checkout page from a menu or tree view control, but not the second checkout page.

The web.sitemap file created from the Site Map template

```xml
<?xml version="1.0" encoding="utf-8" ?>
<siteMap xmlns="http://schemas.microsoft.com/AspNet/SiteMap-File-1.0" >
    <siteMapNode url="" title=""  description="" roles="">
        <siteMapNode url="" title=""  description="" roles="" />
        <siteMapNode url="" title=""  description="" roles="" />
    </siteMapNode>
</siteMap>
```

Attributes of the siteMapNode element

Attribute	Description
url	The url of the page. Each siteMapNode element must specify a unique value for this attribute.
title	The text that will appear in the menu for the page.
description	The tool tip text for the page.
roles	Indicates which users have access to the page.

Description

- To create a web.sitemap file, choose the Website→Add New Item command, select Site Map from the list of available templates, and click Add. You can then use the Code Editor to edit the web.sitemap file.

- The web.sitemap file contains an XML-based description of the navigation hierarchy of an ASP.NET application.

- Each siteMapNode element defines a page in the web site. You can nest siteMapNode elements within other siteMapNode elements to indicate the hierarchy of pages in the web site. But you don't have to include all of the pages in your web site in the site map.

- The roles attribute of the siteMapNode element indicates that the page should be made available only to users that have the specified role or roles. For example, if you create a role for administrators called Admin, you can use this attribute to indicate those pages that should be available only to administrators. For more information about user roles, see chapter 9.

Figure 8-2   How to create a web.sitemap file

The web.sitemap file for the Navigation application

Figure 8-3 shows the complete web.sitemap file for the Navigation application. The site navigation structure defined by this file corresponds to the structure shown in the TreeView control in figure 8-1.

If you compare the siteMapNode elements in this file with the items listed in the TreeView control in figure 8-1, you should see how the nesting of the siteMapNode elements specifies the site's hierarchical structure. For example, the siteMapNode elements for the Order.aspx, Cart.aspx, and Checkout1.aspx pages are contained within the start and end elements of the siteMapNode element for the Shopping.aspx page.

In this case, not all of the pages in the Navigation application are listed in the web.sitemap file. For example, there's a second checkout page and an order confirmation page that aren't in the sitemap file. That's because users shouldn't be allowed to navigate directly to these pages.

The web.sitemap file used for the controls in figure 8-1

```xml
<?xml version="1.0" encoding="utf-8" ?>
<siteMap xmlns="http://schemas.microsoft.com/AspNet/SiteMap-File-1.0" >

  <siteMapNode url="Default.aspx" title="Home"
    description="Home page." roles="">

    <siteMapNode url="Shopping.aspx" title="Shopping"
      description="Shop for your favorite products." roles="">
      <siteMapNode url="Order.aspx" title="Order Products"
        description="Order a product." roles="">
      </siteMapNode>
      <siteMapNode url="Cart.aspx" title="Shopping Cart"
        description="View your shopping cart." roles="">
      </siteMapNode>
      <siteMapNode url="Checkout1.aspx" title="Check Out"
        description="Finalize your purchase." roles="">
      </siteMapNode>
    </siteMapNode>

    <siteMapNode url="Projects.aspx" title="Projects"
      description="Do-it-yourself Halloween projects." roles="">
      <siteMapNode url="Costumes.aspx" title="Costumes"
        description="Costume projects." roles="">
      </siteMapNode>
      <siteMapNode url="Static.aspx" title="Static Props"
        description="Static props." roles="">
      </siteMapNode>
      <siteMapNode url="Animated.aspx" title="Animated Props"
        description="Animated props." roles="">
      </siteMapNode>
    </siteMapNode>

    <siteMapNode url="Service.aspx" title="Service and Support"
      description="Customer service and product support." roles="">
      <siteMapNode url="CustService.aspx" title="Customer Service"
        description="Customer service." roles="">
      </siteMapNode>
      <siteMapNode url="Support.aspx" title="Product Support"
        description="Product support." roles="">
      </siteMapNode>
      <siteMapNode url="Map.aspx" title="Site Map"
        description="A map of all the pages on this web site." roles="">
      </siteMapNode>
    </siteMapNode>

    <siteMapNode url="About.aspx" title="About Us"
      description="All about our company." roles="">
    </siteMapNode>

  </siteMapNode>

</siteMap>
```

Figure 8-3   The web.sitemap file for the Navigation application

How to use the site navigation controls

Once you've created the sitemap file, you're ready to use the site navigation controls. The topics that follow show you how to do that.

How to use the TreeView control

Figure 8-4 shows how to use the TreeView control, which displays the pages in a web site as a hierarchical tree. Each node on the tree is a link that represents a page in the web site. You can click any of these links to go directly to that page. You can also click the + or − icons that appear next to the nodes to expand or collapse the nodes.

The table in this figure lists the attributes you're most likely to use with the TreeView control. The ID attribute provides a name for the TreeView control, and the DataSourceID attribute lists the ID of the data source that provides the site map data. You'll learn how to create a site map data source in the next figure.

The other attributes let you customize the appearance and behavior of the TreeView control. For example, you can use the ExpandDepth attribute to set the number of levels that are initially expanded when the TreeView is first displayed. And you can use the ShowLines attribute to include lines that graphically show the tree's hierarchical structure. The best way to learn how these attributes affect the TreeView control is to experiment with them.

A TreeView control

The aspx code for the TreeView control shown above

```
<asp:TreeView ID="TreeView1" runat="server"
              DataSourceID="SiteMapDataSource1"
              ShowLines="True">
</asp:TreeView>
```

Attributes of the TreeView control

Attribute	Description
ID	The ID of the control.
Runat	Must specify Server.
DataSourceID	The ID of the SiteMapDataSource the tree should be bound to.
ExpandDepth	The number of levels to be automatically expanded when the tree is initially displayed. The default is FullyExpand.
MaxDepthDataBind	Limits the maximum depth of the tree. The default is -1, which places no limit.
NodeIndent	The number of pixels to indent each level. The default is 20.
NodeWrap	Set to True to word-wrap the text of each node. The default is False.
ShowExpandCollapse	Set to False if you want to hide the Expand/Collapse buttons. The default is True.
ShowLines	Set to True to include lines that show the hierarchical structure. The default is False.

Description

- The TreeView control is used to display the site map in a hierarchical tree.
- To display an application's navigation structure, the TreeView control must be bound to a SiteMapDataSource control as described in the next figure.

Figure 8-4   How to use the TreeView control

How to create a SiteMapDataSource control

Figure 8-5 shows two ways to create a SiteMapDataSource control. One way is to drag the SiteMapDataSource control from the Data tab of the Toolbox to a page. Then, you can set the properties for the control.

The other way is to click the Smart Tag icon for a TreeView or Menu control, and choose New Data Source from the menu that appears. This brings up the Data Source Configuration Wizard dialog box shown at the top of this figure. Then, you select Site Map and click OK to create a site map data source.

To customize the behavior of the *site map data source*, you can use the attributes listed in this figure. For example, the ShowStartingNode attribute determines whether the highest-level SiteMapNode element in the web.sitemap file will be included in the tree or menu. Usually, you'll leave this attribute set to its default of True for TreeView controls and you'll set it to False for Menu controls.

The StartFromCurrentNode and StartingNodeUrl attributes let you bind a TreeView or Menu control to just a portion of the site map. If you specify True for the StartFromCurrentNode attribute, the tree or menu will start from the current page. As a result, only child pages of the current page will appear in the tree or menu. The StartingNodeUrl attribute lets you select any node in the site map as the starting node for the tree or menu.

The Data Source Configuration Wizard dialog box

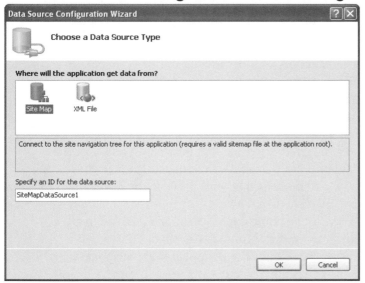

SiteMapDataSource examples

Example 1: A default SiteMapDataSource control

```
<asp:SiteMapDataSource ID="SiteMapDataSource1" runat="server" />
```

Example 2: A SiteMapDataSource control that specifies a starting level

```
<asp:SiteMapDataSource ID="SiteMapDataSource1" runat="server"
StartingNodeUrl="Projects.aspx" />
```

Common attributes of the SiteMapDataSource control

Attribute	Description
ID	The ID of the control.
Runat	Must specify Server.
StartingNodeUrl	The url of the node the SiteMapDataSource should use as its starting node.
ShowStartingNode	Set to False to not include the starting node. The default is True.
StartFromCurrentNode	Set to True to start the navigation from the current node. The default is False, which starts the navigation from the root node specified in the web.sitemap file.

Two ways to create a SiteMapDataSource control

- Drag the control from the Data tab of the Toolbox to a page.
- Click the Smart Tag icon in the upper-right corner of a TreeView or Menu control, then select New Data Source in the Choose Data Source drop-down list.

Description

- You use a SiteMapDataSource control to bind a TreeView or Menu control to the navigation structure defined by the web.sitemap file.

Figure 8-5   How to create a SiteMapDataSource control

How to use the Menu control

Figure 8-6 shows how to use the Menu control, which lets you create menus that are arranged either vertically or horizontally. *Vertical menus* are usually used in a sidebar alongside the content placeholder in a master page. In contrast, *horizontal menus* typically appear beneath a banner image and above the content placeholder.

Each item in a menu can contain a submenu that appears when you hover the mouse over the item for a moment. For example, the Service and Support submenu shown in the examples in this figure doesn't appear until you hover the mouse over the Service and Support item. The part of the menu that is always displayed is called the *static menu*. Submenus that appear when you hover the mouse over a menu item are called *dynamic menus*.

Like the TreeView control, the Menu control must be bound to a site map data source. Then, the other attributes in this figure let you customize the appearance of the menu and specify which items will appear in the menu. For example, the Orientation attribute determines whether the menu is arranged vertically or horizontally. And the MaximumDynamicDisplay attribute determines how many layers of dynamic submenus should be displayed.

As you set the properties for a Menu control, you'll see that it includes many style properties that aren't listed in this figure. You can set these properties to control the formatting that's used to display the menu. Alternatively, you can automatically apply a predefined format to the menu by selecting AutoFormat from the Menu control's smart tag menu. When you select an auto format, Visual Studio generates the style properties that apply the formatting that you selected.

A menu with vertical orientation

A menu with horizontal orientation

Typical aspx code for a Menu control

```
<asp:Menu ID="Menu1" Orientation="Horizontal" runat="server"
    DataSourceID="SiteMapDataSource1">
</asp:Menu>
```

Common attributes of the Menu control

Attribute	Description
ID	The ID of the control.
Runat	Must specify Server.
DataSourceID	The ID of the SiteMapDataSource the menu should be bound to.
ItemWrap	If True, words in the menu items will be word-wrapped if necessary. The default is False.
MaximumDynamicDisplay	The number of levels of dynamic submenus to display.
Orientation	Horizontal or Vertical.
StaticDisplayLevels	The number of levels that should always be displayed. The default is 1.
StaticEnableDefaultPopOutImage	If True, an arrow graphic is displayed next to any menu item that has a pop-out submenu. If false, the arrow graphic is not displayed. The default is True.

Description

- The Menu control displays site navigation information in a menu. Submenus automatically appear when the user hovers the mouse over a menu item that has a submenu.

- To display an application's navigation structure, the Menu control must be bound to a SiteMapDataSource control.

- The Menu control has many formatting attributes that aren't listed in this figure. You can quickly apply a coordinated set of formatting attributes by clicking the Smart Tag icon for the Menu control and choosing AutoFormat from the menu that appears. Then, you can select one of several predefined formats for the menu.

Figure 8-6   How to use the Menu control

How to use the SiteMapPath control

Figure 8-7 shows how to use the SiteMapPath control, which creates a series of links that lead from the application's home page to the current page. These links are sometimes called *bread crumbs* because they let the user find his or her way back to the home page.

Unlike the TreeView and Menu controls, the SiteMapPath control doesn't need to be bound to a data source. Instead, it obtains the site navigation information directly from the web.sitemap file.

The attributes listed in this figure let you customize the appearance of the SiteMapPath control. In particular, you can indicate how many parent nodes to list, which direction the nodes are listed in, what text to use to separate the nodes, and whether the current page should be formatted as a link or just plain text.

Although this figure doesn't show it, the SiteMapPath control includes other style attributes that let you completely customize the appearance of the site map path. And like the Menu control, you can also use the AutoFormat attribute to apply predefined formatting.

A SiteMapPath control

Home > Service and Support > Site Map

Aspx code for a SiteMapPath control

```
<asp:SiteMapPath ID="SiteMapPath1" runat="server">
</asp:SiteMapPath>
```

Common attributes of the SiteMapPath control

Attribute	Description
ID	The ID of the control.
Runat	Must specify Server.
ParentLevelsDisplayed	The maximum number of parent nodes to display. The default is -1, which displays all parent nodes.
PathDirection	Indicates the order in which nodes should be listed. Allowable values are RootToCurrent and CurrentToRoot.
PathSeparator	The string displayed between each node of the path. The default is a greater-than sign.
RenderCurrentNodeAsLink	Set to True if you want the node that represents the current page to be rendered as a link. The default is False.

Description

- The SiteMapPath control displays a list of the links for each node in the site map from the root node to the current page.
- Unlike the TreeView and Menu controls, you don't need to bind the SiteMapPath control to a data source. Instead, it automatically uses the web.sitemap file to determine the current page's position within the web site's navigation structure.

Figure 8-7   How to use the SiteMapPath control

A master page for the Navigation application

To show you how the navigation controls work together, figure 8-8 presents the complete listing for a master page that includes both a navigation menu and a site map path. This is the master page that displays the page shown in figure 8-1.

This master page begins with an Image control that displays a banner at the top of the page. Then, a table is used to control the layout of the rest of the page. This table consists of three rows and three columns. Note that the first cell in the first row specifies the RowSpan attribute, which causes the cell to span two rows. That way, the Menu control occupies the first column of both the first and second rows of the table.

Then, the first column that's defined for the first row contains the Menu control (which will also occupy the first column in second row). The second column in the first row provides ten pixels of white space. And the third column in the first row contains the SiteMapPath control.

After that, you can see that the second column in the second row provides ten pixels of white place, and the third column contains the content placeholder. You can also see how the message label is defined for the third row. In figure 8-1, a Site Map page is displayed within the content placeholder.

Notice also that the asp:Menu element includes several style attributes and elements that specify the appearance of the menu. These attributes and elements were generated by Visual Studio when I selected an auto format for the menu.

In addition, this master page uses a code-behind file named MasterPage.master.vb. But since this code-behind file is the same as the one presented in chapter 3, it's not repeated here.

The body of the master page for the Navigation application

```
<body>
    <form id="form1" runat="server">
    <asp:Image ID="Image1" runat="server" ImageUrl="~/Images/banner.jpg" />
    <br />
    <table cellpadding="0" cellspacing="0">
      <tr>
        <td bgcolor="red" bordercolor="red" style="width: 153px" valign="top"
            rowspan="2" height="400">
        <asp:Menu BackColor="#E3EAEB" DataSourceID="SiteMapDataSource1"
            DynamicHorizontalOffset="2"
            Font-Names="Verdana" Font-Size="0.8em" ForeColor="#666666"
            ID="Menu1" runat="server"
            StaticSubMenuIndent="10px">
          <StaticSelectedStyle BackColor="#1C5E55" />
          <StaticMenuItemStyle HorizontalPadding="5px"
              VerticalPadding="2px" />
          <DynamicMenuStyle BackColor="#E3EAEB" />
          <DynamicSelectedStyle BackColor="#1C5E55" />
          <DynamicMenuItemStyle HorizontalPadding="5px"
              VerticalPadding="2px" />
          <DynamicHoverStyle BackColor="#666666" Font-Bold="True"
              ForeColor="White" />
          <StaticHoverStyle BackColor="#666666" Font-Bold="True"
              ForeColor="White" />
        </asp:Menu>
        <asp:SiteMapDataSource ID="SiteMapDataSource1" runat="server"
            ShowStartingNode="False" />
        </td>
        <td style="width: 10px"></td>
        <td style="width: 704px" valign="top">
            <asp:SiteMapPath ID="SiteMapPath1" runat="server">
            </asp:SiteMapPath>
        </td>
      </tr>
      <tr>
        <td style="width: 10px"></td>
        <td style="width: 704px" valign="top">
            <asp:contentplaceholder id="Main" runat="server">
            </asp:contentplaceholder>
        </td>
      </tr>
      <tr height="25">
        <td bgcolor="red" bordercolor="red">
            style="width: 153px" valign="top"></td>
        <td style="width: 10px"></td>
        <td style="width: 704px" valign="top">
            <asp:Label id="lblMessage" runat="server">
            </asp:Label>
        </td>
      </tr>
      </table>
    </form>
</body>
```

Figure 8-8   A master page that includes navigation controls

Perspective

This should give you a pretty good idea of how useful the new navigation features can be. If you experiment with them, you should quickly see that they're also easy to use.

You'll also discover that the TreeView, Menu, and SiteMapPath controls include many attributes that weren't described in this chapter. However, most of these attributes are designed to let you alter the appearance of the navigation controls, not their behavior. So once you master the basics of using these controls, you shouldn't have any trouble learning how to tweak their appearance by using the other attributes.

Terms

site navigation
site map data source
vertical menu
horizontal menu
static menu
dynamic menu
bread crumbs

9

How to use the login controls

To secure an application, you need to restrict access to some of its pages, but let authorized users access those pages. With ASP.NET 1.x, you had to manually edit XML files and write code to provide this functionality. But with ASP.NET 2.0, you can use the new Web Site Administration Tool and login controls to provide this functionality without having to write a single line of code.

An introduction to authentication

If you want to limit access to all or part of your ASP.NET application to certain users, you can use *authentication* to verify each user's identity. Then, once you have authenticated the user, you can use *authorization* to check if the user has the appropriate privileges for accessing a page. That way, you can prevent unauthorized users from accessing pages that they shouldn't be able to access.

Three types of authentication

Figure 9-1 describes the three types of authentication you can use in ASP.NET applications. The first, called *Windows-based authentication*, requires that you set up a Windows user account for each user. Then, you use standard Windows security features to restrict access to all or part of the application. When a user attempts to access the application, Windows displays a login dialog box that asks the user to supply the username and password of the Windows account.

To use *forms-based authentication*, you add a login page to your application that typically requires the user to enter a username and password. Then, ASP.NET displays this page automatically when it needs to authenticate a user who's trying to access the application. One of the new features of ASP.NET 2.0 is that it automatically creates a database to store user data such as usernames and passwords. In addition, it includes new login controls that automatically generate code that reads data from and writes data to this database. As a result, you can implement forms-based authentication without having to write a single line of code. That makes this type of authentication easy to use, and you'll see how this works as you progress through this chapter.

Passport authentication relies on the *Microsoft Passport* service to authorize users. Passport is a centralized account management service that lets users access multiple web applications with a single user account. Unfortunately, you must pay Microsoft a hefty fee for the right to use Passport in your applications. In addition, Passport has had some problems with security flaws that have caused several major web sites to stop supporting it. As a result, it hasn't become as widely used as Microsoft had originally hoped.

Windows-based authentication

- Causes the browser to display a login dialog box when the user attempts to access a restricted page.
- Is supported by most browsers.
- Is configured through the IIS management console.
- Uses Windows user accounts and directory rights to grant access to restricted pages.

Forms-based authentication

- Lets developers code a login form that gets the username and password.
- The username and password entered by the user are encrypted if the login page uses a secure connection.
- Doesn't rely on Windows user accounts. Instead, the application determines how to authenticate users.

Passport authentication

- *Passport* is a centralized authentication service offered by Microsoft.
- Passport lets users maintain a single user account that lets them access any web site that participates in Passport. The advantage is that the user only has to maintain one username and password.
- Passport authentication isn't free. You must sign up for Passport authentication and pay a significant fee to use it in your applications. For more information, visit www.passport.net.

Description

- *Authentication* refers to the process of validating the identity of a user so the user can be granted access to an application. A user must typically supply a username and password to be authenticated.
- After a user is authenticated, the user must still be authorized to use the requested application. The process of granting user access to an application is called *authorization*.

Figure 9-1   Three types of authentication

How forms-based authentication works

To help you understand how forms-based authentication works, figure 9-2 shows a typical series of exchanges that occur between a web browser and a server when a user attempts to access a page that's protected by forms-based authentication. The authentication process begins when a user requests a page that is part of a protected application. When the server receives the request, it checks to see if the user has already been authenticated. To do that, it looks for a cookie that contains an *authentication ticket* in the request for the page. If it doesn't find the ticket, it redirects the browser to the login page.

Next, the user enters a name and password and posts the login page back to the server. Then, if the username and password are found in the database, which means they are valid, the server creates an authentication ticket and redirects the browser back to the original page. Note that the redirect from the server sends the authentication ticket to the browser as a cookie. As a result, when the browser requests the original page, it sends the cookie back to the server. This time, the server sees that the user has been authenticated and the requested page is sent back to the browser.

By default, the authentication ticket is sent as a session cookie. In that case, the user is authenticated only for that session. However, you also can specify that the ticket be sent as a persistent cookie. Then, the user will be authenticated automatically for future sessions, until the cookie expires.

HTTP requests and responses with forms-based authentication

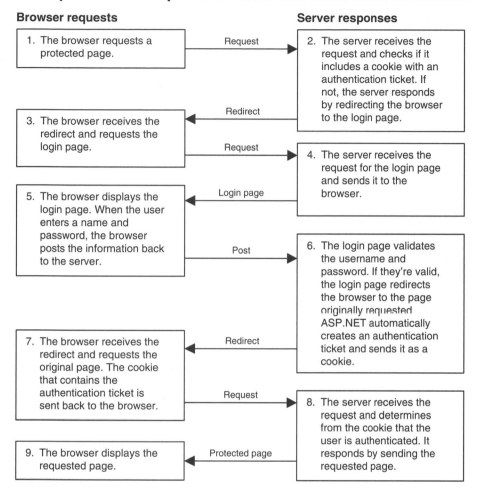

Browser requests

1. The browser requests a protected page.

3. The browser receives the redirect and requests the login page.

5. The browser displays the login page. When the user enters a name and password, the browser posts the information back to the server.

7. The browser receives the redirect and requests the original page. The cookie that contains the authentication ticket is sent back to the browser.

9. The browser displays the requested page.

Server responses

2. The server receives the request and checks if it includes a cookie with an authentication ticket. If not, the server responds by redirecting the browser to the login page.

4. The server receives the request for the login page and sends it to the browser.

6. The login page validates the username and password. If they're valid, the login page redirects the browser to the page originally requested. ASP.NET automatically creates an authentication ticket and sends it as a cookie.

8. The server receives the request and determines from the cookie that the user is authenticated. It responds by sending the requested page.

Arrows: Request, Redirect, Request, Login page, Post, Redirect, Request, Protected page

Discussion

- When ASP.NET receives a request for a page that's protected from a user who has not been authenticated, the server redirects the user to the login page.

- To be authenticated, the user's computer must contain an *authentication ticket*. By default, this ticket is stored as a session cookie.

- ASP.NET automatically creates an authentication ticket when the application indicates that the user should be authenticated. ASP.NET checks for the presence of an authentication ticket any time it receives a request for a restricted page.

- The authentication ticket cookie can be made persistent. Then, the user will be authenticated automatically in future sessions, until the cookie expires.

Figure 9-2   How forms-based authentication works

How to set up authentication and authorization

By default, all pages of a web site can be accessed by all users whether or not they are authenticated. As a result, if you want to restrict access to all or some of the pages of the web site, you need to set up authentication and authorization. In the old days of ASP.NET 1.0, you needed to manually edit the web.config file for a web site to do that. But with ASP.NET 2.0, you can use the ASP.NET Web Site Administration Tool to set up authentication and authorization as shown in the topics that follow.

How to start the Web Site Administration Tool

When you're developing an application, you can start the ASP.NET Web Site Administration Tool by choosing the Website→ASP.NET Configuration command from Visual Studio's menus. This starts a web browser that displays the home page for this tool. Then, you can click on the Security tab to access a web page like the one shown in figure 9-3. This page lets you set up users, create groups of users known as *roles*, and create *access rules* that control access to parts of your application.

To set up authentication for the first time, you can click on the link that starts the Security Setup wizard. This wizard walks you through several steps that allow you to set up the security for your application. Alternatively, you can use the links at the bottom of the page to select the authentication type and manage the users, roles, and access rules for your application.

The Security tab of the Web Site Administration Tool

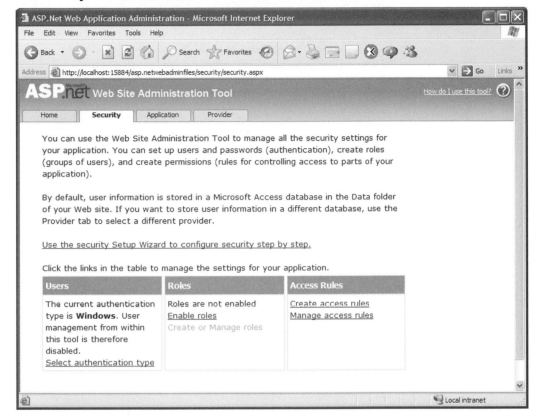

Description

- When developing an application, you can start the ASP.NET Web Site Administration Tool by choosing the Website→ASP.NET Configuration command.

- You can use the ASP.NET Web Site Administration Tool to set up users, roles, and access rules.

Figure 9-3   How to start the Web Site Administration Tool

How to enable forms-based authentication

By default, a web site is set up to use Windows authentication. If all users will be accessing your web site through a private local Windows network (an intranet), this option may be the easiest to implement because it uses built-in Windows dialog boxes to allow users to log in.

However, if any of your users will access your web site from the Internet, you'll need to switch to forms-based authentication. To do that, you can click on the Select Authentication Type link from the Security tab of the Web Site Administration Tool to display the page shown in figure 9-4. Then, you can select the From the Internet option. When you use this option, you'll need to create a web form that allows users to log in as shown later in this chapter.

How to enable forms-based authentication

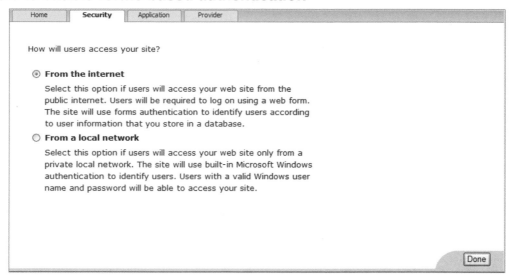

Description

- By default, a web site is set up to use Windows authentication. However, this option is only appropriate for accessing a web site through a local intranet.

- To switch to forms-based authentication, select the From the Internet option. This is the option that you'll need to use if you intend to deploy the application so it's available from the Internet.

Figure 9-4   How to enable forms-based authentication

How to create and manage roles

Roles allow you to apply the same access rules to a group of users. Although roles are optional and are disabled by default, they make it easy to manage authentication. As a result, you'll typically want to enable roles. And since you use roles when you create users and access rules, it's often helpful to set up the roles before you create the users and access rules. That way, you don't have to go back later and edit your users and access rules so they are associated with the correct roles.

To understand how roles work, let's say you create a role named admin for all employees that will be administrators for the web site, and you assign this role to multiple users. Later, if you want to give all users in the admin role additional permissions, you don't have to give the permissions to each user. Instead, you just need to give the additional permissions to the admin role and all users with that role will get the new permissions.

You can use the Web Site Administration Tool to create and manage roles. To do that, you need to click on the link on the Security tab to enable roles. Then, you can click on the Create or Manage Roles link to display a page like the one in figure 9-5.

The first two controls on this page allow you to add roles. To do that, you just enter a name for the role and click on the Add Role button, and the role will appear in the table at the bottom of the page. Then, you can click on the Manage link for the role to add users to the role or to remove users from the role. Or, you can click the Delete link for the role to delete the role entirely.

Usernames and roles

```
Username      Roles
doug          admin
joel          admin, custserv
kelly         custserv
```

How to create and manage roles

Description

- A *role* allows you to apply the same access rules to a group of users.
- Each user may be associated with one or more roles.
- By default, roles are disabled. To enable them, you need to click on the link in the Security tab that enables roles.
- Once you enable roles, you can use the page shown above to add roles, to manage all users associated with the role, or to delete the role.

Figure 9-5   How to create and manage roles

How to create and manage users

The first page displayed in figure 9-6 shows how to use the Web Site Administration Tool to create users. To do that, you start by entering all of the required information for a user. This information includes a username, a password, an email address, and a security question and answer. If you want to associate the user with one or more roles, you can select the check box next to each role that you want to apply to the user. In this figure, for example, the user is associated with the admin role. When you're done, you can click on the Create User button to create the user.

The default password policy for an ASP.NET 2.0 application requires that you enter at least seven characters with one of them being a non-alphanumeric character. If that's too strict for your web site, though, you can relax this policy by adding two attributes to the membership provider, which you'll learn how to do in figure 9-8.

If you want to automatically send the password to the user immediately after you create the user, you can select the Send Password check box. Then, when you click on the Create User button, the username and password will be sent to the user. For this to work, of course, the application must be configured so it can send email. By default, the Web Site Administrator Tool will try to send email to an SMTP server set to localhost on port 25.

If you want to automatically generate a password for the user, you can select the Autogenerate Password check box. Then, you won't need to fill out the password text boxes and the password will be emailed to the user when you click on the Create User button. Again, for this to work, the application must be configured so it can send email.

Once you've created one or more users, you can use the second screen displayed in this figure to manage them. To edit a user's email address, you can click on the Edit User link. (As of Beta 2, though, this link doesn't let you edit the username, password, or security question and answer.) To change the roles assigned to a user, you can select the Edit Roles link for the user and work with the check boxes that are displayed in the Roles column of the table. To prevent a user from logging into your application but retain his or her information in your database, you can set the status to inactive by clearing the Active check box to the left of the username.

If your application contains many users, you may need to use the Search For Users table to search for users. When you use this table, you can search by username or email address. For example, to search by email address, you can select the email address option from the Search By combo box, enter the email address in the For text box, and click on the Find User button. If necessary, you can use the asterisk (*) wildcard for multiple characters, and you can use the question mark (?) wildcard for a single character. Alternatively, you can click on the letters displayed on this page to display all users whose username or email address begins with the specified letter. Either way, you should be able to quickly find the user that you're looking for.

How to create a user

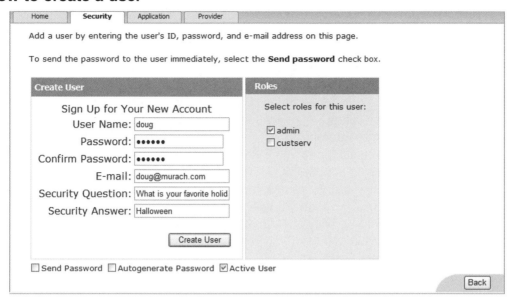

How to manage users

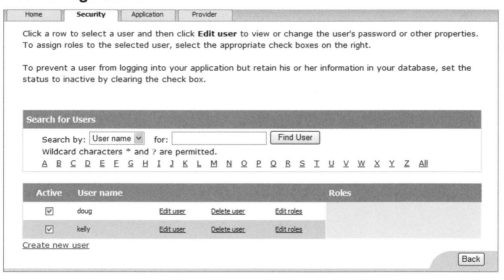

Figure 9-6   How to create and manage users

How to create and manage access rules

The first page in figure 9-7 shows how to create an *access rule* that restricts access to all or part of a web application. If you want to apply an access rule to the entire web application, you can select the root directory for the web application and apply the rule. Then, this rule will apply to all subfolders. For example, if you want to only allow authenticated users to access your web site, you can select the root directory (Ch09Authentication in this example), and create a rule that denies access to anonymous users.

However, it's more common to allow all users including anonymous users to be able to access the pages in the root directory. That way, all users can view your home page and any other pages that you want to make available to the general public. Then, you can restrict access to the pages in your application that are stored in subfolders. For example, this screen shows how to create a rule for the Maintenance folder that denies access to all users.

The second page in this figure shows how to manage the access rules for a folder. To do that, you can select the folder to display all of the access rules for the folder. Then, you can move rules up or down, which is important since they're applied in the order in which they're displayed. Or, you can delete any rules that you no longer want to apply.

On the second page, you can see the rules that restrict access to the Maintenance folder. Here, the bottom rule (which is dimmed) is the rule that's automatically applied to all pages of a web site if you don't create new rules. This rule allows access to all users including anonymous users. Then, the middle rule overrides the bottom rule and denies access to all users including authenticated users. However, the top rule overrides the middle rule and allows access to users in the admin role. As a result, only authenticated users in the admin role are able to access the pages in the Maintenance folder.

How to create an access rule

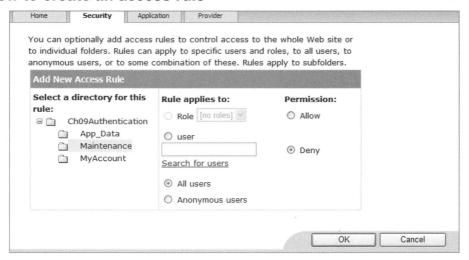

How to manage access rules

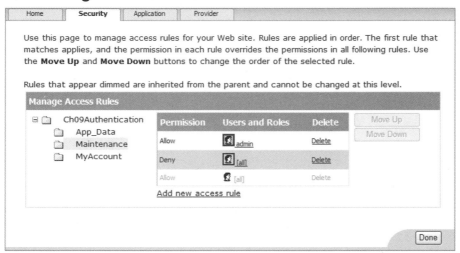

Description

- An *access rule* determines which users have access to portions of a web site.
- Each rule overrides the rules below it. As a result, for the Maintenance directory shown above, users in the admin role are allowed and all other users are denied.

Figure 9-7   How to create and manage access rules

How to modify the membership and role provider

When you add roles and users, a class known as a *data provider* contains the code that reads and writes the data for the users and roles. A data provider that works with membership data is often called a *membership provider*, and a data provider that works with roles data is often called a *role provider*. By default, a data provider named AspNetSqlProvider is used to store both membership and role data in a SQL Server Express database named AspNetDB.mdf that's stored in the App_Data folder of your web site. This database is created for you automatically, and it usually works the way you want, at least for prototyping.

However, the data provider architecture lets you use different data providers if you want to. If, for example, you want to use one data provider for the membership data and another for roles data, you can use the Provider tab shown in figure 9-8 to select separate providers named AspNetSqlMembershipProvider and AspNetSqlRoleProvider. (As of Beta 2, those are the only providers that are available and the only type of database that's supported is SQL Server.)

If the data providers that ship with ASP.NET 2.0 aren't adequate for your application, you may need to write a custom data provider. If, for example, you need to store membership data in an Oracle database, a MySQL database, or even on a midrange or mainframe computer, you can write a custom membership provider to do that. Or, if you need to work with existing membership data that's stored in a SQL Server database, you can write a custom provider to work with that data.

To write a membership provider, you need to code a class that implements the abstract MembershipProvider class. To write a role provider, you need to code a class that implements the abstract RoleProvider class. After you implement all of the necessary properties and methods of these classes, you can edit the machine.config or web.config file to add the providers to the list for all applications or the list for one application. Then, you can use the Provider tab to select the data providers for memberships and roles. Once you do that, the rest of the authentication features should work as described in this chapter.

For more information about writing a custom data provider, see chapter 10. Although that chapter shows how to create a custom data provider for the Profile feature, many of the same concepts apply to creating a custom data provider for memberships and roles.

This figure also shows how you can modify the attributes of a data provider to change the way that the data provider behaves. In particular, it shows how you can relax the strict password requirements for an application. To do that, you can copy the <membership> element from the machine.config file (which applies to all web applications) to the web.config file (which applies to your application). Then, you can edit the Name attribute of the <add> element to create a unique name for the modified provider, and you can add and set the minRequiredPasswordLength and minRequiredNonAlphanumericCharacters attributes. In this case, these attributes are set so each password requires 6 characters and zero special characters. Last, you can add the defaultProvider attribute to the <membership> element so your application uses this provider.

The Provider tab of the Web Site Administration Tool

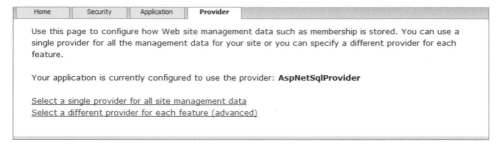

Elements in the web.config file that relax the default password policy

```
<membership defaultProvider="AspNetSqlMembershipProviderRelaxed">
  <providers>
    <add name="AspNetSqlMembershipProviderRelaxed"
         type="System.Web.Security.SqlMembershipProvider,
               System.Web, Version=2.0.0.0, Culture=neutral,
               PublicKeyToken=b03f5f7f11d50a3a"
         connectionStringName="LocalSqlServer"
         enablePasswordRetrieval="false"
         enablePasswordReset="true"
         requiresQuestionAndAnswer="true"
         applicationName="/"
         requiresUniqueEmail="false"
         passwordFormat="Hashed"
         maxInvalidPasswordAttempts="5"
         passwordAttemptWindow="10"
         passwordStrengthRegularExpression=""
         minRequiredPasswordLength="6"
         minRequiredNonalphanumericCharacters="0"/>
  </providers>
</membership>
```

Description

- By default, a *data provider* named AspNetSqlProvider is used to store both membership and role data in a SQL Server Express database named AspNetDB.mdf. However, you can use separate membership and role providers, and you can write your own custom providers.

- To relax the password restrictions for a provider, you can change the attributes for password length and non-alphanumeric characters in the web.config file for an application.

Figure 9-8   How to modify the membership and role provider

How to use the ASP.NET 2.0 login controls

Once you've restricted access to some or all of the pages of your web application, you need to allow users with the proper permissions to log in and access the restricted pages. In addition, you may want to provide other features such as allowing users to log out, to create an account by themselves, to recover a forgotten password, or to change a password. With ASP.NET 2.0, you can use the controls in the Login tab of the Toolbox to automatically handle these tasks.

How to use the Login control

Figure 9-9 shows how to create a login page that contains a Login control. When you create a login page, you should name it Login.aspx. That's because ASP.NET looks for a page with this name when it attempts to authenticate a user. Also, since this page is used for the entire application, you usually want to use a simple format so it works equally well for all parts of the application.

Once you've created a page named Login.aspx, you can add all of the login functionality just by adding a Login control to the page. To do that, drag the Login control that's in the Login tab of the Toolbox onto the page.

Like most login pages, the Login control includes two text boxes that let the user enter a username and a password. In addition, it includes a check box that lets the users indicate whether or not they want to be logged in automatically the next time the application is accessed. If the user selects this check box, the application can create a persistent cookie that contains the authentication ticket.

When the user clicks the Log In button within the Login control, the code for the control tries to authenticate the user. It does that by checking to see whether the username and password are in the membership provider. Then, if the user is authenticated, the code checks the role provider to see whether the user has the proper authorization for the requested page. If so, this code continues by redirecting the browser to that page.

If you want to automatically apply formatting to the Login control, you can right-click on the control and select the AutoFormat command. Then, you can use the resulting Auto Format dialog box to select a format that you like. When you do, Visual Studio will change many of the control's formatting properties. This feature works similarly for the CreateUserWizard, PasswordRecovery, and ChangePassword controls described in the pages that follow.

Although it's not shown in this figure, a login page should always force the page to use a secure connection. Then, if a hacker manages to intercept a user's username and password, your application won't be compromised.

A Login control in the Web Forms Designer

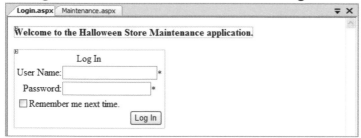

The aspx code for the Login control

```
<asp:Login ID="Login1" runat="server">
</asp:Login>
```

Common attributes of the Login control

Attribute	Description
RememberMeSet	Determines whether the RememberMe check box is displayed. By default, this is set to True.
RememberMeText	The text for the label of the RememberMe text box.
FailureText	The text that's displayed when a login attempt fails.

The AutoFormat dialog box for a Login control

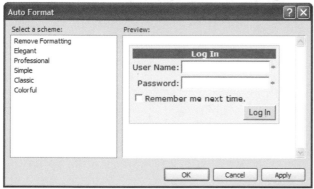

Description

* When a user attempts to access a page that requires authentication, ASP.NET automatically redirects the user to the application's login page. This page must be named Login.aspx.

* To automatically apply formatting to the Login control, right-click on it and select the AutoFormat command.

Figure 9-9   How to use the Login control

How to use the LoginStatus and LoginName controls

Figure 9-10 shows how you can use the LoginStatus and LoginName controls. In the page at the top of this figure, you can see that the LoginName control provides the name of a logged in user and a click here link if the name that's shown isn't correct. In contrast, the LoginStatus control provides a Login link if a user hasn't logged in yet, and a Logout link if the user has logged in.

To use these controls, you just drag them onto the form from the Login tab of the Toolbox. Then, you can change the properties as needed. For instance, you can use the LoginText and LogoutText attributes of the LoginStatus control to change the text that's displayed by the links. And you can use the FormatString property of the LoginName control to add text before or after the placeholder for the username.

When the user clicks on the Login link of a LoginStatus control, the user will be redirected to the Login page and required to enter a username and password. Then, after the user has been authenticated, the user will be redirected to the original page. Conversely, when the user clicks the Logout link, the user will be redirected to the Login page (Login.aspx).

When a user has been authenticated, the LoginName control will display the user name. Otherwise, the control won't display the user name. However, it will display any other text that has been specified in the FormatString attribute.

The LoginName and LoginStatus controls displayed in a browser

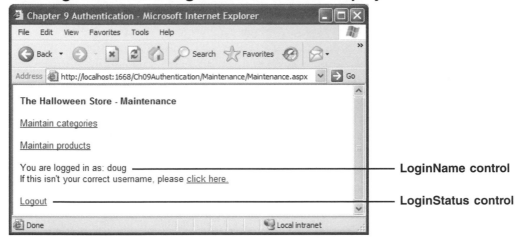

The LoginName and LoginStatus controls in the Web Forms Designer

The aspx code for the LoginName and LoginStatus controls

```
<asp:LoginName ID="LoginName1" runat="server"
    FormatString="You are logged in as: {0}" /><br />

<asp:LoginStatus ID="LoginStatus1" runat="server" />
```

Common attributes of the LoginName control

Attribute	Description
FormatString	The text that's displayed with the username. This string uses "{0}" to identify the UserName parameter, and you can add text before or after this parameter.

Common attributes of the LoginStatus control

Attribute	Description
LoginText	The text that's displayed for the login link.
LogoutText	The text that's displayed for the logout link.

Figure 9-10   How to use the LoginStatus and LoginName controls

How to use the CreateUserWizard control

If you only have a few users for your application, you can use the Web Site Administration Tool to create and manage users as described earlier in this chapter. Then, you can use the Login, LoginStatus, and LoginName controls to allow users to log in and out. Often, though, you'll want to allow users to create user accounts for themselves. To do that, you can use the CreateUserWizard control as shown in figure 9-11.

By default, the CreateUserWizard control uses two steps to create a new user: the Create User step and the Complete step. Usually, these steps work like you want them to. However, if you need to modify their behavior, you can do that by changing the properties of the control.

To do that, select the control and click on the Smart Tag icon to display the smart tag menu. Then, select the appropriate command from the smart tag menu. Often, that means selecting the step that you want to edit. For example, you may need to select the Complete step so you can modify its properties. In particular, you may need to set the PostBackUrl property of the Continue button so the user is redirected to the appropriate page.

When you use the pages that result from the CreateUserWizard control, you should realize that the membership provider is being used to write the data to the appropriate data source. This works the same as it does for the Web Site Administration Tool.

The CreateUserWizard control with the smart tag menu shown

The two steps of the CreateUserWizard control in a browser

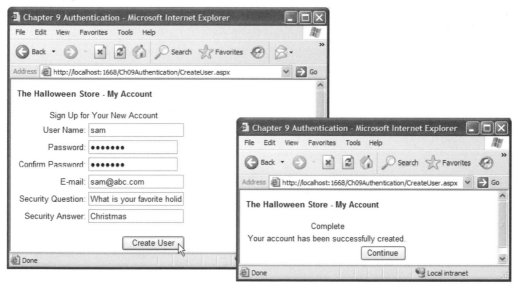

Description

- If you select the CreateUserWizard control in the Web Forms Designer, you can use the smart tag menu to switch between its two steps and reset or customize either step.

- In the Complete step, you need to set the PostBackUrl property of the Continue button so the user is directed to the appropriate page.

Figure 9-11   How to use the CreateUserWizard control

How to use the PasswordRecovery control

It's inevitable that some users will forget their passwords. Fortunately, the PasswordRecovery control makes it easy to automate the process of recovering forgotten passwords. This process is described in figure 9-12, and it's especially useful if you are managing a site with a large number of users.

When you use the PasswordRecovery control, the password is sent to the user via email. As a result, you need to make sure that your system is set up so it can send email before you test this control. By default, an application will try to send email to an SMTP server set to localhost on port 25.

The most important element of the PasswordRecovery control is the MailDefinition element. In particular, you must set the From attribute of the MailDefinition element to the email address that's sending the email message or an error will occur when your system attempts to send the email. Typically, the From email address is set to the email address that's used by the web site administrator. If you set this attribute correctly, a standard message will be sent to the user. To customize the subject line and message body, you can edit the other attributes of the MailDefinition element.

The PasswordRecovery control uses three views. In the Web Forms Designer, you can switch between these three views by using the smart tag menu, and you can edit the properties for any of these views as necessary.

When you display this control in a browser, the first view asks the user to enter a username. Then, the second view requires the user to answer the security question. If the answer to this question is correct, the password is emailed to the address that's associated with the username, and the third view is displayed. This view displays a message that indicates that the password recovery was successful and that the password has been sent to the user via email.

The PasswordRecovery control in the Web Forms Designer

The first two views of the PasswordRecovery control

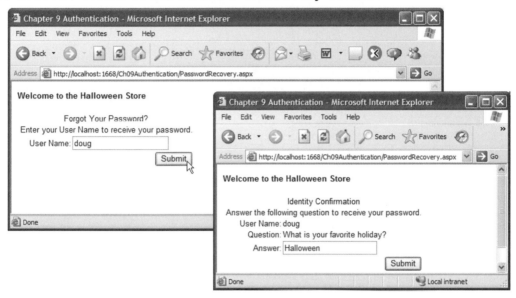

Description

- After the second view is completed, the password is emailed to the user. For this to work, you need to edit the From attribute of the MailDefinition element to supply the from address for this email. In addition, the web server that you're using must be configured to work with a SMTP server.

- By default, an application will try to send email to an SMTP server set to localhost on port 25.

Figure 9-12   How to use the PasswordRecovery control

How to use the ChangePassword control

Another common task associated with the authentication process is allowing users to change their passwords. To make that easy for you, ASP.NET 2.0 provides the ChangePassword control, and figure 9-13 shows how to use it.

The ChangePassword control uses two views. The first view lets the user enter the current password and the new password twice. Then, if the old password is correct and the two new passwords match, the second view is displayed. This view tells the user that the password has been successfully changed.

Once you've placed the PasswordControl on the form, it usually works the way you want it to. However, you may need to edit the Url attributes so they point to the pages that you want to navigate to when the user clicks on the Cancel and Continue buttons.

The first view of the ChangePassword control in the Web Forms Designer

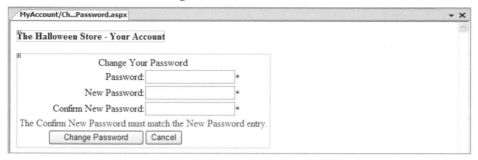

The second view of the ChangePassword control

The aspx code for the ChangePassword control

```
<asp:ChangePassword ID="ChangePassword1" runat="server"
    CancelDestinationPageUrl="MyAccount.aspx"
    ContinueDestinationPageUrl="MyAccount.aspx">
</asp:ChangePassword>
```

Description

- The ChangePassword control uses two views to allow users to change their passwords. The first view lets the user change the password. The second view is displayed when the change has been successful.

- The CancelDestinationPageUrl and ContinueDestinationPageUrl attributes provide the URLs that are navigated to when the Cancel or Continue buttons are clicked.

Figure 9-13   How to use the ChangePassword control

How to use the LoginView control

If your web site uses authentication, you often to need to display one message to users who are logged in and another message to users who aren't logged in. For example, when a user isn't logged in, you may want to display a message that asks the user to log in. Conversely, if a user is logged in, you may want to display a message that welcomes the user back and allows the user to log out. Figure 9-14 shows how to use the LoginView control to accomplish these tasks.

The LoginView control uses two views. The first view contains the controls that are displayed to users who aren't logged in (*anonymous users*). The second view contains the controls that are displayed to users who are logged in (*authenticated users*). In this figure, each view of the LoginView control contains a Label control followed by a LoginStatus control. This is a fairly typical use of the LoginView control. However, the LoginView control can store entire tables if that's necessary. Then, the height and width of the LoginView control will be adjusted automatically to accommodate the controls that you place inside of it.

The LoginView control in the Web Forms Designer

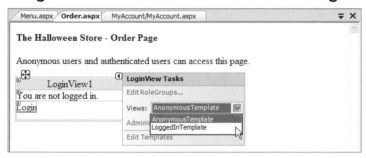

The aspx code for the LoginView control

```
<asp:LoginView ID="LoginView1" runat="server">
    <LoggedInTemplate>
        <asp:Label ID="Label2" runat="server"
            Text="You are logged in." Width="155px"></asp:Label><br />
        <asp:LoginStatus ID="LoginStatus2" runat="server" />
    </LoggedInTemplate>
    <AnonymousTemplate>
        <asp:Label ID="Label1" runat="server"
            Text="You are not logged in." Width="175px"></asp:Label><br />
        <asp:LoginStatus ID="LoginStatus1" runat="server" />
    </AnonymousTemplate>
</asp:LoginView>
```

The LoginView control displayed in a browser

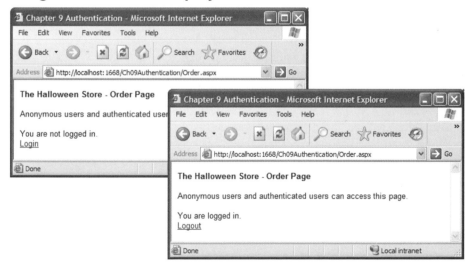

Description

- The LoginView control lets you change what's on the web page depending on whether the user isn't logged in (an *anonymous user*) or is logged in (an *authenticated user*).

Figure 9-14   How to use the LoginView control

The Authentication application

To show how to use forms-based authentication to restrict access to a web application, this topic presents part of a Halloween Store application that we'll refer to as the Authentication application. This application restricts access to all pages in the Maintenance folder to users with admin privileges. In addition, it restricts access to all pages in the MyAccount folder to users who have created an account and logged in.

As you review this application, please keep in mind that the authentication and authorization features don't require any code. That's why the figures that follow show only the pages, the directory structure, the access rules, and the web.config files.

The pages

Figure 9-15 shows just four pages of the Authentication application, but you can also think of the pages in figures 9-11 through 9-13 as part of this application. For instance, the Forgot your Password link on the Login page goes to the page in figure 9-12, and the Need to Create a New Account link goes to the page in figure 9-11. Also, the Change Password link on the MyAccount page goes to a ChangePassword page like the one in figure 9-13.

To start this application, the Menu page in figure 9-15 contains three links that allow you to perform some tests to make sure that the authentication and authorization features are working correctly. The first link on this page lets the user access an Order page to begin placing an order. When the user clicks on this link, the system tries to authenticate the user by checking whether the user has a cookie with a valid authentication ticket. If so, the user will be authenticated automatically. If not, the user can view the Order page as an anonymous user. Either way, the Order page will be displayed. In other words, this page is available to both anonymous and authenticated users.

The second link on the Menu page lets the user access the MyAccount page where the user can edit settings for his or her personal account. To be able to access this page, the user must be authenticated. When the user clicks on this link, the system attempts to authenticate the user by checking if the browser has a cookie with a valid authentication ticket. If so, the user will be authenticated automatically and allowed to access the MyAccount page. If not, the user will be redirected to the Login page so he or she can log in. Once the user supplies a valid username and password to the Login page, the browser will be redirected to the MyAccount page.

The Menu page

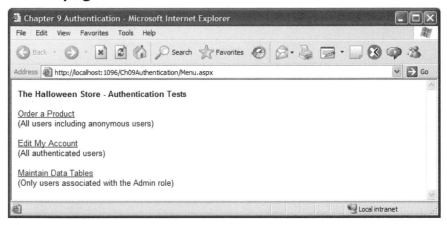

The Login page

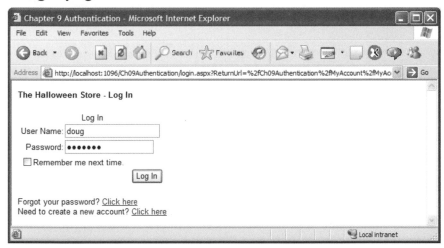

Description

- The Menu page contains three links. The first lets anonymous users or authenticated users access the Order page. The second lets authenticated users access the MyAccount page. The third lets authenticated users who are associated with the Admin role access the Maintenance page.

- The Login page is only displayed if the user clicks on the second or third link and the browser doesn't contain a cookie that authenticates the user.

- If the user clicks on the Forgot your Password link on the Login page, the PasswordRecovery page in figure 9-12 is displayed. If the user clicks on the Need to Create a New Account link, the CreateUser page in figure 9-11 is displayed.

Figure 9-15   The pages of the Authentication application (part 1 of 2)

The third link on the Menu page lets users access the Maintenance page that can be used to manage data that's stored in the Categories and Products tables of the database for the web site. To be able to access this page, the user must be authenticated and the user must be associated with the admin role. When the user clicks on this link, the system attempts to authenticate the user by checking if the browser has a cookie with a valid authentication ticket. If so, the user will be authenticated automatically and allowed to access the Maintenance page. If not, the user will be redirected to the Login page so he or she can log in. Once the user supplies a valid username and password for a user with admin privileges, the browser will be redirected to the Maintenance page.

When you're using the MyAccount and Maintenance pages, the LoginStatus control on these pages allows the users to log out when they're done. This removes the authentication ticket from the browser. As a result, the application won't remember the user the next time the user attempts to access the application, even if the user has selected the Remember Me check box to store the authentication ticket in a persistent cookie.

The MyAccount page

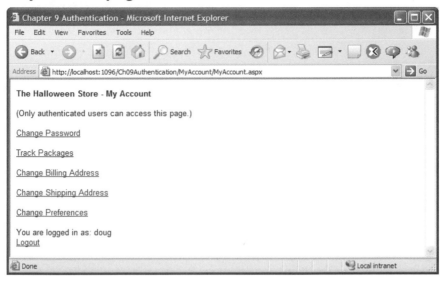

The Maintenance page

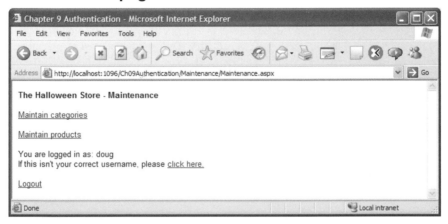

Description

- The MyAccount page lets a user edit account data. The user must be authenticated, but need not be associated with any role. When the user clicks on the Change Password link, a page like the one in figure 9-13 is displayed.

- The Maintenance page lets a user maintain data in the Categories and Products tables. The user must be authenticated and must be associated with the admin role.

- The LoginStatus control on these pages lets the user log out when done. This removes the authentication ticket from the browser. As a result, the application won't be able to remember the user the next time the user attempts to access the application.

Figure 9-15   The pages of the Authentication application (part 2 of 2)

The directory structure

Figure 9-16 shows the directory structure for the Authentication application. This shows the App_Data folder that stores the SQL Server Express database that's used to store the data about the web site's registered users and their roles. In addition, it shows two directories that store web pages that have restricted access. First, it shows the Maintenance directory, which contains the Maintenance page shown in the previous figure. Second, it shows the MyAccount directory, which contains the MyAccount page shown in the previous figure.

In addition, there are three web.config files for this application: one for the root directory, one for the Maintenance directory, and one for the MyAccount directory. The complete listings for these files are shown in figure 9-17.

The access rules

Figure 9-16 also shows the one access rule for the MyAccount directory. This rule denies access to anonymous users. As a result, only users who are authenticated can access the MyAccount directory.

The Maintenance directory, on the other hand, contains two access rules. The first rule denies access to all users. Then, the second rule allows access to authenticated users who are associated with the admin role. To refresh your memory about how this works, please refer back to figure 9-7.

The directory structure for the Authentication application

The access rules for the Maintenance directory

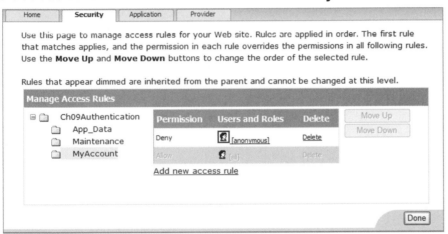

Description

- The MyAccount page lets a user edit personal account data. The user must be authenticated, but doesn't need to be associated with any role.

Figure 9-16   The directory structure and access rules for the Authentication application

The web.config files

Figure 9-17 shows the three web.config files for the Authentication application. When you use the Web Site Administration Tool to create access rules, it automatically creates and modifies these web.config files. As a result, you don't need to be able to manually edit these files. However, it's good to have an idea of what's going on under the hood as you use the Web Site Administration Tool.

In addition, once you become familiar with these files, you may find that you prefer to manually edit or review these files. But first, you need to understand the XML code that's used by these files to store configuration settings.

To enable forms-based authentication, you can use the Mode attribute of the <authentication> element. This attribute is set to "Windows" by default to use Windows authentication, but you can set it to "Forms" to enable forms-based authentication.

Once you've enabled forms-based authentication, you can use the <authorization> element to deny or allow access to specified users. To deny access to users, you can code a <deny> element within the <authorization> element and set the Users and Roles attributes. To allow access to users, you can code an <allow> element within the <authorization> element and set the Users and Roles attributes.

If you want to apply access rules to the root directory for the application, you can code an <authorization> element within the web.config file in the root directory. However, it's more common to apply access rules to subdirectories of the root directory. In that case, you can code a web.config file for each directory as shown in this figure.

The web.config files for the Authentication application

For the root directory

```
<?xml version="1.0"?>
<configuration>
    <system.web>
        <roleManager enabled="True"/>
        <authentication mode="Forms" />
        <compilation debug="true"/>
    </system.web>
</configuration>
```

For the MyAccount directory

```
<?xml version="1.0" encoding="utf-8"?>
<configuration>
    <system.web>
        <authorization>
            <deny users="?" />
        </authorization>
    </system.web>
</configuration>
```

For the Maintenance directory

```
<?xml version="1.0" encoding="utf-8"?>
<configuration>
    <system.web>
        <authorization>
            <allow roles="admin" />
            <deny users="*" />
        </authorization>
    </system.web>
</configuration>
```

Wildcard specifications in the users attribute

Wildcard	Description
*	All users, whether or not they have been authenticated.
?	All unauthenticated users.

Discussion

- When you use the Web Site Administration Tool to create access rules, it automatically creates and modifies the web.config files for an application.

- If you prefer, you can manually edit these files and you can read them to quickly review the settings for an application.

- To enable forms-based authentication, set the Mode attribute of the <authentication> element to "Forms." This attribute is set to "Windows" by default.

- To deny access to users, you can code a <deny> element within the <authorization> element and set the Users and Roles attributes.

- To allow access to users, you can code an <allow> element within the <authorization> element and set the Users and Roles attributes.

Figure 9-17   The web.config files for the Authentication application

How to use code to work with authentication

For most web applications, you can use the Web Site Administration Tool to create users, roles, and access rules. Then, you can use the login controls to allow authorized users to access the restricted pages. And you can do all of this without having to write any code.

However, if you do need to write code to work with authentication, ASP.NET 2.0 provides three new classes that make it easy to do that: the Membership, MembershipUser, and Roles classes. These classes work well with the FormsAuthentication class that was widely used with ASP.NET 1.x. All of these classes are stored in the System.Web.Security namespace.

How to use the Membership class

If you need to work with user data, you can use the Membership class as shown in figure 9-18. This class uses the membership provider that's specified for the application to read and write data from the data store. For more information about how this works, see figure 9-8.

All methods of the Membership class are static. As a result, you never need to create an instance of this class to use its methods. To give you an idea of the types of methods that are available from the Membership class, some of the most commonly used methods are summarized in this figure. However, for a full list of methods, you should consult the documentation for the Membership class.

You can use these methods to create or delete a user. When you use some of these methods, you may need to catch the exceptions that are thrown by them. For example, when you create a user, you need to catch the MembershipCreateUserException that's thrown when the user can't be created.

You can also use these methods to retrieve and update the data that's stored for a user. To do that, you must work with an object created from the MembershipUser class. For example, the GetUser method returns a MembershipUser object that contains the data for the user such as the username, password, email address, security question, and security answer. For more information about working with this class, see the next figure.

If you create a custom login page that doesn't use the Login control shown earlier in this chapter, you can use the ValidateUser method of the Membership class to authenticate the user. Then, if the specified username and password exist in the database and the user has the proper authorization, this method will return a true value. In that case, you can safely redirect the request to the original page that caused the custom login page to be displayed. You can see an example of how this works in figure 9-20.

Common methods of the Membership class

Method	Description
ValidateUser(username, password)	Returns a boolean value that indicates whether the user is authenticated and authorized.
CreateUser(username, password)	Creates a user with the specified username and password.
CreateUser(username, password, email)	Creates a user with the specified username, password, and email address.
GetUser()	Returns a MembershipUser object that contains data about the currently logged-on user. Updates the last activity date-time stamp.
GetUser(username)	Returns a MembershipUser object that contains data about the user with the specified username. Updates the last activity date-time stamp.
GetUserNameByEmail(email)	Returns a string that contains the username that corresponds with the specified email address.
GetAllUsers()	Returns a MembershipUserCollection object that contains MembershipUser objects.
DeleteUser(username)	Deletes the user with the specified username.
UpdateUser(membershipUser)	Updates the user with the data that's stored in the specified MembershipUser object.

A statement that checks if a user is valid

```
Dim bIsValidUser As Boolean
bIsValidUser = Membership.ValidateUser(txtUserName.Text, txtPassword.Text)
```

A statement that creates a user

```
Try
    Membership.CreateUser(txtUserName.Text, txtPassword.Text)
Catch eCreateUser As MembershipCreateUserException
    lblStatus.Text = eCreateUser.Message
End Try
```

A statement that gets the current user and updates the last activity timestamp

```
Dim User As MembershipUser = Membership.GetUser()
```

A statement that deletes a user

```
Membership.DeleteUser(txtUsername.Text)
```

Description

- All methods of the Membership class are static.
- For more information about the MembershipUser class, see the next figure.
- The Membership class is in the System.Web.Security namespace.

Figure 9-18   How to use the Membership class

How to use the MembershipUser class

Figure 9-19 shows how to use the MembershipUser class. To start, you typically use a method of the Membership class to retrieve a MembershipUser object from the data source that's used for authentication. Then, you can use the properties and methods of the MembershipUser object to get or modify the data that's stored in this object.

For example, you might want to use the Email property to get the email address from the MembershipUser object. Or, you might want to set the IsApproved property to False if the user is unsuccessful at logging on a given number of times. Then, the user would not be allowed to log on until the password question was answered correctly, at which time the IsApproved property could be reset to True.

You might also want to use the ChangePassword method to change the password for the object. When you use this and other methods from the MembershipUser object, it updates the data in the MembershipUser object and it updates the data in the membership data store. As a result, you don't need to use the UpdateUser method of the Membership class to update the data in the data store.

Common properties of the MembershipUser class

Property	Description
Username	The username for the membership user.
Email	The email address for the membership user.
PasswordQuestion	The password question for the membership user.
CreationDate	The date and time when the user was added to the membership data store.
LastLoginDate	The date and time when the membership user was last authenticated.
LastActivityDate	The date and time when the membership user was last authenticated or accessed the application.
IsApproved	A boolean value that indicates whether the membership user can be authenticated.

Common methods of the MembershipUser class

Method	Description
GetPassword()	Gets the password for the membership user from the membership data store.
ChangePassword(oldPassword, newPassword)	Updates the password for the membership user in the membership data store.
ResetPassword()	Resets a user's password to a new, automatically generated password.
ChangePasswordQuestionAndAnswer(password, question, answer)	Updates the password question and answer for the membership user in the membership data store.

Code that changes a user's password

```
Dim User As MembershipUser = Membership.GetUser()
Try
    User.ChangePassword(txtOldPassword.Text, txtNewPassword.Text)
Catch eHttp As HttpException
    lblStatus.Text = "An exception occurred. Unable to change password."
End Try
```

Description

- The MembershipUser class is in the System.Web.Security namespace.
- The methods shown here update the MembershipUser object and the data that's stored in the membership data store.

Figure 9-19   How to use the MembershipUser class

How to use the FormsAuthentication class

If you don't want to use the Login control described earlier in this chapter, you can create a login form that includes text boxes that allow the user to enter a username and password. Then, you can write code that authenticates the user and redirects the user from the login page to the page that was originally requested. To do that, you can use the ValidateUser method of the Membership class with the RedirectFromLoginPage method of the FormsAuthentication class as shown in figure 9-20.

When a login page has established that a user has entered a correct username and password, it can use the RedirectFromLoginPage method to create an authentication ticket for the user and redirect the browser to the page that the user originally tried to access. The two arguments for this method specify the username and whether or not the authentication ticket should be saved in a persistent cookie. Because the example in this figure specifies false for the second argument, the authentication ticket will be saved in a session cookie.

Whether the authentication ticket is saved in a session cookie or a persistent cookie, you can use a SignOut method like the one shown in the second statement to log a user off your application. This method removes the authentication ticket from the user's computer. Then, the user will have to be authenticated again the next time the application is accessed.

Common methods of the FormsAuthentication class

Method	Description
`RedirectFromLoginPage(username, createPersistentCookie)`	Issues an authentication ticket for the user and redirects the browser to the page it was attempting to access when the login page was displayed. If the createPersistentCookie argument is True, the cookie that contains the authentication ticket is persistent across browser restarts. Otherwise, the cookie is only available for the current session.
`SignOut()`	Logs the user off by removing the cookie that contains the authentication ticket.

A statement that redirects the browser to the originally requested page

```
If Membership.ValidateUser(txtUserName.Text, txtPassword.Text) Then
    FormsAuthentication.RedirectFromLoginPage(txtUserName.Text, False)
Else
    lblStatus.Text = "Invalid user! Try again."
End If
```

A statement that logs a user off

```
FormsAuthentication.SignOut()
```

Discussion

- After you authenticate a user, you use the RedirectFromLoginPage method of the FormsAuthentication class to redirect the browser to the page that was originally requested. This method creates an authentication ticket that's passed as a cookie to the browser.

- The FormsAuthentication class is in the System.Web.Security namespace.

Figure 9-20   How to use the FormsAuthentication class

How to use the Roles class

The Roles class works similarly to the Membership class. First, all methods of the Roles class are static methods. Second, you can use the Roles class to read data from and write data to the role provider that's specified for the application.

Although you can use the Roles class to add and delete roles from the roles data store, you probably won't need to do that. However, you might need to provide some custom code that works with roles in another way. To illustrate, let's say you've used the Web Site Administration Tool to define a role named premium. Then, when users pay a small fee, they can access the premium pages of the web site. In that case, you might need to write code that adds the current user to the premium role after the user has paid for the premium subscription. To do that, you can use the AddUserToRole method of the Roles class as shown in this figure.

Common methods of the Roles class

Method	Description
CreateRole(rolename)	Adds a new role to the data source.
GetAllRoles()	Gets a list of all the roles for the application.
AddUserToRole(username, rolename)	Adds the specified user to the specified role.
GetRolesForUser(username)	Gets a list of the roles that a user is in.
GetUsersInRole(rolename)	Gets a list of users in the specified role.
IsUserInRole(username, rolename)	Gets a value indicating whether a user is in the specified role.
RemoveUserFromRole(username, rolename)	Removes the specified user from the specified role.
DeleteRole(rolename)	Removes a role from the data source.

Code that creates a role

```
Try
    Roles.CreateRole(txtRoleName.Text)
Catch ex As Exception
    sMessage = "Error creating role: " + ex.Message
End Try
```

Code that gets all roles in the system

```
Dim sRoles As String() = Roles.GetAllRoles
```

A statement that adds a user to a role

```
Roles.AddUserToRole(currentUsername, "premium")
```

A statement that removes a user from a role

```
Roles.RemoveUserFromRole(txtUsername.Text, cboRoles.SelectedValue)
```

Description

- The Roles class is in the System.Web.Security namespace.
- All methods of the Roles class are static.

Figure 9-21 How to use the Roles class

Perspective

This chapter has presented the skills that you need for using forms-based authentication to restrict access to a web application. Although the underlying concepts are the same as they were with ASP.NET 1.x, ASP.NET 2.0 automates many aspects of authentication that were previously tedious and time-consuming. That's why you should be able to implement authentication far more quickly with ASP.NET 2.0 than you could with ASP.NET 1.x, even if you have to develop a custom membership or role provider.

In the next chapter, you'll learn how to develop custom providers. In particular, you'll learn how to develop a custom provider for the profile feature. Once you know how to do that, you should also be able to write any custom providers that you need for memberships and roles.

Terms

authentication
authorization
Windows-based authentication
forms-based authentication
Passport authentication
Microsoft Passport
authentication ticket
role
access rule
data provider
membership provider
role provider
anonymous user
authenticated user

10

How to use profiles

In the last chapter, you learned how to work with authentication. In particular, you learned how to create user accounts that include information about a user such as username, password, and email address. Once you understand how authentication works, you're ready to learn how to use profiles.

You can use the profile feature to store additional information about a user such as the user's mailing address or the preferences that a user has for working with your web application. You can also use it as an easier way to store and retrieve session data like a shopping cart. By default, the profile feature is designed to work with authenticated users, but you can also use it to work with anonymous users.

An introduction to profiles

The *profile feature* is new to ASP.NET 2.0. In the Beta releases, this feature was known as the *personalization feature*, so you may see the term *personalization* used for the profile feature. As you will see, the use of profiles has several advantages, along with a few potential pitfalls.

Profiles compared with session state

The profile feature lets you use the Profile class to store and retrieve data that's associated with a user, which can be referred to as a *profile*. This works similarly to storing user data in the Session class, but the Profile class has several advantages over the Session class. Figure 10-1 describes three of these advantages.

First, the Profile class is designed to store data in a persistent data store that's available for future sessions. In contrast, the Session class is designed to work with temporary data that's available for only the current session.

Second, the Profile class uses strongly typed data. As a result, you can use IntelliSense to discover the properties that are stored in the Profile class, and you typically don't need to use casting when retrieving profile data. In contrast, the Session class uses keys to retrieve an object of the object type. As a result, you must know the name of the key to be able to access an object, and then you must cast the object to its appropriate type when you retrieve it.

Third, the Profile class works more efficiently than the Session class because it only retrieves data when the data is requested. In contrast, all values of the Session object are retrieved on each request, whether or not they're used.

This figure also describes some of the difficulties of working with the Profile class. These difficulties are mainly due to the complexities that are brought on by the challenges of storing persistent data.

First, if you have an existing data store that you want to use, you have to write a significant amount of code to get the Profile class to be able to work with this data. That's because, by default, the Profile class uses a data provider to store profile data in a SQL Server Express database named AspNetDb.mdf. This type of provider is called a *profile provider*. To change the way this works, you need to write a custom profile provider that will use your existing data store, as described later in this chapter, but this is a significant undertaking.

Second, if you decide to use the Profile class to store data about anonymous users, the amount of data in your database can quickly grow so that it contains stale and redundant data that isn't useful and will eventually slow the performance of your site. That's especially true if you have a high volume site with a large number of anonymous users. As a result, you'll need to implement a strategy for managing this data. For example, you'll need to find a way to delete data when it becomes stale or redundant.

Advantages of using the Profile class

Persistent data storage

Unlike the Session class, which only stores data for the current session, the Profile class stores data in a persistent data store. As a result, you can retrieve the data in later sessions.

Strongly typed data access

Unlike the Session class, which requires you to use keys and casting to retrieve data, the Profile class uses properties that have data types. This allows you to use the IntelliSense feature to display the properties that are stored in the Profile class, and it allows you to retrieve data without casting.

Efficient data retrieval

Unlike the Session class, which retrieves data each time a page is posted, the Profile class only retrieves data when necessary.

Disadvantages of using the Profile class

Difficulty accessing legacy data

By default, the profile feature creates a database and allows you to use the Profile class to work with the data in that database. However, if you have data that's stored in an existing database and want to use the Profile class to work with that data, you need to write a custom profile provider and configure your web application to use that profile provider.

Data that's stale and redundant

Since the profile feature stores data persistently about each user, it's easy for your database to become full of stale and redundant data. This is especially true if you store data about anonymous users. If this begins to slow the performance of your site, you'll need to develop a strategy for managing this data.

Description

- The *profile feature* uses the Profile class to persistently store data associated with a user such as first name, birth date, shopping cart, and so on. This data can be referred to as a *profile*.
- To implement the profile feature, ASP.NET 2.0 uses a data provider called a *profile provider*.

Figure 10-1   Profiles compared with session state

An overview of how profiles work

Figure 10-2 gives an overview of how the profile feature works. To start, you define the properties of the Profile class in the web.config file for the application. Once you do that, ASP.NET recompiles the Profile class so it includes these properties. Then, you can write code that uses the Profile class to get and set these properties.

If you take a closer look at the web.config file in this figure, you can see that it uses the <profile>, <properties>, and <add> elements to define the profile properties. Within each <add> element, you must use the Name attribute to specify the name for the property. Then, if you want to specify a data type besides the string type, you can use the Type attribute to specify the data type. In addition, you can use other attributes to specify other behaviors for the profile property. As you progress through this chapter, you'll learn the details for working with the attributes that are available from the <add> element.

By default, the data that's stored by the Profile class can only be read by authenticated users. As a result, the user must log in or submit a cookie with a valid authentication ticket before retrieving or storing profile data. However, it's possible to use the profile feature with another new ASP.NET 2.0 feature known as *anonymous identification* that allows anonymous users to use the profile feature. Anonymous identification lets ASP.NET identify users by storing a unique identifier for each user, usually as a cookie within the user's browser.

In this figure, the web.config file allows anonymous identification by setting the Enabled attribute of the <anonymousIdentification> element to True. Then, to allow the Cart property to use anonymous identification, the AllowAnonymous attribute of the Cart property is set to True. As a result, users can persistently store items in their cart even if they don't log in.

Once you've defined the profile properties in the web.config file, you can use the Profile class to get and set these properties. Since the properties are strongly typed, you don't need to use casting when you retrieve data from the Profile class. However, if you want to display non-string data in a text box, you need to use a ToString method to convert the data type to a string. For example, since the LastActivityDate property is of the DateTime type, the ToShortDateString method is used to convert the property to a string that can be displayed in a text box. Conversely, you may sometimes need to convert a value that's entered as a string to a data type before you can store it in the Profile class.

In some early versions of the Beta release, the Web Site Administration Tool included a Profile tab that allowed you to create and manage the profile properties set in the web.config file. Although this feature was dropped in the final Beta release, it may return in future releases. If so, you can use that tool to edit the web.config file. Until then, you must manually edit the web.config file.

A web.config file that configures a profile

```
<system.web>

  <anonymousIdentification enabled="true" />

  <profile>
    <properties>

      <add name="FirstName"/>

      <add name="LastActivityDate"
           type="System.DateTime"/>

      <add name="Cart"
           type="Cart"
           serializeAs="Binary"
           allowAnonymous="true"/>

    </properties>
  </profile>
</system.web>
```

Visual Basic code that stores profile data

```
Protected Sub btnSave_Click(ByVal sender As Object, _
        ByVal e As System.EventArgs) Handles btnSave.Click
    Profile.FirstName = txtFirstName.Text
    Profile.LastActivityDate = DateTime.Now
    Profile.Cart = cart
End Sub
```

Visual Basic code that retrieves profile data

```
Dim Cart As ShoppingCart

Protected Sub Page_Load(ByVal sender As Object, _
        ByVal e As System.EventArgs) Handles Me.Load
    If Not IsPostBack Then
        txtFirstName.Text = Profile.FirstName
        txtLastActivityDate.Text = Profile.LastActivityDate.ToShortDateString()
        Cart = Profile.Cart;
    End If
End Sub
```

Description

- After you define the properties of a *profile* in the web.config file, you can use the Profile class to store and retrieve the data.

- By default, the profile feature only allows you to access data for users who have been authenticated. However, it's also possible to store data about anonymous users.

- In future versions of ASP.NET, you may be able to use the Web Site Administration Tool to create and manage profile properties. However, in version 2.0, you must manually edit the web.config file.

Figure 10-2   An overview of how profiles work

How the default profile provider works

The machine.config file sets the defaults for all web applications on the current machine. In figure 10-3, you can see the elements that set the default profile provider.

To start, this figure shows the default connection string. This connection string is named LocalSqlServer, and it connects to a SQL Server Express database named AspNetDb.mdf that's stored in the data directory of the application. This is the same connection string and database that's used for the membership and role providers that are described in chapter 9.

Then, this figure shows the code that configures the profile feature so it uses a profile provider named AspNetSqlProfileProvider. This provider uses the LocalSqlServer connection string to connect to the AspNetDb.mdf database using the SqlProfileProvider class that's stored in the System.Web.Profile namespace.

If you're developing a web application from scratch, you may want to use this default provider as is. It works well for prototyping and may be acceptable for some small to medium-sized web applications. Then, since the database is automatically created and configured, you can use the Profile class to store and retrieve data without having to write any data access code.

However, if you need to work with an existing data store, or if you need to gain control over low-level data access details, the default profile provider won't work for your application. If, for example, you need to access data that's stored in an existing SQL Server database that uses a different database schema, the default provider won't work. Or, if you need to access data that's stored in an Oracle database, the default provider won't work.

In that case, one option is to avoid the profile feature altogether. After all, if you have an existing database, you may already have existing classes that read and write profile data to and from the database. If not, you can write this data access code yourself. Typically, that means storing temporary profile data in the Session object. Although this alternative may not be as slick as using the Profile class, it will give you more control over when and how profile data is stored.

Another option is to implement a custom profile provider. To do that, you need to write a class that implements all of the abstract methods of the abstract ProfileProvider class. Then, you need to modify the web.config file for your application so it uses this custom profile provider. For more information about how to do this, please see figures 10-13 and 10-14.

The elements of the machine.config file that are used by the profile feature

The default connection string for SQL Server Express

```
<connectionStrings>
  <add name="LocalSqlServer"
       connectionString="data source=.\SQLEXPRESS;Integrated
           Security=SSPI;AttachDBFilename=|DataDirectory|aspnetdb.mdf;User
           Instance=true"
       providerName="System.Data.SqlClient" />
</connectionStrings>
```

The default profile provider

```
<system.web>

  <profile>
    <providers>
      <add name="AspNetSqlProfileProvider"
           connectionStringName="LocalSqlServer"
           applicationName="/"
           type="System.Web.Profile.SqlProfileProvider,
               System.Web, Version=2.0.0.0, Culture=neutral,
               PublicKeyToken=b03f5f7f11d50a3a" />
    </providers>
  </profile>

</system.web>
```

Description

- To store data, the profile feature uses a *profile provider*.

- By default, the profile feature uses a profile provider named AspNetSqlProfileProvider to store and retrieve data from a SQL Server Express database named AspNetDb.mdf.

- To use the Profile class with data that's stored in an existing database, you must write and configure a custom profile provider as described in figures 10-13 and 10-14.

Figure 10-3   How the default profile provider works

How to use profiles with authenticated users

By default, the profile feature only works for authenticated users. Most of the time, this makes sense. For example, you typically want a user to create an account and log in before you allow the user to read or write personalized data such as first name, last name, or preferences for the web application. The topics that follow show you how to use profiles, but they assume that the user has been authenticated before accessing the specified web pages.

How to define profile properties

Figure 10-4 shows the details of how to define and use a profile property for a string data type. To start, you must code a <profile> element and a <properties> element within the <system.web> element of the web.config file. Within the <properties> element, you can code one or more <add> elements to add profile properties. Then, you can use the Name attribute of the <add> element to specify the name of the property. In this figure, the web.config file contains two properties named FirstName and LastName. Since the <add> elements don't specify a data type, the string data type is used by default.

Once you have defined profile properties in the web.config file, you can write code that uses the Profile class to store and retrieve the profile properties. Remember, though, that these properties can only be accessed for a user after the user has been authenticated. In this figure, for example, let's assume that the code that stores profile data is in the code-behind file for a page named MyAccount.aspx that can only be accessed by an authenticated user. As a result, the user must log in or submit a cookie with a valid authentication ticket before being allowed to access the MyAccount page.

When the user accesses this page, the code that's in the Load event procedure for the page uses the Profile class to read the user's first and last name from the data store. Since this data is stored as the string type, it can be loaded directly into a text box without any casting or conversions. Then, the MyAccount page will be displayed with the data for the current authenticated user displayed in the text boxes for the FirstName and LastName properties. If no data exists for the current user, though, the FirstName and LastName properties will return nulls. In that case, you should leave the text boxes at their default values of empty strings.

At this point, the user can enter or edit his or her first or last name in these text boxes. Then, the user can click on the Save button to execute the event handler for the Click event of the button. This event procedure uses the FirstName and LastName properties of the Profile class to save the data that's in the text boxes for the first and last names. Again, since these properties are of the string type, no casting or conversion is needed.

How to define profile properties in the web.config file

```
<system.web>

  <profile>
    <properties>

      <add name="FirstName"/>
      <add name="LastName"/>

    </properties>
  </profile>

</system.web>
```

Visual Basic code that retrieves profile data

```
Protected Sub Page_Load(ByVal sender As Object, _
      ByVal e As System.EventArgs) Handles Me.Load
    If Not IsPostBack Then
        txtFirstName.Text = Profile.FirstName
        txtLastName.Text = Profile.LastName
    End If
End Sub
```

Visual Basic code that stores profile data

```
Protected Sub btnSave_Click(ByVal sender As Object, _
      ByVal e As System.EventArgs) Handles btnSave.Click
    Profile.FirstName = txtFirstName.Text
    Profile.LastName = txtLastName.Text
End Sub
```

Description

- To define the properties that can be used by a profile in the web.config file, you code an <add> element within the <profile> and <properties> elements. The only attribute that's required within an <add> element is the Name attribute, which specifies the name that's used to access the property.
- By default, all profile properties are stored with the string data type.
- By default, the user must be authenticated before the profile properties can be accessed. If the user isn't authenticated, the property will return an empty string.

Figure 10-4   How to define profile properties

How to specify data types

Figure 10-5 shows how to use the Type attribute of a profile property to specify a data type other than the string type. To start, this figure shows the XML code for the FirstName property displayed in the last figure. Then, it shows the XML code for a property named BirthDate that uses the DateTime data type. Last, it shows the XML code for a property named AccessCount that uses an integer data type.

When you specify a .NET data type, you must qualify it by including the namespace. For example, you must use System.DateTime for the Date data type, and you must use System.Int32 for the Integer type. In contrast, you can use Visual Basic data types like Date and Integer without any qualification.

In addition, if you use a custom data type and that data type is stored within the application's App_Code folder, you don't need to include the namespace. For example, let's assume that you store a class named Customer within the App_Code folder. Let's also assume that this class isn't coded within a namespace. In that case, you can specify the Customer type like this:

```
<add name="Customer" type="Customer">
```

However, if this class is coded within the Business namespace, you must specify the Customer type like this:

```
<add name="Customer" type="Business.Customer">
```

You'll learn more about working with custom data types later in this chapter.

When you work with profile properties that use data types, you need to convert these properties to a different data type so they can be displayed in a control. For example, the BirthDate property in this figure (which is of the DateTime type) is stored in a text box (which takes a string type). That's why the code in this figure uses the ToShortDateString method to convert the BirthDate property to a string, and that's why the ToDateTime method of the Convert class is used to convert the string that's stored in the text box to a valid DateTime object.

However, if you don't need to convert a profile property to get it to work with a control, you can often work with it directly. For example, the last statement in this figure shows how you can update the AccessCount property (which is an Integer type). To do this, you just use the += operator to add 1 to the property. This updates AccessCount and causes the updated count to be stored in the data source.

How to specify data types for profile properties in the web.config file

```
<!— System.String is the default type —>
<add name="FirstName" />

<add name="BirthDate"
    type="System.DateTime" />

<add name="AccessCount"
    type="System.Int32" />
```

Visual Basic code that retrieves typed profile data

```
txtFirstName.Text = Profile.FirstName

txtBirthDate.Text =
    Profile.BirthDate.ToShortDateString()

lblCount.Text =
    Profile.AccessCount.ToString()
```

Visual Basic code that stores typed profile data

```
Profile.FirstName = txtFirstName.Text

Profile.BirthDate =
    Convert.ToDateTime(txtBirthDate.Text)

Profile.AccessCount += 1      ' updates and stores the access count
```

Description

- You can use the Type attribute of the <add> element to specify the data type for a profile property in the web.config file.
- By default, all profile properties are stored with the string data type.
- To specify the Type attribute for a .NET data type, you must include the namespace.
- To specify the Type attribute for a custom data type that's in the App_Code folder, you don't need to include the namespace for the data type (see figure 10-8).

Figure 10-5   How to use data types with profile properties

How to group profile properties

Figure 10-6 shows how to group profile properties. To do that, you code a <group> element within the <profile> and <properties> elements. Within this <group> element, you must code a Name attribute that specifies the name of the group. In this figure, for example, the Name attribute creates a group named Preferences.

Within the <group> element, you can code one or more <add> elements to specify the properties for the group. In this figure, for example, the Preferences group contains two properties of the Boolean type named SendPromotions and SendNewProducts. These properties can be used to determine whether to send a user emails about special product promotions or announcements for new products. Please note, however, that you can't nest one group within another.

Once you've defined a group and its properties within the web.config file, you can access them just as you would any other property. The only difference is that you need to specify the name of the group before the name of the property. To illustrate, the examples in this figure show how to use the SendPromotions and SendNewProducts properties with the Checked property of a check box. Since the Checked property expects a Boolean value, no casting or conversion is required to synchronize the check box with the profile property.

This figure also shows that the IntelliSense feature works with groups just as it does for regular properties. To access it, you just type "Profile" followed by a period to display a list that includes all of the groups that are available from the Profile class. Then, you can select a group by typing the first few letters of the group's name and pressing the Tab key. Finally, you can enter a period and then select a property within the group.

How to group profile properties

```
<group name="Preferences">

    <add name="SendPromotions"
        type="System.Boolean" />

    <add name="SendNewProducts"
        type="System.Boolean" />

</group>
```

Visual Basic code that retrieves grouped profile properties

```
chkPromotions.Checked = Profile.Preferences.SendPromotions
chkNewProducts.Checked = Profile.Preferences.SendNewProducts
```

Visual Basic code that stores grouped profile properties

```
Profile.Preferences.SendPromotions = chkPromotions.Checked
Profile.Preferences.SendNewProducts = chkNewProducts.Checked
```

How IntelliSense makes it easy to work with profile properties

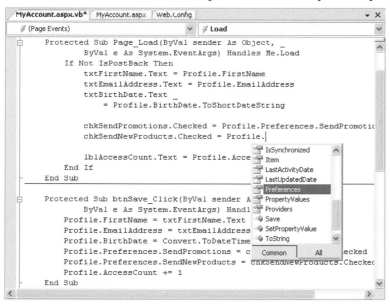

Description

- To group properties, you can code a <group> element around any <add> elements within the <profile> and <properties> elements in the web.config file. The only attribute that's required within a <group> element is the Name attribute, which specifies the name for the group.

- You can't nest a second <group> element within the first <group> element.

Figure 10-6   How to group profile properties

How to specify default values

The first example in figure 10-7 shows how to use the DefaultValue attribute of the <add> element to specify a default value for a profile property. Here, the default value for the Boolean SendPromotions property is set to True. As a result, the first time you use the Profile class to retrieve this property it will be a True value. If you don't code a default value, a blank value will be displayed for this property.

How to specify read-only properties

By default, you can read and write all profile properties. However, if you want to make a profile property read-only, you can set the ReadOnly attribute of the <add> element to True. This is shown in the second example in this figure.

How to specify default values for profile properties

```
<add name="SendPromotions"
     type="System.Boolean"
     defaultValue="true" />
```

How to specify read-only profile properties

```
<add name="DisplayName"
     readOnly="true" />
```

Description

- You can use the DefaultValue attribute of the <add> element to initialize the value of a property.

- You can set the ReadOnly attribute of the <add> element to True to prevent the application from writing to that property.

Figure 10-7   How to specify two more profile property attributes

How to use custom types

Figure 10-8 shows how to use a custom data type named Customer. To start, this figure shows the Customer class. This class specifies the types of data that are stored within each Customer object. To store a Customer class like this one in a database, you mark the class as serializable by coding the Serializable attribute at the start of the class. This lets the .NET Framework know that it's OK to convert this class to binary data.

In this example, each of the eight properties of the Customer class store string data. However, you can use any of the data types for a class like this. If, for example, you want to store a Date data type, you can do that. Or, if you want to store a custom data type named Address to store street address information, you can do that as long as you use the Serializable attribute at the start of that class to mark it as serializable.

By default, the SerializeAs attribute of the <add> element stores data as strings. For most data types, this setting is adequate. However, for a custom data type such as the Customer type, this setting won't work. As a result, you'll need to set the SerializeAs attribute to binary. That way, the Profile class knows to convert the Customer object to binary data before saving this field to the database. Conversely, it knows to convert the binary data stored in the database to a Customer object when reading this field from the database.

The Visual Basic code in the examples shows how to work with the Customer data type. To start, you can retrieve the Customer object for a user just as you would retrieve any other type of profile property for a user. But note that if you try to retrieve a Customer object and no object exists, one is created using the default constructor. Conversely, you can save the Customer object for a user just as you would save any other type of profile property.

Since the profile property named Customer is of the Customer data type, you can use it to directly access any of the properties stored within the Customer object. For example, to retrieve the Email property of the Customer object for the user, you can use this statement:

```
txtEmail.Text = Profile.Customer.Email
```

This retrieves the Customer object for the user, accesses the Email property, and stores it in the email text box. Conversely, to store a change that's made in the email text box, you can use this statement:

```
Profile.Customer.Email = txtEmail.Text
```

Although you can also set the SerializeAs attribute to XML or ProviderSpecific, you probably won't need to use these settings unless you create a custom profile provider. In that case, you may want to set the SerializeAs attribute to ProviderSpecific so the profile provider can determine how to store and retrieve each object. To see an example of this, refer to figures 10-13 and 10-14.

The Customer class in the App_Code folder

```
<Serializable()> _
Public Class Customer
    Public Email As String
    Public LastName As String
    Public FirstName As String
    Public Address As String
    Public City As String
    Public State As String
    Public ZipCode As String
    Public Phone As String
End Class
```

How to specify a custom data type

```
<add name="Customer"
    type="Customer"
    serializeAs="Binary"/>
```

Possible values for the SerializeAs attribute

Value	Description
String	Converts the object to a string (if necessary) and stores it within the specified data store for the application. This is the default setting.
Binary	Converts the object to binary data and stores it within the specified data store for the application. For this to work, the .NET Framework must be able to serialize the object.
XML	Converts the object to XML and stores it in the specified data store for the application.
ProviderSpecific	Allows a custom profile provider to decide how to store the object. To see an example, refer to figure 10-13.

Visual Basic code that retrieves typed data

```
Dim Customer As Customer = Profile.Customer
```

Visual Basic code that stores profile data

```
Dim Customer As Customer = Profile.Customer
Customer.Email = txtEmail.Text
Customer.LastName = txtLastName.Text
Customer.FirstName = txtFirstName.Text
Profile.Customer = Customer
```

Description

- To specify the Type attribute of the <add> element for a custom data type that's in the App_Code folder, you can code just the name of the class. However, if the class is coded within a namespace, you must include the name of the namespace.

- To store a custom data type as binary data, you need to mark it as serializable by coding the Serializable attribute just before the declaration of the class. Then, you can set the SerializeAs attribute of the <add> element to binary to specify that the data should be stored as binary data.

Figure 10-8   How to use custom data types

How to use profiles with anonymous users

By default, the profile feature only works with authenticated users. However, there are times when you may want to use profiles with anonymous users. For example, you probably don't want to force a user to log in before he or she can add items to a shopping cart. Fortunately, the new *anonymous identification* feature that came with ASP.NET 2.0 lets you use profiles with anonymous users.

The topics that follow show how to enable anonymous identification and how to specify which properties can be accessed by anonymous users. In addition, they show how to deal with an issue that arises when you allow anonymous users to use profiles. In particular, it shows how you can migrate the data that's stored for a user from an anonymous account to an authenticated account if the anonymous user creates an account and logs in.

How to enable anonymous identification

Before you can identify anonymous users, you need to enable the anonymous identification feature as shown in figure 10-9. To do that, you just code an <anonymousIdentification> element with an Enabled attribute set to True. Once you do that, a cookie will be stored for each user that visits your web site. This cookie will be named .ASPXANONYMOUS, and it will be stored on the user's machine for 100,000 minutes, which is almost 70 days. That way, each time an anonymous user visits your site, the user's browser passes a cookie to the site that contains an identifier that uniquely identifies the user.

Most of the time, that's all you need to do to enable anonymous identification. However, if you want to change the name of the cookie, you can use the CookieName attribute. Or, if you want to shorten or lengthen the amount of time that the cookie is stored on the user's system, you can use the CookieTimeout attribute. Or, if you need to make sure that this works even if the user's browser doesn't support cookies (which is rare), you can use the Cookieless attribute. In that case, you typically set the Cookieless attribute to AutoDetect so cookies can be used if they're available.

How to allow anonymous users to access profile properties

Once you've enabled anonymous identification, you must specify which profile properties can be accessed by an anonymous user. To do that, you can set the AllowAnonymous attribute of the <add> element to True. In this figure, for example, the Cart property can be accessed by anonymous users, but the Customer property can't. Note that the Cart property uses a ShoppingCart data type that's defined by the ShoppingCart class shown in figure 10-12.

How to use profile properties with anonymous users

```
<system.web>

  <anonymousIdentification enabled="true" />

  <profile>
    <properties>

      <add name="Customer"
           type="Customer"
           serializeAs="Binary"/>

      <add name="Cart"
           type="ShoppingCart"
           serializeAs="Binary"
           allowAnonymous="true"/>

    </properties>
  </profile>

</system.web>
```

Attributes of the <AnonymousIdentification> element

Attribute	Description
Enabled	Enables or disables anonymous identification. The default setting is False.
CookieName	Sets the name of the cookie that's stored for each anonymous user. The default setting is .ASPXANONYMOUS.
CookieTimeout	Sets the length of time that the cookie will be stored on the user's machine in minutes. The default setting is 100,000 minutes, which is almost 70 days.
Cookieless	Specifies how to identify anonymous users. You can use one of the four values shown below.

Possible values for the Cookieless attribute

Value	Description
UseCookies	Uses cookies to store the anonymous identifier. This is the default setting.
UseUrl	Stores the anonymous identifier in the URL.
AutoDetect	Allows ASP.NET to detect whether the browser can support cookies. If so, it uses cookies to store the anonymous identifier. If not, it uses the URL.
UseDeviceProfile	Configures the anonymous identifier for the device or browser.

Description

- Once you've enabled *anonymous identification*, you can set the AllowAnonymous attribute of any <add> element to True to allow anonymous users to access the specified profile property.

Figure 10-9   How to enable anonymous identification

How to migrate data from anonymous to authenticated users

Once you begin storing personalized data for anonymous users, you need to develop a strategy for what to do if the anonymous user creates an account and authenticates. To illustrate, let's assume an anonymous user has added items to his or her cart and that this cart has been saved to the data store. Then, the anonymous user decides to purchase the items in his or her cart. At this point, the user must get authenticated by creating an account or by logging in, and you must decide what to do with the data that's stored in the anonymous user's cart.

Figure 10-10 shows how you can use the Profile_MigrateAnonymous event procedure to handle this situation. To start, you can create a global.asax file for your application if one doesn't already exist. Then, you can code the Profile_MigrateAnonymous event procedure in this file. Because Profile_MigrateAnonymous is an application-wide event, it will be called whenever a user authenticates. In fact, unless you remove the cookie that contains the anonymous identifier as shown in the second example in this figure, this method may be called twice each time the user authenticates.

One way to migrate data is to copy the data that's stored in the Cart property for the anonymous user to the Cart property for the authenticated user as shown in the first example in this figure. Here, the first statement retrieves the profile for the anonymous user and stores it in a ProfileCommon object named ProfileCommon. To accomplish this, this statement uses the AnonymousId property of the ProfileMigrateEventsArg object to retrieve the unique identifier for the user, and it uses the static GetProfile method of the Profile class. Then, the second statement copies the Cart property from the anonymous user's profile to the Cart property for the newly authenticated user's profile. This will replace any items in the authenticated user's cart with the items in the anonymous cart.

At this point, the data for the ShoppingCart object is stored for both the anonymous user and the authenticated user. As a result, if the user logs out and becomes anonymous again, the user's cart will still contain all of the same items. On the other hand, if the user logs in and becomes authenticated, the user's cart will be replaced by whatever items are stored in the anonymous cart.

Although this solution works, it doesn't provide for an anonymous user that already has stored items in the cart for his authenticated account. In that case, you may not want to replace the authenticated Cart property with the anonymous Cart property. Instead, you may want to merge the items in the two carts as shown in the second example in this figure. In this case, if the same item is in both carts, the code in the AddItem method of the ShoppingCart class increases the quantity for the item appropriately.

After the items in the two carts have been merged, this code uses a method of the ProfileManager class to delete the anonymous profile from the data store. Then, it uses a method of the AnonymousIdentificationModel class to clear the cookie that stores the anonymous identifier from the client's browser. This reduces the size of the data store, it deletes all items from the anonymous cart, and it prevents the Profile_MigrateAnonymous event procedure from being run twice each time a user authenticates.

Code that copies the data for an anonymous user to an authenticated user

```
Public Sub Profile_MigrateAnonymous(ByVal sender As Object, _
        ByVal e As ProfileMigrateEventArgs)
    Dim ProfileCommon As ProfileCommon = Profile.GetProfile(e.AnonymousID)
    Profile.Cart = ProfileCommon.Cart
End Sub
```

Code that merges data for an anonymous user with data for an authenticated user

```
Public Sub Profile_MigrateAnonymous(ByVal sender As Object, _
        ByVal e As ProfileMigrateEventArgs)

    ' get the anonymous profile
    Dim ProfileCommon As ProfileCommon = Profile.GetProfile(e.AnonymousID)

    If ProfileCommon.Cart.Count > 0 And Profile.Cart.Count = 0 Then
        ' swap carts
        Profile.Cart = ProfileCommon.Cart
    ElseIf Profile.Cart.Count > 0 And ProfileCommon.Cart.Count > 0 Then
        ' put all anonymous items in the authenticated cart
        Dim Item As CartItem
        For Each Item In ProfileCommon.Cart.GetItems
            If Not Item Is Nothing Then
                Profile.Cart.AddItem(Item)
            End If
        Next Item
    End If

    ' delete the anonymous profile data from the data store
    ProfileManager.DeleteProfile(e.AnonymousID)

    ' clear the cookie that identifies the anonymous user
    AnonymousIdentificationModule.ClearAnonymousIdentifier()
End Sub
```

Description

- Since the Profile_MigrateAnonymous event procedure may be called from multiple web pages, it is often stored in the global.asax file. This event procedure is executed whenever a user is authenticated.
- If you don't delete the profile data for the anonymous user and remove the anonymous identifier after the data for an anonymous user has been migrated to the authenticated user, the Profile_MigrateAnonymous procedure will be executed twice each time a user is authenticated.
- The code for the GetItems and AddItem procedures of the ShoppingCart class is shown in figure 10-12.

Figure 10-10   How to migrate data from anonymous to authenticated users

The Cart Profile application

Now that you've seen the details for how to use profiles to work with authenticated users and anonymous users, you're ready to see how these details fit together within an application. In particular, you're ready to see how the Halloween Store application can use profiles to provide for a shopping cart that persists across sessions for both anonymous and authenticated users, and you're ready to see how this application can use profiles to store other user data for authenticated users. We'll call this the Cart Profile application.

The pages

Part 1 of figure 10-11 shows how the Cart page of this application can be displayed for an anonymous user or an authenticated user. The first Cart page contains a single item, and you can tell that the user is an anonymous user because the Login control at the bottom of the page says, "Login."

The second Cart page shows that the user is an authenticated user because the Login control at the bottom of the page says, "Logout." In addition, you can tell that this authenticated user has previously saved first name data because the page displays "Doug's shopping cart" instead of "Your shopping cart" above the list box that's used for the shopping cart. Last, the cart for the authenticated user contains two items instead of one because the application has merged the anonymous cart with the authenticated cart.

The Cart page before the user logs in

The Cart page after the user logs in

Figure 10-11   The pages of the Cart Profile application (part 1 of 2)

Part 2 of figure 10-11 shows the CheckOut1 page that's displayed when the user clicks on the Check Out button on the Cart page. This page can only be accessed by an authenticated user, which is appropriate since this page allows the user to enter and edit personalized customer data. If an anonymous user tries to access this page, the user is transferred to the Login page using the techniques of the last chapter.

In this application, you can only display the CheckOut1 page by clicking on the Check Out button from the Cart page. However, in a more full-featured application, you might want to add a "My Account" link that allows a user to edit this type of information at his or her convenience. That way, a user can create an account, authenticate, and begin storing personalized data like the data shown in this figure without having to begin the check out process.

The CheckOut1 page

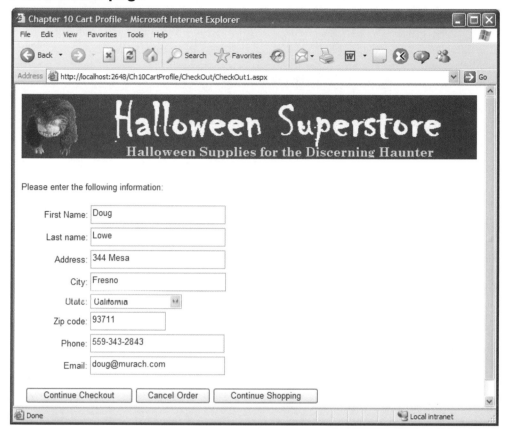

Description

- The Cart page can display the cart for an anonymous user or an authenticated user. When an anonymous user logs in, all items in the anonymous user's cart are copied into the authenticated user's cart, adding to the quantity as necessary for duplicate items.

- The CheckOut1 page can only be accessed by an authenticated user. This page allows the user to enter or edit personalized user data.

- If an anonymous user clicks on the Check Out button on the Cart page, the Login page is automatically displayed by using the techniques presented in chapter 9.

Figure 10-11   The pages of the Cart Profile application (part 2 of 2)

The code

Part 1 of figure 10-12 shows the code for the ShoppingCart class. Since this is a typical business class, you shouldn't have any trouble understanding it. However, there are a few points to notice.

First, the Serializable attribute is coded at the top of this class to mark it as serializable. This allows the Profile class to store and retrieve ShoppingCart objects from the data store. However, the ShoppingCart class uses the CartItem and Product classes that were presented in chapter 2. As a result, for the ShoppingCart class to be serialized successfully, the CartItem and Product classes must also be marked as serializable.

Second, the AddItem method contains all of the logic that's used to add an item to the cart. In particular, if the item already exists in the cart, the quantity of that item is increased appropriately. As a result, you can access this code from any point in the application. For example, the Order page calls this method to add an item to the cart, and the global.asax file calls this method to migrate items from the anonymous cart to the authenticated cart.

Third, the ShoppingCart class works with strongly typed data. For example, the AddItem method only accepts objects of the CartItem type. As a result, it's impossible for a programmer to accidentally add another type of object to the cart (which could cause a nasty debugging problem). Conversely, the GetItems method returns an array of CartItem objects. As a result, you don't need to use casting to retrieve the CartItem objects.

The code for the ShoppingCart class

```
Imports Microsoft.VisualBasic

<Serializable()> _
Public Class ShoppingCart

    Private Cart As SortedList = New SortedList()

    Public ReadOnly Property Count() As Integer
        Get
            Return Cart.Count
        End Get
    End Property

    Public Sub AddItem(ByVal Item As CartItem)
        Dim sProductID As String = Item.Product.ProductID
        If (Cart.ContainsKey(sProductID)) Then
            Dim ExistingItem As CartItem
            ExistingItem = CType(Cart.Item(sProductID), CartItem)
            ExistingItem.Quantity += Item.Quantity
        Else
            Cart.Add(sProductID, Item)
        End If
    End Sub

    Public Function GetItems() As CartItem()
        Dim Items(Cart.Count) As CartItem
        Dim i As Integer
        If (Cart.Count > 0) Then
            For i = 0 To Cart.Count - 1
                Items(i) = CType(Cart.GetByIndex(i), CartItem)
            Next
        End If
        Return Items
    End Function

    Public Sub Clear()
        Cart.Clear()
    End Sub

    Public Sub RemoveAt(ByVal i As Integer)
        Cart.RemoveAt(i)
    End Sub

End Class
```

Description

- The ShoppingCart class uses the CartItem and Product classes that were presented in chapter 2. The only difference is that the Serializable attribute has been added to these classes to mark them as serializable.

Figure 10-12   The code for the Cart Profile application (part 1 of 3)

Part 2 of figure 10-12 presents a partial listing of the code for the Cart page. To start, when the page is loaded, the Page_Load event procedure sets the title for the cart. First, this procedure declares the default title that's displayed for anonymous users and for authenticated users who have not saved their first names in the data store. Then, this procedure uses the Profile class to check if the FirstName property of the Customer object contains a null value or an empty string. If not, the first name data is used to personalize the title for the cart. Finally, the DisplayCart procedure is called to load all items in the cart into the list box for the cart.

The DisplayCart procedure begins by clearing any existing items from the list box. Then, it uses a For Each...Next loop to add each item in the cart to the list box. To do that, it uses the GetItems method of the Cart property of the Profile class to get an array of CartItem objects.

The btnRemove_Click and the btnEmpty_Click procedures both use the Cart property of the Profile class to update the items that are stored in the cart. These updates are automatically made to the data store as soon as the statements are executed. If, for example, you click the Empty Cart button, the code that's in the btnEmpty_Click procedure will clear all items from the Cart property of the Profile class, which will delete all cart items from the data store.

The code for the Cart page

```
Partial Class Cart
    Inherits System.Web.UI.Page

    Protected Sub Page_Load(ByVal sender As Object, _
            ByVal e As System.EventArgs) Handles Me.Load
        If Not IsPostBack Then
            Dim sTitle As String = "Your shopping cart:"
            Dim sFirstName As String = Profile.Customer.FirstName
            If Not sFirstName Is Nothing And Not sFirstName = "" Then
                sTitle = sFirstName & "'s shopping cart:"
            End If
            lblCartTitle.Text = sTitle
            Me.DisplayCart()
        End If
    End Sub

    Private Sub DisplayCart()
        lstCart.Items.Clear()
        Dim CartItem As CartItem
        For Each CartItem In Profile.Cart.GetItems
            If Not CartItem Is Nothing Then
                lstCart.Items.Add(CartItem.Display)
            End If
        Next CartItem
    End Sub

    Protected Sub btnRemove_Click(ByVal sender As Object, _
            ByVal e As System.EventArgs) Handles btnRemove.Click
        If lstCart.SelectedIndex > -1 And Profile.Cart.Count > 0 Then
            Profile.Cart.RemoveAt(lstCart.SelectedIndex)
            Me.DisplayCart()
        End If
    End Sub

    Protected Sub btnEmpty_Click(ByVal sender As Object, _
            ByVal e As System.EventArgs) Handles btnEmpty.Click
        Profile.Cart.Clear()
        lstCart.Items.Clear()
    End Sub

    Protected Sub btnCheckOut_Click(ByVal sender As Object, _
            ByVal e As System.EventArgs) Handles btnCheckOut.Click
        Response.Redirect("~/CheckOut/CheckOut1.aspx")
    End Sub

End Class
```

Description

- Within the Page_Load event procedure, the Profile.Customer property is used to display a different title for the cart if the user is authenticated and has stored a first name in the database.

- Within the other procedures, the Profile.Cart property is used to work with the items that are stored in the cart for the current user. Since this property is of the ShoppingCart type, you can use the methods defined in the ShoppingCart class to work with it.

Figure 10-12   The code for the Cart Profile application (part 2 of 3)

Part 3 of figure 10-12 presents a partial listing of the code for the CheckOut1 page. To start, when this page loads, it binds the states data to the State combo box. Then, it uses the Profile class to return a Customer object and display the properties of the Customer object within the text boxes on the page. Remember that the first statement shown here will create a Customer object if one doesn't already exist. Because of that, you need to check this object to be sure it isn't null before you assign its properties to the text boxes. If you don't, an error will occur because the properties of the object will be null.

On the CheckOut1 page, if the user clicks the Continue Checkout or Continue Shopping button, the UpdateCustomer procecure is called. This procedure begins by creating a new Customer object. Then, it sets the properties of this Customer object to the string values that are stored in the text boxes on the page. Last, it uses the Profile class to save the updated Customer object.

If, on the other hand, the user clicks on the Cancel button, the UpdateCustomer procedure isn't called. Instead, the user is immediately redirected to the Order page. As a result, the Profile class isn't called, and the customer data on the CheckOut1 page isn't saved.

The code for the CheckOut1 page

```
Partial Class CheckOut1
    Inherits System.Web.UI.Page

    Protected Sub Page_Load(ByVal sender As Object, _
            ByVal e As System.EventArgs) Handles Me.Load

        If Not IsPostBack Then

            ' Code that binds data to the State combo box goes here

            Dim Customer As Customer = Profile.Customer
            If Not Customer Is Nothing Then
                txtLastName.Text = Customer.LastName
                txtFirstName.Text = Customer.FirstName
                txtAddress.Text = Customer.Address
                txtCity.Text = Customer.City
                ddlState.SelectedValue = Customer.State
                txtZipCode.Text = Customer.ZipCode
                txtPhone.Text = Customer.Phone
                txtEmail.Text = Customer.Email
            End If
        End If
    End Sub

    Protected Sub UpdateCustomer()
        Dim Customer As New Customer
        Customer.LastName = txtLastName.Text
        Customer.FirstName = txtFirstName.Text
        Customer.Address = txtAddress.Text
        Customer.City = txtCity.Text
        Customer.State = ddlState.SelectedValue
        Customer.ZipCode = txtZipCode.Text
        Customer.Phone = txtPhone.Text
        Customer.Email = txtEmail.Text
        Profile.Customer = Customer
    End Sub

    Protected Sub btnContinue_Click(ByVal sender As Object, _
            ByVal e As System.EventArgs) Handles btnContinue.Click
        UpdateCustomer()
        Response.Redirect("../Order.aspx")
    End Sub

    Protected Sub btnCheckout_Click(ByVal sender As Object, _
            ByVal e As System.EventArgs) Handles btnCheckout.Click
        UpdateCustomer()
        lblMessage.Text = "Sorry, that function hasn't been implemented yet."
    End Sub

    Protected Sub btnCancel_Click(ByVal sender As Object, _
            ByVal e As System.EventArgs) Handles btnCancel.Click
        Response.Redirect("../Order.aspx")
    End Sub

End Class
```

Description

- This page uses the Profile.Customer property to store and retrieve Customer objects.

Figure 10-12   The code for the Cart Profile application (part 3 of 3)

How to use a custom profile provider

In some cases, the default profile provider won't work for your application. If, for example, you need to use data that's stored in an existing database, you won't be able to use the default provider. Then, if you want to use profiles with that database, you'll need to write a custom profile provider. This lets you get under the hood and gain control over what database is used and how the profile properties are read from and written to the database.

How to edit the web.config file so it uses a custom profile provider

Figure 10-13 shows the web.config file for an application that uses the custom profile provider shown in figure 10-14. To start, the web.config file includes an <add> element within a <connectionStrings> element. This element defines the connection string that the custom profile provider uses to connect to the database. In this case, the database is the SQL Server Express database named Halloween.mdf that's used throughout this book.

Once the connection string for the database is defined, another <add> element is coded within the <profile> and <providers> elements to add the custom profile provider to the list of profile providers. Within this <add> element, the Name attribute specifies the name of the ProfileProvider class, the Type attribute specifies the type, and the ConnectionStringName attribute specifies the name of the connection string (which is defined within the <connectionStrings> element earlier in the file).

In this application, the Cart property uses the default profile provider described in figure 10-3. However, the Customer property uses the custom profile provider. This makes sense because the existing Halloween database contains data about customers, but not about carts. To specify a custom profile provider for the Customer property, the Provider attribute specifies the name of the custom profile provider. In addition, the SerializeAs attribute specifies that the custom profile provider should be used to determine how to write and read the Customer object.

If you want to set the default provider for all profile properties, you can code a DefaultProvider attribute within the <profile> element like this:

```
<profile defaultProvider="MyProfileProvider">
```

Then, both the Cart and Customer properties will use the same profile provider. As a result, whenever you call one of these properties, the data for both properties is retrieved. For example, when you call the Customer property to retrieve customer data, the cart data for that customer is also retrieved. Often, this is okay. But if you don't want all profile properties to be retrieved each time you call another profile property, you can code a custom provider for each property or group of properties.

A web.config file that uses a custom profile provider

```
<appSettings>
  <add key="applicationName" value="Chapter 10 Customer Profile Provider"/>
</appSettings>

<connectionStrings>
  <add name="HalloweenConnection"
      connectionString="Data Source=localhost\SQLExpress;
      Initial Catalog=Halloween;
      Integrated Security=True" />
</connectionStrings>

<system.web>

  <authentication mode="Forms" />
  <roleManager enabled="true"/>
  <anonymousIdentification enabled="true"/>
  <compilation debug="true"/>

  <profile>

      <providers>
        <add name="CustomerProfileProvider"
            type="Murach.CustomerProfileProvider"
            connectionStringName="HalloweenConnection" />
      </providers>

      <properties>
        <add name="Cart"
            type="Cart"
            serializeAs="Binary"
            allowAnonymous="True"/>
        <add name="Customer"
            type="Customer"
            serializeAs="ProviderSpecific"
            provider="CustomerProfileProvider"/>

      </properties>
  </profile>

</system.web>
```

Description

- For more information about coding the web.config file to use a custom provider, look up the "Sample Profile Provider Implementation" topic in the Visual Studio help system and scroll down to the "Using the Sample Provider in an ASP.NET Application" topic.

- You can use a single profile provider for all profile properties by coding a DefaultProvider attribute for the <profile> element that specifies the profile provider.

- Within the <add> element of a profile property, you can use the Provider attribute to specify a different profile provider for each property, and you can use the SerializeAs property to specify that the profile provider should determine how the object is saved and retrieved from the database.

Figure 10-13   How to edit the web.config file so it uses a custom profile provider

How to write the class for the provider

To give you some idea of how to write a class for a custom profile provider, figure 10-14 shows a class that provides a bare bones implementation for a custom provider. This class has over 250 lines of code and takes five pages to print. And that's for a class that only supports one property! So, obviously, writing a custom provider is no walk in the park. Then again, if you have a solid understanding of ADO.NET, you should be able to follow this code without much trouble.

The declaration for this class specifies that the class is stored within the Murach namespace, is named CustomerProfileProvider, and inherits the abstract ProfileProvider class. As a result, the CustomerProfileProvider class must implement all abstract members of the ProfileProvider class. In addition, since the ProfileProvider class inherits the abstract SettingsProvider class and the SettingsProvider class inherits the abstract ProviderBase class, you must also implement the abstract members of the SettingsProvider and ProviderBase classes.

In all, this means that you must provide implementations for 11 methods and 2 properties if you want to provide a fully functional profile provider. However, to get a partially functional custom provider that works adequately for the Cart Profile application, you only need to implement 2 properties (Name and ApplicationName) and 3 methods (Initialize, GetPropertyValues, and SetPropertyValues).

To start, the Initialize method sets the default values for the Name property, the ApplicationName property, and the connection string. To do that, it uses the ConfigurationManager class to read values from the web.config file.

Then, the GetPropertyValues method reads data from the database. To do that, this method uses the GetEmail and GetCustomer methods. Note that the GetEmail method uses the Membership class to read the user's email address from the membership data store (which is stored in the default AspNetDB.mdf database). This email address is the key that's used to store and retrieve customer records in the Halloween database.

Conversely, the SetPropertyValues method writes data to the Halloween database. To do that, this method uses the SetCustomer method, which uses the stored procedure shown in figure 10-15 to add or update customers. This stored procedure allows more of the SQL code to be stored in the database layer.

Finally, the last eight methods of the CustomerProfileProvider class throw exceptions. As a result, if you invoke one of these methods, an appropriate exception will be thrown. When that happens, you can implement the method so it works correctly.

For more information about implementing these methods and properties, look up the ProfileProvider class in the Visual Studio documentation and navigate to the "Implementing a Profile Provider" topic in the help system. There you can find detailed descriptions of each method along with sample code for a custom profile provider in the "Sample Profile Provider Implementation" topic.

A class that implements a custom profile provider   **Page 1**

```
Imports Microsoft.VisualBasic
Imports System.Configuration
Imports System.Data
Imports System.Data.SqlClient

Namespace Murach

    Public Class CustomerProfileProvider
        Inherits ProfileProvider

        Private sProviderName As String
        Private sAppName As String
        Private sConnection As String

        '****************************************************
        ' ProviderBase members
        '****************************************************/

        ' System.Configuration.Provider.ProviderBase.Name Property
        Public Overrides ReadOnly Property Name() As String
            Get
                If sProviderName Is Nothing Then
                    Return "CustomerProfileProvider"
                End If
                Return sProviderName
            End Get
        End Property

        ' System.Configuration.Provider.ProviderBase.Initialize Method
        Public Overrides Sub Initialize(ByVal Name As String, _
                ByVal Config As NameValueCollection)
            ' Initialize values from Web.config
            sProviderName = Name

            sAppName = ConfigurationManager. _
                AppSettings("ApplicationName").ToString()

            If sAppName Is Nothing Or sAppName.Trim().Equals("") Then
                sAppName = HttpContext.Current.Request.ApplicationPath
            End If

            sConnection = ConfigurationManager. _
                ConnectionStrings("HalloweenConnection").ConnectionString

        End Sub
```

Figure 10-14   A class for a custom profile provider (part 1 of 5)

A class that implements a custom profile provider

```vb
'***************************************************
' System.Configuration.SettingsProvider Members
'***************************************************

' System.Configuration.SettingsProvider.ApplicationName Property
Public Overrides Property ApplicationName() As String
    Get
        Return sAppName
    End Get
    Set(ByVal value As String)
        sAppName = value
    End Set
End Property

' SettingsProvider.GetPropertyValues Method
Public Overrides Function GetPropertyValues( _
    ByVal Context As SettingsContext, _
    ByVal Collection As SettingsPropertyCollection) _
        As SettingsPropertyValueCollection

    Dim sUsername As String = CType(Context("UserName"), String)
    Dim bAuthenticated As Boolean = CType(Context("IsAuthenticated"), _
        Boolean)

    Dim spvCollection As SettingsPropertyValueCollection = _
        New SettingsPropertyValueCollection()

    Dim setProperty As SettingsProperty
    For Each setProperty In Collection
        Dim spValue As SettingsPropertyValue _
            = New SettingsPropertyValue(setProperty)

        Select Case setProperty.Name
            Case "Customer"
                spValue.PropertyValue _
                    = GetCustomer(sUsername, bAuthenticated)

                ' Add other profile properties here

            Case Else
                Throw New HttpException("Unsupported property.")
        End Select
        spvCollection.Add(spValue)
    Next
    Return spvCollection
End Function

' Get the user's email address from the Membership data source
Private Function GetEmail(ByVal Username As String) As String
    Dim User As MembershipUser = Membership.GetUser(UserName)
    If User Is Nothing Then
        Return Nothing
    End If
    Return User.Email
End Function
```

Figure 10-14   A class for a custom profile provider (part 2 of 5)

A class that implements a custom profile provider   Page 3

```vb
' Retrieve a Customer object from the Halloween DB
Private Function GetCustomer(ByVal Username As String, _
        ByVal Authenticated As Boolean) As Customer
    If Authenticated Then
        Dim Email As String = GetEmail(Username)
        If Email Is Nothing Or Email.Trim().Equals("") Then
            Throw New HttpException("No email address for " + Username)
        End If

        Dim sSelect As String = "SELECT Email, LastName, FirstName, " _
            & "Address, City, State, ZipCode, PhoneNumber " _
            & "FROM Customers WHERE Email = @Email"
        Dim cmd As SqlCommand _
            = New SqlCommand(sSelect, New SqlConnection(sConnection))

        cmd.Parameters.AddWithValue("Email", Email)
        cmd.CommandType = CommandType.Text
        Dim Customer As Customer = New Customer()
        Dim dr As SqlDataReader
        Try
            cmd.Connection.Open()
            dr = cmd.ExecuteReader(CommandBehavior.CloseConnection)
            If (dr.Read()) Then
                Customer.Email = CType(dr("Email"), String)
                Customer.LastName = CType(dr("LastName"), String)
                Customer.FirstName = CType(dr("FirstName"), String)
                Customer.Address = CType(dr("Address"), String)
                Customer.City = CType(dr("City"), String)
                Customer.State = CType(dr("State"), String)
                Customer.ZipCode = CType(dr("ZipCode"), String)
                Customer.Phone = CType(dr("PhoneNumber"), String)
            End If
        Catch ex As Exception
            Throw ex
        Finally
            If Not dr Is Nothing Then
                dr.Close()
            End If
        End Try
        Return Customer
    Else ' Not authenticated, return empty Customer object
        Return New Customer()
    End If
End Function
```

Figure 10-14   A class for a custom profile provider (part 3 of 5)

A class that implements a custom profile provider

```vb
' SettingsProvider.SetPropertyValues Method
Public Overrides Sub SetPropertyValues( _
    ByVal Context As SettingsContext, _
    ByVal Collection As SettingsPropertyValueCollection)

    Dim sUsername As String = CType(Context("UserName"), String)
    Dim bAuthenticated As Boolean = CType(Context("IsAuthenticated"), _
        Boolean)

    Dim spValue As SettingsPropertyValue
    For Each spValue In Collection
        Select Case spValue.Property.Name
            Case "Customer"
                SetCustomer(sUsername, CType(spValue.PropertyValue, _
                    Customer), bAuthenticated)

                ' add other profile properties here

            Case Else
                Throw New HttpException("Unsupported property.")
        End Select
    Next spValue
End Sub

' Store or update a Customer object in the Halloween DB
Public Sub SetCustomer(ByVal Username As String, _
        ByVal Customer As Customer, ByVal Authenticated As Boolean)
    If Authenticated Then
        If Customer.Email Is Nothing _
                Or Customer.Email.Trim.Equals("") Then
            Throw New HttpException("No email address for " & Username)
        End If

        Dim cmd As SqlCommand = New SqlCommand( _
            "AddOrUpdateCustomer", New SqlConnection(sConnection))

        cmd.CommandType = CommandType.StoredProcedure
        cmd.Parameters.AddWithValue("Email", Customer.Email)
        cmd.Parameters.AddWithValue("LastName", Customer.LastName)
        cmd.Parameters.AddWithValue("FirstName", Customer.FirstName)
        cmd.Parameters.AddWithValue("Address", Customer.Address)
        cmd.Parameters.AddWithValue("City", Customer.City)
        cmd.Parameters.AddWithValue("State", Customer.State)
        cmd.Parameters.AddWithValue("ZipCode", Customer.ZipCode)
        cmd.Parameters.AddWithValue("PhoneNumber", Customer.Phone)

        Try
            cmd.Connection.Open()
            cmd.ExecuteNonQuery()
        Catch ex As Exception
            Throw ex
        Finally
            cmd.Connection.Close()
        End Try
    End If
End Sub
```

Figure 10-14   A class for a custom profile provider (part 4 of 5)

A class that implements a custom profile provider   **Page 5**

```
'**************************************************
' System.Web.Profile.ProfileProvider methods
'**************************************************
Public Overrides Function DeleteInactiveProfiles(ByVal _
authenticationOption As System.Web.Profile.ProfileAuthenticationOption, _
ByVal userInactiveSinceDate As Date) As Integer
    Throw New Exception("The method or operation is not implemented.")
End Function

Public Overloads Overrides Function DeleteProfiles( ByVal _
usernames() As String) As Integer
    Throw New Exception("The method or operation is not implemented.")
End Function

Public Overloads Overrides Function DeleteProfiles(ByVal profiles _
As System.Web.Profile.ProfileInfoCollection) As Integer
    Throw New Exception("The method or operation is not implemented.")
End Function

Public Overrides Function FindInactiveProfilesByUserName(ByVal _
authenticationOption As System.Web.Profile.ProfileAuthenticationOption, _
ByVal usernameToMatch As String, ByVal userInactiveSinceDate As Date, _
ByVal pageIndex As Integer, ByVal pageSize As Integer, _
ByRef totalRecords As Integer) As System.Web.Profile.ProfileInfoCollection
    Throw New Exception("The method or operation is not implemented.")
End Function

Public Overrides Function FindProfilesByUserName(ByVal _
authenticationOption As System.Web.Profile.ProfileAuthenticationOption, _
ByVal usernameToMatch As String, ByVal pageIndex As Integer, _
ByVal pageSize As Integer, ByRef totalRecords As Integer) _
As System.Web.Profile.ProfileInfoCollection
    Throw New Exception("The method or operation is not implemented.")
End Function

Public Overrides Function GetAllInactiveProfiles(ByVal _
authenticationOption As System.Web.Profile.ProfileAuthenticationOption, _
ByVal userInactiveSinceDate As Date, ByVal pageIndex As Integer, _
ByVal pageSize As Integer, ByRef totalRecords As Integer) _
As System.Web.Profile.ProfileInfoCollection
    Throw New Exception("The method or operation is not implemented.")
End Function

Public Overrides Function GetAllProfiles(ByVal authenticationOption _
As System.Web.Profile.ProfileAuthenticationOption, _
ByVal pageIndex As Integer, ByVal pageSize As Integer, _
ByRef totalRecords As Integer) As System.Web.Profile.ProfileInfoCollection
    Throw New Exception("The method or operation is not implemented.")
End Function

Public Overrides Function GetNumberOfInactiveProfiles(ByVal _
authenticationOption As System.Web.Profile.ProfileAuthenticationOption, _
ByVal userInactiveSinceDate As Date) As Integer
    Throw New Exception("The method or operation is not implemented.")
End Function
    End Class
End Namespace
```

Figure 10-14   A class for a custom profile provider (part 5 of 5)

The stored procedure that's used by the custom profile provider

Figure 10-15 shows the stored procedure that's used by the SetCustomer method of the CustomerProfileProvider class. This stored procedure executes two SQL statements within a transaction. To start, if the customer record exists, the first SQL statement deletes it. Then, the second SQL statement inserts the record. If either statement fails, the transaction is rolled back. Although there are other techniques for adding and updating customer records, this technique works adequately for the Halloween Store application, and it has the added benefit of illustrating the use of transactions.

The stored procedure that's used by the CustomerProfileProvider class

```
CREATE PROCEDURE dbo.AddOrUpdateCustomer
        ( @Email varchar(25),
          @LastName varchar(20),
          @FirstName varchar(20),
          @Address varchar(40),
          @City varchar(30),
          @State char(2),
          @ZipCode varchar(9),
          @PhoneNumber varchar(20) )
AS
        BEGIN TRAN
        DELETE FROM Customers WHERE Email = @Email
        IF @@ERROR = 0
            BEGIN
                INSERT INTO Customers
                    (Email, LastName, FirstName, Address,
                     City, State, ZipCode, PhoneNumber)
                VALUES (@Email, @LastName, @FirstName, @Address,
                        @City, @State, @ZipCode, @PhoneNumber)
                IF @@ERROR = 0
                    COMMIT TRAN
                ELSE
                    ROLLBACK TRAN
            END
        ELSE
            ROLLBACK TRAN

        RETURN
```

Description

- The SetCustomer method in the CustomerProfileProvider class calls this stored procedure, which uses transactions to add or update a customer record.

Figure 10-15   The stored procedure that's used by the CustomerProfileProvider class

Perspective

This chapter has presented the skills you need for using the profiles feature to store data for authenticated and anonymous users. It has also shown you how to go about writing a custom profile provider.

Now, you should be able to use profiles to quickly prototype a new application without writing any of the data access code. That is one of the strengths of this feature. Then, once you get the prototype working, you can decide whether you need to write a custom profile provider to gain control of how this feature stores your data.

Terms

profile feature
personalization feature
profile
profile provider
anonymous identification

11

How to use the MultiView and Wizard controls

The MultiView and Wizard controls are new ASP.NET 2.0 controls. These controls provide two ways to divide a page into multiple views or steps. Both of these controls let you navigate between views or steps without writing any Visual Basic code, and they make it easy to work with the data that's stored within these views or steps.

How to use the MultiView control

In the topics that follow, you'll see how a MultiView control can be used as part of a Checkout application. Of course, the MultiView control can also be used for any application that lets the user navigate between related pages.

How the MultiView control works

Figure 11-1 shows a Checkout application that uses three *views* of a MultiView control. Although each of these views appears to be a separate page, each view is actually on the same page (the Checkout.aspx page). When the user clicks on any of the buttons within a MultiView control, the page requires a postback. As a result, all of the data on the page is posted each time the user clicks on a navigation button to switch views. For example, when the user clicks on the Next button in the first view, the data that's stored in all three views is posted. Although this isn't as efficient as coding three separate pages, the MultiView control makes it easier to develop and maintain these pages.

The first view of a MultiView control

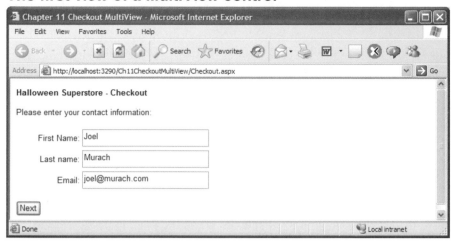

The second view of a MultiView control

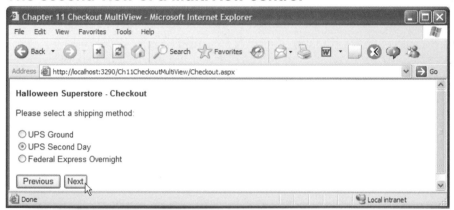

The third view of a MultiView control

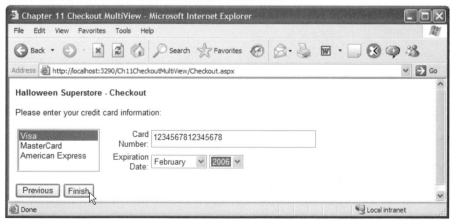

Figure 11-1   How the MultiView control works

How to add views

Figure 11-2 shows how to add views to a MultiView control. To do that, you begin by placing a MultiView control on the form. Then, you can add multiple View controls within the MultiView control. Finally, you can place other controls within each View control.

In this figure, the MultiView control is named mvCheckout, and it contains three View controls named vContact, vShippingMethod, and vCreditCard. To keep this figure simple, each view only contains some plain text and a Button control or two. This allows you to get the navigation for the views set up correctly before adding other controls to each view.

The MultiView control allows you navigate between views without writing any Visual Basic code. To start, you can set the ActiveViewIndex attribute of the MultiView control to select the view that's displayed when the page is first loaded. For example, in this figure, this attribute is set to 0 to display the first view. Then, you can set a button's CommandName attribute to one of the commands that work with the MultiView control. For example, in this figure, the CommandName attribute of the Next button is set to NextView, and the CommandName attribute of the Previous button is set to PrevView. This is all the code that's needed to get these buttons to work! For more information about using the CommandName attribute, see figure 11-4.

A MultiView control with three View controls

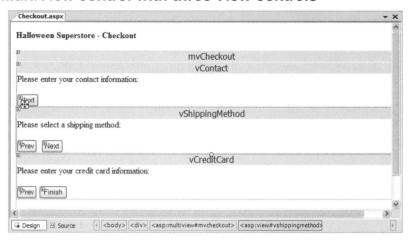

The ASP.NET tags for these controls

```
<strong>Halloween Superstore - Checkout</strong><br /><br />
<asp:MultiView ID="mvCheckout" runat="server" ActiveViewIndex="0">
    <asp:View ID="vContact" runat="server">
        Please enter your contact information:<br /><br />
        <asp:Button ID="Button1" runat="server"
            CommandName="NextView" Text="Next" />
    </asp:View>
    <asp:View ID="vShippingMethod" runat="server">
        Please select a shipping method:<br /><br />
        <asp:Button ID="Button2" runat="server"
            CommandName="PrevView" Text="Prev" /> 
        <asp:Button ID="Button3" runat="server"
            CommandName="NextView" Text="Next" />
    </asp:View>
    <asp:View ID="vCreditCard" runat="server">
        Please enter your credit card information:<br /><br />
        <asp:Button ID="Button4" runat="server"
            Text="Prev" CommandName="PrevView" />
        <asp:Button ID="btnFinish" runat="server"
            Text="Finish" PostBackUrl="~/Completion.aspx" />
    </asp:View>
</asp:MultiView>
```

Description

- Once you add a MultiView control to a page, you can add one or more View controls within the MultiView control, and you can add other controls such as labels, text boxes, and buttons within the View control.

- To display the first view when the page is loaded, set the ActiveViewIndex attribute of the MultiView control to 0.

- To use commands to navigate to the next or previous view, you can add any control that has a CommandName attribute such as a Button control. Then, you can set the CommandName attribute to NextView or PrevView.

Figure 11-2   How to add views

How to add controls to a view

Figure 11-3 shows a View control after several other controls have been added to it. In this figure, a Panel control, three RadioButton controls, and two Button controls have been added to the View control named vShippingMethod. However, you can add just about any type of control to a View control.

The second view of figure 11-1

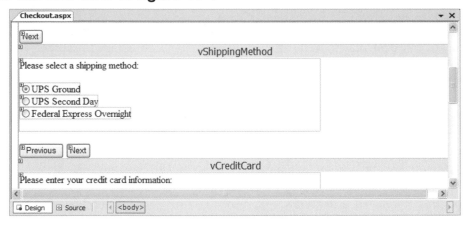

The ASP.NET tags for the second View control

```
<asp:MultiView ID="mvCheckout" Runat="server" ActiveViewIndex="0">

    <asp:View ID="vContactInfo" Runat="server">
        <!-- code for the first view goes here -->
    </asp:View>

    <asp:View ID="vShippingMethod" Runat="server">
        <asp:Panel ID="Panel1" Runat="server" Width="492">
            Please select a shipping method:<br /><br />
            <asp:RadioButton ID="rdoUPSGround" Runat="server"
                Text="UPS Ground" GroupName="ShipVia"
                Checked="True" /><br />
            <asp:RadioButton ID="rdoUPS2Day" Runat="server"
                Text="UPS Second Day" GroupName="ShipVia" /><br />
            <asp:RadioButton ID="rdoFedEx" Runat="server"
                Text="Federal Express Overnight" GroupName="ShipVia" /><br />
        </asp:Panel><br />
        <asp:Button ID="Button2" runat="server"
            CommandName="PrevView" Text="Previous" />
        <asp:Button ID="Button3" runat="server"
            CommandName="NextView" Text="Next" />
    </asp:View>

    <asp:View ID="vCreditCard" Runat="server">
        <!-- code for the third view goes here -->
    </asp:View>

</asp:MultiView>
```

Description

- Within a View control, you can add any other controls including controls such as panels and tables that contain other controls such as labels, text boxes, radio buttons, check boxes, combo boxes, buttons, and so on.

Figure 11-3   How to add controls to a view

How to navigate between views with commands

For most MultiView controls, you can navigate between the views by adding one or more buttons to each view and using the ASP.NET tags to set the CommandName attribute of each button to NextView or PrevView as shown in figure 11-2. However, in some cases, you'll need to be able to navigate to any view on the page. To do that, you can use the CommandName and CommandArgument attributes of a button as shown in figure 11-4.

If you need to navigate to a view with a specified index, you can set the CommandName attribute to SwitchViewByIndex. Then, you can set the CommandArgument attribute to the appropriate index (where 0 is the first view, 1 is the second view, and so on).

If you prefer to navigate to a view with a specified ID, you can set the CommandName attribute to SwitchViewByID. Then, you can set the CommandArgument attribute to the ID.

Within a MultiView control, you can use any control that has CommandName and CommandArgument attributes to navigate between the views. All button controls (Button, ImageButton, and LinkButton) have both of these attributes. That's why this figure can use LinkButton controls instead of the Button controls that were used in figure 11-2.

A view that allows you to navigate to other views

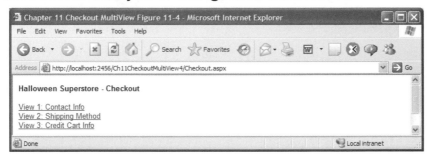

How to navigate by index

```
<asp:View ID="vNavigate" runat="server">
    <asp:LinkButton ID="LinkButton1" runat="server"
        CommandName="SwitchViewByIndex" CommandArgument="0" >
        View 1: Contact Info</asp:LinkButton><br />
    <asp:LinkButton ID="LinkButton2" runat="server"
        CommandName="SwitchViewByIndex" CommandArgument="1" >
        View 2: Shipping Method</asp:LinkButton><br />
    <asp:LinkButton ID="LinkButton3" runat="server"
        CommandName="SwitchViewByIndex" CommandArgument="2" >
        View 3: Credit Cart Info</asp:LinkButton>
</asp:View>
```

How to navigate by name

```
<asp:View ID="vNavigate" runat="server">
    <asp:LinkButton ID="LinkButton1" runat="server"
        CommandName="SwitchViewByID" CommandArgument="vContact" >
        View 1: Contact Info</asp:LinkButton><br />
    <asp:LinkButton ID="LinkButton2" runat="server"
        CommandName="SwitchViewByID" CommandArgument="vShippingMethod" >
        View 2: Shipping Method</asp:LinkButton><br />
    <asp:LinkButton ID="LinkButton3" runat="server"
        CommandName="SwitchViewByID" CommandArgument="vCreditCart" >
        View 3: Credit Cart Info</asp:LinkButton>
</asp:View>
```

Description

- If a control within a MultiView control has CommandName and CommandArgument attributes, you can use those attributes to navigate between the available views. For example, both the Button and LinkButton controls have CommandName and CommandArgument attributes.

- To navigate to the next or previous view, you can set the CommandName attribute to NextView or PrevView as shown in figure 11-2.

- To navigate to the view with the specified index, you can set the CommandName attribute to SwitchViewByIndex, and you can set the CommandArgument attribute to the appropriate index where 0 is the first view, 1 is the second view, and so on.

- To navigate to the view with the specified ID, you can set the CommandName attribute to SwitchViewByID, and you can set the CommandArgument attribute to the ID.

Figure 11-4   How to navigate between views with commands

How to access the data stored in a MultiView control

To show how to access the data that's stored within a MultiView control, figure 11-5 presents a fourth and final view that displays all of the data that's entered in the three views shown in figure 11-1. This final view is displayed when the user clicks on the Finish button that's available from the third view. Since the data for each of the previous views is automatically stored in the view state of the page, the code for this final view can access that data. In other words, the state of these controls is automatically maintained. And since all of the controls are on the same page, you can directly access them just as you would any control.

For example, the code in the DisplayMessage procedure begins by getting the shipping type from the radio buttons that are in the second view. Then, this code builds a string that contains the data that's stored in the first three views. To do that, it directly accesses the text box, list box, and drop-down list controls from the first and third views. Finally, it displays this message in the multi-line text box of the fourth and final view.

In this figure, the code only converts the text to a string and displays it in a text box. However, this code could store this data in the Session object so it's available to other pages within the current session. Or, this code could store this data in a database so it's available for future sessions. Regardless, this figure shows how the MultiView control makes it easy to access the data that's stored within any of its views.

A view that displays the data of the MultiView control

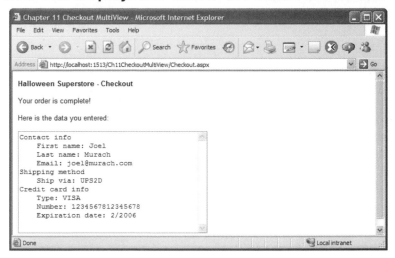

Code that accesses the data that's stored in the MultiView control

```
Protected Sub btnFinish_Click(ByVal sender As Object, _
        ByVal e As System.EventArgs) Handles btnFinish.Click
    Me.DisplayMessage()
End Sub

Protected Sub DisplayMessage()
    Dim sShipVia As String = ""
    If (rdoUPSGround.Checked) Then
        sShipVia = "UPSG"
    ElseIf (rdoUPS2Day.Checked) Then
        sShipVia = "UPS2D"
    ElseIf (rdoFedEx.Checked) Then
        sShipVia = "FEDEX"
    End If
    Dim sMessage As String
    sMessage = _
        "Contact info" & ControlChars.CrLf & _
        "    First name: " & txtFirstName.Text & ControlChars.CrLf & _
        "    Last name: " & txtLastName.Text & ControlChars.CrLf & _
        "    Email: " & txtEmail.Text & ControlChars.CrLf & _
        "Shipping method" & ControlChars.CrLf & _
        "    Ship via: " & sShipVia & ControlChars.CrLf & _
        "Credit card info" & ControlChars.CrLf & _
        "    Type: " & listCardType.SelectedValue & ControlChars.CrLf & _
        "    Number: " & txtCardNumber.Text & ControlChars.CrLf & _
        "    Expiration date: " & ddlExpirationMonth.SelectedValue & "/" & _
                            ddlExpirationYear.SelectedValue
    txtMessage.Text = sMessage
End Sub
```

Description

- Because the state of each control in the MultiView and View controls is stored in view state, it's easy to access the data for the controls from the code-behind file.

Figure 11-5   How to access the data stored in a MultiView control

Properties and events of the MultiView and View controls

Figure 11-6 starts by showing two useful properties of the MultiView control. You can use the first of these properties, the ActiveViewIndex property, to get or set the zero-based index for the active view. This is useful if you need to write code to display the index of the active view or if you need to write code to change the active view. For example, the code shown at the bottom of this figure uses the ActiveViewIndex to display the number of the current view. However, you could also set the ActiveViewIndex to 0 to display the first view.

You can use the second of these properties, the Views property, to access the collection of View objects that are stored in the MultiView control. Although this property allows you to perform complex operations such as adding or removing a view at runtime, it's more commonly used to get a count of the total number of views. For example, the code shown at the bottom of this figure uses the Count property of the Views collection to display the total number views.

For a MultiView control like the one presented in figure 11-1, you don't usually need to use the events of the MultiView or View controls. However, if you add controls outside of the MultiView control that need to be synchronized with the MultiView control, you may need to code event procedures for the events shown in this figure. For example, the code shown at the bottom of this figure is an event procedure for the ActiveViewChanged event of the MultiView control. The code within this event procedure changes the text that's displayed in a label that's placed outside of the MultiView control. This causes the label to display a message for each view like this:

```
View 1 of 4
```

Since this event procedure is executed every time the active view changes, the text within this label will always be synchronized with the view that's displayed.

Properties of the MultiView control

Property	Description
ActiveViewIndex	Gets or sets the index for the active view where 0 is the first view, 1 is the second view, and so on. By default, this is set to -1 so no view is selected as the active view.
Views	Gets the collection of View objects contained within the MultiView control. The Count property of this collection can be used to determine the total number of View controls in the MultiView control.

Button properties that work with the MultiView control

Property	Description
CommandName	Sets the navigation command for the button. This property can be set to NextView, PrevView, SwitchViewByIndex, or SwitchViewByID. For more information, see figure 11-2 and figure 11-4.
CommandArgument	Sets the arguments required by the SwitchViewByIndex and SwitchViewByID commands. For more information, see figure 11-4.

An event of the MultiView control

Event	Description
ActiveViewChanged	Fires every time the active view changes.

Events of the View control

Event	Description
Activate	Fires every time the view is activated.
Deactivate	Fires every time the view is deactivated.

The ActiveViewChanged event of the MultiView control

```
Protected Sub mvCheckout_ActiveViewChanged(ByVal sender As Object, _
        ByVal e As System.EventArgs) Handles mvCheckout.ActiveViewChanged
    Dim viewNumber As Integer = mvCheckout.ActiveViewIndex + 1
    lblStatus.Text = "View " & viewNumber & " of " & mvCheckout.Views.Count
End Sub
```

Figure 11-6   Properties and events of the MultiView and View controls

How to use the Wizard control

In the topics that follow, you'll see how a Wizard control can be used to code a Checkout application that's similar to the one presented earlier in this chapter. This will help you compare the MultiView control to the Wizard control.

How the Wizard control works

Figure 11-7 shows a Checkout application that uses three *steps* of a Wizard control. Although each of these steps appears to be a separate page, each step is actually part of the same page (Checkout.aspx). This works like the views within a MultiView control. The main difference is that, by default, the Wizard control includes a *side bar* on the left side of the control, which provides links to each step in the control. As a result, you can easily navigate to any step in the wizard.

In addition, by default, the Wizard control automatically includes the Next, Previous, and Finish buttons shown on these steps. As a result, if you want to include these features, you may prefer using a Wizard control over a MultiView control.

Step 1 of a Wizard control

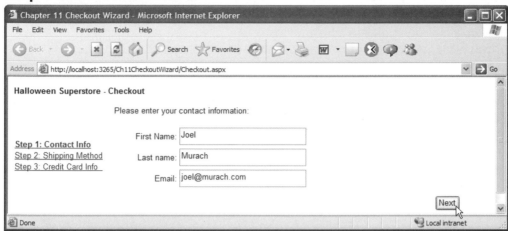

Step 2 of a Wizard control

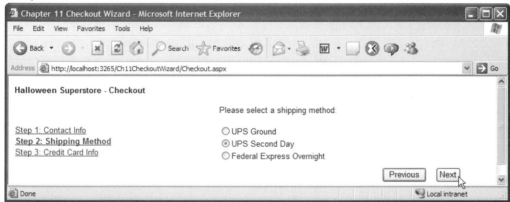

Step 3 of a Wizard control

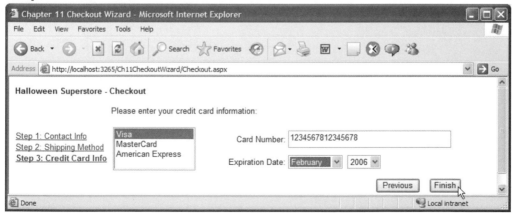

Figure 11-7   How a Wizard control works

How to add or remove steps

Figure 11-8 shows how to add or remove steps from a Wizard control. To start, you place a Wizard control on a page. Next, you select the Add/Remove WizardSteps command from the smart tag menu to display the WizardStep Collection Editor. Then, you can use the Add and Remove buttons on this editor to add or remove steps. In addition, you can use this dialog box to edit the properties for each step.

Once you get the correct number of steps for your wizard, you can add controls to each step. To do that, you can use the smart tag menu to select and display the step. Then, you can use any standard technique to add controls to the step. In this figure, for example, a TextBox control has been placed on the first step immediately after some plain text.

Whenever you prefer, you can use the ASP.NET tags to work with the steps of a wizard. For example, this figure shows the ASP.NET tags for the beginning of a Wizard control with three steps. Here, three WizardStep tags are coded within the WizardSteps tag, which is coded within the Wizard tag. The first step contains some plain text and a text box, and the next two steps contain only plain text. However, you can add other types of controls to each step, even container controls such as panels and tables that contain other controls such as labels, text boxes, drop-down lists, and so on.

Unlike the MultiView control, you don't need to add buttons to provide for navigation features for the Wizard control. That's because the Wizard control displays the appropriate Next, Previous, and Finish buttons by default. You'll learn more about how this works as you progress through this chapter.

A wizard with three steps

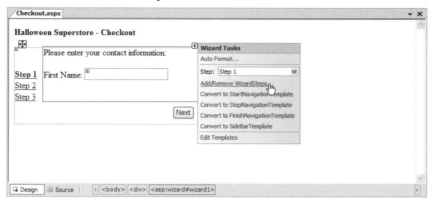

The WizardStep Collection Editor

The ASP.NET tags for a Wizard control

```
<asp:Wizard ID="Wizard1" runat="server" ActiveStepIndex="0" Width="344px">
    <WizardSteps>
        <asp:WizardStep runat="server" Title="Step 1">
            Please enter your contact information:<br /><br />
            First Name: <asp:TextBox ID="txtFirstName" runat="server">
                </asp:TextBox><br /><br />
        </asp:WizardStep>
        <asp:WizardStep runat="server" Title="Step 2">
            Please select a shipping method:</asp:WizardStep>
        <asp:WizardStep runat="server" Title="Step 3">
            Please enter your credit card information:</asp:WizardStep>
    </WizardSteps>
</asp:Wizard>
```

Description

- To access the WizardStep Collection Editor, you can select the Add/Remove WizardSteps command from the smart tag menu for the Wizard control.
- To add or remove steps or to edit the properties for a step, you can edit the ASP.NET tags, or you can use the WizardStep Collection Editor.

Figure 11-8   How to add or remove steps

How to add a Cancel button

Figure 11-9 shows how to add a Cancel button to each step in a Wizard control. To do that, you set the DisplayCancelButton attribute of the wizard to True. Once you display the Cancel button, you can code an event procedure to handle the CancelButtonClick event that occurs when the user clicks this button. You can see an example of this in the event procedure in this figure.

The code within this event procedure displays the first step and clears all of the text from the text box controls on this page. To display the first step, this code sets the ActiveStepIndex property of the wizard to 0. Then, it sets the Text property of the three text box controls on this page to an empty string. This shows that you can directly access all of the controls within the wizard from the code-behind file for the page.

A wizard with a Cancel button

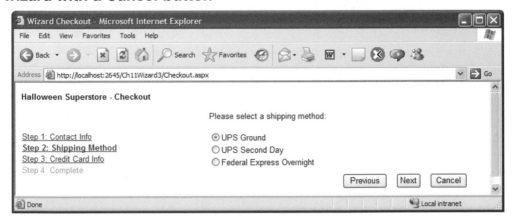

A Wizard tag that works with a Cancel button

```
<asp:Wizard ID="wizCheckout" runat="server" Width="739px"
    DisplayCancelButton="true">
```

Visual Basic code that works with the Cancel button

```
Protected Sub wizCheckout_CancelButtonClick(ByVal sender As Object, _
        ByVal e As System.EventArgs) Handles wizCheckout.CancelButtonClick
    wizCheckout.ActiveStepIndex = 0
    txtFirstName.Text = ""
    txtLastName.Text = ""
    txtEmail.Text = ""
End Sub
```

Description

- You can display a Cancel button for each step of a wizard by setting the DisplayCancelButton attribute of the Wizard control to True. By default, this attribute is set to False.

- You can use the CancelButtonClick event of the Wizard control to respond to the user clicking on the Cancel button.

- You can use the ActiveStepIndex property of the Wizard control to get or set the active step where 0 is the first step, 1 is the second step, and so on.

Figure 11-9   How to add a Cancel button

How to add a completion step

Figure 11-10 shows how to add a fourth and final step to the wizard that's displayed in figure 11-7. This step is displayed when the user clicks on the Finish button in the third step. But first, the event procedure that handles the FinishButtonClick event of the wizard is executed. In this figure, this event procedure calls the DisplayMessage procedure, which displays all of the data that's been entered in the first three steps in the multiline text box of the fourth step.

The DisplayMessage procedure called by this event procedure contains the same code as the DisplayMessage procedure that was presented in figure 11-5. This shows that the technique for accessing the data that's stored in a Wizard control is the same as the technique for accessing the data that's stored in a MultiView control. That's because, like the MultiView control, the Wizard control stores its data in the view state for the page.

The primary difference between the fourth step and the first three steps is that it doesn't have a side bar or navigation buttons. That's because the StepType attribute for this step has been set to Complete. This attribute is left at the default setting of Auto for the first three steps. As a result, the first step only contains a Next button, the second step contains Previous and Next buttons, and the third step contains Previous and Finish buttons. That's usually what you want, but if it isn't, you can use the StepType attribute to change it.

A wizard with a completion step

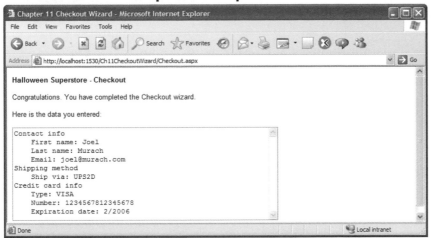

A WizardStep tag that defines a completion step

```
<asp:WizardStep runat="server"
    StepType="Complete" Title="Step 4: Complete">
        Congratulations. You have completed the Checkout wizard.<br /><br />
    <asp:Label ID="Label1" runat="server"
        Text="Here is the data you entered:"></asp:Label><br />
    <asp:TextBox ID="txtMessage" runat="server" Height="166px"
        TextMode="MultiLine" Width="489px"></asp:TextBox>
</asp:WizardStep>
```

Visual Basic code that displays a message on the completion page

```
Protected Sub wizCheckout_FinishButtonClick(ByVal sender As Object, _
        ByVal e As System.Web.UI.WebControls.WizardNavigationEventArgs) _
        Handles wizCheckout.FinishButtonClick
    Me.DisplayMessage()
End Sub
```

Possible values for the StepType attribute

Value	Description
Auto	Automatically sets the first step to Start, the last step to Finish, and any intermediate steps to Step. This is the default.
Start	Defines a step that doesn't have a Previous button.
Step	Defines a step that has Previous and Next buttons.
Finish	Defines a step that has Previous and Finish buttons.
Complete	Defines a step that doesn't have a side bar or any buttons. This step is typically used to display a completion message.

Description

- To add a completion step, you can add a final WizardStep tag and set its StepType attribute to Complete.

Figure 11-10   How to add a completion step

Properties and events of the Wizard and WizardStep controls

Figure 11-11 starts by summarizing three useful properties of the Wizard control. First, you can use the ActiveStepIndex property to get or set the active step. For example, the event procedure for the Cancel button shown in figure 11-9 sets this property to 0 to display the first step. Second, you can set the DisplayCancelButton property to True to display a Cancel button for each step of the wizard as described in figure 11-9. Third, if you don't want to display the side bar, you can set the DisplaySideBar property to False.

Besides these properties, there are many other properties of the Wizard control that you can use to control the appearance and function of the wizard. For example, you can edit the text that's displayed on the navigation buttons. Or, you can edit the type of button that's used for the navigation buttons. By default, the wizard uses regular Button controls, but it's also possible to use ImageButton or LinkButton controls. If you use the AutoFormat command that's available from the smart tag menu for a wizard, you can automatically change many of these properties.

In a typical wizard, you only need to handle the FinishButtonClick event that's fired when the user clicks on the Finish button. An example of this is shown in figure 11-10. Within this event procedure, you can store the data that has been gathered by the wizard and redirect the application to the next page. However, if you add a Cancel button, you'll probably want to add an event procedure for the CancelButtonClick event of the wizard that's executed when the Cancel button is clicked as shown in figure 11-9. And, if necessary, you can write event procedures for any of the other events shown in this figure. For example, you may want to write an event procedure for the ActiveStepChanged event to synchronize any controls that are placed outside of the Wizard control with the wizard's current step.

This figure finishes by presenting two properties of the WizardStep control that can be used to control the types of buttons that are displayed on the step. First, you can set the StepType property to any of the values shown in figure 11-10. Second, you can set the AllowReturn property to False to remove the Previous button from the step. However, the user can still return to the previous step by clicking the browser's Back button or by clicking on the links in the side bar if it's displayed. As a result, if it's critical to your application to prevent the user from returning to the previous step, you'll need to remove the side bar and disable the browser's Back button.

Properties of the Wizard control

Property	Description
ActiveStepIndex	Gets or sets the index for the active page where 0 is the first page, 1 is the second page, and so on. By default, this property is set to the page that's selected in Design View.
DisplayCancelButton	To show a Cancel button on every step, you can set this property to True. The default is False.
DisplaySideBar	To hide the side bar, you can set this property to False. The default is True.

Events of the Wizard control

Event	Description
ActiveStepChanged	Fires every time the active step changes.
NextButtonClick	Fires every time a Next button is clicked.
PreviousButtonClick	Fires every time a Previous button is clicked.
CancelButtonClick	Fires every time a Cancel button is clicked.
FinishButtonClick	Fires every time the Finish button is clicked.
SideBarButtonClick	Fires every time one of the side bar links is clicked.

Properties of the WizardStep control

Property	Description
StepType	Changes the types of buttons (Previous, Next, Finish) that are available for the step (see figure 11-10).
AllowReturn	To remove the Previous button from the step, you can set this property to False. The default is True.

Description

- You can use other properties of the Wizard control to control the formatting options for a wizard.
- You can use the AutoFormat command that's available from the smart tag menu for a wizard to automatically apply many formatting options for the wizard.

Figure 11-11   Properties and events of the Wizard and WizardStep controls

How to use templates and styles with wizards

Figure 11-12 shows how you can use templates and styles to customize the default controls and formatting for your wizard. For example, you can use templates to override the default controls for the parts of a wizard. Or, you can use styles to change the formatting for the parts of a wizard.

To begin working with templates, you can select the Edit Templates command from the wizard's smart tag menu to enter Template Editing mode. In Template Editing mode, you can select the template that you want to edit from the smart tag menu. In this figure, for example, you can see the start navigation template that contains the navigation buttons for the start step.

Once you've displayed a template, you can use standard techniques to add controls to the template. In this figure, for example, the LinkButton control has been added to the StartNavigationTemplate. This causes the LinkButton control on this template to override the Button control that's used by default.

When you're done modifying the templates, you can select the End Template Editing command from the smart menu. Then, you can run the application and see how the new template works.

Once you understand how to modify one template, you shouldn't have much trouble modifying the other ones. You can use the three navigation templates to modify the navigation buttons for the start, step, and finish steps. You can use the side bar template to modify the links displayed in the side bar template. And you can use the header template to add a header to the wizard control. By default, the header template doesn't contain any controls, so adding controls to this template activates a new part of the wizard.

To work with styles, you can begin entering the tag for the style in the HTML Editor. Then, you can use the IntelliSense feature to select the style and attributes that you want to modify. In this figure, for example, the first style tag uses the navigation style to set the horizontal alignment for all navigation buttons to left. Then, the second style tag uses the side bar style to make the font size smaller for the links in the side bar. As a result, the side bar will use a smaller font and won't take up as much horizontal space.

Although it might seem like a lot of extra work to set up templates and styles for an application, the extra work might pay off in certain situations. For example, you might want to use templates and styles if you have an application where you need to develop multiple wizards with custom formatting. Then, you can apply a consistent format to all of these wizards by copying the tags for the templates and styles to all pages that contain a wizard.

A Wizard control in Template Editing Mode

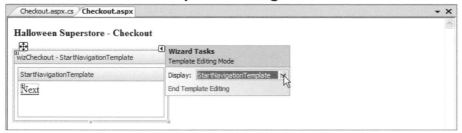

ASP.NET tags for wizard templates and styles

```
<asp:Wizard ID="wizCheckout" runat="server" >

    <StartNavigationTemplate>
        <asp:LinkButton ID="LinkButton1" runat="server" >Next
        </asp:LinkButton>
    </StartNavigationTemplate>

    <NavigationStyle HorizontalAlign="Left" />
    <SideBarStyle Font-Size="Small" />

    <WizardSteps>
        <!-- wizard steps go here -->
    </WizardSteps>
</asp:Wizard>
```

Wizard templates and styles

Template	Style
HeaderTemplate	HeaderStyle
StartNavigationTemplate	StartNextButtonStyle
StepNavigationTemplate	StepNextButtonStyle
	StepPreviousButtonStyle
FinishNavigationTemplate	FinishCompleteButtonStyle
	FinishPreviousButtonStyle
SideBarTemplate	SideBarButtonStyle
	SideBarStyle
	CancelButtonStyle
	NavigationButtonStyle
	NavigationStyle

Description

- You can use templates and styles to customize the default controls and formatting for your wizard.

Figure 11-12   How to use templates and styles with wizards

Perspective

Although the new MultiView and Wizard controls don't let you do anything that wasn't possible using ASP.NET 1.x, they sure make it easier to develop a set of related views or steps that gather or display information. They also make it easy to access the data that's gathered by these views. In short, they're useful additions to the features that are available to the ASP.NET 2.0 developer.

Terms

view
step
side bar

12

How to use themes

When you develop a web site, you usually want to apply consistent formatting to all of its pages so the entire site has a cohesive look and feel. In addition, it's generally considered a good programming practice to separate the formatting of the web pages from the content of the web pages whenever that's possible. That way, web designers can focus on making the site look good, and programmers can focus on making the site work the way it should.

To make this easier and more flexible, ASP.NET 2.0 introduces a new feature known as *themes* that builds upon older formatting technologies such as cascading style sheets (CSS). This new feature allows you to create multiple themes for a web site, and it makes it easy to switch between themes. If you want, you can even write code that allows a user to customize a web site by choosing a preferred theme.

An introduction to themes

When you work with standard HTML, it is a common practice to store the global formatting information for a web site in a file known as a *cascading style sheet (CSS)*. Then, the styles in this sheet are applied to all pages in the application unless they are overridden by individual pages or by individual elements.

Although this works well for HTML elements, it can be tricky to get this to work correctly with ASP.NET server controls since this requires the programmer and web designer to understand how server controls are rendered to HTML before being returned to the browser. But now, ASP.NET 2.0 introduces a new feature known as *themes* that allows you to specify the formatting for both HTML elements and server controls. To start, a theme includes a cascading style sheet. In addition, a theme includes information that specifies the formatting for the ASP.NET server controls.

A page before and after a theme has been applied

Figure 12-1 shows the Order page for the Halloween Store application before and after a theme has been applied to it. If you could see these pages in color, you would clearly see the differences between them. In particular, you would see that the second page uses a different font, font color, and font size for all of the elements and controls on the page. In addition, the buttons that are defined on the second page look different than the buttons on the first page because they don't have rounded corners and do use a different background color.

This Order page includes both HTML elements and server-side ASP.NET controls. To start, this page includes two HTML tags that define the heading and subheading for the page like this:

```
<h1>Halloween Superstore</h1>
<h4>Halloween supplies for the discerning haunter</h4>
```

The custom formatting for these tags is stored in the cascading style sheet for the theme. Then, this page uses ASP.NET tags to define the server controls that are on the rest of the page. However, the custom formatting for these server controls isn't stored in the Order page. Instead, this formatting is stored in an external file as described in the next figure.

Before: The Order page without a theme

After: The Order page with a theme

Figure 12-1   A page before and after a theme has been applied

How themes work

Figure 12-2 gives an overview of how themes work. To start, it shows the Solution Explorer for an application that contains an App_Themes folder. This folder can contain multiple subfolders with each subfolder defining one theme.

For example, the App_Themes folder in this figure contains two folders that define themes. The first folder contains the Classic theme. To help identify this folder as a theme folder, Visual Studio adds a paintbrush to the folder icon. The second folder contains the SmokeAndGlass theme.

The SmokeAndGlass folder shows the three types of files that can be contained by a theme. First, a theme folder can contain a file for the cascading style sheet that defines the styles that define the appearance of the HTML elements. This file must have an extension of css. In addition, it typically has the same name as the theme folder, although that's not required.

Second, a theme folder can contain a file for the *skins* that define the appearance of the ASP.NET server controls. A skin specifies the formatting attributes for a server control, and a file that contains skins must have an extension of skin. In addition, if the theme only has one skin file, this file typically has the same name as the theme folder, although that's not required. In fact, as you'll see later in this chapter, it's possible to store skin definitions in multiple skin files within a theme folder.

Third, a theme folder can contain the files for any images that are used by the theme. These files can be stored in the theme folder, or they can be stored in any subfolder of the theme folder. In this figure, for example, all of the GIF files that are used by the SmokeAndGlass theme are stored in the Images subfolder of the SmokeAndGlass folder.

The partial SmokeAndGlass.css file shown in this figure shows how formatting information for HTML elements is stored in a cascading style sheet. To start, the BODY style sets the default formatting for any text in the body of an HTML page. This formatting includes specifying the font family, the font size, the line height relative to the font size, and the color. Then, the H1 style sets the formatting for any text within an H1 tag. This style inherits some settings such as font size from the predefined H1 style and it inherits other settings such as font family and font color from the BODY style. With a little bit of experimenting, you can typically set up a css file to get your pages to look the way you want.

The partial SmokeAndGlass.skin file shown in this figure shows how formatting information for server controls is stored in skins. In particular, this file contains one skin for each type of control that's used on the Order page shown in figure 12-1. For example, the skin for the Label control specifies the font name and font color that are used for labels. The skins for the other controls also specify font attributes, and the TextBox and Button controls specify some other attributes that control the appearance of the border and background color.

The directory structure for a theme

Part of the SmokeAndGlass.css file

```
BODY {
    FONT-FAMILY: Verdana, Geneva, Arial, Helvetica, sans-serif;
    FONT-SIZE: 11pt;
    LINE-HEIGHT: 110%;
    COLOR : #585880;
}

H1 {
    font-family: Verdana, Geneva, Arial, Helvetica, sans-serif;
    COLOR: #585880;
    margin-top: 3px;
}
```

Part of the SmokeAndGlass.skin file

```
<asp:Label   runat="server"         ForeColor="#585880"
             Font-Names="Verdana" />

<asp:DropDownList
             runat="server"         ForeColor="#585880"
             Font-Names="Verdana" />

<asp:TextBox runat="server"         BackColor="#FFFFFF"
             BorderStyle="Solid"    Font-Names="Verdana"
             ForeColor="#585880"    BorderColor="#585880"
             BorderWidth="1pt" />

<asp:Button  runat="server"         BorderColor="#585880"
             Font-Bold="true"       BorderWidth="1pt"
             ForeColor="#585880"    BackColor="#F8F7F4" />
```

Description

- The App_Themes folder can contain multiple subfolders with each subfolder defining one *theme*.

- Each theme folder can contain a file that contains the *cascading style sheet* (CSS) that defines the appearance of the HTML elements, files that define the *skins* that control the appearance of the ASP.NET server controls, and files for any images that are used by the cascading style sheet or the skins.

Figure 12-2   How themes work

How to make an existing theme available to an application

Designing a theme that looks good isn't an easy task, even for an experienced web designer. It requires coding a cascading style sheet that defines the formatting for all of the HTML elements, coding skins that define all of the server controls, and creating any graphics that are used by the style sheets or the skins. As a result, the easiest way to get started with themes is to use an existing theme.

To obtain an existing theme, you can download the SmokeAndGlass theme that's included with the application for this chapter. This theme was included with the Beta 1 version of ASP.NET 2.0 to show how themes work, and I have made some minor modifications to it. Or, you can try to download another theme from the web. For example, Microsoft has suggested that they may provide an online theme gallery on www.asp.net that will enable developers to find and share themes for their sites. As more developers began to create themes, the availability and quality of themes available from the web should improve.

Once you have a theme folder on your computer that contains the files for a theme, it's easy to make the theme available to an application. To do that, you can use Visual Studio to create the App_Themes folder. Then, you can use the Windows Explorer to copy the theme folder into the App_Themes folder as described in figure 12-3. After you do that, you may need to refresh the App_Themes folder before you'll see the new folder.

How to apply a theme to an application

Once the theme has been added to the App_Themes folder, you can apply it to the entire application by editing the web.config file as shown in figure 12-3. To do that, you add a <pages> element within the <system.web> element. Then, you code a Theme attribute within the <pages> element that specifies the name of the theme.

For most applications, you'll want to apply a single theme to the entire application as shown in this figure. When you do that, you can't override the formatting that has been specified by the theme for an individual element or control. If, for example, you want to set the color for a label to red, you can't do that because that attribute has already been specified by the theme. However, if an attribute isn't specified by the theme, you can change it for a control. For example, since the theme doesn't specify the Font-Bold attribute for labels, you can apply or remove boldfacing from individual labels.

Most of the time, this is how you want themes to work. However, if you need to apply a different theme to a page or control, if you need to remove a theme from a page or control, or if you want to change the way overriding works, you can learn how to do that later in this chapter.

How to make an existing theme available to an application

1. Create the App_Themes folder. To do that, you can right-click on the root folder, select the Add Folder submenu, and select the Theme Folder item. This creates the App_Themes folder and a subfolder with a default name of Theme1. You can delete this Theme1 folder since you will be using an existing theme.

2. Copy the folder that contains the theme into the App_Themes folder. To do that, you can use the Windows Explorer.

A web.config file that specifies a theme

```
<configuration>
  <system.web>
    <pages theme="SmokeAndGlass" />
  </system.web>
</configuration>
```

Description

- You can get the SmokeAndGlass theme shown in the previous figure by downloading the applications for this book. You may also be able to download themes from the Internet.

- To apply a theme to the current application, you can edit the web.config file for the application. Within the web.config file, you can use the Theme attribute of the <pages> element to specify the name of the theme.

- When you use the Theme attribute of the <pages> element to apply a theme to a page, you can't override any of the formatting attributes specified by the theme for individual controls. However, you can change attributes that aren't specified by the theme.

- Figures 12-8 and 12-9 show other techniques for applying and removing themes from individual pages and controls.

- Figure 12-10 shows how to allow controls to override attributes that are specified by a theme.

Figure 12-3   How to apply a theme to the entire application

How to create your own themes

In the topics that follow, you'll learn the basic skills for creating your own themes. Even if you never need to create your own themes, you should read through these topics since they show the details of how themes work. In addition, they present skills that you can use to edit an existing theme.

How to use cascading style sheets

Figure 12-4 shows how to create and use a cascading style sheet. If you're familiar with HTML and cascading style sheets, you shouldn't have any problem understanding this figure. The cascading style sheet for a theme is just a regular HTML style sheet. However, it must be stored in the folder for the theme. In addition, when you use Visual Studio to enter or edit a style sheet, you can use Visual Studio's IntelliSense and Style Builder features.

You can add a new style sheet to a theme by right-clicking on the theme folder and selecting the Add New Item command. Then, you can select the template for a style sheet and enter the name for the style sheet. In this figure, for example, you can see a newly created style sheet named Classic.css.

If you aren't familiar with cascading style sheets, you can get the general idea of how one works by studying the one in this figure. However, for complete details, you should get a book about HTML that has a chapter or two about cascading style sheets.

The Body style in this figure sets the default color for any text in the body of an HTML page to blue. Here, the Color attribute of the standard HTML Body style is set to a value of #000066. This value specifies a blue color using a standard HTML palette for specifying colors. It's also possible to set the Color attribute to a keyword such as Blue or Navy that corresponds with one of the colors from the web palette. However, these keywords limit the number of colors that are available. As a result, web designers typically use the #000000 format to specify colors.

The H1 and H4 styles in this figure use the Font-Size attribute to specify a font size in points. In addition, the H4 style uses the Font-Style attribute to specify that the heading should be italicized. The rest of the attributes for the H1 and H4 styles use the default settings, except that they use the Color attribute that's specified by the Body style. If you want to specify a different color, though, you can use the Color attribute of these tags to override the Color attribute of the Body style.

The style sheet in this figure also defines a *CSS class* named Highlighted that can be used to change the background color of any HTML element to light gray. To identify this class, a period is coded before the name of the class. Then, the Background-Color class is used to set the background to light grey.

To use the styles in a style sheet, you can code the tag as you would normally. However, to use a CSS class, you must specify the name of the class. To do that, you use the Class attribute for HTML tags and the CssClass attribute for ASP.NET tags.

The start of a cascading style sheet

A .css file that defines three styles and one HTML class

```
body
{
    color: #000066;
}
h1
{
    font-size: 18pt;
}
h4
{
    font-size: 12pt;
    font-style: italic;
}
.highlighted
{
    background-color: #CCCCCC;
}
```

An HTML tag that uses a style

```
<h1>Halloween Superstore</h1>
```

An HTML tag that specifies an HTML class

```
<h4 class="highlighted">Halloween supplies for the discerning haunter</h4>
```

An ASP.NET tag that specifies an HTML class

```
<asp:Label ID="lblName" runat="server" CssClass="highlighted"></asp:Label>
```

Description

- To add a new .css file to a theme, you can right-click on the folder for the theme and select the Add New Item command. Then, you can use the Add New Item dialog box to select the Style Sheet template and enter the name for the .css file.
- When using Visual Studio to work with a css file, you can use IntelliSense to select from lists of HTML elements and attributes.
- When using Visual Studio to work with a css file, you can access the Style Builder dialog box by right-clicking on a style and selecting the Build Style command. Then, you can use that dialog box to edit the attributes for the style.

Figure 12-4   How to use cascading style sheets

How to use skins

Figure 12-5 shows how to create and use a file that contains skins for the controls of an application. As you would hope, this works similarly to cascading style sheets, but it allows you to define styles for ASP.NET server controls.

You can add a new skin file to a theme by right-clicking on the theme folder and selecting the Add New Item command. Then, you can select the template for a skin file and enter the name for the file. In this figure, for example, you can see a newly created skin file named Classic.skin.

Once you create a skin file, you can add skins to the file by opening the tag, entering the name of the control, entering a RunAt attribute, and closing the tag. For example, you can begin a tag for the Label control like this:

```
<asp:Label runat="server" />
```

Then, you can set other attributes to control the formatting for the control. For example, you can change the ForeColor attribute for a Label control like this:

```
<asp:Label runat="server" ForeColor="#000066" />
```

Since this uses the standard ASP.NET syntax for setting control attributes, you shouldn't have much trouble understanding how this works.

When you use themes, you typically need to define one skin for each type of control that you use in your application. In this figure, for example, you can see the skin files for the Label, TextBox, Button, and DropDownList controls. These are all the controls that are used by the Order page shown in figure 12-1. However, for a more robust application, you'd probably need to include skins for many more types of controls. Otherwise, a control that doesn't have a skin probably won't look like the rest of the controls.

The first four skins in this skin file don't include a SkinID attribute. As a result, they're the *default skins* that are used when a control of that type doesn't include a SkinID attribute. For example, the default skin for a label is applied to the Label control that's defined by the first ASP.NET tag shown in this figure.

If you need to supply multiple skins for a control, you can code a *named skin* that includes a SkinID attribute that uniquely identifies the skin. For example, the named skin in this figure provides a second skin for the Label control with a SkinID of Head1. This skin adds boldfacing to the font and sets the font size to large to make the label have the appearance of a heading. To apply this skin to a Label control, you can add a Label control to a form and set its SkinID attribute to Head1 as shown by the second Label control defined in this figure.

All of the skins in this figure specify the color of the font. However, this is already done by the Body style in the cascading style sheet for the Classic theme and is automatically applied to all HTML elements. Since all of the ASP.NET sever controls are eventually rendered as HTML elements before being returned to the client, the color specified in the Body style is automatically applied to the server controls. As a result, you don't need to set the ForeColor attribute for these controls unless you want to make sure that the color specified for these server controls overrides the color that's set by the Body style.

The start of a skin file

A skin file that defines four default skins and one named skin

```
<asp:Label
    runat="server"              ForeColor="#000066"/>

<asp:DropDownList
    runat="server"              ForeColor="#000066"/>

<asp:TextBox
    runat="server"              ForeColor="#000066"
    BorderStyle="Solid"         BorderWidth="1pt" />

<asp:Button
    runat="server"              ForeColor="#000066"
    Font-Bold="true"            BackColor="#EEEEEE"
    BorderColor="#000066"       BorderWidth="1pt" />

<%-- a named skin for labels --%>
<asp:Label
    runat="server"              ForeColor="#000066"
    Font-Bold="true"            Font-Size="large"
    SkinID="Head1"/>
```

An ASP.NET tag that uses the default skin for a label

```
<asp:Label ID="Label3" Runat="server" Text="Quantity:"></asp:Label>
```

An ASP.NET tag that specifies a named skin for a label

```
<asp:Label ID="lblName" runat="server" SkinID="Head1"></asp:Label>
```

Description

- To add a new skin file to a theme, you can right-click on the folder for the theme, and select the Add New Item command. Then, you can use the Add New Item dialog box to select the Skin File template and enter the name for the skin file.

- To specify a comment within a skin file, you must use the <%-- and --%> tags.

- To create a *default skin*, don't specify the SkinID attribute for the skin. Then, the skin will automatically be applied to any control of that type whose SkinID property isn't set.

- To create a *named skin*, specify the SkinID attribute for the skin. Then, you can use the SkinID property to apply the skin to a control of that type.

Figure 12-5   How to use skins

Another way to store skins

In figure 12-5, all of the skins for the application were stored in a single skin file. However, it's also possible to split skins up into multiple files. For example, figure 12-6 shows how you can store the skins in figure 12-5 in separate files. Here, both of the skins for the Label control are stored in a file named Label.skin, the skin for the DropDownList control is stored in a file named DropDownList.skin, and so on.

The choice of how to store your skins depends on your preferences and on the number of skins used by your application. If you have a large number of skins with multiple skins for each type of control, you may find it easier to organize and manage them by splitting them into separate files. This can make it easier to find skins and to copy them from one application to another. On the other hand, you might find that the additional skin files create a file management headache. As a result, you might prefer to keep all skins in a single file even if that file becomes very long.

A theme that uses multiple skin files

The Label.skin file

```
<asp:Label
    runat="server"              ForeColor="#000066"/>

<asp:Label
    runat="server"              ForeColor="#000066"
    Font-Bold="true"            Font-Size="large"
    SkinID="Head1"/>
```

The DropDownList.skin file

```
<asp:DropDownList
    runat="server"              ForeColor="#000066"/>
```

The TextBox.skin file

```
<asp:TextBox
    runat="server"              ForeColor="#000066"
    BorderStyle="Solid"         BorderWidth="1pt" />
```

The Button.skin file

```
<asp:Button
    runat="server"              ForeColor="#000066"
    Font-Bold="true"            BackColor="#EEEEEE"
    BorderColor="#000066"       BorderWidth="1pt" />
```

Description

- Skins can be stored in a single file as shown in the previous figure or in separate files as shown in this figure.

Figure 12-6   Another way to store skins

How to use images

Each theme can use its own images. These images can be stored directly in the theme folder or in subfolders of the theme folder. For example, in this figure, the folder for the Classic theme contains an Images subfolder that contains two gif files. Once you have added images to a theme, you can use a relative URL to refer to the images from the css and skin files as shown in figure 12-7. That way, if you switch themes, the images associated with the css and skin files will also be switched.

The brownfadetop.gif file can be used as the background for an HTML element or a server control to create a shading effect that isn't possible using a regular colored background. This is an HTML trick that was developed by web designers to get around the limitations of plain HTML, and it's typical of the types of hacks that are often used by web designers. If you look at this image, you can see that it's very narrow. In fact, it's only 5 pixels wide and 100 pixels tall. Although it's difficult to tell from this black-and-white figure, this image contains a brown background that fades to a lighter brown as it nears the top of the image.

The Classic.css style sheet includes a CSS class named BrownFadeTopBack that sets the BackGround-Image tag to the brownfadetop.gif file in the Images subfolder. As a result, if this CSS class is used to apply this image to an HTML element or server control, the image will be sized and repeated as necessary to fill the entire background for that HTML element or server control. For example, the H4 tag shown in this figure specifies the BrownFadeTopBack CSS class. As a result, this HTML element's background is shaded accordingly.

The bullet.gif file can be used to customize controls that use bullets. For example, the skin for the BulletedList control uses the BulletImageURL attribute to specify that this control should use the bullet.gif file stored in the Images subfolder of the current theme. In addition, this skin uses the BulletStyle attribute to specify that the bullet should use a custom image. As a result, the BulletedList control shown in this figure uses this custom bullet.gif image instead of the default bullet style, which is a small black circle.

The images for the Classic theme

The brownfadetop.gif image

A CSS class that uses this image

```
.brownfadetopback
{
    background-image: url(images/brownfadetop.gif);
}
```

An HTML tag that uses the image

```
<h4 class="brownfadetopback">Halloween supplies for the discerning
haunter</h4>
```

How the H4 tag appears on the page

Halloween supplies for the discerning haunter

The bullet.gif image

The skin for a BulletedList control that uses this image

```
<asp:BulletedList runat="server"
    BulletImageURL="images/bullet.gif"
    BulletStyle="CustomImage" />
```

An ASP.NET tag that uses the image

```
<asp:BulletedList ID="BulletedList1" runat="server">
    <asp:ListItem Value="Item1">Austin Powers</asp:ListItem>
    <asp:ListItem Value="Item2">Freddy</asp:ListItem>
</asp:BulletedList>
```

How the BulletedList control appears on the page

○ Austin Powers
○ Freddy

Figure 12-7   How to use images

More skills for working with themes

Most of the time, you want to apply a single theme to all pages of an application as described in figure 12-3. However, there may be times when you want to apply a theme to individual pages or controls. For example, you may want to allow each user to select a preferred theme for a page. Conversely, there may be times when you want to remove a theme from individual pages or controls. And there may be times when you want to allow individual controls to override attributes that are specified by the theme.

How to apply a theme to a page

Figure 12-8 starts by showing how you can use the Theme attribute of the Page directive to apply a theme to a single page at design time. Then, it shows how you can use the Theme property of the Page class to apply a theme to a single page at runtime.

At runtime, you must make sure the code that applies the theme is executed before the HTML element or ASP.NET control is added to the page. To do that, you can code an event procedure for the PreInit event of the Page class as shown in this figure. This event procedure is executed before the Init event that adds the controls to the page. As a result, this is a good event to use to apply a theme to a page.

The code within the event procedure for the PreInit event sets the Theme for the Page equal to a string for a theme that has been stored in the Session object. That way, if the user has selected a theme earlier in the session, the theme for this page will be changed to the theme selected by the user. However, unless you store this theme in a persistent data store, this theme will be lost when the user ends the current session.

To make the theme available for future sessions, you can use the profile feature described in chapter 10. To do that, you can configure the profile feature so it includes a Theme property that stores a string for the user's preferred theme. Then, you can use the Profile class to get the theme like this:

```
Page.Theme = Profile.Theme
```

How to apply a skin to a control

In figure 12-5, you saw how to use the SkinID attribute to apply a named skin to a server control at design time. Now, figure 12-8 reviews this skill, and it shows how to use the SkinID property of a server control to apply a named skin at runtime. To do that, you can use the PreInit event of the page to make sure that this skin is applied before the control is added to the page and displayed. This works the same as it does for applying a theme to a page.

How to apply a theme to a page

At design time

```
<%@ Page Language="VB" Theme="SmokeAndGlass" %>
```

At runtime

```
Protected Sub Page_PreInit(ByVal sender As Object, ByVal e As EventArgs) _
        Handles Me.PreInit
    Page.Theme = CType(Session("myTheme"), String)
End Sub
```

How to apply a skin to a control

At design time

```
<asp:Label ID="lblName" runat="server" SkinID="Head1"></asp:Label>
```

At runtime

```
Protected Sub Page_PreInit(ByVal sender As Object, ByVal e As EventArgs) _
        Handles Me.PreInit
    lblName.SkinID = CType(Session("mySkinID"), String)
End Sub
```

Description

- To apply a theme to a single page, you can use the Theme attribute of the Page directive or the Theme property of the Page class.

- To apply a skin to a control, you can use the SkinID attribute or property of the control.

- The code that applies a theme or skin at runtime should be coded in the event procedure for the PreInit event of the Page class so the code is executed before the HTML elements and ASP.NET controls are added to the page.

Figure 12-8   How to apply themes and skins

How to remove a theme from an application

Although it isn't shown in this chapter, it's possible for a web site administrator to set a global theme that applies to all web applications running on the server. In that case, you may want to remove the global theme from all pages of your application. To do that, you can open the web.config file for your application and set the Theme attribute of the <pages> element to an empty string as shown in figure 12-9.

How to remove a theme from a page

Figure 12-9 also shows how to remove a theme from a single page. At design time, you can set the Theme attribute of the Page directive to an empty string. At runtime, you can set the Theme property of the Page class to an empty string. To do that, you can use the PreInit event of the page to make sure that this theme is removed before the HTML elements and controls are added to the page and displayed. This works the same as it does for applying a theme to a page.

How to remove a theme from a control

By default, the EnableTheming property is set to True for all controls. As a result, any themes that are applied to a page are applied to all controls on the page. Typically, that's what you want. However, since you can't override an attribute that's set in a skin by setting it at the control level, you may want to remove the theme from the control so you can apply custom formatting to a control. To do that, you can set the EnableTheming attribute for the control to False as shown in figure 12-9. Then, you can use standard ASP.NET formatting techniques to format that control. In this figure, for example, the ForeColor attribute is used to change the color of a label to red.

If you need to set the EnableTheming property at runtime, you can use the PreInit event of the page to make sure that this skin is removed before the HTML elements and controls are added to the page and displayed. This works the same as it does for applying a theme to a page.

How to remove themes from the entire application

At design time

```
<system.web>
  <pages theme="" />
</system.web>
```

How to remove themes from the current page

At design time

```
<%@ Page Language="VB" Theme="" %>
```

At runtime

```
Protected Sub Page_PreInit(ByVal sender As Object, ByVal e As EventArgs) _
        Handles Me.PreInit
    Page.Theme = ""
End Sub
```

How to remove a theme from a control

At design time

```
<asp:Label ID="lblName" runat="server"
    EnableTheming="False" ForeColor="red">
</asp:Label>
```

At runtime

```
Protected Sub Page_PreInit(ByVal sender As Object, ByVal e As EventArgs) _
        Handles Me.PreInit
    lblName.EnableTheming = false
    lblName.ForeColor = System.Drawing.Color.Red
End Sub
```

Description

- To remove a theme from all of the pages in an application, you can set the Theme attribute of the <pages> element to an empty string.

- To remove a theme from a single page, you can set the Theme attribute of the Page directive or the Theme property of the Page class to an empty string.

- To remove a theme from a control, you can set the EnableTheming attribute or property to False.

- The code that removes a theme at runtime should be coded in the event procedure for the PreInit event of the Page class so the code is executed before the HTML elements and ASP.NET controls are added to the page.

Figure 12-9   How to remove themes and skins

How to use style sheet themes

When you use the Theme attribute or property to apply a theme, the theme is known as a *customization theme*. So far, all of examples in this chapter have worked with customization themes. When you use a customization theme, you can't override any of attributes that are set by the theme. For example, since the Classic theme sets the color of a label to blue, you can't set the color of an individual label to red unless you remove the theme from the label as shown in figure 12-9. This often isn't ideal because it also removes all other formatting that was applied by the theme.

If you want to be able to override the attributes specified by a theme, you can use the StyleSheetTheme attribute to apply the theme to all pages as shown in figure 12-10. Then, the theme is known as a *style sheet theme*, and you can override any of the attributes specified in this theme by setting them at the control level. For the most part, you can use the same skills for working with style sheet themes that you use for customization themes.

However, to apply a style sheet theme to a single page at runtime, you don't use the PreInit event. Instead, you override the StyleSheetTheme property of the page to get and set the name of the theme. Then, when a page loads, it automatically calls the StyleSheetTheme property to set the style sheet theme. In this figure, for example, the StyleSheetTheme property for the page gets the name of the style sheet theme from the Session object and sets the name of the style sheet theme in the Session object.

To understand how themes work, you need to understand the order in which the attributes of a theme are applied. First, all attributes specified by the style sheet theme are applied. Then, the custom attributes specified for individual controls are applied, overriding the style sheet theme if necessary. Finally, the attributes specified by the customization theme are applied, overriding the style sheet theme if necessary. That's why you can't override a customization theme by setting attributes for a control.

Although it's uncommon, it's possible to apply both types of themes to an application. For example, this figure shows how to apply the SmokeAndGlass theme as the style sheet theme while also applying the Classic theme as the customization theme. As a result, if the same attribute is specified in both themes, the attribute specified in the Classic theme will override the attribute in the SmokeAndGlass theme. However, if an attribute is specified in the SmokeAndGlass theme and it isn't specified in the Classic theme, that attribute will be applied to the page unless, of course, it is overridden by a custom attribute for a control.

How to apply a style sheet theme to all pages in the application

```
<system.web>
  <pages styleSheetTheme="SmokeAndGlass" />
</system.web>
```

How to apply a style sheet theme to a single page

At design time

```
<%@ Page Language="VB" StylesheetTheme="SmokeAndGlass" %>
```

At runtime by overriding the StyleSheetTheme property in the code-behind file

```
Public Overrides Property StyleSheetTheme() As String
    Get
        Return CType(Session("myTheme"), String)
    End Get
    Set(ByVal value As String)
        Session("myTheme") = value
    End Set
End Property
```

How to remove a style sheet theme from a single page

At design time

```
<%@ Page Language="VB" StylesheetTheme="" %>
```

The order in which themes are applied

1. Style sheet theme attributes
2. Control attributes
3. Customization theme attributes

How to apply both a customization theme and a style sheet theme

At design time

```
<%@ Page Language="VB" StylesheetTheme="SmokeAndGlass" Theme="Classic" %>
```

Description

- A *customization theme* can't be overridden by custom settings on controls. A *style sheet theme* can be overridden at the control level.

- To apply or remove a style sheet theme at design time, you can use the StyleSheetTheme property. This works just like the Theme property does for customization themes.

- To apply or remove a style sheet theme at runtime, you can override the StyleSheetTheme property of the page.

Figure 12-10   How to work with style sheet themes

Perspective

In this chapter, you learned how themes work and how they can be used to separate the formatting of an application from the code of an application. In addition, you learned enough about creating a theme from scratch to realize that it isn't an easy task, even for an experienced web designer.

Now, you should have all the skills you need to work with a web designer to create a suitable theme for your application. Also, as themes become more widely used, you may be able to download an appropriate theme for your application from the Internet. Either way, once you have the theme you want, you can use the skills of this chapter to get the most from it.

Terms

theme
cascading style sheet (CSS)
skin
default skin
named skin
CSS class
customization theme
style sheet theme

13

How to use web parts to build portals

Portals are web pages that display modular content that can be customized by the user. In the past, developing a portal was a difficult proposition that involved writing a lot of code. But now, with ASP.NET 2.0, you only need to write a few lines of code to be able to develop a portal.

To make this possible, ASP.NET 2.0 provides a built-in portal framework that's conceptually similar to the framework that's used by Microsoft SharePoint. In addition, Visual Studio 2005 provides full support for building portals, and the .NET Framework exposes an API that can be used to work with portals.

An introduction to the portal framework

The topics that follow introduce you to the ASP.NET 2.0 portal framework that allows you to easily develop *portals*, which are web pages that provide modular content that can be customized by each user of the page. To start, you'll see five screens that illustrate some of the features for a portal that might be used by a salesperson employed by the company that runs the Halloween Store web site. Then, you'll learn how portal configurations are stored, and you'll learn how the ASP.NET portal framework compares with the Microsoft SharePoint portal framework. Finally, you'll learn about the types of controls that can be used as *web parts*, which are the controls that provide modular content that can be used by a portal.

A portal that uses web parts

Each portal page contains one or more web parts. In part 1 of figure 13-1, for example, the Sales Portal page contains three web parts: Order Calculator, Days to Halloween, and Product List. In the first screen, the user has pulled down the control menu for the Product List part and is about to minimize it. In the second screen, the Product List has been minimized. As a result, only its title bar is displayed. In addition, the user is about to click on a radio button to switch to another display mode that allows the user to move web parts.

A portal page that displays three web parts

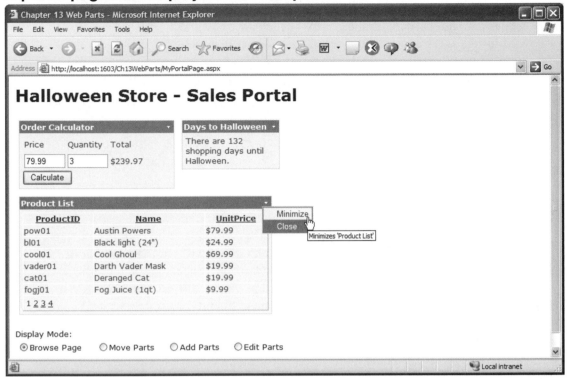

The same page after one web part has been minimized

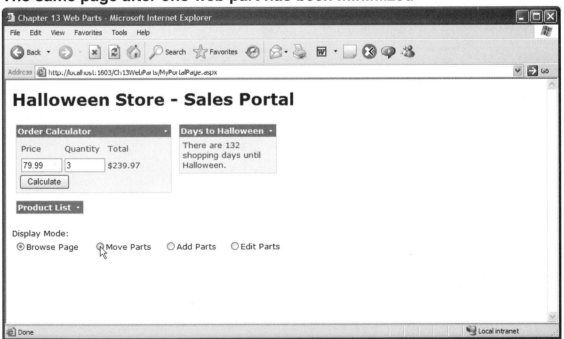

Figure 13-1   A page that uses web parts (part 1 of 3)

In part 2 of figure 13-1, the user has switched to the mode that allows the user to move web parts between different areas of the page. This causes the header text and borders for these areas, which are known as *web part zones*, to be displayed. For example, the header text for the first web part zone is "Zone 1 – Horizontal Layout." That's because this zone lays out web parts horizontally from left to right. In contrast, the header text for the second web part zone is "Zone 2 – Vertical Layout." That's because this zone lays out the web parts vertically from top to bottom.

Once the user has switched to a mode that allows the web parts to be moved, the user can drag a web part from one zone to another. For instance, in part 2 of this figure, the user drags the Days to Halloween part from the first web part zone to the second one.

Although this figure doesn't illustrate it, this portal also lets a user add web parts to a web part zone, and it lets a user edit the appearance and behavior of web parts. If, for example, the user clicks on the Add Parts radio button, the page displays a zone that lets the user add a part by selecting it from a catalog that contains all available parts for the page. Or, if the user clicks on the Edit Parts radio button, an Edit command is added to the control list menu for each web part. Then, the user can select this command to edit the appearance and behavior of this web part. Later in this chapter, you'll see examples that show how both of these features work.

The same page as a web part is being moved

The same page after the move has been completed

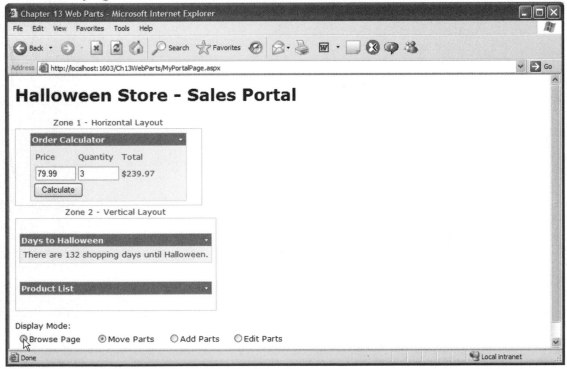

Figure 13-1   A page that uses web parts (part 2 of 3)

How user configurations are stored

To store the portal configuration for each user, the Web Parts feature uses the profile and anonymous identification features described in chapter 10. As a result, the portal framework automatically adds the AspNetDb.mdf database file to the project and uses this database to store the user configurations. Then, whenever a user moves a web part to a new zone, minimizes a web part, or modifies the portal configuration in some other way, the new configuration is saved in this database. That way, the customized page can be displayed the next time the user visits the site.

SharePoint and ASP.NET 2.0

Microsoft SharePoint is an older technology that provides a robust portal framework that can, among other things, be used to develop web parts. Although the ASP.NET 2.0 portal framework can also be used to develop web parts, web parts aren't interchangeable between these two technologies. However, these technologies are similar from a conceptual point of view, and the ASP.NET 2.0 portal framework has been designed so it can support SharePoint web parts in the future.

If you already know how to use SharePoint web parts, you'll be able to use many of the same skills for building portals with ASP.NET 2.0. Conversely, many of the skills that you learn for building web parts with ASP.NET 2.0 also apply to building web parts with SharePoint.

The same page after the minimized part has been restored

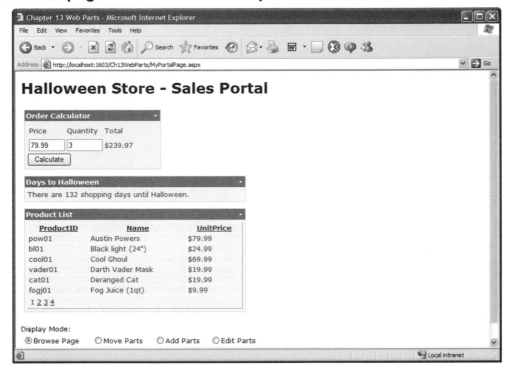

Description

- ASP.NET 2.0 comes with a built-in portal framework that allows you to easily develop *portals*, which are web pages that can be customized by users.

- A *web part* is a special type of control that can be displayed within a *web part zone*. Most portals let the user customize the appearance of the portal by minimizing, restoring, closing, and moving the web parts. In addition, most applications let the user add web parts to the page, and some applications let the user edit the properties of the web parts.

- To store the layout of a portal for each user, the web parts feature uses the profile and anonymous identification features described in chapter 10. This automatically adds the AspNetDb.mdf database file to the project and uses this database to store the data about how the portal is configured for each user.

Figure 13-1   A page that uses web parts (part 3 of 3)

Types of controls that can be used as web parts

Figure 13-2 shows the types of controls that can be placed within a web part zone. To start, you can place any ASP.NET control within a web part zone. This includes standard ASP.NET controls such as Label and Calendar controls, it includes user controls, and it includes custom server controls. When you add one of these controls to a web part zone, the control is automatically wrapped by the GenericWebPart class. This class allows the control to behave like a web part.

The advantage of this approach is that you can use the ASP.NET skills that you're already familiar with to quickly develop controls that can be used as web parts. The disadvantage is that the GenericWebPart class doesn't let you take advantage of several advanced features of web parts. For example, when you use the GenericWebPart class, you can't create a connection between two web parts and share data between them.

If you need to use any of the advanced features, you can develop custom WebPart controls that inherit the WebPart class. Keep in mind, though, that custom WebPart controls are significantly more difficult to develop than the user controls that are used in this chapter.

The WebPart hierarchy in this figure shows that all web parts begin by inheriting the Panel class. Then, the Part and WebPart classes provide additional members that can be used to work with web parts. Finally, the GenericWebPart class provides the functionality that's necessary to wrap ASP.NET controls so they can appear and behave as WebPart controls at runtime.

Types of controls that can be used as web parts

ASP.NET controls that can be placed in a web part zone

- Standard controls (such as the Label control in figure 13-3)
- User controls (such as the ProductList control in figure 13-4)
- Custom server controls

Custom WebPart controls

- Custom WebPart controls (such as the HalloweenCounter control in figure 13-10)

The WebPart hierarchy

```
Panel
    Part
        WebPart
            GenericWebPart
```

Description

- When you add an ASP.NET control such as a user control to a web part zone, the control is automatically wrapped by the GenericWebPart class. This class allows ASP.NET controls to behave like web parts.

- A custom WebPart control inherits the WebPart class. As a result, custom WebPart controls let you take advantage of several advanced web part features that aren't available for standard ASP.NET controls. However, custom WebPart controls are significantly more difficult to develop than user controls.

- Since user controls and custom server controls aren't new with ASP.NET 2.0, this book doesn't show how to develop them. To learn how to create them, please refer to *Murach's ASP.NET Web Programming with VB.NET*, or check our web site for the availability of a new ASP.NET 2.0 book for Visual Basic users that includes both the old and the new features.

Figure 13-2   Types of controls that can be used as web parts

How to use web parts

Now that you have a general idea of what web parts are and how they work, you're ready to learn how to use Visual Studio to create portals that use web parts. As you'll see in a moment, you only need to write a few lines of code to create a fully functional portal.

How to create a page that uses web parts

Figure 13-3 shows how to create a page that uses two web part zones and three web part controls. To start, you open the page in Design view, go to the WebParts tab of the Toolbox, and drag a WebPartManager control onto the page. This control manages the web parts and zones, and each portal page must include one of these controls.

Once you've added a WebPartManager control to a page, you can add WebPartZone controls by dragging them from the Toolbox onto the page. To keep things simple, the page in this figure contains only two zones, but it's common to place several web part zones on a page. Often, these web part zones are added within a table. Then, you can add a web part zone to each cell of the table to give the user more flexibility for how the page can be organized.

Once you've added the WebPartZone controls to the page, you can add web parts to the web part zones. In this figure, for example, two Label controls have been added to the first web part zone, and one Label control has been added to the second web part zone. These controls are coded within the ZoneTemplate element of the WebPartZone controls. This template specifies the web parts that are displayed the first time a user accesses the portal. However, if the user closes or moves these web parts, the user's changes will be stored in the database, and the changes will be displayed the next time the user accesses the portal.

Any control that's placed within a WebPartZone control is automatically wrapped by the GenericWebPart class so it can behave like a web part. As a result, for the Label controls in this figure, you can set any attributes that are available to the GenericWebPart class. Of these attributes, the Title attribute is commonly used to set the title of a web part. This attribute is stored in the Part class, which is ultimately inherited by the GenericWebPart class.

A page that contains two web part zones and three web parts

The tags for the page

```
<h1>Halloween Store - Sales Portal</h1>

<asp:WebPartManager ID="WebPartManager1" runat="server">
</asp:WebPartManager>

<asp:WebPartZone ID="WebPartZone1" runat="server"
    LayoutOrientation="Horizontal"
    HeaderText="Web Part Zone 1 - Horizontal Layout">
    <ZoneTemplate>
        <asp:Label ID="Label1" runat="server" Title="Part 1 Title"
            Text="Part 1 Content"></asp:Label>
        <asp:Label ID="Label2" runat="server" Title="Part 2 Title"
            Text="Part 2 Content"></asp:Label>
    </ZoneTemplate>
</asp:WebPartZone><br />

<asp:WebPartZone ID="WebPartZone2" runat="server"
    HeaderText="Web Part Zone 2 - Vertical Layout">
    <ZoneTemplate>
        <asp:Label ID="Label3" runat="server" Title="Part 3 Title"
            Text="Part 3 Content"></asp:Label>
    </ZoneTemplate>
</asp:WebPartZone>
```

Figure 13-3   How to create a page that uses web parts (part 1 of 2)

If necessary, you can use the HeaderText attribute of a WebPartZone element to specify the header text for the web part zone. Then, this text will be displayed above the control in Design view, and it will be displayed above the control at runtime whenever the portal enters certain modes such as the mode that allows the user to move web parts between zones.

You may also want to set the LayoutOrientation attribute of a WebPartZone element to specify the layout orientation. In this figure, for example, the first web part zone specifies a horizontal orientation, so the web parts are displayed from left to right. In contrast, the second web part zone doesn't specify a layout orientation, so the default orientation is used to display the web parts vertically.

When you run a page like the one in this figure, the default features provide a lot of built-in functionality. For example, the control menu for each web part will contain Minimize and Close commands for any parts that haven't been minimized and Restore and Close commands for any parts that have been minimized. So, if you use the Minimize command to minimize a web part, you can use the Restore command to restore that web part. However, if you select the Close command, the web part will be removed from the page. In that case, there's no way for the user to add that part back to the page unless the page provides for it as described in figure 13-6.

The page when it's displayed in a browser

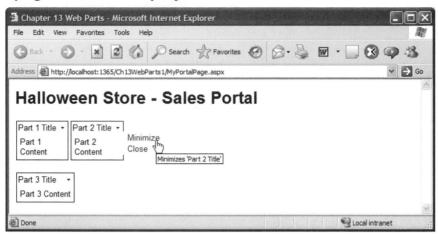

Description

- In the Toolbox, all of the controls for working with web parts are stored in the WebParts tab.

- Each portal must have one (and only one) WebPartManager control. This control manages the web parts and zones on the page.

- Most portals have two or more WebPartZone controls that define the web part zones that are available on the page. These controls are often coded within a table that specifies the number of rows and columns to be used for the page.

- The ZoneTemplate element of a WebPartZone control specifies the web parts that are displayed the first time a user accesses the portal.

- The HeaderText attribute of a WebPartZone control specifies the header text that's used for the zone when it's displayed in Design view. This text is also displayed at runtime when the portal enters certain modes such as the mode that allows the user to move web parts between zones.

- The Title attribute can be added to any control in a web part zone. That's because each control added to a web part zone is automatically wrapped by the GenericWebPart class, which provides access to the Title attribute of the Part class. In the Beta 2 version of Visual Studio, this attribute didn't work correctly with IntelliSense, but this should be fixed in the final release of the product.

Figure 13-3   How to create a page that uses web parts (part 2 of 2)

How to add a user control to a web part zone

Although figure 13-3 shows how to add a standard Label control to a web part zone, it's more common to add a user control to a web part zone as shown in figure 13-4. Then, this user control will automatically be wrapped by the GenericWebPart class so it behaves like a web part.

To make this work, you must start by creating a user control. In case you aren't already familiar with how to do that, this figure reviews this skill by showing how to create a user control that displays a list of products. In summary, you (1) add a user control (ascx file) to the project, (2) use the User Control Designer to design the control, and (3) use the Code Editor to write any code that's necessary to get the control to work.

In this figure, for example, a user control file named ProductList.ascx has been added to the project. This user control contains a SqlDataSource control that specifies the connection string and the Select statement needed to retrieve the data for the user control. In addition, it contains a GridView control that displays a list of the products that are retrieved by the SqlDataSource control.

The ProductList user control in Design view

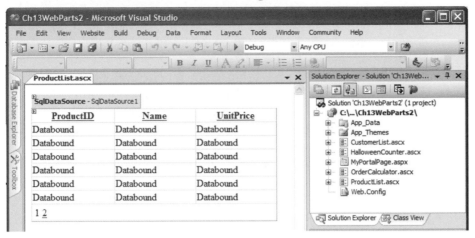

The ProductList control in Source view

```
<%@ Control Language="VB" AutoEventWireup="false" CodeFile="ProductList.ascx.vb"
         Inherits="ProductList" %>

<asp:SqlDataSource ID="SqlDataSource1" runat="server"
    ConnectionString="Data Source=localhost\SQLExpress;
        Initial Catalog=Halloween;Integrated Security=True"
    SelectCommand="SELECT ProductID, Name, UnitPrice
        FROM Products ORDER BY Name">
</asp:SqlDataSource>

<asp:GridView ID="GridView1" runat="server" DataSourceID="SqlDataSource1"
    AllowPaging="True" AllowSorting="True" AutoGenerateColumns="False"
    PageSize="6" Width="400px">
    <Columns>
        <asp:BoundField DataField="ProductID" HeaderText="ProductID"
            ReadOnly="True" SortExpression="ProductID" />
        <asp:BoundField DataField="Name" HeaderText="Name"
            SortExpression="Name" />
        <asp:BoundField DataField="UnitPrice" DataFormatString="{0:c}"
            HeaderText="UnitPrice" SortExpression="UnitPrice" />
    </Columns>
</asp:GridView>
```

Description

- To create a user control, you must add a user control (ascx file) to the project, use the User Control Designer to design the control, and use the Code Editor to write any code that's necessary to get the control to work.

- Since user controls aren't new with ASP.NET 2.0, this book doesn't show how to develop them.

Figure 13-4   How to add a user control to a web part zone (part 1 of 2)

Once you've created a user control and added it to your project, you can add it to your portal page. The easiest way to do that is to view the page in Design view. Then, you can drag the user control from the Solution Explorer onto the page. This automatically generates the Register directive that registers the control and the ASP.NET tag that displays the control.

Once you add the user control to the web part zone, you can switch to Source view and add a Title attribute to the control. In this figure, for example, the Title attribute for the ProductList control has been set to "Product List." This works the same for user controls as for the Label controls described in figure 13-3.

Although this figure only shows the code for the ProductList user control, you can use the same coding techniques to create other user controls such as the Order Calculator and Days to Halloween controls. In many ways, these controls are easier to develop than the ProductList user control since they don't access a database. Instead, the Order Calculator control allows the user to calculate a total based on quantity and price, and the Days to Halloween control calculates the number of days to Halloween and displays the result within a label.

A page that includes three user controls

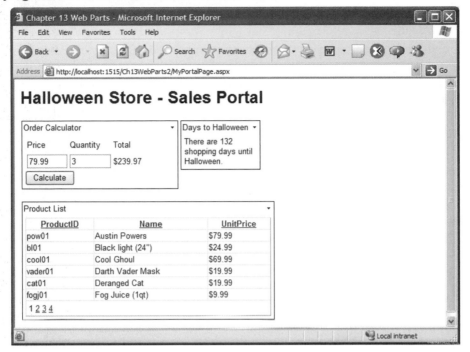

The code that registers a user control for a page

```
<%@ Register Src="ProductList.ascx" TagName="ProductList" TagPrefix="ucl" %>
```

The code that adds a user control to a web zone

```
<asp:WebPartZone ID="WebPartZone2" runat="server"
    HeaderText="Web Part Zone 2 - Vertical Layout">
    <ZoneTemplate>
        <ucl:ProductList ID="ProductList1" runat="server" Title="Product List">
        </ucl:ProductList>
    </ZoneTemplate>
</asp:WebPartZone>
```

Description

- In Design view, you can register a user control and add it to the page by dragging it from the Solution Explorer onto the page.

- In Source view, you can register a user control and add it to the page by coding the Register directive and by coding the tag for the user control.

Figure 13-4   How to add a user control to a web part zone (part 2 of 2)

How to let the user move web parts between zones

By default, a page that contains web parts runs in *browse display mode*. In this mode, you can only minimize, restore, and close web parts. Then, if you want to allow the user to be able to move web parts between zones, you must switch into *design display mode*. In this mode, which is shown in figure 13-5, the header text and borders appear for each web part zone, and the user can move web parts between zones by dragging them from one zone to another.

To switch between display modes in the code-behind file for a page, you set the DisplayMode property of the WebPartManager class equal to one of the DisplayMode constants that are available from that class. In this figure, for example, the page includes a RadioButtonList control that allows the user to choose between browse display mode and design display mode. If the user chooses the second option, the page enters design display mode so the user can move web parts between zones. Then, when the user is done moving web parts, the user can select the first option. This will cause the page to enter browse display mode, which is the optimal mode for browsing the data that's displayed on a page.

A page that lets the user move web parts between zones

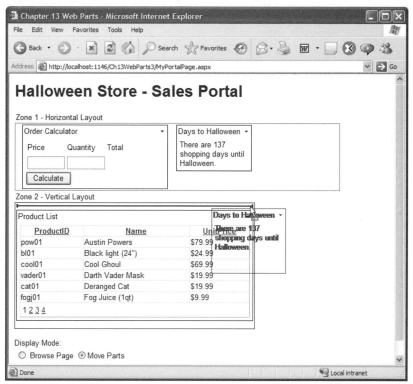

A radio button list that switches between display modes

```
<asp:RadioButtonList ID="rdoDisplayMode" runat="server" AutoPostBack="True"
    RepeatDirection="Horizontal">
        <asp:ListItem Selected="True">Browse Page</asp:ListItem>
        <asp:ListItem>Move Parts</asp:ListItem>
</asp:RadioButtonList>
```

The event procedure for the radio button list

```
Protected Sub rdoDisplayMode_SelectedIndexChanged(ByVal sender As Object, _
        ByVal e As System.EventArgs) _
        Handles rdoDisplayMode.SelectedIndexChanged
    If rdoDisplayMode.SelectedIndex = 0 Then
        WebPartManager1.DisplayMode = WebPartManager.BrowseDisplayMode
    ElseIf rdoDisplayMode.SelectedIndex = 1 Then
        WebPartManager1.DisplayMode = WebPartManager.DesignDisplayMode
    End If
End Sub
```

Description

- You can use the DisplayMode property of the WebPartManager class to switch between display modes. To do that, you can set this property equal to any of the constant values stored in the WebPartManager class such as BrowseDisplayMode and DesignDisplayMode.

Figure 13-5   How to let the user move web parts between zones

How to let the user add web parts to a zone

If a user closes a web part when working in browse or design display mode, the part is removed from the page and there's no way for the user to add the web part back to the page. However, you can add functionality to the page that lets the user add web parts that have been closed back to the page and add web parts that aren't on the page by default. To do this, you must perform three tasks.

First, you must provide a way for the user to switch to the *catalog display mode* that's shown in figure 13-6. To do that, you can extend the RadioButtonList control shown in figure 13-5 so it includes a third option that allows the user to switch into catalog display mode.

Second, you must add a CatalogZone control to the page. To do that, you can drag the CatalogZone control from the Toolbox onto the page.

Third, you must add one or more of the CatalogPart controls within the CatalogZone control. In this figure, for example, the CatalogZone control contains a PageCatalogPart control followed by a DeclarativeCatalogPart control. The DeclarativeCatalogPart control includes a WebPartsTemplate element that declares any web parts that aren't on the default page but should also be available. In this example, the CustomerList part is the only part in this catalog, but you can code multiple parts for this catalog.

When the page is running in browse display mode, the catalogs of available web parts that are defined by the CatalogZone and CatalogPart controls aren't displayed. However, if the user switches to catalog display mode, the catalog is displayed. In this figure, for example, the CatalogZone control is displayed in the bottom half of the page, starting with the heading (Catalog of Web Parts) that's provided by the HeaderText attribute.

After the heading, the CatalogZone control displays "Select the catalog you would like to browse" and a menu that lets you switch between the CatalogPart controls within the zone. In this figure, the choices are Page Catalog and Declarative Catalog, and the user has selected Page Catalog. This displays a list of all the web parts that were on the page by default, but were closed by the user (this list includes just the Product List part). In contrast, if the user selects Declarative Catalog, the list displays all of the web parts in that catalog. The number in parentheses after each menu item for the catalog zone indicates the number of items in each list (one each).

Under the catalog list, the CatalogZone control generates controls for adding a selected web part. Here, the user is using the drop-down list to specify the zone that the selected web part should be added to. Then, when the user clicks the Add button, the selected part is added to that zone.

By default, the CatalogZone control also displays a Close link in its header and a Close button next to the Add button. This provides the user with a way to close the CatalogZone control and exit catalog display mode. However, this also causes the display mode to get out of synch with the RadioButtonList control. As a result, the Visible attribute of the HeaderCloseVerb and CloseVerb elements has been used to hide these elements. (When working with web parts, the term *verb* is used to refer to the actions that are executed by the buttons, links, and menu items that are available from a web part.)

A page that lets the user add web parts to a zone

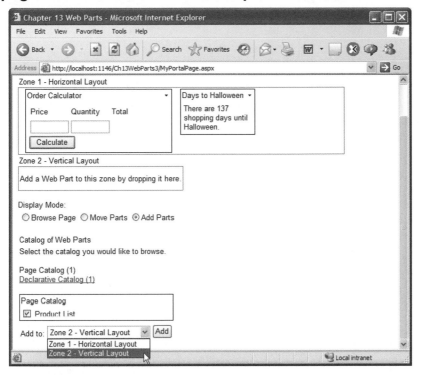

The ASP.NET tags for the catalog

```
<asp:CatalogZone ID="CatalogZone1" runat="server"
    HeaderText="Catalog of Web Parts">
    <ZoneTemplate>
        <asp:PageCatalogPart ID="PageCatalogPart1" runat="server" />
        <asp:DeclarativeCatalogPart ID="DeclarativeCatalogPart1" runat="server">
            <WebPartsTemplate>
                <ucl:CustomerList ID="CustomerList1" runat="server"
                    Title="Customer List"/>
            </WebPartsTemplate>
        </asp:DeclarativeCatalogPart>
    </ZoneTemplate>
    <HeaderCloseVerb Visible="False" />
    <CloseVerb Visible="False" />
</asp:CatalogZone>
```

The code that switches to catalog display mode

```
WebPartManager1.DisplayMode = WebPartManager.CatalogDisplayMode
```

Description

- To let the user add web parts to a page, you must (1) provide a way to switch to *catalog display mode*, (2) add a CatalogZone control to the page, and (3) place one or more of the CatalogPart controls within the CatalogZone control. (The CatalogPart controls are the PageCatalogPart, DeclarativeCatalogPart, and ImportCatalogPart controls.)

Figure 13-6   How to let the user add web parts to a zone

How to let the user edit the properties of a web part

Most of the time, you can provide all of the customization that's necessary for a portal by letting the user minimize, restore, close, move, and add web parts as described in the last three figures. However, there are times when you may also want to let the user edit the properties that control the appearance and behavior of a web part. To do this, you must perform three tasks that are similar to the three tasks for letting the user add a web part to a page.

First, you must provide a way for the user to switch to the *edit display mode* that's shown in figure 13-7. To do that, you can extend the RadioButtonList control shown in figure 13-5 so it includes a fourth option that lets the user switch to this mode. Once the switch has been made, this mode adds an Edit command to the drop-down control menu for each web part. Then, the user can edit a web part by selecting this command, which displays the properties that can be edited, as shown in the second screen in this figure.

Second, you must add an EditorZone control to the page. To do that, you can drag the EditorZone control from the Toolbox onto the page. This control is a container control that works similarly to the WebPartZone and CatalogZone controls.

Third, you must add one or more of the EditorPart controls within the EditorZone control. In this figure, for example, the EditorZone control contains just one EditorPart control, the AppearanceEditorPart control. But you could add other EditorPart controls such as the BehaviorEditorPart, LayoutEditorPart, or PropertyGridEditorPart control.

By default, the EditorZone control displays a Close link in its header. This lets the user close the EditorZone control, which hides this control and any subordinate EditorPart controls, but doesn't exit edit display mode. As a result, the Edit command is still available from each of the web parts on the page.

A page that lets the user edit web parts

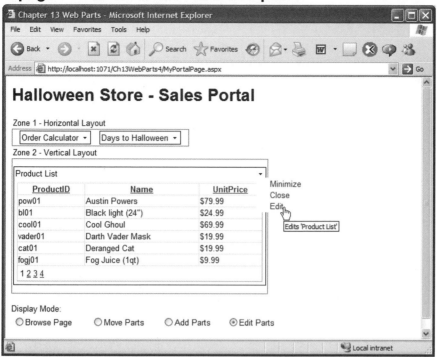

An editor zone for the Product List part

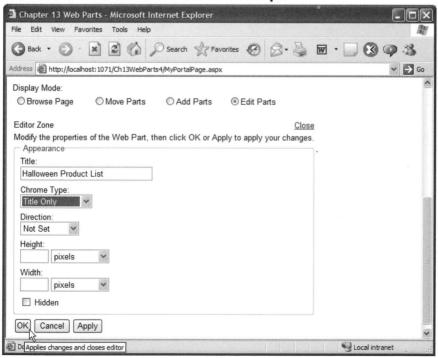

Figure 13-7   How to let the user edit the properties of a web part (part 1 of 2)

Although the EditorPart controls let the user modify the properties of a web part, most of these properties only provide for minor cosmetic changes. In this figure, for example, the user has modified the Product List web part by changing the title from "Product List" to "Halloween Product List" and by turning off the border. Since this type of change is so trivial, you may not want to bother with this type of editing support.

When working with web parts, the term *chrome* is used to refer to the non-content area of a web part such as the border, title bar, minimize/close buttons, and so on. In this figure, for example, the user can use the Chrome Type combo box to change the type of chrome that's used for the Product List web part. In the next figure, you'll see how you can use the PartChromeStyle element of the WebPartZone element to change the style of the chrome for each web part within a web part zone.

A page after the appearance of the product list part has been edited

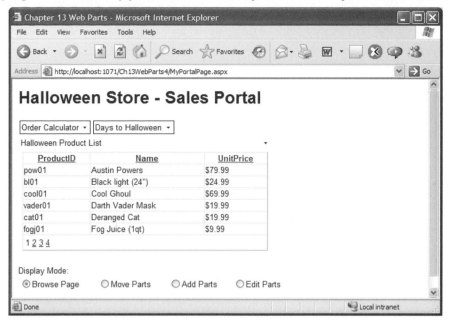

The ASP.NET tags for the editor zone

```
<asp:EditorZone ID="EditorZone1" runat="server">
    <ZoneTemplate>
        <asp:AppearanceEditorPart ID="AppearanceEditorPart1" runat="server" />
    </ZoneTemplate>
</asp:EditorZone>
```

The code that switches to EditDisplayMode

```
WebPartManager1.DisplayMode = WebPartManager.EditDisplayMode
```

The EditorPart controls

```
AppearanceEditorPart
BehaviorEditorPart
LayoutEditorPart
PropertyGridEditorPart
```

Description

- To let the user edit the web parts on a page, you must (1) provide a way to switch to *edit display mode*, (2) add an EditorZone control to the page, and (3) place one or more of the EditorPart controls within the EditorZone control.

- When a page enters edit display mode, an Edit command becomes available from the drop-down control menu for each web part. When a user selects this command, the properties of the web part will be displayed so the user can edit them.

- When working with web parts, the term *chrome* is used to refer to the non-content area of a web part such as the border, title bar, minimize/close buttons, and so on.

Figure 13-7   How to let the user edit the properties of a web part (part 2 of 2)

How to apply formatting to web parts

So far, the examples in this topic haven't included any formatting. That's why they appear as white controls with black borders. However, for a typical portal, each web part should be formatted in a way that's appropriate for that portal. Most of the time, that means applying formatting that gives the portal a professional and pleasing appearance as shown in figure 13-8.

The easiest way to apply formatting to all of the web parts in a web part zone is to use the AutoFormat feature. To do that, select the AutoFormat command from the web part zone's smart tag menu and choose a format. When you do, you'll be able to pick from a variety of formats and the appropriate attributes and elements will be added to the WebPartZone tag. Then, if necessary, you can edit these tags. In this figure, for example, I applied the Professional format to the first web part zone, and then I modified the attributes and elements slightly to make them more appropriate for the application.

If you want to apply the same formatting to multiple web part zones, you can store the formatting for the WebPartZone in a skin file within a theme as described in chapter 12. To get the formatting for a web part zone into a skin file, you can copy the tag for the WebPartZone control from the aspx file into the skin file. Then, you can delete any attributes or elements that aren't used to control the formatting of web parts such as the ID attribute, the LayoutOrientation attribute, the HeaderText attribute, and the ZoneTemplate element. When that's done, you end up with a WebPartZone tag like the one in this figure that only contains the attributes and elements that apply formatting. Then, this formatting can automatically be applied to all web part zones on the page or to all web part zones in the entire application.

As you might expect, you can use similar techniques to apply formatting to the CatalogZone and EditorZone controls, which will change the appearance of the CatalogPart and EditorPart controls within these zones. For example, you can use the AutoFormat feature to automatically apply formatting to a catalog or editor zone. Although the tags that apply this type of formatting aren't shown in this figure, you can see them in the application for this chapter that you can download from our web site.

A page after formatting has been applied to the web parts

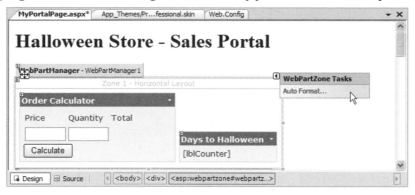

The ASP.NET tags that apply formatting to a web part zone

```
<asp:WebPartZone runat="server"
    BorderColor="#CCCCCC"
    Font-Names="Verdana"
    Padding="6">
    <PartChromeStyle
        BackColor="#F7F6F3"              BorderColor="#E2DED6"
        Font-Names="Verdana"            ForeColor="White" />
    <MenuLabelHoverStyle                ForeColor="#E2DED6" />
    <MenuLabelStyle                     ForeColor="White" />
    <MenuVerbHoverStyle
        BackColor="#F7F6F3"              BorderColor="#CCCCCC"
        BorderStyle="Solid"             BorderWidth="1px"
        ForeColor="#333333" />
    <HeaderStyle
        ForeColor="#CCCCCC"              HorizontalAlign="Center" />
    <MenuVerbStyle
        BorderColor="#5D7B9D"           BorderStyle="Solid"
        BorderWidth="1px"               ForeColor="White" />
    <PartStyle
        ForeColor="#333333" />
    <TitleBarVerbStyle
        Font-Underline="False"          ForeColor="White" />
    <MenuPopupStyle
        BackColor="#5D7B9D"             BorderColor="#CCCCCC"
        BorderWidth="1px"/>
    <PartTitleStyle
        BackColor="#5D7B9D"             Font-Bold="True"
        ForeColor="White" />
</asp:WebPartZone>
```

Description

- You can use the AutoFormat feature to automatically format all of the parts in a web part zone, catalog zone, or editor zone. To do that, select the AutoFormat command from the zone's smart tag menu and choose a format.

- You can use a theme to apply formatting to all of the zones on a page (or to the entire web site). For more information about themes, see chapter 12.

Figure 13-8   How to apply formatting to web parts

How to write code that works with web parts

You can develop most portals using just the skills that have already been presented in this chapter. However, if you need to customize a portal beyond what has been shown, the portal framework exposes an API that lets you write code that works with web parts. This API also lets you develop custom WebPart controls that can take advantage of some of the advanced features of the portal framework. What follows is just an introduction to this subject, but it should get you started if you're an experienced programmer.

Classes for working with web parts

Figure 13-9 shows some of the classes that are commonly used to work with web parts. Of these classes, the WebPartManager class is the one that's most commonly used to work with portals. As you learned earlier in this chapter, you can use this class to switch between display modes. In addition, you can use this class to access a collection of WebPart and WebPartZone objects that correspond to the web parts and zones available from the page. And you can use this class to respond to the events that occur to a web portal such as switching display modes or adding or removing a web part or zone.

In general, the classes described in this figure correspond with the controls that are available from the WebParts tab in Visual Studio's Toolbox. Most of the time, you can use Visual Studio to set the properties for these controls at design time. Whenever necessary, though, you can write code that uses these classes to work with these controls at runtime. To do that, you often need to get a more complete description of the class for the control by looking it up in the documentation for the .NET Framework class library.

Classes for working with web parts

Class	Description
WebPartManager	Can be used to work with all of the zones and web parts on the page, to change display modes for the page, and to respond to events that are raised by the zones and web parts on the page.
WebPartZone	Can be used to modify the properties of a web part zone. Many of these properties control the appearance of the web parts within this zone.
CatalogZone	Can be used to modify the properties of a catalog zone. Many of these properties control the appearance of the catalog parts within this zone.
EditorZone	Can be used to modify the properties of an editor zone. Many of these properties control the appearance of the editor parts within this zone.
ConnectionsZone	Can be used to work with connections between custom WebPart controls.
WebPartVerb	Can be used to work with a *verb*, which is a button, link, or menu item in the title bar of a web part.
WebPart	Can be used to work with web parts at runtime, or it can be overridden to create a custom WebPart that takes advantage of the advanced features of the portal framework (see figure 13-10).
GenericWebPart	Can be used to work with user controls and custom server controls within a web part zone. Many of its properties are inherited from the Panel and Part classes. The ASP.NET 2.0 portal framework automatically uses this class whenever it needs to wrap web parts that are created from ASP.NET controls such as standard controls, user controls, and custom server controls.
PageCatalogPart	Can be used to work with the web parts in the page catalog, including parts that a user has closed.
DeclarativeCatalogPart	Can be used to work with the web parts in the declarative catalog.
ImportCatalogPart	Can be used to import a catalog of web parts.
BehaviorEditorPart	Can be used to apply behavior changes to an associated web part.
AppearanceEditorPart	Can be used to apply appearance changes to an associated web part.
LayoutEditorPart	Can be used to apply layout changes to web parts.
PropertyGridEditorPart	Can be used to change the property grid of a web part.

Description

- For a complete description of each class, including its constructors, properties, methods, and events, look up the class in the documentation for the .NET Framework class library.

Figure 13-9   Classes for working with web parts

How to develop and use a custom WebPart control

To show you how to develop a custom WebPart control, figure 13-10 presents the HalloweenCounter class, which defines a custom WebPart control that displays a message that indicates the number of shopping days until Halloween. To start, this class inherits the WebPart class. Since this WebPart class inherits the Panel class and the Part class, the HalloweenCounter class inherits these classes too.

Next, the constructor for the HalloweenCounter class sets the Title property to "Days to Halloween." This is possible because the Title property is available from the Part class, which is inherited by the WebPart class and the HalloweenCounter class.

Then, the HalloweenCounter class overrides the RenderContents method of the WebControl class. This method is called by the web page whenever the page needs to display the control. The code within this method calculates the number of shopping days to Halloween, creates a message that includes the results of this calculation, and uses the HtmlTextWriter object to write that message to the page.

Since the message doesn't include any HTML tags, this HalloweenCounter class causes plain text to be displayed as the content of the web part. However, you can include HTML tags in the message if you want to format it. Also, if you know how to render controls as HTML, you can create complex controls using this method. In this regard, the skills for developing a custom WebPart control are similar to the skills for developing a custom server control.

The last two statements in this figure show how to register a custom WebPart control and place it on the page. First, you code a Register directive that specifies the namespace for the control and a prefix for the control's tag. Then, you code the tag for the control, using the prefix followed by the name of the class that defines the control. Once you do that, the page will display the custom WebPart just as it would display a user control that was wrapped in the GenericWebPart class.

The code that defines the custom WebPart control

```
Imports Microsoft.VisualBasic

Namespace murach

    Public Class HalloweenCounter
        Inherits WebPart

        Public Sub New()
            Me.Title = "Days to Halloween"
        End Sub

        Protected Overrides Sub RenderContents _
                (ByVal writer As HtmlTextWriter)
            Dim dtmToday As Date = Date.Today
            Dim dtmHalloween As Date = New Date(Date.Today.Year, 10, 31)
            If dtmToday > dtmHalloween Then
                dtmHalloween.AddYears(1)
            End If

            Dim tsSpan As TimeSpan = dtmHalloween - dtmToday
            Dim sContent As String = "There are " & tsSpan.Days _
             & " shopping days until Halloween."

            writer.Write(sContent)
        End Sub

    End Class

End Namespace
```

Code that registers a custom WebPart control for a page

```
<%@ Register TagPrefix="mma" Namespace="murach" %>
```

Code that places a custom WebPart control on a page

```
<mma:HalloweenCounter ID="HalloweenCounter1" runat="server" />
```

Description

- To develop a custom WebPart control, code a class that inherits the WebPart class. Then, override the RenderContents method of the WebControl class to render the contents of the web part.
- To use a custom WebPart control, code a Register directive that specifies the namespace for the control and a prefix for the control's tag. Then, code the tag for the control using the prefix followed by the name of the class that defines the control.

Figure 13-10   How to develop and use a custom WebPart control

Perspective

Now that you've finished this chapter, you should have the skills you need to develop portals with web parts. In particular, you should be able to develop a portal that lets the user move web parts between zones, add web parts to a page, and even edit the properties of a web part. You should also be able to develop some custom web parts.

Of course, there's more to developing portals than has been presented in this chapter. For instance, one of the most difficult aspects of developing portals is developing the web parts for them. But since ASP.NET 1.x provided for user controls and custom server controls, this book doesn't show how to develop those types of web parts. Also, if you want to do something like share data between web parts, you're going to have to dig into the documentation for the classes that let you work with web parts. For many portals, though, this chapter should provide all of the skills that you're going to need.

Terms

portal
web part
web part zone
browse display mode
design display mode
catalog display mode
verb
edit display mode
chrome

14

New ways to work with pages and other new web controls

The first 13 chapters in this book have presented the major new features of ASP.NET 2.0. But ASP.NET 2.0 also provides some minor new features that you should be aware of. In this chapter, then, you'll learn three new techniques for working with pages, and you'll learn how to use five more new controls.

New features for working with pages

You've already learned about many new features of ASP.NET 2.0 that are designed to make it easier to work with ASP.NET pages. For example, the new code-behind model simplifies the relationship between the aspx code that declares web controls and the Visual Basic code that handles events raised by those controls. Now, the topics that follow present three more new features for working with pages.

How to use URL mapping

As figure 14-1 shows, *URL mapping* is a new feature that lets you map an incoming URL request to a different URL. For example, URL mapping lets you map a simple URL such as www.halloweenstore.com/props.aspx to a more complicated URL such as www.halloweenstore.com/products/props/index.aspx. Then, when a user requests the props.aspx page, the mapped page is retrieved instead.

To provide for URL mapping, you add entries to the <urlMapping> element of the application's web.config file. Then, each <add> element provides a URL and the URL that it should be mapped to. Each of these URLs must be specified relative to the application's root directory, and you must use the tilde character (~) to represent the root directory. For example, the first entry in the example in this figure maps any request for the default.aspx page in the application root to the order.aspx page in that directory.

One common use of URL mapping is to provide a simple URL for a page that actually has a more complicated address. That makes the URL easier for the user to understand, and it also hides the actual structure of the application from users. If, for example, you organize your web site into directories that are nested several layers deep, URL mapping lets you create the appearance of a flat structure. The second entry in this figure's example shows this type of mapping.

Another benefit of URL mapping is that it lets you reorganize your web site without changing existing code. To illustrate, suppose your application's root directory contains an image file named banner.jpg, and this image is displayed with an Image control at the top of each page. If you don't use URL mapping and later decide to move this file to a directory named Images, the URLs in the Image controls will be broken. If you use URL mapping, though, you can map the directory change so you don't have to change any of the existing pages that refer to the banner.jpg file in the root directory. The third entry in the example in this figure shows this type of mapping.

The syntax of the <urlMapping> element

```
<urlMapping enabled="true">
    <add url=original-URL mappedUrl=mapped-URL />
</urlMapping>
```

Attributes of the <urlMapping> and <add> elements

<urlMapping> attribute	Description
enabled	Must be set to True to enable URL mapping.
<add> attributes	**Description**
url	The incoming URL that will be remapped.
mappedUrl	The URL that will be used in place of the incoming URL.

An example of URL mapping

```
<system.web>
    <urlMapping enabled="true">
        <add url="~/default.aspx" mappedUrl="~/order.aspx" />
        <add url="~/props.aspx" mappedUrl="~/Products/Props/index.aspx" />
        <add url="~/banner.jpg" mappedUrl="~/Images/banner.jpg" />
    </urlMapping>
        .
        .
        .
</system.web>
```

Three common reasons to use URL mapping

- To provide more friendly names for the application's pages.
- To hide the actual structure of your application from your users.
- So you can change the internal structure of an application without breaking existing code.

Description

- *URL mapping* uses configuration settings in the web.config file to map incoming URL requests to different URLs.
- The <urlMapping> element must be coded between the <system.web> and </system.web> tags.
- When a browser displays a page that has been mapped, the original URL, not the mapped URL, is displayed as the address of the page.
- You can't use URL mapping to map an .html file to an .aspx file. For example, you can't remap "~/default.html" to "~/default.aspx".
- You can use the tilde character (~) to represent the application's root directory.

Figure 14-1   How to use URL mapping

How to use access keys

Most Windows applications use *access keys* (also called *accelerator keys*) that let the user select controls by using keyboard shortcuts. If, for example, you designate F as the access key for an input field that accepts a customer's first name, the user can move the focus directly to this field by pressing Alt+F.

As figure 14-2 shows, ASP.NET 2.0 now lets you create access keys for web applications too. To create an access key, you simply add the AccessKey attribute to the control you want to create the keyboard shortcut for. Since the AccessKey attribute is defined by the System.Web.UI.WebControls.WebControl class, you can use it with any web control.

For text boxes and other controls that are identified by labels, it's common to specify the access key for the label rather than the control itself. Then, you can underline the letter that serves as the access key by using the <u> and </u> HTML tags to underline the access key. In this case, you should also code the AssociatedControlID attribute to specify the control that should receive the focus when the user uses the access key. This is illustrated by the code for the three labels in this figure.

Unfortunately, ASP.NET doesn't provide a way to underline the access key in a button control. That's because buttons are rendered using the <input type=submit> HTML element, which doesn't provide a way to format the text displayed by the button. You can still specify an access key, though, as illustrated by the last line of code in this figure.

A web page that uses access keys

The aspx code for the page shown above

```
<h2>Halloween Superstore</h2>
Please enter your contact information:<br /><br />

<asp:Label ID="Label1" runat="server" width="100px" BorderStyle="None"
    AccessKey="F" AssociatedControlID="txtFirstName"
    Text="<u>F</u>irst name:" /> 
<asp:TextBox ID="txtFirstName" Runat="server"
    Width="200px" Height="22px" /> <br />

<asp:Label ID="Label2" runat="server" width="100px" BorderStyle="None"
    AccessKey="L" AssociatedControlID="txtLastName"
    Text="<u>L</u>ast name:" /> 
<asp:TextBox ID="txtLastName" Runat="server"
    Width="200px" Height="22px" /> <br />

<asp:Label ID="Label3" runat="server" width="100px" BorderStyle="None"
    AccessKey="E" AssociatedControlID="txtEmail"
    Text="<u>E</u>mail:" /> 
<asp:TextBox ID="txtEmail" Runat="server"
    Width="200px" Height="22px" /><br /><br />

<asp:Button ID="btnNext" runat="server" AccessKey="N" Text="Next"/>
```

Description

- In ASP.NET 2.0, you can use the AccessKey attribute on any web control to specify a keyboard shortcut for the control. To use the keyboard shortcut, the user holds down the Alt key and presses the access key.

- You can specify the AssociatedControlID attribute on a label control to associate the label with another control. When the user presses the access key for the label, the focus will be moved to the associated control.

Figure 14-2   How to use access keys

How to use validation groups

The new *validation group* feature lets you group validation controls and specify which group should be validated when a page is posted. I introduced this feature back in chapter 5 because the Category Maintenance application in that chapter required it. Now, figure 14-3 presents the additional details you need to know to take full advantage of this useful new feature.

To illustrate how you might use validation groups, consider a page that requires the user to enter a bill-to address and an optional ship-to address, with a checkbox to indicate whether the ship-to address should be the same as the bill-to address. Then, if the checkbox is checked, the ship-to address isn't required. As a result, the validators for the ship-to fields shouldn't be executed. To implement this type of validation, you can use two validation groups: one for the bill-to fields, the other for the ship-to fields.

The first example in this figure shows just one of the ship-to address text boxes and a validator that's assigned to a validation group named ShipTo. For the purpose of this example, though, you can assume that the other ship-to fields also have validators assigned to the ShipTo group. And you can assume that the bill-to fields have validators assigned to a group named BillTo.

The second example in this figure shows the button that submits the page. Here, the button specifies BillTo as its validation group so the bill-to text fields will be validated when the user submits the form. Although the CausesValidation attribute is set to True in this example, this isn't actually necessary because it is set to True by default.

The third example in this figure shows how you can invoke the ShipTo validators in code if the checkbox is left unchecked. As a result, the ship-to fields will be validated only if the checkbox isn't checked.

Unfortunately, the fact that validators are executed with client-side script whenever possible can complicate the way validation groups work. If, for example, the user leaves the checkbox unchecked but doesn't enter any data at all, only the bill-to validations will be executed. That's because those validators are executed on the client side when the user clicks the submit button. But when they detect that required data is missing, they display their error messages and stop the page from being posted. As a result, the code that calls the validators for the ship-to fields is never executed. (The only way around this limitation is to write your own client-side validation script to validate the ship-to fields if the checkbox is unchecked.)

Note that any validation controls that don't specify the ValidationGroup attribute are considered part of the *default group*. The validators in this group are executed only when the page is posted with a button or other control that causes validation but doesn't specify a validation group, or when the Page.Validate method is called without specifying a validation group.

Attributes used to cause validation when a button is clicked

Attribute	Description
CausesValidation	Specifies whether validation should be performed when the user clicks the button.
ValidationGroup	Specifies the name of the group to be validated if CausesValidation is True. This is used on the validation controls to indicate which group each validator belongs to and on the button control to indicate which group should be validated when the user clicks the button.

Page class methods and properties for working with validation groups

Property	Description
IsValid	Returns True if all of the validators that have been called have returned True. The validators in the validation group specified by the control that caused the postback are automatically called. Validators in other validation groups can be manually called by using the Validate method.

Method	Description
boolean Validate(string)	Calls the Validate method for each validation control in the specified validation group.

Examples

A text box with a validator that specifies a validation group

```
<asp:TextBox ID="txtShipToLastName" runat="server" /> 
<asp:RequiredFieldValidator ID="RequiredFieldValidator1" runat="server"
    ControlToValidate="txtShipToLastName"
    ErrorMessage="Last Name is a required field."
    ValidationGroup="ShipTo" />
```

A button that specifies a validation group

```
<asp:Button ID="btnNext" runat="server" Text="Post"
    CausesValidation="true" ValidationGroup="BillTo" />
```

Visual Basic code that conditionally validates a group

```
If chkShipToSameAsBillTo.Checked = False Then
    Page.Validate("ShipTo")
End If
```

Description

- A *validation group* is a group of validators that are run when a page is posted.

- You use the ValidationGroup attribute on each validator to specify which group it belongs to. Then, you use the ValidationGroup attribute on each control that causes a postback (such as a button or a list box) to specify which group should be executed.

- You can use Visual Basic code to force the execution of a particular group by using the Validate method.

- Any validators that don't specify the ValidationGroup are part of the *default group*. This group is executed only when posted by a button or control that doesn't specify a validation group.

Figure 14-3   How to use validation groups

Other new web controls

In earlier chapters, you've learned about new web controls like the GridView control in chapter 5, the TreeView and Menu controls in chapter 8, and the Wizard and MultiView controls in chapter 11. Now, you'll learn about five more controls that are new with ASP.NET 2.0.

How to use the FileUpload control

The FileUpload control, shown in figure 14-4, is designed for applications that let the user upload files to the web site. This control displays a text box that lets the user enter the path for the file to be uploaded, plus a Browse button that displays a dialog box that lets the user locate and select the file.

To upload the selected file, you must also provide a separate button or control that results in a postback, like the Upload button in this figure. Then, when the user clicks this button, the page is posted and the file selected by the user is sent to the server along with the HTTP request.

The first example in this figure shows the aspx code that declares the FileUpload control and the Upload button shown at the top of this figure. Note here that the FileUpload control doesn't include an attribute that specifies where the file should be saved on the server. That's because the FileUpload control doesn't automatically save the uploaded file. Instead, you must write code that calls the SaveAs method of the FileUpload control. The second example in this figure shows how to write this code.

Before you call the SaveAs method, you should test the HasFile property to make sure the user has selected a file. If the user has selected a valid file and it was successfully uploaded to the server, the HasFile property will be True. Then, you can use the FileName property to get the name of the selected file, and you can combine the file name with the path where you want the file saved. In this figure, the file is stored in the C:\Uploads directory.

For this code to work, the user account that ASP.NET runs under must have write access to the directory that the file is saved to. To grant that access, use the Windows Explorer to navigate to the directory, right-click it, and choose Properties. Then, click the Security tab, click the Add button, add the ASP.NET Machine Account (*machinename*\ASPNET), and grant Modify and Write access to the account.

To illustrate the use of the PostedFile.ContentLength property, the event procedure in the figure uses this property to determine the size of the uploaded file. Then, if this value exceeds the limit set by the sizeLimit variable, the file isn't saved. Instead, an error message is displayed.

A part of a web page that includes a FileUpload control

The aspx code

```
File upload:<br /><br />
<asp:FileUpload ID="FileUpload1" runat="server" /><br /><br />
<asp:Button ID="btnUpload" runat="server" Text="Upload" /><br /><br />
<asp:Label ID="lblMessage" runat="server"></asp:Label>
```

The Click event procedure for the Upload button

```
Protected Sub btnUpload_Click(ByVal sender As Object, _
        ByVal e As System.EventArgs) Handles btnUpload.Click
    Dim iSizeLimit As Integer = 5242880    ' 5,242,880 is 5MB
    If FileUpload1.HasFile Then
        If FileUpload1.PostedFile.ContentLength <= iSizeLimit Then
            Dim sPath As String = "C:\uploads\" & FileUpload1.FileName
            FileUpload1.SaveAs(sPath)
            lblMessage.Text = "File uploaded to " & sPath
        Else
            lblMessage.Text = "File exceeds size limit."
        End If
    End If
End Sub
```

Properties and methods of the FileUpload class

Property	Description
HasFile	If True, the user has selected a file to upload.
FileName	The name of the file to be uploaded.
PostedFile	The HttpPostedFile object that represents the file that was posted. You can use this object's ContentLength property to determine the size of the posted file.

Method	Description
SaveAs(string)	Saves the posted file to the specified path.

Description

- The FileUpload control displays a text box and a button that lets the user browse the client computer's file system to locate a file to be uploaded.

- Because the FileUpload control doesn't provide a button to upload the file, you must provide a button or other control to post the page. Then, in the button's Click event procedure, you must call the SaveAs method of the FileUpload control to save the file on the server.

- To use the SaveAs method, the user must have write access to the specified directory.

Figure 14-4   How to use the FileUpload control

How to use the BulletedList control

Figure 14-5 shows how to use the BulletedList control, which provides an easy way to create lists. In spite of its name, this control can be used to create both *bulleted lists* and *numbered lists*. Bulleted lists can have one of four different bullet styles, including Disc, Circle, Square, or CustomImage. And numbered lists can have normal numbers (Numbered), letters (LowerAlpha or UpperAlpha), or Roman numerals (LowerRoman or UpperRoman).

The first example in this figure shows how you can hard-code the list items in a list by using ListItem elements. In this case, the ListItem elements provide the text to be displayed by the list.

Alternatively, you can use data binding to retrieve the data for the list from a data source. The second example in this figure uses this technique to display data retrieved from the Categories table in the Halloween database. Here, an AccessDataSource control is used to retrieve the data.

Both of these examples format the list as simple text. However, you can use the DisplayMode attribute to format the list items as hyperlinks or link buttons. If you format the list items as hyperlinks, the value of the field specified by the DataValueField attribute is used as the URL for each list item. If you format the list items as link buttons, you can provide an event procedure for the Click event of the list. Then, you can use the value of the e argument's Index property to determine which list item the user clicked.

Two bulleted lists displayed on a web page

Materials you will need: Categories:

- Styrofoam panel   1. Costumes
- Gray and black latex paint   2. FX
- Stone texture paint   3. Masks
- Rotary tool   4. Props

BulletedList attributes

Attribute	Description
AppendDataBoundItems	If True, data bound items are added to any existing list items.
BulletImageUrl	Specifies the URL of the image used to display the bullets if the BulletStyle attribute is set to CustomImage.
BulletStyle	Specifies the bullet style. For a bulleted list, allowable values are Disc, Circle, Square, or CustomImage. For a numbered list, allowable values are Numbered, LowerAlpha, UpperAlpha, LowerRoman, or UpperRoman.
DataSourceID	The name of the data source the list is bound to.
DataTextField	The name of the data source field displayed by the list.
DataTextFormatString	A format string that's applied to the text before it's displayed.
DataValueField	The name of the data source field to use as the URL for a hyperlink list.
DisplayMode	Specifies how the text for each item should be displayed. Allowable values are Text, HyperLink, or LinkButton.
FirstBulletNumber	Specifies the starting number if numbers are displayed.

Example 1: A BulletedList with hard-coded items

```
Materials you will need:<br />
<asp:BulletedList ID="BulletedList1" runat="server" BulletStyle="Disc">
    <asp:ListItem>Styrofoam panel</asp:ListItem>
    <asp:ListItem>Gray and black latex paint</asp:ListItem>
    <asp:ListItem>Stone texture paint</asp:ListItem>
    <asp:ListItem>Rotary tool</asp:ListItem>
</asp:BulletedList>
```

Example 2: A BulletedList bound to an AccessDataSource control

```
Categories:<br />
<asp:BulletedList ID="BulletedList2" runat="server" BulletStyle="Numbered"
    DataSourceID="AccessDataSource1"
    DataTextField="ShortName" >
</asp:BulletedList>
<asp:AccessDataSource ID="AccessDataSource1" runat="server"
    DataFile="~/App_Data/Halloween.mdb"
    SelectCommand="SELECT [ShortName] FROM [Categories]">
</asp:AccessDataSource>
```

Description

- The BulletedList control creates *bulleted lists* or *numbered lists*. The list items can be supplied with ListItem elements or from a data source.

Figure 14-5   How to use the BulletedList control

How to use the HiddenField control

ASP.NET applications have long relied on *hidden fields* to save information across posts to the server. In fact, ASP.NET's view state feature relies on hidden fields to store information between posts. But now, as figure 14-6 shows, ASP.NET 2.0 introduces a new HiddenField control that lets you create a hidden field on a web page and use it to save information that will be sent back to the server when the user re-posts the page.

To illustrate, the application in this figure uses a HiddenField control to keep track of the value previously entered into a text box. Then, when the user enters a value and clicks the Post button, the page is posted to the server and the Click event procedure is executed. This procedure sets the value of the hidden field to the value entered by the user, and clears the text box. As a result, when the page is sent back to the user, the text box is empty. However, if the user clicks the "Recall previous value" button, the Click event procedure of the Recall button sets the text box value to the value that was saved in the hidden field.

Quite frankly, I doubt that you'll find much reason to use the HiddenField control. That's because ASP.NET provides better ways to save data across page posts. One alternative, for example, is to add the data to a page's view state. Then, the data will be automatically saved on the page in a hidden field. Another alternative is to add the data to session state, which saves the data on the server.

A page that uses a hidden field

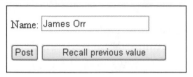

The aspx code for the hidden field page

```
<body>
    <form id="form1" runat="server">
    <div>
        Name: <asp:TextBox ID="txtCustomer" runat="server"></asp:TextBox>
            <br /><br />
        <asp:HiddenField ID="HiddenCustomer" runat="server" />
        <asp:Button ID="btnPost" runat="server" Text="Post" />
        <asp:Button ID="btnRecall" runat="server" Enabled="false"
            Text="Recall previous value" />
    </div>
    </form>
</body>
```

The code-behind class for the page with the hidden field

```
Partial Class _Default
    Inherits System.Web.UI.Page

    Protected Sub btnPost_Click(ByVal sender As Object, _
            ByVal e As System.EventArgs) Handles btnPost.Click
        HiddenCustomer.Value = txtCustomer.Text
        txtCustomer.Text = ""
        btnRecall.Enabled = True
    End Sub

    Protected Sub btnRecall_Click(ByVal sender As Object, _
            ByVal e As System.EventArgs) Handles btnRecall.Click
        txtCustomer.Text = HiddenCustomer.Value
    End Sub

End Class
```

Description

- The new HiddenField control lets you save *hidden fields* on a page without displaying the data. When the page is posted back to the server, the data in the hidden fields will be accessible from the code-behind file.
- The value of the hidden field is specified by the Value property. Since this property is a string type, you can't use it to store objects unless you convert them to strings.
- The application above saves the value entered in the text box when the user clicks the Post button. If the user clicks the Recall button (which is enabled the first time the user clicks the Post button), the text box is restored using the data saved in the hidden field.
- For most applications, it's better to use session state or view state than it is to use HiddenField controls.

Figure 14-6   How to use the HiddenField control

How to use the ImageMap control

An *image map* is an image that has several clickable regions, called *hot spots*. Although HTML has supported image maps since around 1995, ASP.NET hasn't directly supported image maps until now. Figure 14-7 shows how the new ImageMap control provides a simple way to create image maps in ASP.NET 2.0.

The ImageMap control lets you create three types of hot spots: rectangles, circles, and polygons. The example in this figure displays a map of California with two polygon hot spots: one for Northern California, the other for Southern California. Each hot spot is defined by a PolygonHotSpot element, and the polygon shapes are defined by a list of x and y coordinates that indicate the corners of the hotspot.

Unfortunately, Visual Studio doesn't provide a convenient point-and-click editor to define hot spots. As a result, you'll need to use a separate graphics program to determine the x and y coordinates for the map's hot spots. Once you've determined those coordinates, you can return to Visual Studio to create the hot spot elements for the ImageMap control.

In the Click event procedure for an ImageMap control, you can use the PostBackValue property to determine which hot spot the user clicked. In the example in this figure, this event procedure uses this property to determine whether the sRegion variable is set to NorthernCalifornia or SouthernCalifornia.

The California.gif image

An ImageMap control that defines two hot spots

```
<asp:ImageMap ID="ImageMap1" runat="server" ImageUrl="~/Images/California.GIF">
    <asp:PolygonHotSpot Coordinates="76, 228, 177, 158, 121, 111,
        121, 3, 0, 3, 0, 83, 76, 228"
        HotSpotMode="PostBack" PostBackValue="North" />
    <asp:PolygonHotSpot Coordinates="76, 229, 177, 159, 301, 275,
        296, 347, 215, 358, 111, 295, 76, 229"
        HotSpotMode="PostBack" PostBackValue="South" />
</asp:ImageMap>
```

The ImageMap1_Click event procedure

```
Protected Sub ImageMap1_Click(ByVal sender As Object, _
        ByVal e As System.Web.UI.WebControls.ImageMapEventArgs) _
        Handles ImageMap1.Click
    Dim sRegion As String
    If e.PostBackValue = "North" Then
        sRegion = "NorthernCalifornia"
    Else
        sRegion = "SouthernCalifornia"
    End If
End Sub
```

ImageMap attributes

Attribute	Description
ImageUrl	The URL of the image to be displayed.
HotSpotMode	Sets the behavior for the hot spots. PostBack causes the page to be posted and Navigate links to a different page.

Three elements that define hotspots

Element	Attributes that define the hot spot boundary
CircleHotSpot	X, Y, and Radius
RectangleHotSpot	Top, Left, Bottom, and Right
PolygonHotSpot	Coordinates

Description

- The new ImageMap control lets you display an *image map* with one or more *hot spots*. The page either posts back or links to another page when the user clicks one of the hot spots.

Figure 14-7   How to use the ImageMap control

How to use the Substitution control for improved caching

As you may know, ASP.NET 1.x can cache pages to improve the performance for busy web sites. Then, whenever a user requests an ASP.NET page, ASP.NET first checks to see if a copy of the page is available in the page cache. If so, the cached copy of the page is sent to the user. However, this feature works only for static pages, so each user who receives a page from the page cache gets exactly the same page.

But now, ASP.NET 2.0 provides a Subtitution control that lets you provide different content for each user and still take advantage of page caching. As figure 14-8 shows, this control is designed for pages that contain mostly static information that can be cached. For instance, the page in this figure shows a GridView control with a product list that will only change if a new product is added or the price of one of the products is changed. This is the type of data that can typically be cached.

However, this page also displays a greeting that includes the name of the user, and this name will change for every user that views the page. Because the Subtitution control is used to display the name, though, the page can still be cached.

As this figure shows, the Substitution control simply provides the name of a shared method in the code-behind class that should be called whenever the page is retrieved. This method will be called even if the page is retrieved from the page cache. Then, the string value that's returned by the method is inserted into the page in place of the Substitution control. In this case, the method is named ShowGreeting, and it simply returns a greeting message that includes the user's name retrieved from session state.

Note that the method must be declared as shared. That's because when the page is retrieved from the page cache, an instance of the page object isn't created. However, the HTTP context is passed to the shared method as a parameter. You can then use this context object to retrieve page items such as session state.

Note also that the return value of the method is a string that can include HTML tags. As a result, the substituted text can return HTML elements as well as simple text.

A page that uses a Substitution control

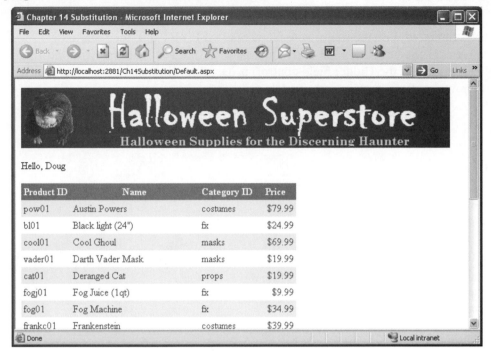

The aspx code for the Substitution control

```
<asp:Substitution ID="Greeting" runat="server" MethodName="ShowGreeting" />
```

The ShowGreeting method in the code-behind file

```
Public Shared Function ShowGreeting(ByVal Context As HttpContext) As String
    Return "Hello, " & Context.Session("FirstName").ToString
End Function
```

Description

- The Substitution control lets you create a small region of dynamic content for a page that's mostly static. Then, the page can take advantage of ASP.NET 2.0's page caching features.

- The Substitution control includes a MethodName attribute that provides the name of a method in the code-behind file. This method is called during the rendering phase of the page and returns a string value that is inserted into the final page.

- The method for a Substitution control must be defined as shared and must accept an HttpContext object. Then, you can use the HttpContext object to access page items such as Session state.

Figure 14-8   How to use the Substitution control for improved caching

Perspective

When compared with the major new features of ASP.NET 2.0, the features presented in this chapter are minor. Nevertheless, each of these features (with the possible exception of the HiddenField control) is useful in some situations, and it's good to know that these features are available.

Terms

URL mapping
access key
accelerator key
validation group
default group
bulleted list
numbered list
hidden field
image map
hot spot

Section 4

ASP.NET 2.0 in practice

The two chapters in this section deal with two practical issues that you encounter when you switch to ASP.NET 2.0. First, chapter 15 describes the ways that you can deal with your old applications once you make that switch. Then, chapter 16 shows you how to deploy your new applications.

15

How to migrate from ASP.NET 1.x to ASP.NET 2.0

If you decide to develop your new applications in ASP.NET 2.0, then you've got to decide how to handle your old applications. Do you keep running them under ASP.NET 1.x? Do you convert them to ASP.NET 2.0? Or are there other options? The goal of this chapter is to give you the information and skills that you need for making the right decisions.

An introduction to migration

If you decide that you're going to develop all new web applications with ASP.NET 2.0, you also have to decide how you're going to handle your old 1.x applications. The three topics that follow present the options you have and the problems you face as you migrate your old applications to ASP.NET 2.0.

Four options for running ASP.NET 1.x applications

Figure 15-1 describes the four options for running your existing 1.x applications along with ASP.NET 2.0 applications. These options aren't listed in order of preference. Instead, I listed them in order from the least amount of change to the most. Which of these options you choose for your own applications will depend on the details of your situation.

The first option is to do nothing. In other words, you continue to run your existing applications on their current servers without migrating them to ASP.NET 2.0. Then, you won't have to worry about any compatibility issues and you won't have to devote time to the migration effort. Of course, you'll want to use ASP.NET 2.0 for new application development. But any new ASP.NET 2.0 applications can be deployed to separate servers. This, of course, is the simplest solution, and it's often the most reasonable one.

The second option is to run your existing 1.x applications under ASP.NET 2.0. Since ASP.NET 2.0 is designed to be fully backward-compatible, you should be able to run those applications under ASP.NET 2.0 without modification. And because ASP.NET 2.0's internal operations have been improved, you can often improve the performance of an ASP.NET 1.x application simply by running it under ASP.NET 2.0.

To make this work, you need to force your old applications to run under ASP.NET 2.0. Otherwise, they will continue to run under the old version of ASP.NET. One way to force your old applications to run under ASP.NET 2.0 is to remove ASP.NET 1.x from the server. Alternatively, you can configure your old applications so they will run under ASP.NET 2.0, as shown in figure 15-2.

Note too that you must thoroughly re-test your old applications under ASP.NET 2.0 before you deploy them. Although Microsoft has gone to great lengths to ensure that ASP.NET 2.0 is backward-compatible with ASP.NET 1.x applications, figure 15-3 describes two common compatibility problems that you might encounter when you run a 1.x application under 2.0. If you do encounter problems, you will either have to modify the application to make it compatible with ASP.NET 2.0 or revert the applications to ASP.NET 1.x.

A third option is to run both ASP.NET 1.x and 2.0 on the same server, which is called *side-by-side execution*. This of course enables you to run both ASP.NET 1.x and 2.0 applications on the same server. This is especially useful if you have several applications hosted on a single server because it lets you switch the applications to ASP.NET 2.0 one at a time. This option also lets you keep your existing applications on ASP.NET 1.x, but use the same server to deploy new applications that run under ASP.NET 2.0.

Run your ASP.NET 1.x and 2.0 applications on separate servers

- ASP.NET 1.x applications can continue to run on servers with ASP.NET 1.x installed, while ASP.NET 2.0 applications can run on separate servers with ASP.NET 2.0 installed. Then, you don't have to worry about compatibility issues.

- This is often the best strategy for existing applications that are already deployed to ASP.NET 1.x servers.

Run your ASP.NET 1.x applications under ASP.NET 2.0

- Since ASP.NET 2.0 is backward-compatible with previous versions, most ASP.NET 1.x applications should run under ASP.NET 2.0 without any modifications. This lets existing applications take advantage of ASP.NET 2.0's better performance without recoding.

- To run an ASP.NET 1.x application under ASP.NET 2.0, you must configure it to do so, as described in figure 15-2.

- In rare cases, ASP.NET 1.x applications won't run correctly under ASP.NET 2.0. Figure 15-3 lists two of the most common compatibility problems.

- Because of performance and other benefits, this is the preferred way to run ASP.NET 1.x applications.

Run your ASP.NET 1.x applications side-by-side with your ASP.NET 2.0 applications

- Since a single server can run multiple versions of ASP.NET, all three versions of ASP.NET applications (1.0, 1.1, and 2.0) can run on the same server.

- If ASP.NET 1.0, 1.1, and 2.0 are all installed on the same server, each application will run under the ASP.NET version the application was developed for. If you want an application developed for a previous version to run under a later version, you must configure it to do so as described in figure 15-3.

- This option should be used only if you encounter compatibility problems when you run your ASP.NET 1.x applications under ASP.NET 2.0. It's better to run existing ASP.NET 1.x applications under ASP.NET 2.0 if possible.

Convert your ASP.NET 1.x applications to ASP.NET 2.0

- Visual Studio 2005 includes a conversion tool that can convert ASP.NET 1.x applications to ASP.NET 2.0.

- The Conversion Wizard converts applications so they use the new code-behind model, but doesn't implement new features such as master pages or themes.

- Conversion is a good option for applications that are still in the early phases of development or that would benefit from the new features of ASP.NET 2.0.

Description

- There are four basic approaches for migrating existing applications to ASP.NET 2.0. No one approach is best for all applications, so you must weigh the benefits and drawbacks of each to decide which is the best choice for a particular application.

Figure 15-1   Four options for running ASP.NET 1.x applications

The fourth option is to convert a 1.x application to ASP.NET 2.0. You can do that by using the Conversion Wizard that's built into Visual Studio 2005, as shown in figures 15-4 through 15-6. Conversion often makes sense for applications that are being developed under version 1.x, but haven't yet been completed. Of course, if an application is nearly complete, you should probably just finish it under the old version. But if you're early in the development cycle, now might be a good time to upgrade the entire application to ASP.NET 2.0.

Converting an application to ASP.NET 2.0 also upgrades the application to work with Visual Studio 2005. That means that all of the developers working on the application will need Visual Studio 2005 to continue working on the application once it has been converted. Fortunately, Visual Studio 2005 can co-exist with previous versions of Visual Studio without a problem. As a result, you can use Visual Studio 2002 or 2003 to work on your existing ASP.NET 1.0 or 1.1 applications and use Visual Studio 2005 to work on ASP.NET 2.0 applications.

How to set the ASP.NET version for a web site

Simply installing ASP.NET 2.0 on a server that already has ASP.NET 1.x won't cause the 1.x applications to run under the new version. If you want to run an application that was developed for ASP.NET 1.x under ASP.NET 2.0, you must also configure the applications to run under ASP.NET 2.0. Figure 15-2 shows you how to do that.

One benefit of installing two or more versions of ASP.NET on the same server is that you can gradually migrate your applications to ASP.NET 2.0. For example, if a server hosts several ASP.NET 1.1 applications, you can install ASP.NET 2.0 on that server and configure just one of the applications to run under ASP.NET 2.0. Once you've thoroughly tested that application, you can migrate the other applications to ASP.NET 2.0 one at a time.

In fact, if an application includes one or more virtual directories, you can switch the virtual directories to ASP.NET 2.0 one at a time. This allows you to migrate a large application in phases rather than all at once. That, in turn, can simplify the testing effort that's required to ensure that the application operates correctly under the new version.

The ASP.NET tab of the Properties dialog box for a web site

How to use the IIS Management Console

- To display the IIS Management Console in Windows XP, open the Control Panel and double-click Administrative Tools, then double-click Internet Information Services.

- To display the IIS Management Console in Windows Server 2003, choose Start→Administrative Tools→Internet Information Services (IIS) Manager.

- To open the Properties dialog box for a web site, use the tree pane to locate the web site in the IIS Management Console. Then, right-click the web site and choose Properties.

- The ASP.NET Version drop-down list in the ASP.NET tab of the Properties dialog box displays all installed versions of ASP.NET so you can select the version you want to use for an application.

Description

- When you install ASP.NET 2.0 on a system that already has a previous ASP.NET version installed on it, existing applications will continue to run under the previous version unless you use the Properties dialog box to specify that the application should use the new version.

- You can use the IIS Management Console to specify the ASP.NET version that an application should use as described above.

Figure 15-2   How to set the ASP.NET version for a web site

Two common compatibility problems

Although Microsoft has put a lot of effort into ensuring that ASP.NET 1.x applications will operate under ASP.NET 2.0, there are a few issues that might cause compatibility problems. Figure 15-3 describes two of the most common problems.

First, ASP.NET 2.0 is designed to render HTML that complies with a newer set of standards called XHTML. The trouble is that ASP.NET 1.x often renders HTML that isn't compliant with this standard. In most cases, the differences are subtle and don't affect the application's operation. But some of the XHTML differences can cause problems for existing ASP.NET 1.x applications.

Some ASP.NET 1.x applications, for example, include custom JavaScript code that runs in the browser. The problem is that the Form element that's generated for these pages includes a non-standard attribute called Name that provides a name for the form, and the JavaScript code sometimes uses this attribute to access controls on the form. However, because ASP.NET 2.0 renders HTML that's compliant with the XHTML standard, and the XHTML standard doesn't allow a Name attribute for the Form element, the JavaScript code that refers to the Name attribute won't work under ASP.NET 2.0.

As this figure shows, you can work around this problem by adding an entry to the web.config file that forces the application to render old-style HTML. Although adding this entry will get the application working again, you should consider it a temporary solution. Eventually, you'll want to revise the application's JavaScript code so it doesn't use the Name attribute.

Another source of ASP.NET 2.0 compatibility problems is the fact that Microsoft has added more than 2,000 new classes to the .NET Framework. As a result, it's possible that the names you've used for your own classes might conflict with the names of one or more of these new classes. For example, ASP.NET 2.0 includes a new class named Membership. So if you've developed a membership feature for an ASP.NET 1.x application that includes a class named Membership, you may encounter problems if you recompile the application. If so, you'll need to fully qualify any references to the custom classes.

As this figure points out, some compatibility problems won't become apparent until pages are recompiled. So keep in mind that ASP.NET automatically recompiles a page whenever you make even the smallest change to it. That's why I recommend that you rebuild the entire application when you migrate it to ASP.NET 2.0. That way, you'll discover any compatibility problems right away.

Problem 1: XHTML differences

- ASP.NET 2.0 renders HTML that is compliant with the XHTML standard.

- Although most pages should render the same with XHTML as they did with HTML, there may be some minor differences.

- Since ASP.NET 2.0 doesn't include a Name attribute for the Form element, client-side JavaScript code that uses this attribute will fail.

- You can force ASP.NET 2.0 to revert to HTML rendering by adding this line to the system.web section of the web.config file:

```
<xhtml11Conformance enableLegacyRendering="true" />
```

Problem 2: Naming conflicts

- Since .NET 2.0 provides 2,000 new classes, you may discover that you've used a name for one of your classes that is now used by one of the classes for .NET 2.0.

- Although compiled classes (binaries) should work, naming conflicts may occur when the pages are recompiled.

- If naming conflicts occur, you should fully qualify references to avoid the conflict.

Description

- Most applications developed for ASP.NET 1.x will run under ASP.NET 2.0. However, some applications may have compatibility problems.

- The two most common compatibility problems are detailed above.

- If you encounter compatibility problems, you can either modify the application to correct the problems or configure the application to run under ASP.NET 1.0 or 1.1 as described in figure 15-2.

Figure 15-3   Two common compatibility problems

How to convert an ASP.NET 1.x application to ASP.NET 2.0

Although ASP.NET 2.0 can run most ASP.NET 1.x applications unchanged, you may find the need to convert an ASP.NET 1.x application to ASP.NET 2.0. If so, the following topics show you how to use the Visual Studio 2005 Conversion Wizard to do that.

How to use the Conversion Wizard

Figure 15-4 shows how to use the Conversion Wizard, which launches automatically whenever you open an application created with Visual Studio 2002 or 2003 with Visual Studio 2005. This wizard automatically converts ASP.NET 1.x applications to ASP.NET 2.0, often without any problems.

Please note, though, that the conversion isn't reversible. In other words, once you convert an application, you won't be able to open the application in Visual Studio 2002 or 2003 or run the application under ASP.NET 1.x. As a result, you should always make a backup copy of the application before you convert it. (Although the Conversion Wizard will also make a backup copy, I recommend that you make your own just to be on the safe side.)

As you can see from this figure, the Conversion Wizard is simple to use. The only option you must select is whether or not to create a backup copy. Once the conversion is finished, a report will be displayed that details what changes were made and any errors that were encountered during the conversion.

The opening screen of the Conversion Wizard

Pages displayed by the Conversion Wizard

- **Welcome:** Displays the welcome message shown above.
- **Choose Whether To Create a Backup:** Lets you create a backup of the application before converting it. Because the conversion isn't reversible, it's a good idea to let the wizard create that backup.
- **Ready To Convert:** Displays a summary of the steps that will be taken to convert the application.
- **Conversion Complete:** Displays the results of the conversion and lets you choose whether or not you want to display the conversion report when you leave the wizard.

Description

- The Conversion Wizard converts a Visual Studio 2002 or 2003 web application to a Visual Studio 2005 web application.
- To start the Conversion Wizard, just open a Visual Studio 2002 or 2003 web application in Visual Studio 2005. This automatically launches the Conversion Wizard.

Note

- The conversion that's done by the Conversion Wizard isn't reversible. Once you've converted a web application to Visual Studio 2005, you won't be able to open it in Visual Studio 2002 or 2003.

Figure 15-4   How to use the Conversion Wizard

Changes made by the Conversion Wizard

Figure 15-5 describes the changes made by the Conversion Wizard as it converts an old web application to ASP.NET 2.0. As you can see, the most extensive changes are to implement the new code-behind model. To do that, the wizard makes several major changes to the .aspx and .aspx.vb files. For example, the attributes in the Page directives of the .aspx files are changed so they use the new CodeFile attribute instead of the old CodeBehind attribute. Also, the code-behind file is changed to a partial class, and its event procedures are changed from private to protected.

In addition, most of the generated code that appeared in the code-behind file under ASP.NET 1.x is removed. This code was generated by Visual Studio at design time in previous versions, but this code is generated at compile time under ASP.NET 2.0. As a result, it doesn't have to be placed in the code-behind file.

Of course, the Conversion Wizard also makes other changes to the application. For example, all non-page classes (such as custom business objects, utility classes, and so on) are moved to the App_Code folder and the web.config file is modified so it complies with the new format.

One of the most significant changes is that the project file is removed during the conversion process. In contrast, Visual Studio 2002 and 2003 both relied on the project file to keep track of the files that made up the project, and many important project settings were kept in that file. In Visual Studio 2005, though, any file that's contained in the application's folder or one of its subfolders is considered part of the project, and the project settings that were stored in the project file have been moved to the web.config file. As a result, Visual Studio 2005 doesn't use project files at all.

Changes made to implement the new code-behind model

- The CodeBehind attribute is replaced with the CodeFile attribute.
- The code-behind file is changed to a partial class.
- Event procedures that were declared as private are changed to protected.
- Most of the code in the code-behind file that was generated by the Web Forms Designer is removed.

Other changes made by the Conversion Wizard

- Non-page classes are moved to the App_Code folder.
- The web.config file is changed to the new format.
- The project file is removed.

Description

- The Conversion Wizard makes many major and minor changes to an ASP.NET 1.x application when it converts it to ASP.NET 2.0.

Figure 15-5   Changes made by the Conversion Wizard

How to use the conversion report

When the Conversion Wizard finishes converting a web site to ASP.NET 2.0, a report that details the Wizard's activities is displayed, as shown in figure 15-6. Then, you should read this report carefully to make sure the wizard didn't encounter any problems that it couldn't deal with.

When you first look at the report, you'll discover that it includes many informational and warning messages. Fortunately, you can safely ignore most of them. For example, the conversion report in this figure includes five warning messages that indicate that the private keyword has been changed to protected. Because event procedures must be declared with the protected keyword so they will work with the new code-behind model, this change shouldn't cause a problem. The only reason this warning message is generated is that this change can cause problems in some unusual cases. If, for example, you create a class that inherits one of your page classes, the event procedures that were private will now become protected, thus making them accessible to the derived class.

The conversion report is stored in the application's root folder as a text file named ConversionReport.txt. As a result, you can redisplay it at any time by double-clicking on it in the Solution Explorer.

A typical conversion report

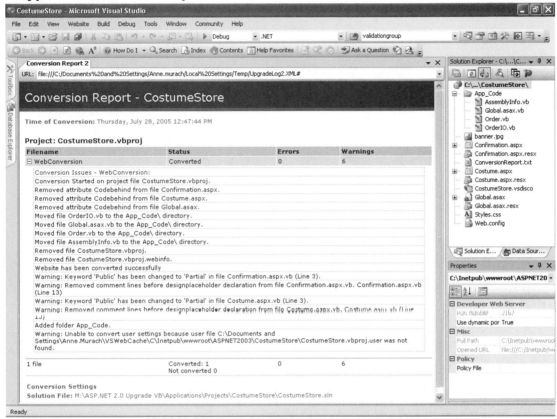

Description

- The conversion report is displayed by default when the Conversion Wizard finishes.
- Most of the messages simply let you know what actions the wizard took as it converted the application.
- Warning messages indicate conversions that can sometimes result in problems. You should review each of these messages to make sure a problem isn't indicated.
- Error messages indicate portions of the application that couldn't be converted.
- The conversion report is stored in the ConversionReport.txt file in the application's root directory.

Note

- The conversion report shown here was generated by Beta 2. However, Microsoft says that it has made major improvements to the Conversion Wizard since Beta 2 was released. As a result, the conversion report may have a different appearance in the final release of the product.

Figure 15-6   How to use the conversion report

Perspective

To be honest, there's little reason to convert existing ASP.NET 1.x applications to ASP.NET 2.0. As the old adage says, "If it ain't broke, don't fix it." To take advantage of the more efficient operation of ASP.NET 2.0, though, you may want to migrate your IIS servers to ASP.NET 2.0. But since the vast majority of ASP.NET 1.x applications will run just fine under ASP.NET 2.0, there's no reason to convert the applications themselves.

For applications that are still under development, though, you have a more difficult decision to make: Do you continue to develop the application using ASP.NET 1.x? Or do you convert the work you've done to ASP.NET 2.0 and finish the application that way? Of course, the answer will depend on a variety of factors, including how near the application is to completion, how difficult the conversion will be, and whether the application will benefit from many new features of ASP.NET 2.0. My hope is that this book has given you the information that you need for making that decision.

Term

side-by-side execution

16

How to configure and deploy ASP.NET 2.0 applications

This chapter presents the ways that ASP.NET 2.0 applications can be configured and deployed, including the new features that help you do that. After this chapter presents two new tools for configuring an application, it presents three general ways to deploy an application. Then, it presents four specific deployment techniques.

How to configure an ASP.NET 2.0 application

As with previous versions of ASP.NET, the web.config file controls the configuration of an ASP.NET 2.0 application. As a result, you usually need to change this file not only during the development of an application but also when it is deployed. For example, you need to create a connection string to access the application's database when you develop the application. But if you move the database to another server when the application is deployed, you need to adjust the connection string to point to the correct database.

With previous versions of ASP.NET, you had to manually edit the web.config file whenever you wanted to change an application's configuration. But now, ASP.NET 2.0 provides two new GUI tools that let you change the settings in this file. These tools are presented in the topics that follow.

How to use the Web Site Administration Tool

As figure 16-1 shows, the Web Site Administration Tool is a web-based editor that lets you specify certain configuration options. This tool uses a tabbed interface that lets you switch between the home page and the pages that configure security, application, and provider settings.

The Security and Provider tabs let you configure the ASP.NET authentication and provider features. You can refer to chapter 9 for more information on using the Security tab. And if you ever create your own custom providers, you shouldn't have any trouble using the Provider tab.

The Application tab lets you create custom application settings that appear in the <appSettings> element of the web.config file and can be accessed in code by using the System.Configuration.ConfigurationManager class. This tab also lets you configure a web site to work with an SMTP server so it can send and receive email. It lets you configure debugging options for the site. And it lets you start and stop the site.

When you use the Web Site Administration Tool, you need to remember that it has two limitations. First, it doesn't let you set all of the configuration options that are available via the web.config file. For example, you can't use it to change the connection strings stored in the file or specify custom error pages. To edit these configuration settings, you must manually edit the web.config file or use the IIS Management Console that's described in the next figure.

The second limitation is that you can only use the Web Site Administration Tool from within Visual Studio 2005. As a result, you can't use this tool for a web site that's been deployed to a production server unless you can open the web site in Visual Studio 2005. (Although Microsoft originally intended to let you open the Web Site Administration Tool directly from a web browser, they dropped that feature because of security concerns.)

The home page of the Web Site Administration Tool

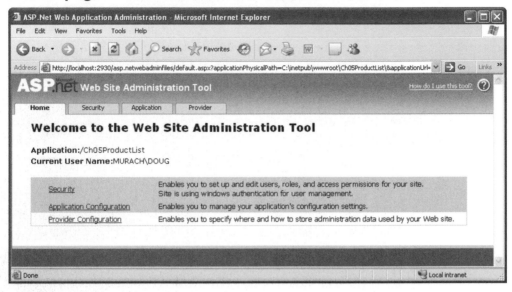

The four tabs of the Web Site Administration Tool

- **Home:** Displays the home page.
- **Security:** Lets you configure security features. For more information, see chapter 9.
- **Application:** Lets you create custom application settings, configure SMTP email support, control debugging and tracing settings, and start or stop the application.
- **Provider:** Lets you configure providers for features such as membership and profiles.

Description

- The Web Site Administration Tool lets you configure certain web.config settings using a browser-based interface.
- To start the Web Site Administration Tool, open the project in Visual Studio 2005 and choose Website→ASP.NET Configuration.

Figure 16-1   How to use the Web Site Administration Tool to configure an ASP.NET 2.0 application

How to use the IIS Management Console

Another new feature of ASP.NET 2.0 is the ASP.NET tab that has been added to the Properties dialog box of the IIS Management Console. In chapter 15 (figure 15-2), you learned how to use this tab to set the ASP.NET version that an application should run under. In addition, this tab provides an Edit Configuration button that displays the dialog box in figure 16-2.

With this dialog box, you can configure most of the settings that are specified via the web.config file. However, to use this dialog box, you must have the authorization to run the IIS Management Console on the server that hosts the application.

The ASP.NET Configuration Settings dialog box

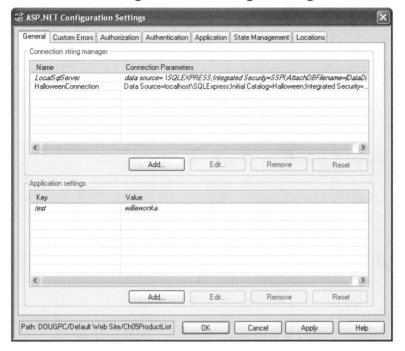

The seven tabs of the ASP.NET Configuration Settings dialog box

- **General:** Creates connection strings and application setting strings.
- **Custom Errors:** Configures custom error pages.
- **Authorization:** Creates authorization rules.
- **Authentication:** Specifies the authentication mode and configures membership providers.
- **Application:** Configures application settings such as the default master page and theme.
- **State management:** Configures session state settings.
- **Locations:** Adds <Location> elements to the web.config file that let you apply configuration settings to specific parts of the application.

Description

- The IIS Management Console includes an ASP.NET Configuration Settings dialog box that lets you configure the web.config file for an ASP.NET application.
- The ASP.NET Configuration Settings dialog box lets you configure more web.config settings than the Web Site Administration Tool, but it only works for IIS-based applications.
- To open the ASP.NET Configuration Settings dialog box, open the IIS Management Console, right-click the web site, and choose Properties. Then, click the ASP.NET tab and click the Edit Configuration button.

Figure 16-2   How to use the IIS Management Console to configure an ASP.NET 2.0 application

How to deploy an ASP.NET 2.0 application

Deployment refers to the process of copying an ASP.NET web application from the development system to the production server on which the application will be run. As the following topics explain, ASP.NET 2.0 provides several alternatives for deploying web applications.

Three ways to deploy an ASP.NET 2.0 application

Figure 16-3 lists the three basic approaches to deploying an ASP.NET 2.0 application. The first is commonly called *XCopy deployment* because it simply copies the files required by the application to the production server. To do that, you can use the DOS XCopy command, or you can use the Copy Web Site command from within Visual Studio 2005 as described in figure 16-4.

The second way to deploy a web site is called *precompiled deployment*. This is a new type of deployment that lets you compile the pages of an application before deploying the application to the production server. Then, the precompiled assemblies are copied to the server. To use this method of deployment, you can use the Publish Web Site command from within Visual Studio 2005 as shown in figure 16-5. Or, you can use the aspnet_compiler command from a command prompt as shown in figure 16-6.

The third way to deploy a web application is to develop a Web Setup project that creates a Windows *Setup program* for the application. Then, you can run this Setup program on the production server to install the application. This approach is described in figure 16-7.

Which of these deployment alternatives is the best choice depends on the particular needs of each application. XCopy deployment is the easiest, and is often used during development to create copies of an application on different servers for testing purposes. For small applications, XCopy deployment may also be the best choice for production deployment.

Precompiled deployment has several advantages over XCopy deployment. For example, precompiled deployment provides better performance for the first users that access the site. In addition, it provides increased security because you don't have to copy the application's source files to the server.

For applications that are deployed to one or just a few servers, precompiled deployment is usually the best choice. However, if you're distributing an application to many different servers, you should consider creating a Setup program for the application. Although creating this program can involve considerable work, the effort will be repaid each time you use the program to install the application.

XCopy deployment

- To manually copy the files of an ASP.NET web site to a server, you can use the XCopy command from a command prompt. Then, you can use the IIS Management Console to create a virtual directory that's mapped to the directory that you copied the web site to.
- To automate the deployment, you can create a batch file for the XCopy command. Then, you can run the batch file any time you make changes to the application and want to deploy the updated code.
- You can also do XCopy deployment from Visual Studio 2005 by using the Copy Web Site command (see figure 16-4).

Precompiled deployment

- Deploys precompiled assemblies to the specified server.
- Lets you deploy the web site with or without the source files.
- Can be done from within Visual Studio using the Publish Web Site command (see figure 16-5) or from a command prompt using the aspnet_compiler command (see figure 16-6).

Setup program deployment

- Uses a Web Setup project to build a Windows Setup program that can be run to deploy a web application to a server (see figure 16-7).
- Useful if you want to distribute a web application to multiple servers.
- Can be used to deploy precompiled assemblies and can be configured to include or omit the source files.
- An application that's installed by a Setup program can be removed by using the Add or Remove Programs applet that can be accessed from the Control Panel.

Description

- There are three general methods for deploying ASP.NET 2.0 applications: *XCopy deployment*, *precompiled deployment*, and *Setup program* deployment.
- The method you should use for deployment depends on how often the application will need to be deployed and whether you want to include the source code with the deployed application.

Figure 16-3   Three ways to deploy an ASP.NET 2.0 application

How to use the Copy Web Site command for XCopy deployment

Although previous versions of Visual Studio have provided a Copy Project command, figure 16-4 shows that this command has been replaced in Visual Studio 2005 with the more powerful Copy Web Site command. This command lets you copy a web site to a file system, local IIS, FTP, or remote IIS web site. In addition, it lets you copy all of the files in the web site or just selected files, and you can use it to synchronize web sites so that both sites have the most recently updated versions of each file.

To use this command, open the web site you want to copy and start the command to display the dialog box shown in this figure. Here, the Source Web site section lists the files in the current web site. Next, click the Connect button to display an Open Web Site dialog box that lets you pick the location you want to copy the web site to. If you're copying to a local or remote IIS system, you can also use this dialog box to create a virtual directory on the server if the virtual directory doesn't already exist.

Once you select the remote web site, its files will appear in the Remote Web site section of the dialog box. You can then select the files you want to copy in the Source Web site list and click the right-arrow button that appears between the lists to copy the files from the source web site to the remote web site. You can use the other buttons to copy files from the remote web site to the source web site, to synchronize files in the web sites, or to stop a lengthy copy operation.

The Copy Web Site dialog box

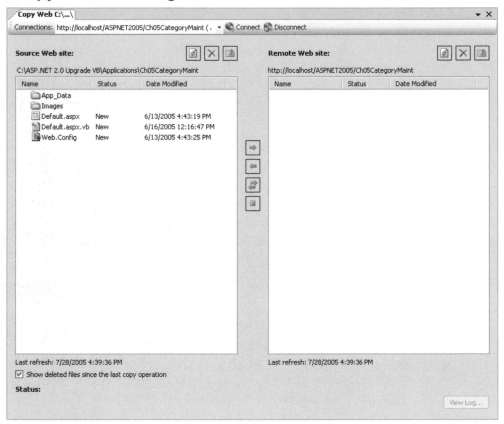

How to use the Copy Web Site command

1. In Visual Studio, open the web site you want to deploy and choose the Website➔Copy Web Site command.

2. Click the Connect button to display an Open Web Site dialog box that lets you choose the destination you want to copy the web site to.

3. Select the files you want to copy. (Press Ctrl+A to select all of the site's files.)

4. Click the ➔ button to copy the files from the source web site to the remote web site.

Description

*   You can use the Copy Web Site command to deploy an ASP.NET 2.0 application with XCopy deployment.

Figure 16-4   How to use the Copy Web Site command for XCopy deployment

How to use the Publish Web Site command for precompiled deployment

The new Publish Web Site command that's available with Visual Studio 2005 lets you precompile an ASP.NET 2.0 application and copy the precompiled assemblies to a target server. This is the easiest way to use the new precompiled deployment feature, and figure 16-5 shows how to use this command.

As this figure indicates, there are three main advantages to using precompiled deployment. First, because all of the pages are compiled before the web site is deployed to the server, this avoids the delays that can be encountered by the first visitors to the web site. In contrast, when precompiled deployment isn't used, each page is compiled by the ASP.NET runtime the first time the page is accessed by a user. As a result, the first user to retrieve each page will encounter a delay while the page is compiled.

A second advantage is that any compiler errors will be found before the application is deployed. Although unlikely, it's possible for pages in a production web site to become out of sync when the application is deployed. For example, a supporting class might be accidentally omitted. Then, when a page that uses that class is first accessed by a user, a compiler error will occur. By precompiling the entire application, though, you can eliminate the chance of users encountering these errors.

A third advantage is that you can deploy a precompiled application without the source files. This can be useful for two main reasons. First, it avoids the security risk that's inherent when you place your application's source code on the production server because there's always the possibility that a talented hacker might exploit a vulnerability in IIS and access your code. Second, if you develop a commercial application and don't want your customers to be able to access your source code, this makes that possible.

To omit the source code from a precompiled application, you uncheck the Allow This Precompiled Site to be Updateable box. Then, the source files won't be copied to the production server. Instead, dummy files with the same names as the source files will be copied to the server. If you open one of these files, you'll find that it contains a single line with the following text:

```
This is a marker file generated by the precompilation tool,
and should not be deleted!
```

Although these dummy files are required for the application to work, their contents are ignored by the ASP.NET runtime.

The Publish Web Site dialog box

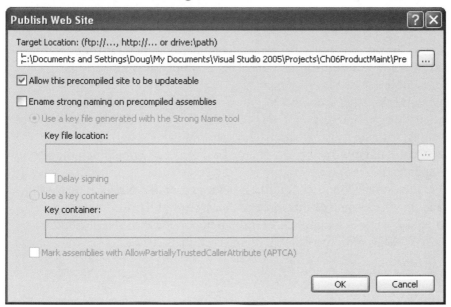

Publish Web Site   [?][X]

Target Location: (ftp://..., http://... or drive:\path)

C:\Documents and Settings\Doug\My Documents\Visual Studio 2005\Projects\Ch06ProductMaint\Pre   [...]

☑ Allow this precompiled site to be updateable

☐ Ename strong naming on precompiled assemblies

   ⦿ Use a key file generated with the Strong Name tool

     Key file location:

     [   ] [...]

     ☐ Delay signing

   ○ Use a key container

     Key container:

     [   ]

☐ Mark assemblies with AllowPartiallyTrustedCallerAttribute (APTCA)

[OK]   [Cancel]

Advantages of precompiling a web site

- Avoids delays caused by compiling web pages when they are first accessed by a user.
- Finds compile errors before the site is deployed.
- Can copy just the executable files and not the source files to the server.

Description

- The Build→Publish *web site* command compiles all of the files that make up an ASP.NET 2.0 application, then deploys the compiled assemblies to the server you specify.
- If you check the Allow This Precompiled Site To Be Updateable box, the source files are deployed to the server along with the executable files. If you leave this box unchecked, the source files aren't copied to the server.

Figure 16-5   How to use the Publish Web Site command for precompiled deployment

How to use the aspnet_compiler command for precompiled deployment

Figure 16-6 shows how to use the aspnet_compiler command from a command prompt to precompile a web site. This is simply a command-line version of the Publish Web Site command.

When you use the aspnet_compiler command, the precompiled assemblies are copied to the target directory. If you specify the –u switch, the source files are copied along with the precompiled assemblies and the site will be updateable. If you omit this switch, the source files won't be copied and the site will not be updateable.

Note that the aspnet_compiler command is located in the .NET Framework directory, and the exact name of this directory may be slightly different on your system. On my system, for example, under the Beta 2 release of .NET 2.0, this directory is c:\Windows\Microsoft.NET\Framework\v2.0.20152.

The syntax of the aspnet_compiler command

```
aspnet_compiler -v virtual-directory [-u] [-d] [-f] [target-directory]
```

Switches

Switch	Description
-v	Precedes the name of the virtual directory of the existing web site to be precompiled.
-u	The precompiled web site will be updateable.
-d	Debug information will be included in the compiled assemblies.
-f	Overwrites the target directory if it already exists.

Examples

Precompiles an existing web site

```
aspnet_compiler -v Ch05ProductList c:\Deploy\Ch05ProductList
```

Precompiles a web site in place

```
aspnet_compiler -v Ch05ProductList
```

Creates an updateable precompiled web site with debugging info

```
aspnet_compiler -v Ch05ProductList -u -d c:\Deploy\Ch05ProductList
```

Description

- You can use the aspnet_compiler command to precompile a web site from a command prompt.
- If you specify a target directory, the precompiled web site is stored in the directory you specify. If you don't specify a target directory, the web site is precompiled in place.
- If the target directory isn't the final destination for an application, you can use XCopy deployment to move the precompiled web site to that destination.

Note

- The aspnet_compiler command is located in the .NET Framework directory, which is %systemroot%\Microsoft.NET\Framework\v2.0.xxxxx, where *xxxxx* is the five-digit build number. This location may vary depending on the release of ASP.NET 2.0 that you're using.

Figure 16-6   How to use the aspnet_compiler command for precompiled deployment

How to create and use a Setup program

Another way to deploy a web application is to develop a *Web Setup project* that creates a standard Windows *Setup program* that you can use to install the web application on an IIS server. As figure 16-7 shows, you start by adding a Web Setup project to an existing web site. Then, you configure the Web Setup project so it installs the files required by the web application. You can also configure many custom options that control how the application will be installed.

Once you've configured the Web Setup project, you can build the project. This creates the setup files (Setup.exe and Setup.msi) in the Debug or Release folder of the Web Setup project, depending on whether you've configured Visual Studio to compile the debug or release version of the Setup program. (To change from the debug to the release configuration, use the Build→Configuration Manager command.)

In most cases, you'll want to copy the Setup.exe and Setup.msi files to a network server or burn them to a CD. Then, you can install the application by running the Setup.exe program from the server that will host the application.

Note that the Setup program itself is a standard Windows application, not a web application. As a result, the Setup.exe and Setup.msi files aren't found in the Websites directory along with other web applications. Instead, you'll find these files in the project directory for the Web Setup project, which you can find under My Documents\Visual Studio 2005\Projects.

When you run a Setup program to install the web application on the host server, it steps you through the installation process. In this figure, for example, you can see the screen for one of the steps of a typical Setup program.

Because Web Setup projects haven't changed much from the Setup projects for previous versions of ASP.NET, you shouldn't have much trouble creating and using one. For more information, though, please refer to our ASP.NET 1.x book, *Murach's ASP.NET Web Programming with VB.NET.*

The Select Installation Address step of a typical Setup program

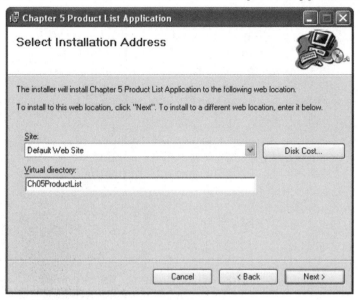

How to create a Setup program

- Choose the File→Add→New Project command to display the Add New Project dialog box. Then, choose Setup and Deployment in the Other Project Types list, select Web Setup Project as the template, enter a name for the Web Setup project, and click OK.

- In the Solution Explorer, right-click the Web Setup project and choose the Add→Project Output command. This displays the Add Project Output Group dialog box. Then, click OK to add the content files from your web site to the Web Setup project.

- When the Web Setup project is selected, a row of buttons appears at the top of the Solution Explorer. These buttons access setup editors that let you customize various aspects of the Web Setup project. For example, you can use the User Interface Editor to customize the user interface, and you can use the Custom Actions Editor to specify additional installation actions such as running a SQL script to install a database.

- To build the Web Setup project, use the Build→Build command. Then, Visual Studio creates files named Setup.exe and Setup.msi in the Web Setup project's Debug or Release folder. After you copy these files to a network server or burn them to a CD, you can run the Setup program to install the web application.

Description

- A *Web Setup project* creates a standard Windows *Setup program* that installs the web application on an IIS server.

- To create a Web Setup project, add a Web Setup project to the web site that you want to deploy. When you build the Web Setup project, the Setup program is created.

- To install the web application, run the Setup program on the server that will host the application. This program steps you through the installation process.

Figure 16-7   How to create and use a Setup program

Perspective

As you develop a web application, you'll probably find yourself working with both the new Web Site Administration Tool and the new ASP.NET Configuration dialog box of the IIS Management Console. In addition, you'll often find yourself editing the web.config file directly.

As for deployment, you'll probably spend a surprising amount of time developing procedures for deploying even relatively small applications. So for large applications, I recommend that you develop a Setup program early in the project's development cycle. Then, you can use this program to install the application on multiple servers during testing, and you can use that experience to fine-tune the Setup program as you go along. As a side benefit, you may discover installation issues that affect the application's design.

* * *

In this book, we've done our best to emphasize the new features that we think will help you the most and to focus on the skills that you need for using these features effectively. Now, if you've read all 16 chapters of this book, we hope that you've found at least a few new features that you want to use in your new applications and that you've learned the skills you need for using them. Because we haven't tried to present all of the advanced options for every feature, we also hope this book has left you well prepared to dig deeper into them.

Terms

deployment
XCopy deployment
precompiled deployment
Web Setup project
Setup program

Appendix A

How to install and use the software and downloadable files

To develop ASP.NET 2.0 applications, you need to have Visual Studio 2005 or Visual Web Developer Express Edition installed on your PC. Both of these products include a development web server that you can use to run your applications. However, because of the limitations of this server, you'll also want to test your applications using IIS. The easiest way to do that is to install IIS on your own PC.

This appendix shows you how to download, install, and use the applications and databases that can be downloaded from our web site. It also describes the installation procedures for Visual Studio 2005 and IIS.

How to download and install the files for this book

Throughout this book, you'll see complete applications that illustrate the material presented in each chapter. To help you understand how these applications work, you can download the source code and data for these applications from our web site at www.murach.com. Then, you can open and run them in Visual Studio. These files come in a single download, as summarized in figure A-1. This figure also describes how you download and install these files.

When you download the single install file and execute it, it will install all of the files for this book in the Murach\ASP2VBUpgrade folder on your C drive. Within this folder, you'll find a folder named Apps that contains all the applications in this book. You can open and run these applications in Visual Studio as file-system applications as described in figure A-3. You can also convert them to local IIS applications as described in that figure.

The download also includes Access and SQL Server Express versions of the Halloween database used by many of the applications. Since the Access database is small, we've included it in the App_Data folder of each application that uses it so you can run these applications without any trouble. Before you can run the applications that use the SQL Server database, however, you must attach this database to SQL Server Express, and you must grant ASP.NET access to this database.

To attach the database to SQL Server Express, you can use Windows Explorer to find and run the db_attach.bat file in the C:\Murach\ASP2VBUpgrade\Database directory. This batch file runs a SQL Server script named db_attach.sql that attaches the database to your local server.

To grant ASP.NET access to the SQL Server database, you can run the db_grant_access.bat file in the Database directory. But first, you must modify the db_grant_access.sql file that this batch file runs so it uses the name of your computer. To do that, open the file in a text editor, and replace each occurrence of [machineName] with the name of your computer. Then, save and close this file, and run the db_grant_access.bat file to grant ASP.NET access to the Halloween database.

If you run into any trouble attaching the Halloween database or granting ASP.NET access to it, you can read the Readme file that's included with this download. This file describes alternate techniques you can use that can help you troubleshoot the cause of a problem. It also describes the other batch and script files that are included in this download. And it explains how to set the start page for an application so it works the way you want it to.

What the downloadable application file for this book contains

- The source code for all of the applications presented in the book

- Access and SQL Server Express versions of the Halloween database used in these applications

- Files you can use to work with the SQL Server Express version of the Halloween database

- A Readme file that contains additional information about working with the SQL Server database and the applications

How to download and install the files for this book

- Go to www.murach.com, and go to the page for *Murach's ASP.NET 2.0 Upgrader's Guide VB Edition.*

- Click on the link for "FREE download of the book applications." Then, download "All book files." This will download one file named ugvb_allfiles.exe to your C drive.

- Use Windows Explorer to find the downloaded file on your C drive. Then, double-click on this file and respond to the dialog boxes that follow. This installs the files in folders that start with C:\Murach\ASP2VBUpgrade.

How to install the SQL Server database

- Use Windows Explorer to navigate to the C:\Murach\ASP2VBUpgrade\Database directory.

- Double-click the db_attach.bat file to run it. This will attach the Halloween database to the SQL Server Express database server on your local machine.

- Right-click the db_grant_access.sql file and select Edit to open it in a text editor. Then, replace all occurrences of [machineName] with the name of your computer. When you're done, save the file.

- Double-click the db_grant_access.bat file to run it. This will grant a user named ASPNET owner access to the Halloween database.

- For more information on the db_attach.bat, db_grant_access.sql, and db_grant_access.bat files, please see the Readme file for this download.

Description

- You can download the sample applications and database for this book from www.murach.com.

- The Access version of the Halloween database is included in the App_Data folder of each application that uses it.

Figure A-1   How to download and install the files for this book

How to install Visual Studio 2005 and IIS

Figure A-2 describes how to install Visual Studio 2005. Note that these instructions also apply to Visual Web Developer Express Edition with only minor variations. Also, notice that the Setup program illustrated in this figure is for the Beta 2 version of Visual Studio 2005. The final release of the Setup program should be similar, but there may be minor variations.

When you install Visual Studio 2005, the Options page of the Setup program lets you select which Visual Studio options you want to install. Be sure to select Visual Web Developer and the language or languages you want to use to develop ASP.NET applications. Also, select Microsoft SQL Server Express so that you can develop and test applications that work with SQL Server databases.

Before you install Visual Studio 2005, I recommend you install IIS on your computer. That way, the Visual Studio Setup program will automatically register ASP.NET 2.0 with IIS. If you don't install IIS until after Visual Studio is already installed, you'll have to manually register ASP.NET 2.0 with IIS by following the procedure described in this figure.

By the way, you should know that you don't have to have IIS installed to develop the applications in this book or to run the applications that you download from our web site. Instead, you can use Visual Studio and its built-in development server to develop and run these applications. Keep in mind, however, that this server has some limitations, which you'll learn about in chapter 2. Because of that, you'll want to install IIS so that you can thoroughly test the applications you develop.

You'll also need to install Service Pack 2 for Windows XP before you install Visual Studio 2005. If you don't, the Visual Studio 2005 Setup program will alert you to the fact that the service pack hasn't been installed, and it won't let you continue.

The Visual Studio 2005 Setup program

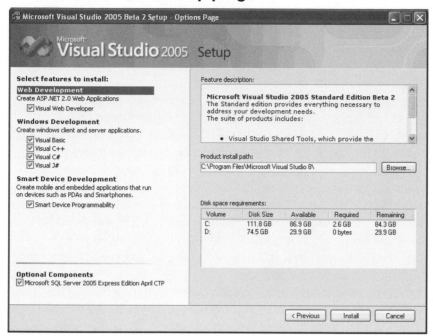

How to install IIS

- To install IIS, double-click Add or Remove Programs in the Control Panel. Then, click on Add/Remove Windows Components to display the Windows Components Wizard, select Internet Information Services (IIS) from the list of components that are displayed, and click on the Next button to complete the installation.

How to install Visual Studio 2005

- Insert the DVD or Disc 1 of the CDs. The setup program will start automatically.
- When the Options page is displayed, make sure Visual Web Developer, the language you want to develop your applications in, and Microsoft SQL Server Express are selected.

How to register ASP.NET with IIS

- If you install Visual Studio 2005 before you install IIS, you need to register ASP.NET 2.0 with IIS. To do that, open a command prompt and go to %systemroot%\Microsoft.NET\Framework\v2.0.xxxxx, where xxxxx is the .NET build number. Then, enter the command aspnet_regiis –i.

Description

- The Visual Studio 2005 Setup program installs not only Visual Studio, but also the .NET Framework, the development web server, and SQL Server Express.
- If you want to run applications from a local IIS server, install IIS before you install Visual Studio.

Figure A-2   How to install Visual Studio 2005 and IIS

How to use the downloaded web applications

You can use two techniques to run the downloaded web applications for this book. First, you can open the applications in Visual Studio and then run them using the built-in development server. Second, you can run them with a local IIS server. Figure A-3 describes both of these techniques.

Before you can run an application with a local IIS server, you must create a virtual directory for the application. To do that, open the Internet Information Services Management Console by double-clicking Administrative Tools in the Control Panel, then double-clicking Internet Information Services. Locate the Default Web Site node in the tree list on the left side of the console window. Right-click this node, then choose New→Virtual Directory. When the Virtual Directory Creation Wizard asks for them, enter the name you want to use to refer to the application (the virtual directory name) and the path to the directory that contains the application. When you're done, the directories will appear under the Default Web Site node. In this figure, for example, you can see virtual directories named Ch03Master and Ch02Cart.

Note that the first time you convert a file-system application to a local IIS application, you'll have to follow the procedure described in this figure to grant IIS access to the folder that contains your web sites. Two user accounts need access to this folder: *machinename*\ASPNET and *machinename*\IUSR_*machinename*. Here, *machinename* refers to your computer's machine name, so you'll need to replace it with the appropriate name. For example, my computer's machine name is DOUGPC, so I granted access to the DOUGPC\ASPNET and DOUGPC\IUSR_DOUGPC accounts.

Once you have created a virtual directory for an application, you can run the application by opening a browser window and specifying //localhost/ followed by the virtual directory name and the starting page. For example, if the virtual directory name is Ch02Cart and the starting page is Order.aspx, you can run the application by entering //localhost/Ch02Cart/Order.aspx in the browser's address bar.

The IIS Management Console

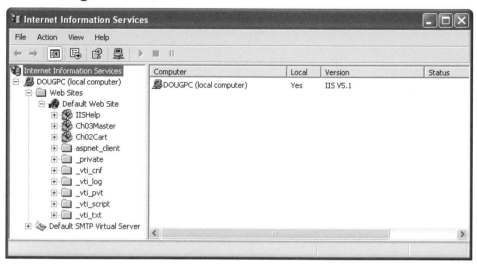

How to open and run a file-system web site from Visual Studio

- Open the web site using the File→Open→Web Site command.
- Run the application on the development server using the Debug→Start command.

How to create a virtual directory for a file-system web site

- Open the Control Panel, double-click Administrative Tools, then double-click Internet Information Services. This opens the IIS Management Console.
- Use the tree to locate the Default Web Site node, right-click Default Web Site, and choose New→Virtual Directory to start the Virtual Directory Creation Wizard.
- Enter the name you want to use for the virtual directory on the Virtual Directory Alias page of the wizard, enter the path for the directory that contains the web site on the Web Site Content Directory page, and accept the defaults on the Access Permissions page.

How to grant IIS access to the downloaded applications

- Open the C:\Murach\ASP2VBUpgrade folder in Windows Explorer, then right-click the Apps folder and choose Properties. Click the Security tab, then click Add and enter *machinename*\ASPNET and click OK. Then, click Add again and enter *machinename*\IUSR_*machinename*. Click OK to close the Properties dialog box.

How to run an application using the local IIS server

- Open the browser you want to use to test the application, and enter //localhost/ followed by the virtual directory you created for the application and the starting page. For example, //localhost/Ch04ProductList/Default.aspx.

Figure A-3   How to use the downloaded web applications

Index

S

What software you need for this book

- Any full edition of Microsoft Visual Studio 2005 or the inexpensive Visual Web Developer Express Edition.

- These editions include everything you need for developing ASP.NET 2.0 applications, including .NET Framework 2.0, ASP.NET 2.0, Visual Basic 2005, a built-in web server, and a scaled-back version of SQL Server called SQL Server Express.

- If you want to use IIS (Internet Information Services) instead of the built-in web server to run web applications on your own PC, you also need to install IIS. You need to do this to test some aspects of web applications, and IIS comes with Windows 2000 or XP (except the XP Home Edition).

- To learn more about installing these products, please read appendix A.

The downloadable files for this book

- The source code for all the applications presented in this book.

- Access and SQL Server Express versions of the Halloween database used by these applications.

- Files you can use to work with the SQL Server Express version of the Halloween database.

- A Readme file that contains additional information about working with the SQL Server database and the applications.

- To learn more about downloading and installing these applications and databases, please read appendix A.

The C# edition of this book

- If this book looks interesting but you're a C# developer, please see *Murach's ASP.NET 2.0 Upgrader's Guide: C# Edition*. It covers all of the same features but uses C# coding examples.

New .NET 2.0 books

- During the next several months, we'll be publishing new books on .NET 2.0 subjects like Visual Basic 2005, C# 2005, basic ASP.NET 2.0 skills, building Windows Forms applications, and database programming.

- So please check our web site periodically for information about our new .NET books.

www.murach.com